IMPROVING
WRITTEN
COMMUNICATION
IN
LIBRARIES

IMPROVING WRITTEN COMMUNICATION IN LIBRARIES

Jana Bradley
Larry Bradley

American Library Association
Chicago and London 1988

Cover designed by Marcia Lange
  Text designed by Kirk George Panikas

Composed by Compositors in Baskerville
  and American Typewriter Medium on an
  Autologic Micro-composer output to an
  Autologic APS-5

Printed on 50-pound Glatfelter,
  a pH-neutral stock and bound in
  C-grade Holliston Roxite by
  Port City Press

The paper used in this publication meets the minimum requirements of American National
Standard for Information Sciences—Permanence of Paper for Printed Library Materials,
ANSI Z39.48-1984. ⊚

Library of Congress Cataloging-in-Publication Data

Bradley, Jana.
  Improving written communication in libraries / Jana Bradley, Larry Bradley.
    p.   cm.
  Bibliography: p.
  Includes index.
  ISBN 0-8389-0497-1
  1. Communication in library administration.   2. Communication in
library science.   3. Library science—Authorship.   4. Written
communication.   I. Bradley, Larry.   II. Title.
Z678.B815 1988
025.1—dc19

                                                          88-10059
                                                          CIP

Printed in the United States of America.

To Our Parents

Gilbert and Marion Bradley
Joseph and Hazel Rediger

CONTENTS

FIGURES   ix
PREFACE   xi

Chapter *1:* PROFESSIONAL WRITING IN LIBRARIES   1

Chapter *2:* THE PROFESSIONAL WRITING PROCESS: Planning and Drafting   20

Chapter *3:* THE PROFESSIONAL WRITING PROCESS: Revising and Editing   48

Chapter *4:* PRODUCING THE DOCUMENT   73

Chapter *5:* MEMOS   94

Chapter *6:* POLICIES   125

Chapter *7:* PROCEDURES   150

Chapter *8:* LETTERS   174

Chapter *9:* ANALYTICAL REPORTS   197

Chapter *10:* MONTHLY REPORTS   212

Chapter *11:* ANNUAL REPORTS   231

Chapter *12:* MISCELLANEOUS FORMATS   253

Chapter *13:* WRITING ARTICLES FOR PUBLICATION   291

APPENDIX: TEST YOUR SKILLS
Discussion and Answers
 A: Revising Weak and Passive Verbs (Answers)   321
 B: Common Problems with Sentence Structure   323
 C: Revising Sentences (Answers)   327

D: Word Choice (Answers)   328

E: Diagnostic Test for Problems in Grammar and Usage (Answers)   328

F: Diagnostic Test for Problems in Grammar and Usage (Discussion)   330

G: Evaluating the Effectiveness of Memos   341

H: Using the Direct Approach   343

 I: Writing Policies   346

 J: Writing Effective Monthly Reports   349

K: Writing an Annual Report   352

SELECTED READINGS   353

INDEX   357

FIGURES

1 Analyzing the Communication Preferences of Individuals
2 Traditional Outline Form
3 Decimal Outline Form
4 Identifying Problem Areas in Your Draft
5 Checking for Unintended Offenses
6 Test Your Skills: Revising Sentences
7 Test Your Skills: Word Choice
8 Test Your Skills: A Diagnostic Test for Problems in Grammar and Usage
9 General Checklist for Grammar and Usage
10 Test Your Skills: Evaluating the Effectiveness of Memos
11 Organizing Memos: Direct Approach
12 Organizing Memos: Indirect Approach
13 Format for Memos
14 Transmittal Memo
15 Informational Memo
16 Update Memo
17 Memo Updating Policy
18 Writing Memos: A Checklist
19 Choosing an Approach to Documenting Policies
20 Sample Policy
21 Test Your Skills: Writing Policies
22 Writing Policies: A Checklist
23 Sample Procedure for a Complex Activity
24 Sample Procedure for a Single Task
25 Writing Procedures: A Checklist
26 Sample Letter Containing Positive Information
27 Sample Letter Containing Neutral Information
28 Sample Letter Containing Negative Information
29 Organizing a Persuasive Letter: Model I
30 Parts of a Letter
31 Writing Letters: A Checklist

32 Analytical Report
33 Writing Analytical Reports: A Checklist
34 Sections for a Monthly Report Using Topical or Activity
    Headings
35 Sections for a Monthly Report Using Genre Headings
36 Test Your Skills: Designing a Format for a Monthly Report
37 Test Your Skills: Writing Effective Monthly Reports
38 Writing Monthly Reports: A Checklist
39 Test Your Skills: Writing an Annual Report
40 Writing Annual Reports: A Checklist
41 Informational Report
42 Proposal (1)
43 Proposal (2)
44 Executive Summary
45 Job Description: Reference Librarian
46 Chronological Resume
47 Functional Resume
48 Writing Articles: A Process
49 Analyzing a Periodical from a Writer's Perspective
50 Indicative Abstract
51 Informative Abstract

PREFACE

This book grew out of workshops on professional writing presented to library audiences and groups of other professionals. In the workshops devoted to written communication in libraries, the participants felt relatively competent in composition but wanted to improve the effectiveness of their written messages and write good documents more quickly. This book developed in response to that need.

The principles of effective writing presented here are not new to most professionals, and yet documents written in libraries and other organizations often do not employ them effectively. Our purpose in this book is not so much to present new information on writing as to apply the perspective of professional writing to libraries. This perspective focuses on achieving specific results, writing for defined audiences, and adapting written communication to the context in which you are writing. Applying these (and other) principles to the written formats typically used in libraries, we have attempted to develop practical guidelines that will be useful for librarians in all types of libraries.

To achieve these goals, we have approached professional writing as a process that can be divided into a series of activities, each of which contributes to the whole. Not everyone needs, or wants, detailed guidance for each activity, so the process approach allows readers to get an overview of the steps and then to concentrate on areas that interest them. We expect that most readers will use the book for reference, reviewing the general process and using the discussions of specific formats as a guide when writing. The checklists at the back of each chapter can be used as a summary of main points or as an aid when starting to write. We have also included exercises and diagnostic tests, so that the book can be used as a study aid for improving professional writing.

Because we felt that many people would be using the book for reference, we have made the discussion of each type of writing self-sufficient. This approach results in some repetition of concepts from chapter to chapter, although in each chapter the discussion is tailored to a specific type of writing. This repetition will be most obvious to people who read from cover to cover in a short time. The points frequently stressed, such as writing for the reader, are the themes of the book, so we have viewed the redundancy as necessary, if the chapters are to stand on their own, and as useful for reinforcement of key ideas.

Our assumption that the book would be used primarily for reference also prompted us to include basic treatments of most types of professional writing and most writing problems; so readers will find in this volume material on common problems of grammar, style, and usage. We realize that most librarians know *most* of this material. However, in our experience, almost everyone is uncertain about a few matters of grammar and usage. We also know from experience that even when writers have a sound understanding of these areas, errors may occur in the rough draft through haste and then march on undetected into the final copy. Therefore, we have provided diagnostic tests, brief descriptions of common problems, and exercises in the text, with fuller discussions in the appendix. Our assumption is that in the text and the appendix readers will concentrate on what is useful to them and skip over what they already have under control.

We envision our audience as librarians in all types of libraries who are interested in improving their written communication or in helping others improve theirs. As we were writing, we had in mind several overlapping subdivisions of this group: librarians working on a specific writing project and looking for guidance; recent library school graduates (and library school students) who may be unfamiliar with accepted practices for written communication in libraries; and librarians in supervisory or administrative positions who are interested in helping their staffs write more effectively. With these audiences in mind, the book is designed to be useful as a guide for individual study and practical application of principles, an aid in informal mentoring, and a basis for more organized study of written formats.

The overriding purpose of this book is to guide librarians in choosing the writing practices that will work best in whatever situation they find themselves, not to dictate that certain practices be followed invariably. We have tried to indicate typical practice, but for every piece of advice we give, we can guarantee that someone, somewhere, is doing something else and succeeding. Communicating, whether in writing or orally, is a process that emerges out of specific situations; similar situations may foster communications that are similar, but success depends on being able to analyze unique elements and respond to them.

This book addresses writing in all libraries. We have tried to distribute our examples evenly across fields of interest, and, in the process, point toward considerations that arise for each type of library. However, we hope that readers will look for the principles behind the examples, even if the details occur in unfamiliar settings, and will extrapolate from them to the type of library they know. Analyzing the differences in written communication that can arise from various types of users, or various organizational structures, is good practice for developing skills in professional writing.

To illustrate our discussion, we have provided samples of written documents, both those highlighting areas for improvement and those illustrating the application of principles. We reviewed many samples of actual documents in preparing the book, but the examples that appear in the text are entirely fictional, created by drawing on our observations of typical writing patterns, but representing the writing of no specific individuals other than ourselves.

Two perspectives have merged to produce this book. Although our purpose in collaborating was to incorporate both practical and theoretical views of language (one of us is an editor turned librarian and the other a professor of literature and composition), we soon discovered that the distinction was an artificial one. In most instances the practical was derived from applying the theoretical to the specific demands of writing in the work place. From both our perspectives, the subject under study was using the strengths of written English to communicate effectively in libraries. We hope that our readers will experience the same pleasures we found in exploring how the expressiveness, the power, and the flexibility of written language can contribute to better practice of librarianship.

Many people have contributed to the development of this book. Participants in our professional writing workshops, both librarians and other professionals, provided valuable insight into what works, and what doesn't work, when writing on the job. The librarians in these workshops were invaluable sources of information about the similarities and differences of writing in different types of libraries. Throughout the preparation of this book, we collected samples of writing from so many different sources that it is impossible to thank each writer individually. For special help in collecting samples of effective writing, we especially wish to thank Barbara Fischler, Director of Libraries, Indiana University-Purdue University at Indianapolis; John Kondelik, Director of Libraries, Butler University in Indianapolis; and Imre Meszaros, Director of the Library, Villa Julie College, in Stevenson, Maryland.

We are particularly indebted to the following librarians who read the manuscript in draft form and provided much useful direction for revision: Alison Bunting, Director, Louise Darling Biomedical Library, Center for the Health Sciences, University of California at Los Angeles; Michael Freeman, Librarian of the College, Haverford College, Haverford, Pennsylvania; Catherine Gibson, Coordinator of Adult Services, Indianapolis–Marion County Public Library, Indianapolis; Ann Bristow, Head of Reference Department, Indiana University, Bloomington, Indiana; and Lorie Sprague, Reference Librarian, DePauw University, Greencastle, Indiana. Their advice added immeasurably to the final text.

Grateful thanks are also due to Marcia Foxx for heroic efforts on the word processor through seemingly endless drafts, and to Kathy Davis, Jill Gremmels, Dan Smith, Wesley Wilson, Pei-Ling Wu and all the library staff of DePauw University for their advice, suggestions, and support, and for the provision of outstanding library services.

Jana Bradley
Larry Bradley
Indianapolis, Indiana

Chapter 1

PROFESSIONAL WRITING IN LIBRARIES

CHAPTER OUTLINE

WRITING TO ACCOMPLISH A PURPOSE

CONTEXT IN PROFESSIONAL WRITING

FAILURES IN PROFESSIONAL WRITING
    Common Causes of Failures in Writing
    Responsibility for Writing Failures

PRINCIPLES OF PROFESSIONAL WRITING
    Professional Writing Is Goal-Oriented
    Professional Writing Is Consumer-Oriented
    Professional Writing Is Clear
    Professional Writing Is Concise

WHEN TO WRITE
    Characteristics of Oral Communication
    Characteristics of Nonverbal Communication
    Characteristics of Writing as a Communication Tool
    Guidelines for Deciding When to Write
    Combining Writing with Other Means of Communication
    Writing Too Much
    Writing Too Little

MOTIVATION AND PERSUASION

TONE AND PERSONALITY

COMMUNICATION SYSTEMS IN LIBRARIES

ETHICS IN PROFESSIONAL WRITING

Like many other professionals, librarians are also writers, although that may not be the way they usually view themselves. Most library positions re-

1

quire some writing, and many involve a significant amount of paperwork. In fact, a surprising amount of writing goes on in libraries.

Much of that writing is designed to keep library operations going. Librarians write memos and reports to keep others informed, to recommend courses of action, and to seek approval for those actions; and they write policies and procedures to guide the provision of library services. Communication with the library's parent institution, the library's users, and the community at large also requires writing, in the form of memos, letters, flyers, fact sheets, newsletters, pamphlets, public service announcements, and articles. Interaction with professional colleagues, both within the institution and outside it, also takes written form: more letters, more memos, minutes of committee meetings, professional documents (such as standards and position papers), and, of course, articles in professional publications.

Writing done as part of professional practice, whether by librarians or other professionals, can be called professional writing. The term, although somewhat ambiguous, has value because it links writing with the performance of professional responsibilities. Skill in professional writing is more than proficiency with language, although that level of competence is important. Effective professional writing results from combining language skills with the understanding of effective library and management practice. Success in professional writing depends on defining what you want to achieve through written communication, analyzing the specific situation, and choosing the language that will communicate effectively in that context.

Topics traditionally covered in instruction about writing, such as organization, sentence structure, and word choice, are important in professional writing; the focus, however, is on how to use these elements of good writing to create a document that communicates effectively in the situation where it is used. Traditional standards of composition are not slighted or diluted by this pragmatic approach. Rather, in professional writing, traditions of effective use of language are used in the service of accomplishing professional goals.

WRITING TO ACCOMPLISH A PURPOSE

Writing in libraries is done for a reason, to accomplish a purpose. That purpose might be to inform staff or library users about activities, policies, or procedures; to secure approval from administrators for resources or policies; to maintain positive relations with library staff and library users; to share ideas with colleagues; or to achieve a variety of other communication goals. A piece of writing, or a document, as we will call it in this book, is effective when it accomplishes the communication purpose intended by the writer. For example, if you choose to communicate a new circulation policy to the staff via a memo, your communication is effective when the policy is understood and implemented by all. A letter written to the library's users announcing restricted hours may be considered successful if the library's patrons are aware of the new hours, understand the reasons behind the decision, and retain positive attitudes toward the library.

Judging the effectiveness of a document by its outcome involves viewing written communication as a tool for achieving a broader purpose. When that purpose is not achieved, or only partially fulfilled, many reasons are possible for the failure. In this book, we are primarily concerned with the reasons written communication fails, and so it is helpful to measure achievement against expectation. Obviously, however, factors outside the influence of written communication can affect its outcome. Even the most effective solution to a professional problem, communicated in the most appropriate way for a given situation, may run up against implacable obstacles. However, by focusing on how communication can be used to achieve specific outcomes, you have the best chance of achieving your purpose when you write.

CONTEXT IN PROFESSIONAL WRITING

Your decision about what you wish to accomplish in a professional situation and the shape you give the document that communicates that purpose depends on the context in which you are acting and writing. Context can be defined as the set of variables that make up the specific situation you are facing. The context of a writing situation begins with your organization and its communication personality: its formal and informal channels of communication, the predominant tone of institutional communication, and the formats used for specific purposes. When a library is part of a parent institution, like a university, a hospital, a corporation, or a governmental unit, the characteristics of that institution form a part of the context, and they influence written communication.

The context for professional writing also includes many other variables: the size, complexity, and cost of what you are attempting to accomplish; the relationship between you and those who will read your writing; things that are going on in the library and the parent institution; and much more. When you write, you must make judgments about the factors in your environment that might affect the success of your efforts to reach the goal you are pursuing and tailor your approach, content, and style accordingly.

The personalities and attitudes of the people who will read the document are also an important part of the context for your writing, as is their knowledge of the subject of the document and their attitudes toward the subject and toward you. For example, suppose the administrator to whom you report becomes impatient with documents that are longer than one page. As a pragmatist, you will want to write one-page documents whenever possible.

Most librarians would agree that on-the-job writing must take context into account. Yet under the pressure of daily activity, it is easy for writers to see only that part of the environment that harmonizes with what they want to accomplish and to overlook situations or attitudes that could produce dissonance. Every writing situation needs to be viewed carefully to determine the approach that will be most successful.

FAILURES IN PROFESSIONAL WRITING

Professional writing in libraries is ineffective when it fails to achieve the writer's goals. Writing failures, like other communication failures, have many causes and may not be dramatic. The goal is not achieved, but the factors contributing to the failure are not always clear, especially to the writer. In fact, the writer may be certain that the responsibility for the failure lies solely with the reader, who did not understand, did not care, or did not listen to reason.

Suppose that the director of a special library runs out of interlibrary loan funds in midyear because of a number of reasonable, but complicated circumstances beyond the director's control. He or she writes a memo to the administrator requesting additional money to continue interlibrary loan service for the year. Let's further suppose that this administrator, in charge of the library and eight other departments, has some contingency funds intended for midyear requests like this one. The administrator gives the memo a rapid reading and rejects the request, with a note on the bottom of the memo: "See what you can do with what you have for the rest of the year, and we'll make an adjustment in next year's budget."

The library director may see the rejection as evidence of the administrator's recalcitrance or thickheadedness, or worse, without wondering how well the memo presented the issues and choices. Many reasons could account for the administrator's negative decision, including the causes diagnosed by the director. Nevertheless, the library director has the *best chance* of getting a positive decision if the memo presents the case briefly, clearly, and in terms that are meaningful and important to the administrator.

Common Causes of Failures in Writing

Although each situation is different, we can generalize about the most common causes of writing failures.

The Intended Audience May Not Read the Document

More frequently than we would like to think, professional writing is simply not read. It is axiomatic in the field of business writing that administrators and executives want everything written in a page or less, and that more lengthy documents run the risk of not being read from start to finish. Managers, though, are not unique in their preference for short documents. All employees have pressures on their time, and few people will curl up with a long memo the way they might with a novel. Almost everyone finds it easier to read attentively when the document is short. And almost all of us will admit that we tend to skim long documents, rather than read every word carefully.

Documents are ignored for reasons other than length. If the importance of the subject to the reader is not immediately apparent, he or she may choose to do other things with valuable time. Readers frequently start documents, and if the information at the beginning seems irrelevant, they may stop, perhaps before getting to the points that were intended to interest them. Other readers may not care much about the subject; if the first few sentences do not motivate them sufficiently to continue, they stop reading.

Recent attention to reading and learning disabilities has made it clear that not everyone understands the written word easily and quickly. In a library, where the written word is like life's blood, people who do not read with ease may be even more reluctant to admit the difficulty than in other situations.

Readers May Not Fully Understand the Content

Even when a document is read, it may fail because readers come away with an imperfect understanding of what the writer intended to say. They may not grasp the main points of the message nor understand the supporting arguments. They may miss vital information or misunderstand what is being said. Or they may not retain the information that the writer wants them to remember.

Readers May Not See the Relevance of the Message to Their Interests

If readers do not perceive that the content of the document affects them, they may not care enough to read thoughtfully. If the document does not clearly indicate what the writer expects from its readers, they may not realize that they should respond.

Readers May Not Be Convinced by the Document

People may read the document but not accept what they find there. When readers remain skeptical about the information in the document, the writer's goals are in jeopardy.

Readers May Be Antagonized by the Document's Message
If readers are annoyed or angered by any element of the message, the success of the document is compromised. The negative reaction may be caused by a misreading of the writer's meaning and may not reflect the writer's intentions at all; nevertheless, the reader may not give the writer the benefit of the doubt, and further communication on the same subject may become more difficult.

Readers May Not Act in the Way That the Writer Wishes
Any of the problems mentioned above can result in the failure of a written document: the failure to get results. When the reader does not do what the writer desires or does not react in the way the writer wishes, the document does not accomplish its purpose.

Responsibility for Writing Failures

Writers may sometimes be tempted to view these failures as the reader's fault, but, in fact, skillful professional writing can reduce the chances of these writing failures. The skill with which the writer analyzes the communication situation, formulates the content, motivates the reader, organizes the ideas, and expresses them affects whether or not the document is read, understood, accepted, and acted upon in the way the writer intends.

Writing prose that succeeds in a specific situation is not an easy task. The writer must take the responsibility for writing so that the recipient reads and understands the message. Creating a document that accomplishes a specific purpose is the essence of professional writing in libraries, and the writer is responsible for bringing librarianship and language skills together to do the job effectively.

PRINCIPLES OF PROFESSIONAL WRITING

Good writing in libraries shares basic principles with effective writing in business and other professions.

Professional Writing Is Goal-Oriented

Your goal for a specific document may be very general, like increasing the library committee's understanding of the value of library automation. Or it may be very specific, like securing approval of a travel request or obtaining compliance with a new policy about smoking in the staff room. If you, as writer, have a clear notion of what you want to accomplish by writing a memo or a report, you will be better able to shape a document that will do that job. You will also be in a better position to judge whether or not the memo accomplishes what you had in mind.

Professional Writing Is Consumer-Oriented

To be successful, professional writing must "speak" clearly and persuasively to the person who reads it. The same memo about the benefits of an online catalog may not communicate effectively with administrators, reference librarians, technical services librarians, library committee members, boards of trustees, library support staff, and users. For each group, the concept of library automation and its benefits must be presented in ways that make sense to that group. Tailoring your writing for the person who will read your document is one of the most important, and most difficult, skills in professional writing.

Professional Writing Is Clear

Good professional writing makes the meaning intended by the writer *clear* to the reader. What will be clear to one reader will not necessarily be clear to another, so clarity must be judged by what the *reader understands*, not by what the writer intends.

Texts on business and professional writing advocate relatively short sentences and plain-English vocabulary because these characteristics usually produce clearer sentences and because most writers benefit from simplifying their sentence structure and vocabulary. This advice does not suggest that you should write all "Dick-and-Jane" sentences. It simply reflects the fact that long sentences and sentences using highly specialized vocabulary are generally much harder to understand.

Professional Writing Is Concise

Most writers find it much more difficult to write a clear one-page document than a five-page report. Yet the evidence is overwhelming that length affects reading behavior. Writing concise, short documents is a technical skill that improves with practice. Advice on writing summaries and abstracts appears in chapters 12 and 13.

WHEN TO WRITE

Writing is a useful means of communicating in libraries, but it is not the only vehicle for effective professional communication. Oral communication is essential to the effective practice of librarianship, and nonverbal communication plays an important role in library practice, as it does in other human endeavors. This book focuses on written communication; however, a vital part of writing effectively is knowing when to write and when to use other methods of communicating, either alone or combined with writing.

The types of oral and written communication most often found in libraries are listed below:

▲ Oral Communication
   telephone calls
   scheduled meetings
   unscheduled encounters
   presentations
   speeches

▲ Written Formats
   memos   forms
   short reports   agendas
   informational reports   minutes
   analytical reports   newsletters
   proposals   booklets
   policies   information sheets
   procedures   articles
   letters

To communicate a specific message effectively, you need to choose the type of communication that is most appropriate for your purpose, your audience, and your message. Many people make this choice from habit or from their perception of convenience. The chances of successful communication improve, however, if you consciously match the characteristics of specific types of communication with your communication needs. While lengthy discussions of the characteristics of oral and nonverbal communication are beyond the scope of this book, a short summary may be useful in deciding which messages should be put in writing. The list of selected readings at the end of the book includes more information about these complex areas of communication.

Characteristics of Oral Communication

Under this category, we are grouping face-to-face communication with communication over the telephone. In these situations, immediate interaction is possible. The opportunity to interpret reactions to your messages and modify your behavior can lead to either positive or negative effects, depending in some measure on the communication skills of both parties. On the positive side, you have the opportunity to read overt and covert clues and to improve communication accordingly. On the other hand, immediate interaction can sometimes decrease the effectiveness of communication, especially with issues involving differences of opinion or conflict of interest. The personality traits of both communicators can also affect oral communication both positively and negatively.

In most instances, oral communication involves simultaneous composition and communication. It requires effort and foresight to plan content, and, if planning is done at all, it is usually limited to outlining a few major points to cover. Except in unusual cases, oral communication leaves no permanent record. For this reason, and because of difficulties inherent in all communication, both parties can retain different ideas of what was said. In oral communication, many other factors, such as cadence, inflection, accent, and nonverbal considerations such as facial expression, gestures, and appearance, affect the meaning of words. For this reason alone, oral communication can be a powerful and effective means of communication.

Characteristics of Nonverbal Communication

Nonverbal communication has been the subject of both research studies and popular works. Clearly, we all send messages by our expressions, our gestures, and our posture. Our actions send messages, too, as we are all well aware. Although we will not be considering nonverbal communication in this book, a few general statements might be useful, if only for comparison with verbal forms of interaction. Books treating nonverbal communication in greater detail are listed in the suggested readings.

Nonverbal communication occurs, most people agree, whether or not the communicator is conscious of it. Others receive messages from our actions and our bodily gestures, whether we intend to send these messages or not, and the range of interpretation can be very broad. Some gestures, like a frown or a smile, have commonly understood meanings, but the significance of even these gestures is far from certain. Nonverbal communication, one can safely say, offers less precision than communication through words, although the message received can be as indelible as ink.

Characteristics of Writing as a Communication Tool

Writing leaves a permanent record. This "paper trail" provides documentation for later reference and can be useful for accountability. Writing can be reproduced in a variety of ways, and so it can deliver the same message to an unlimited number of people in different locations. Traditional methods for producing, reproducing, and delivering written messages usually take some time to reach the recipient; however, rapid delivery options, such as overnight delivery services, telefacsimile, or computer links, mean that the written word can also be transmitted quickly.

Writing can be prepared in advance, thus offering a level of control not possible in oral communication, except in speeches and memorized performances. Complex ideas can be laid out clearly, and repetition and reinforcement of ideas can be structured into the presentation. Probably the least intrusive of communication formats, writing can be received at the reader's convenience. Unfortunately, the reader can also choose not to read the message at all.

A final characteristic of writing is its position as a traditional management skill. Skill in developing the content of budgets, memos, reports, performance reviews, and so forth is very difficult to distinguish from skill in expressing these ideas in writing. Many administrators use proficiency in written communication as one measure of managerial ability.

Guidelines for Deciding When to Write

Writing is overused in some libraries and underused in others. Two factors should influence your decision about whether to communicate in writing or orally: your purpose for communicating and the customary practices within your institution.

Consider communicating in writing when you wish to

▲ request action or approval
▲ create a permanent record for historical purposes
▲ create a permanent record for purposes of control and accountability
▲ send the same message to many people
▲ reach an audience that is difficult to reach in person
▲ plan the details of your message in advance
▲ present your message without interruption
▲ make complex information available in an organized form
▲ allow your readers to receive the message at their convenience
▲ encourage a thoughtful response
▲ conform to expected institutional practice.

Institutional practice will also affect your decision about whether to communicate in writing or in person. Some institutions have formal policies or guidelines for written communication. In the absence of policies, you can often determine institutional practice by observation or inquiry. When you are familiar with an organization and its communication practices, you should be able to decide when you wish to follow the organizational norm for written communication and when you can be more effective by departing from it, perhaps becoming a model for others to follow.

Combining Writing with Other Means of Communication

In actual practice, other means of communication are almost always used in combination with writing: to introduce a subject, to reinforce the message, or to follow up on the content of the written document. For example, a reference librarian presenting a proposal to the head of Reference Services for a pilot program to teach users how to do their own computer searches would undoubtedly discuss the idea both formally and informally with various members of the reference department, including his or her supervisor, before the idea reached written form. In one scenario, the librarian might then send a one-page proposal for the pilot program to the head of Reference and schedule a meeting to discuss the written document. After that meeting, conversations on the telephone might confirm details of the proposal and develop plans for implementation.

Writing Too Much

Writing can be overused when it becomes a vehicle for communications that could be more effectively carried out in person or over the telephone. For example, short, straightforward messages for which a permanent record is not required are good candidates for telephone calls. The telephone is also well suited for questions, discussions of issues, and explorations of ideas. Excessive documentation and explanation are other common examples of the overuse of writing.

When writing is overused, staff feel inundated with written material. Documents are often pushed aside, read but not understood, or filed away never to be consulted away. Another major drawback of communicating excessively in writing is that chances for good personal interaction may decrease.

You can avoid overuse of writing by having a clear notion of both *what* you want to accomplish by writing and *why* a written communication will do the job better than an oral one. For example, a director of a large technical services department may choose to write a departmental newsletter once a month *to provide all staff with the same level of departmental information*. By having a clear idea of the advantage you will gain by writing a message down, you are taking the best precaution possible against writing unnecessarily.

Writing Too Little

It is easy to recognize the dangers of writing too much. The difficulties inherent in writing too little are perhaps less obvious. They can best be appreciated if they are considered as missed opportunities. If information is passed on orally, the chance to have one permanent, verifiable record is lost. If instructions are given orally and then not followed, the opportunity to enforce accountability is weakened by the absence of a clear statement of what should have been done. If a complex, unfamiliar subject is explained at a meeting and handouts are not provided, participants lose the opportunity to review, and remember, the main issues.

The most common example of writing too little is failure to record policies, decisions, expectations, or actions. When communication problems or disagreements arise, ask yourself whether a written record would have been useful and compare the benefit to the effort it would have taken to write it down.

MOTIVATION AND PERSUASION

Professional writing frequently fails to accomplish its purpose simply because the person to whom it is directed does not read the document or reads it with such inattention that little is understood and remembered. By providing your readers with a reason to read your document, you are increasing the chances that they will respond well to what you have written.

Motivating readers is an important consideration in all types of writing, but fiction writers, journalists, and essayists have more techniques at their disposal than do writers of job-related prose. In professional writing, a strong motivator to read is the importance or relevance of the subject to the reader. Ask yourself *why* your readers should want to read what you have written. Is the subject of intrinsic interest to them? Will it affect their routines or procedures? Does it support, or perhaps work against, issues your readers care about? Will it affect the successful performance of their jobs? When you have viewed this question from your perspective and determined why you think the reader *should* be interested, move behind your reader's desk and ask how he or she will feel. What about this subject *will* be important to your reader?

Understanding your reader's perspective will help you organize your document so that its importance is clear at or near the beginning of your document. You will also use your understanding of people and your managerial skills to help you express ideas in ways that motivate others. You would not write the following statements, any more than you would say them: "Read this procedure, because, if you don't, you will make significant mistakes in the performance of your job," or "Read my budget justification and grant my request, because, if you don't, I won't have enough money to run the library in the way that you expect." But, in both cases, you would want to find ways to make clear connections between the content of your document and topics that are important to the reader.

Professional writing relies heavily on the motivational effect of the reader's job responsibilities. People read memos and reports because these documents affect what they have to do. But we all know that the strength of "duty" as a motivator can vary, depending on the time available, the perceived importance of that responsibility compared to others, the reader's attitude toward the writer, and many more factors.

Even readers with the best intentions may, because of the pressures of time, be reluctant readers of messages that you feel they must read. After writing a document that represents your best effort at presenting the issue in the way most likely to be read, you may wish to consider some external motivators, such as scheduling meetings to talk about the content, asking the readers informally for their opinions on the topic, or following up with additional formal communication.

Motivating the reader to read, or holding the reader's attention so that he or she will finish the document, is one half of the problem of motivation in professional writing. Once you decide how to get readers to move their eyes over the page with their minds alert, you must consider how they will react to what they find there. Your document will also need to provide cogent reasons for acting in ways that will accomplish your purpose. These reasons can be either explicitly stated or implicit in the organization of information and the wording of your document, but, in either case, these reasons must be convincing.

Motivation, in the sense of providing reasons for acting in a specific way, can be considered a form of persuasion. In our view, *the most effective tool for persuasion in professional writing is the logic of the case, as understood by the reader.* In some cases, your readers will have no philosophical, practical, or emotional differences with the issues in your document, and your task as writer will be to make the intrinsic logic of your argument clear to the reader.

In other cases, however, what you want readers to understand, feel, or do may run counter to the logic of the situation *as they see it.* You may feel that their "logic" is merely emotional and not at all logical; however, their reactions are based on *their* understanding and *their* thinking, and that system of ideas and feelings is "logic" as they see it. Persuasion in these situations involves identifying the reader's "logic" and moving the reader from that point to some degree of acceptance of the logic that you see as the basis for the actions and reactions you are seeking.

Logical persuasion, to be most effective, must be presented in terms that make sense to the reader, starting from positions that are either logical or important to them and then drawing the connections between those ideas and the ones you are proposing. Finding the connectors or the common ground between your logic and the readers', the real points of agreement between diverse assumptions, and then identifying the "logical" steps, in your terms and theirs, to get to mutual agreement is the real task of persuasion in professional writing.

When great divergence exists between the assumptions on which you base your argument and the assumptions by which your reader judges your case, one document alone may not provide enough scope to develop a shared understanding. In these cases, you may wish to use multiple means of communicating, such as having personal meetings, holding informal conversations, sending your readers copies of articles, writing short summaries of important issues, or using counseling and problem-solving sessions.

TONE AND PERSONALITY

Tone in writing refers to the cumulative effect of all your writing decisions: the length of the document, the way it is organized, and the language you use in expressing your ideas. Tone strongly affects the way people react to your writing, and controlling tone is a frequent problem for professional writers, including librarians. The biggest obstacle to controlling tone is failure to recognize when it is a problem. As the creator of your writing, you understand exactly how you feel and the logic of what you want to say, so you may not be aware when your methods of expression are sending other signals.

A very useful technique for spotting problems with tone is to assess the kind of "personality" that your writing projects. When people read a piece of writing, they instinctively form impressions of the writer. That impression is your personality in a piece of professional writing.

Personality in writing is like the temperature of the air. Whether you notice it or not, it is always there. A personality is projected by the content of your document, its length, vocabulary, appearance, and many other characteristics. You may not be aware of what that personality is, but you cannot avoid having one.

To practice recognizing personality in writing, read through a document written by someone you do not know, and ask yourself: "Based on this writing, what kind of a person do I think the writer is?" Bland? Objective?

Clear-thinking? Logical? Pretentious? Wordy? Pedantic? Flighty? Then try to pinpoint the characteristics in the writing that can account for the impressions you formed.

Writers cannot eliminate personality from their writing. Making sure that the personality you project does not work against you and the goal you are trying to achieve is an important professional writing skill.

Establishing a consistent personality and tone, sometimes called "voice" in composition classes, comes with time and writing practice. If you avoid extremes in language, if you keep your content and your word choice suited to your goals, and if you strive for a natural tone, your individual "voice" and writing personality will surface. Reading your own writing with an awareness of the personality that your writing projects can alert you to potential difficulties.

COMMUNICATION SYSTEMS IN LIBRARIES

Your organizational environment—the department, library, and institution or organization where you work—has its unique systems for written communication. There are systems for getting approvals for actions, systems for the flow of information, and systems for instructions on how things should be done. Depending on where you work, the use of the word system may make you smile or murmur under your breath, "Don't I wish!" By "system," we are referring to the sum of all the patterns for communication, regardless of how unsystematic, chaotic, or numerous those patterns are.

The patterns or channels for communication that make up a system may be rigidly defined, either by relationships in the hierarchy or by the nature of the communication. For example, all requests for any action might have to flow through your immediate supervisor, or requests for certain types of actions might have to go through certain departments. Alternatively, channels may be more fluid and subject to many variables. When channels are not rigidly prescribed, choosing the most effective ones becomes important and often difficult. In most institutions, formal channels for written communication exist, but other, informal ones sometimes work as well or better.

Analyzing the way communication flows in your library or its parent organization can be extremely useful. When you are planning to write a document, you may wish to determine which channels of communication will work best in accomplishing your goal. For example, suppose you are an academic librarian and wish to inform all faculty members of special funds available to buy books to support new courses. You may have several communication channels to choose from: letters to department chairs, an item in the library newsletter, announcements at faculty meetings, or individual mailings to faculty. Your choice would depend on your assessment of the effectiveness of each channel in reaching individual faculty, the importance or desirability of reaching everyone, and the relative costs. As another example, a hospital librarian may wish to establish a media center but may not have enough space within the confines of the library. He or she might wish to consider the channels through which decisions about space allocations are made, noting both the formal channels for requesting space and the political dynamics of those communications.

You and other members of the library staff may also find it useful to analyze patterns of communication in your library as a basis for establishing policies governing written communications. Many libraries, especially large ones, find it useful to define appropriate channels for types of communications, particularly for policies, procedures, and communications that go outside the library. Identifying present patterns and their strengths and weaknesses is an excellent starting point for developing policies on communications.

Although each library has its own channels for communication, some generalizations are possible. Communications in libraries, as in other institutions, can be differentiated by the organizational direction in which they travel: upward, downward, laterally, or outside the organization altogether. Upward communication most frequently travels to the person to whom the writer reports, but it can also skip rungs in the hierarchical ladder. While traditional organizational wisdom decrees that it can be risky to communicate above or around your administrative supervisor, common sense and your knowledge of your own environment will help you assess when that is appropriate and will also prompt you to keep your supervisor informed. Upward communication typically serves one of two purposes: seeking approvals and providing information, either as general knowledge about your activities or as a response to specific issues of immediate concern. Memos, reports, and proposals are the formats most frequently used for upward communication.

Downward communication can move directly down the organizational ladder, or it can branch out in several downward directions. Messages moving downward typically contain information, instructions, or requests for action. Typical formats include memos, newsletters, policies, and procedures.

Lateral communication can move between departments, between professionals in the library, between professional peers in the institution, and between the library and its users. Memos, flyers, fact sheets, newsletters, and other informational formats typically move laterally. Communication outside the library usually consists of letters and, to a lesser extent, memos and publications.

In addition to channels for specific types of communication, institutions have conventions about the formats for written communication. Formats for specific purposes may be prescribed by an institution, either through use of a printed form or by the use of a standard organizational structure. These institutional conventions can be easy to identify from observation of practice or from the presence of written instructions. Sometimes, however, these conventions are informal, and, instead of being written down, are passed on by word of mouth. Libraries vary widely in their adaptation and use of the formats typically used by businesses and other organizations. Some libraries have a highly structured and prescribed system of formats, while others use notes or memos for almost all purposes.

Learning to understand your institution's communication personality, including both channels and formats, is a matter of observation and analysis. The size of the institution may offer some clues to the relative formality of the communication system. When large numbers of people are involved, the communication process is usually more complex and often more difficult to fathom. However, small institutions can also have complex systems. Then, too, the lack of consistent systems may create as much confusion as an overly convoluted setup. Rather than rely on generalizations about communication systems in libraries, you will probably find it most helpful to turn your powers of observation and analysis to written communication in your own library.

As part of your analysis, you may want to

▲ identify any prescribed channels and formats that may exist
▲ look at the channels and formats used by others who have been successful
▲ examine what has worked well, and not so well, for you in the past
▲ consider the special nature of your present circumstances and decide on the blend of following the norm and creative variation that will work best.

ETHICS IN PROFESSIONAL WRITING

Professional writing is a communication tool used as a means for accomplishing tasks and achieving goals in libraries. In making decisions about professional writing, librarians should apply ethical considerations to the ends they are pursuing and to the means that they are employing to reach those ends.

In considering the ethics of your goals, you may wish to consider the "Librarians' Code of Ethics" (*American Libraries*, October, 1982) as a statement of principles to guide actions. The "Librarians' Code of Ethics" spells out ethical considerations for librarians, including providing the highest level of service (through actions defined in the code); resisting efforts at censorship of library materials; protecting the user's right to privacy of information; adhering to principles of due process and equality of opportunity in peer relationships and personnel actions; distinguishing between personal and institutional philosophies; and avoiding personal gain at the expense of users, colleagues, or the institution.

In addition to considering the ethics of the ends, you will want to examine ethical issues in your choice of means. All professional writing involves some elements of persuasion. Persuasion is the act of influencing others by reasons, arguments, or appeals. Policies are designed to influence the actions of those covered by the policy. Any request for funds, for staffing, or for approval of any course of action involves persuading those in authority that your request is valid. Publicity announcing a film series for young adults hopes to persuade teenagers to attend.

Whether or not persuasion is ethical can be measured by the "end," by the action or belief that you are persuading others to perform or accept, and by the means used in persuasion. Both should also be assessed by ethical criteria, by standards of truth and honesty, the common good, and individual rights.

In professional writing, the selection of the content of the document is an important principle of effective writing. No document can cover a topic completely; for all documents, the writer must select relevant information. Based on knowledge of the reader, the writer chooses those details that the reader should know and will want to know. The selection of details must be truthful and must accurately represent the important elements in a situation, as the librarian understands them to apply to the reader. The selection of detail should not mislead the reader and should reflect the writer's honest judgment of what the reader should know. Suppose, for example, that the library director, in consultation with a library consultant and the library automation committee, recommends a library automation vendor. The library director's recommendation to his or her administrator should include an appraisal of the company's financial condition. If that information were deliberately withheld from the institution on the grounds that it might negatively influence the administration's decision, serious questions of ethical impropriety would arise. On the other hand, the report announcing the company's selection to users would not ordinarily contain the same open discussion of any financial risks involved.

The organization of content also should be governed by ethical considerations. When content is organized deductively or directly, important information is presented first. When content is arranged inductively or indirectly, details are presented first, leading to major statements or conclusions. Each is a different way of ordering the information, and ethical use of each pattern requires that it reflect the truth and not mislead the reader.

The writer's choice of words should also be ethical. Words should be used according to their accepted meanings. Using generalizations or abstract words to mislead seriously compromises ethical standards. Clearly, describing a library's finances as "healthy" when it has overrun its budget by 25 percent deceives the reader.

Ethics in library practice and ethics in communication are complex issues and require much more detailed consideration than we can provide here. Our brief discussion is intended to raise these concerns and to encourage you to think about them in your professional writing.

Chapter 2

THE PROFESSIONAL WRITING PROCESS: Planning and Drafting

CHAPTER OUTLINE

THE PROCESS APPROACH

THE PROFESSIONAL WRITING PROCESS

DEFINING YOUR PURPOSE
   Goals for Action
   Goals for Providing Information
   Goals for Fostering Good Human Relations

UNDERSTANDING YOUR READER'S PERSPECTIVE
   Your Reader's Point of View
   Your Reader's Communication Preferences
   Your Reader's Stance on a Specific Issue

PLANNING YOUR COMMUNICATION STRATEGY
   Channels of Communication
   Characteristics of the Format Chosen

DEVELOPING YOUR MATERIAL
   Invention
   Gathering Material
   Making Lists
   Making Maps
   Freewriting
   Writing a Dialogue
   Brainstorming

ORGANIZING YOUR MATERIAL
   Early Organizational Ideas
   Outlining
   Types of Outlines
   Wording the Formal Outline
   Traditional Alpha-Numeric Outline Form
   Decimal Outline Form
   Developing Outlining Skills

DRAFTING YOUR DOCUMENT
   Getting Started
   Deciding on a Beginning
   Constructing "Signposts" for the Reader
   Rewarding Yourself

Jonathan Swift provides a model of concise definition when he describes good writing as the proper words in the proper place. In the previous chapter we defined professional writing as writing that accomplishes a purpose within a specific context. Finding the proper words and putting them in the proper place depend upon goals and circumstances that are constantly changing.

Good professional writing is more than a return to the expository style that was successful during your undergraduate and graduate education. That style was adapted to special circumstances, and professional writing, in its turn, takes its shape from your professional goals and the environment in which you work. The writing principles and techniques you learned in the classroom are the foundation of professional writing, but they must be molded by you, as a professional writer, to fit the task at hand.

The essence of professional writing, then, is shaping your content, your organization, and your expression to accomplish your purpose within a given context. The number of variables involved is mind-boggling, and they change with each writing situation. How, exactly, can professionals develop the ability to tailor their writing to each situation, and to each reader, without taking a leave of absence from their jobs to work on the task?

There are two answers, process and practice. By becoming familiar with the process (the activities that produce successful results), you can develop a mental checklist, giving each step the attention warranted by the situation. Practice makes each step easier and faster.

Before moving to a detailed look at the process for professional writing, we should discuss the pressures of time that are a fact of on-the-job writing. Time is a valuable resource for most professionals, and deciding where to spend it has many ramifications. In this book, we are making two claims. First, the way documents are planned and written strongly affects whether or not they accomplish the task for which they were intended. The success of projects can be in jeopardy if written communication about them is ineffective. If you spend months rethinking the process for selecting journals in an academic library, and you do not communicate the rationale behind this policy effectively to the library committee who must approve it, then a good project may flounder because enough time was not spent on communication. From our first claim, it follows that librarians are wise to spend the time it takes to develop documents that have the best chance of accomplishing their purposes.

Our second claim is that using the process approach can help writers produce better results, frequently in less time than writing without such a structure. Many writers waste a great deal of time stewing over writing tasks, worrying about everything from how to start to what to say. Having a sequence of steps to consider provides a structure for decisions that can save you from having to organize the whole project *ad hoc* each time you write. A skeptic may question how a process that takes two long chapters to discuss can be used to save time in actual situations. Most librarians will not need to follow the process as an inexperienced cook follows a new recipe, with one hand stirring the pot and the other holding the cookbook open. A thoughtful reading of the general process should stimulate renewed awareness of the issues. Then chapters on specific formats can be read when a need arises. The checklists of each process can be reviewed in a few minutes before beginning a document to refresh your memory of important considerations. Obviously, not every step needs thorough attention all the time. Each writer can decide when certain projects warrant more attention to specific steps, and when his or her own skills need developing in specific areas.

Much professional writing tends to be done at one sitting, perhaps on the assumption that doing it all at once will get the job done faster. Both quality and speed can usually be improved by spreading the task over two or three sessions. Even a few hours separating the stages of organizing, drafting and revising can give you an objectivity that will enable you to make improvements more quickly.

THE PROCESS APPROACH

The process approach to professional writing defines the activities that need to take place to produce an effective result. These activities require analysis and decision making from the writer. They focus the writer's attention on one aspect of the situation at a time and ask for consciously formed writing decisions. The process of recognizing choices and writing from intention (rather than from habit) usually produces more effective results immediately.

Successful professional writing requires decisions in each activity of the process. Some skilled professional writers may make these decisions automatically, without thinking about the process they are using, but the purpose of each activity is accomplished, in one way or another. Some writers, for example, consider the perspective of their reader so instinctively that they do not need to make a special effort to identify that perspective and write for it. Other skilled professional writers may have to pay close attention to all activities in the process, although they may do so simultaneously rather than sequentially, knowing by experience the importance of each in the total picture. Every professional writer, no matter how skilled, can benefit from renewed awareness of some aspect of the writing process, and every document can benefit from careful attention to each activity.

The activities in the writing process are listed sequentially, yet every writer knows that every stage can be revisited, reassessed, and modified throughout the writing process. The advantage of considering each of the activities separately, both in discussion and when you are actually writing, is to bring each one into special focus, to give it attention and to understand its importance in the development of the whole.

We have taken a process approach in this book. Chapters 2 and 3 present a general process for professional writing, considering each step by itself. Subsequent chapters focus on individual formats in professional writing, discussing the special characteristics of each format and presenting a version of the general writing process, modified for that format. We envision that librarians will use the discussion of both the general and the specific processes in two ways: reading through them to review the general ideas and techniques involved, and using them as guidelines when working on specific writing projects. The writing process is less a formula or recipe than a map, pointing out places to go in a reasonable sequence but leaving the exploration of the terrain to each traveler.

The more that you practice each step in the process, the more natural it will seem and the easier it will be to incorporate these ways of thinking about writing into your writing routines.

THE PROFESSIONAL WRITING PROCESS

The process for professional writing consists of the following steps:

▲ Defining your purpose
▲ Understanding your reader's perspective
▲ Planning your communication strategy
▲ Developing your material
▲ Organizing your document
▲ Drafting your document
▲ Revising for effectiveness
▲ Editing for correctness
▲ Producing the document.

DEFINING YOUR PURPOSE

Most documents that you write as part of your professional responsibility are communication tools that you will design to do a specific job. Before you can start designing the document, you will need to have a clear understanding of what that job is, why you are writing, and what you expect to accomplish.

Stating to yourself exactly what you are trying to accomplish through writing focuses your thinking on the results you want to achieve. It is sometimes useful to break these results down even further and consider what you want your readers to do, to know, and to feel as a result of your writing.

Goals for Action

What do you want your reader to do as a result of reading your writing? This question centers on the behavior you want to bring about in your reader. Do you want him or her to approve a budget, to order a personal computer for your department, to stop student shelvers from attempting to answer reference questions, to check a patron's ID before charging out books, or to return videotapes in person before the library closes?

Once you have defined the behavior that you want from the reader of your writing, you can make decisions about communication format, content, organization, and wording, based on how effective these will be in eliciting the behavior you want. Stating your goals in behavioral terms has another salutary effect. It can help you be realistic about the results you can expect to achieve through a given document, and it can alert you to the need for additional communication. It is easy to write a memo explaining a new policy and then to assume that, because the memo has been written, the policy will be followed. Defining specific staff behavior as the desired outcome can reveal the need for several communication tools—perhaps a memo, a procedure manual, meetings, or a personal conference—to achieve that goal.

Goals for Providing Information

Some documents do not request action; they simply impart information. However, in most cases, you, as writer, are providing that information for a reason, perhaps to lay the groundwork for future action or to shape attitudes. Asking yourself what you want your reader to know, and why, helps you focus on your real goals for writing.

You may wish to go a step further and ask yourself which facts or ideas you wish your readers to assimilate thoroughly, to have as part of their long-term understanding. Merely reading something does not ensure that it will be remembered. If you define clearly what facts you want your reader to retain, you can tailor your message to emphasize those ideas that are important.

Goals for Fostering Good Human Relations

In every document, you are concerned with both substantive issues and the attitudes and feelings that surround those issues. The issues themselves involve human relations. For example, the issue of reducing the hours that the library is open is fraught with the potential for sparking conflicts. And then the language in which that issue is presented introduces still more possibilities for strong emotional responses.

Language by its very nature shapes attitudes and sways emotions. This affective power can work for you or against you, depending on your skill in using language. Very ticklish subjects can be handled in positive ways. Yet the most innocuous memo can also stir intensely negative feelings if it is worded clumsily.

Every document has the potential for good or ill in the cause of maintaining positive human relations. We suggest that you try to identify the human relations issues in each communication and then formulate goals that respond to these issues. Particularly in situations where you are communicating unwelcome information or in situations involving conflict of interest, you will benefit from setting positive human relations goals and then working to embody them in your writing.

Consider, for example, the situation where several librarians within your institution have applied for a position that you eventually fill with an applicant from outside the library. By identifying the potential for personal and professional conflict in this situation, you can define the human relations goals you wish to achieve. Such goals might include maintaining positive, collegial relationships with the unsuccessful internal applicants and laying the foundations for good working relationships between the existing staff and the newcomer. When you view your communication tasks in light of these goals, the letters that you will write to the unsuccessful applicants, as well as your face-to-face communications with them, take on a new complexity and importance.

In every communication situation, you should be able to identify human relations issues and then formulate goals that respond to these issues. Making this an automatic part of planning your writing will go a long way toward ensuring its effectiveness.

UNDERSTANDING YOUR READER'S PERSPECTIVE

Professional writing is aimed at the reader—to impart information to him or her, to motivate that person to do something, and to foster positive human relations. To accomplish these purposes, writing must be reader-centered; it must respond to the reader's understanding of the situation and motivate the reader on his or her terms. This fundamental concept, writing for your reader, is easy to accept intellectually but very difficult to put into practice. In fact, most of us unconsciously write for clones of ourselves. We construct arguments that make sense to us, use examples that help clarify our own thinking, and select words that are persuasive for people who believe as we do. Overcoming this natural tendency to write from, and for, your own perspective requires that you become much more aware of your reader's point of view. Taking the time to analyze your reader's opinions and attitudes, as well as his or her understanding of an issue, gives you a better chance of writing a document that will be effective.

Your Reader's Point of View

Looking at the reader's position in your organization and the issues that concern him or her will help you understand the reader's perspective. What are your reader's job responsibilities? Who judges his or her performance and on what basis? What attitudes does your reader express in public? What is his or her perception of your role in the organization and of your effectiveness? What job-related issues concern your reader most? Answering these questions can help you understand the situation your reader faces. This knowledge is especially important when your organizational role is significantly different from your reader's, as when you are writing to the person to whom you report or to the people who report to you.

Your Reader's Communication Preferences

People differ in their communication preferences. The way someone prefers to *send* messages is usually apparent from the way he or she chooses to communicate most frequently. The way that same person prefers to *receive* information is not always so obvious. Determining the communication techniques that are most effective in reaching an individual increases the chances that your communication will accomplish its goals.

You may find it useful to analyze the communication preferences of the person to whom you report. The exercise is good practice and is applicable in many situations.

Think back over your communications with this person. What frustrations have you encountered? What has worked well, and not so well, and in what situations? Look at the experience others have had in communicating with this person. Does he or she prefer to receive information in writing, over the telephone, or in person? What frequency of communication is preferred and what level of detail of information is required?

It is probably good to remember at this point that what works in communicating with your boss, or anyone else, depends not only on the medium, but also on the way that medium is used and on the content of your message. For example, the person to whom you report may be receptive to information presented in reports if those reports contain highly relevant information worded clearly and succinctly. In your analysis, you will want to focus not only on the medium that works best, but on the characteristics of communication in that medium that produce good results with your reader. Do short, concise reports work better than lengthy ones? Do frequent, brief, informal phone calls work better than longer, less frequent calls with a more highly structured agenda? Figure 1 presents some questions that you may find helpful in analyzing the communication preferences of people with whom you communicate frequently.

Telephone Calls

- ▲ Is he or she readily available by telephone?
- ▲ Does he or she seem receptive to discussing all types of issues on the spur of the moment?
- ▲ Can you categorize the types of issues that he or she is comfortable discussing on the spur of the moment?
- ▲ What times of the day is he or she most likely to be available? To be receptive?
- ▲ How does he or she respond to the idea of telephone appointments (specific times set in advance to discuss a specific agenda)?
- ▲ Does he or she appreciate receiving a brief, written summary of complex issues, with a note that you will call later to discuss them?
- ▲ If you send a summary in advance, does he or she read it?
- ▲ Are you generally pleased with the results of phone calls? If not, what generally happens? Do you have enough time to discuss the issue thoroughly? Do you feel you are effective in presenting your ideas?
- ▲ Summarize your conclusions about the use of the telephone as a means of communicating with this person.

Written Communication

- ▲ Does he or she request information in writing? What types of information?
- ▲ Can you tell if he or she reads your written documents?
- ▲ Do you receive timely responses?
- ▲ What method for follow-up works best? What gets the best results?
- ▲ Are one-page summaries read more often than long reports?
- ▲ Can you generalize about the level of detail he or she requires from you? Are there differences by types of issue?
- ▲ Have you experimented with different formats and layouts? Can you generalize about which work best?
- ▲ What tone seems most effective? Informal? Formal?
- ▲ Does he or she have a purist's attitude toward grammar and usage? A free-wheeling attitude? Or no strong feelings?
- ▲ What documents does he or she require from others?
- ▲ Summarize your conclusions about writing to this person.

Face-to-Face Meetings

- ▲ Are they hard to schedule?
- ▲ Are you pleased with the results?
- ▲ Do you feel as if you have communicated your ideas effectively?
- ▲ Are you able to present all the information you feel is necessary?
- ▲ Have you tried bringing written summaries with you, either to read from or to leave? Is that effective?
- ▲ Summarize your conclusions about the effectiveness of face-to-face meetings in communicating with this person.

Figure 1. **Analyzing the Communication Preferences of Individuals**

Your Reader's Stance on a Specific Issue

Your analysis of the reader's perspective and communication preferences will be useful background for all your communication decisions. When you are planning to send a document, you will also want to examine your reader's stance in relation to that issue. Before you begin to write, you should be aware of your reader's understanding of the subject, his or her vested interests in the area, and the preconceptions that may affect his or her attitude toward the issue.

What does your reader know about the subject already? This question is worth some thought, even if at first the answer seems obvious. Suppose, for example, that you are writing a report recommending a strategy for converting your library's bibliographic records to machine-readable form. The extent of your reader's knowledge of retrospective conversion should determine the content of your report. You will want to assess what your audience knows about the purposes of this activity, the possible methods, their effects on the final automated product, and the costs. Technical services librarians, public services librarians, library directors, administrators outside the library, and the library's users all have various levels of understanding that should be clearly recognized before you attempt to communicate with them.

Factual knowledge alone does not account for all of your reader's stance on a particular issue. Previous experience, preconceptions, and perceptions of how an issue will affect him or her all play important roles. A series of examples will illustrate attitudes that can affect communication. A new user of a special library, fresh from a graduate program, may have been accustomed to an environment where students do their own library work. In that case, the user may not realize that part of the reference librarian's function in the institution is to assist professionals with research. A faculty member at a university may have difficulty believing that someone without a doctorate in economics can assess the quality of a book in that field. Stereotypes about librarians may limit an administrator's perception of the library director's administrative role in the institution. Or the head of collection development may have serious concerns about the long-range impact of automation on the budget for library materials, and this perception of vested interest may affect attitudes toward computerization.

Preconceptions and attitudes like these should not be seen as hostile viewpoints or as insurmountable barriers, but rather as part of an environment in which you need to write effectively. Your job as a writer is to shape your message so that it responds to these concerns. If you have an unclouded understanding of these attitudes, you will be able to deal with them more effectively.

How should you go about obtaining such an understanding of your reader's ideas, attitudes, and vested interests? This is a legitimate question, and one that has many answers, all revolving around one theme: understanding the people with whom you communicate. Learning about your readers is a continuous process that involves asking questions, listening, observing, and analyzing, not only as part of a specific writing task, but also as an everyday part of the way you do your job.

The questions below may help you in writing effectively to a specific reader.

1. Do you have a clear sense of your reader's point of view? Describe to yourself your reader's position within the organization, including his or her responsibilities and pressures. How might these affect his or her attitude toward your subject?
2. What communication methods does your reader prefer for receiving information?
3. What does your reader understand about the subject of your document?
4. What preconceptions or attitudes affecting this subject does he or she have?
5. What are your reader's vested interests in this subject?
6. Can you describe the level of trust or confidence the reader has in you?
7. How do you predict your readers will react to the document you are planning to send? Are those reactions consistent with your goals?

PLANNING YOUR COMMUNICATION STRATEGY

After you are sure about what you want to accomplish and have a sense of your reader's perspective, you are in a position to plan the communication strategy that will work best. Two activities should go on here. First, you will want to block out, in a general way, your total communication strategy on this issue. You have already identified your goals and your audience. Now you want to review the kinds of communication that will be necessary to achieve your goals. You may wish to think in terms of the following functions:

▲ introducing the topic or issue
▲ presenting the main message
▲ providing background or supplementary information
▲ reinforcing a previous main message
▲ following up on requests in the main message.

Not all these functions are needed in every situation, and several functions are often combined in one message. Planning your total communication strategy involves anticipating the kinds of communication you will need and choosing the media that will do the job best.

Chapter 1 discusses the factors that can help you select the most appropriate communication medium: the content of the message, the characteristics of the medium, your purpose in communication, normal practice in your institution, and your audience. Written documents can be used for any of the functions in the list above. When a document is used to convey the main message, oral communication is often used for supplementary purposes, such as introducing the main message or following up on it.

Once you have considered your total communication strategy and have confirmed the role writing will play in it, your next task is to plan the approach your document will take. You will be making several kinds of decisions: choosing the channels of communication that are most suited to your purposes and deciding on characteristics of the format you will be using, such as the appropriate length, level of formality, and tone.

Channels of Communication

Choosing channels of communication refers to selecting the best method for accomplishing your purpose in your organization, including selecting the people to whom you should communicate and, frequently, the means you should use. In many cases, decisions on both these issues are implicit in the formulation of your purpose. You already have a reasonably good idea that you will write a certain kind of document to a specific person. Although you may have considered possible channels before you formulated your purpose, you may have made the initial decisions out of habit. At some point, you will want to review this choice systematically (if briefly) in light of established practice in your organization. You will want to understand how the specific type of communication is typically handled: to whom it should be sent first and who else should be informed.

For example, if you were planning to ask for an additional staff position, you would review the accepted channels for this kind of request, note the budget cycle, and observe how others have handled requests that were ultimately successful. If you wished to communicate a change in policy to the library staff, you might review the methods you have for reaching everyone: announcements to department heads, discussion at general staff meetings, items in the library newsletter, and individual memos or letters to all staff. Your choice of the most appropriate channel of communication will depend on the nature and content of the policy, whom it affects, the level of detail you want each individual to receive, and the costs you are willing to incur.

Characteristics of the Format Chosen

Your analysis of the channels of communication that will work best for your message will help you decide which written format to use: memo, report, proposal, or other format. Once the format is chosen, you can decide on characteristics that format should have in this situation. In other words, you can decide on some of the "givens" of your document before you begin to collect and organize your material. In particular, you will want to consider the ideal length of your document, the use of a specialized format or organizational structure, and the tone of the document, including the level of formality.

For example, if you are requesting additional space by using a special form that your institution has designed, you know the questions you have to answer and approximately how long each answer should be. In other situations, your knowledge of the person you are writing to may lead you to conclude that a report should be no longer than one page, or that an informal tone will be most effective. You may also decide that your audience has a limited knowledge of library jargon and that your explanations will have to be in plain English.

There is no strict rule about what you should decide when planning your general approach, but by deciding on several important characteristics of the document in advance, you can focus your writing directly on your goals and save yourself time later on.

DEVELOPING YOUR MATERIAL

Developing your material refers to the process of determining the content of your document. Letting your mind consider many possibilities is essential to choosing this content, yet this activity is often truncated or simply skipped. Some writers attempt to develop their ideas at the same time that they are organizing them, and others work out the content of what they want to say as they are writing the first draft. When you are organizing, and when you are writing, you are limiting and narrowing your ideas and making the choices that will shape the character of your document. It is extremely difficult to perform these tasks efficiently while allowing your mind to "expatiate free" over the range of possibilities; to skip the development step is to cut yourself off from alternatives that might be more effective than the ones that first occurred to you.

Developing your ideas involves giving yourself the opportunity to explore the range of possibilities implicit in any subject without leaping immediately into a confining outline or a restricting sentence. This opportunity to discover, create, collect, and consider your ideas is what we will call invention.

Invention

Although this term may call up images of Thomas Edison, the word *invention* traditionally has been used to cover a range of rhetorical activities, from collecting ideas that are already at hand to creating something entirely new. It is the process of formulating your ideas about your material and the best ways of presenting it to your reader.

At its simplest level of application, it describes gathering information from observation, conversation, reading, and memory. At a more complex level, it also describes the formation of ideas and their clarification, including logical connections, judgments, and evaluations that determine not only the content of your writing, but also the shape you will give it and the stance you will take toward it.

Professional writers use invention even when they are very familiar with the subject at hand. Invention is necessary, if only to move from the way you see a subject to the view of your subject that will be most effective with your reader. In most cases, invention involves taking an expansive rather than a restrictive look at ways of accomplishing your goals through writing.

The need for invention is not always immediately clear. It may contradict the pleasing impression that you already know exactly what needs to be said or that there is only one way to say it. But the adaptability, complexity, and expressive power of language make it almost certain that any such assumption is wrong. In almost every writing situation, we have choices, and they make a difference. If writers use the invention stage properly, they recognize that what they want to say can be said in many ways, all of which will do something slightly different.

As writers collect and develop ideas, they review their earlier conclusions about their purpose, their approach, and the response they hope to achieve from their writing. You should be prepared to consider the possibility that your purpose was not as simple as it seemed. What were you hoping to do through this piece of writing? Is this the most appropriate way to do it? Is your focus more specialized, or more general, than your readers will need or want? What could you cut? What should you add? Do you need to find more data to support your conclusions or more examples to interest the people you are writing for?

Whatever helps you, as a writer, formulate your ideas is, *de facto*, a valuable technique for invention. Some tools, both traditional and innovative, that can help with this stage of discovery are listed below:

▲ research (gathering material)   ▲ freewriting
▲ lists   ▲ dialogues
▲ "maps"   ▲ brainstorming

These techniques represent different ways of exploring what you want to include in your document. It would take a rather desperate writer to try them all for one writing project, but writers should feel free to use them in any combination that seems useful.

It is particularly important to keep in mind the reason you are using these invention techniques. You are not simply exploring ideas for their own sake, though you want to encourage the generation of as many as you conveniently can represent. At some point, you will want to look at the results from your readers' point of view. What aspects of the topic that you are dealing with are most likely to be useful and important to them? What will they need to know? What can be safely deleted or summarized?

Gathering Material

Helping others gather material and do research should be second nature to librarians, but when it comes to their own writing, librarians, like other professionals, may be tempted to skip this step. For this reason, it may be useful to review both the value and the sources of published and unpublished information.

Information, both published and unpublished, can serve you by providing additional ideas, facts, opinions, and perspectives. It can be a powerful stimulant to your thinking during the invention stage. Information can also be valuable as evidence when you write your document. As you search for information, you will want to keep this dual perspective in mind: What information could be useful to you as you explore this subject? What information could be useful in communicating your ideas to your reader?

A lengthy discussion of sources is obviously not necessary for librarians, but a brief summary of major external and internal sources of information may serve as a reminder of the variety of information that exists in both published and unpublished formats.

Published Sources of Information

The range of published information on library topics is at least as rich as in other areas, and librarians need not limit themselves to the library literature. Indexes to the journal literature, encyclopedias, dictionaries and handbooks, texts, and statistical compilations are the familiar tools of the trade, and you merely need to remind yourself that they can be as useful to you as they are to the people you serve. Sometimes librarians, like other professional writers, find they need published information quickly, for immediate writing projects. You should not hesitate to ask for help from the information experts, other librarians. Colleagues in your institution, librarians at state libraries or library associations, or reference staffs in specialized libraries can often save time for you, either by guiding your search or by supplying information.

Unpublished Information outside the Institution

Experts with specialized knowledge abound, in agencies, in libraries, in universities, and in specialized industries and businesses. Identifying the appropriate experts can begin with the simple question: Who would know? Obviously, judgment is needed in deciding what information is where, and whom to call, but most people do not mind providing information if they are approached appropriately. If, for example, you need more recent library statistics than appear in published sources, you may try to locate an appropriate compilation prepared by library associations, state libraries, or individual librarians. Failing there, and lacking the time or the courage to send out a questionnaire, you might wish to narrow your needs to a few questions and call libraries directly.

Unpublished Information within Your Institution
Your institution contains a wealth of potentially useful information: in filing cabinets, in statistical reports, in the experience of others, and in the day-to-day operation of your library. To gather this information, you can review files, observe activity directly, interview staff members, or ask questions informally.

Making Lists

Making lists can be helpful for organizing material generated by research, for exploring aspects of a topic, or for getting started. Every day people fend off chaos by making lists, yet people who are convinced they could not get through the day, or even the supermarket, without a list may hesitate to use one when they are grappling with extremely complicated clusters of ideas.

Lists ease the strain on your memory and allow you to take advantage of momentum and chance association. You are not committed to the ideas you generate, so they can be as illogical as you please. In fact, you are better served by lists if you are willing to approach them playfully, secure in the knowledge that you want possibilities *now*, and that you can always become critical and rigorous at a later stage. Work quickly,using your private shorthand, and do not worry about correctness, parallelism, or even usefulness. Later, you can refine or restructure the lists or use them as the basis for further invention or outlining.

It is usually best to provide yourself with some focus for the list, perhaps a title, a heading, or a question. The items in a list can be individual words, phrases, or whole sentences. Questions are useful, especially when you need to consider possibilities or objections that might not occur to you under ordinary circumstances. When you are listing questions, do not stop to answer them until you feel that you have run out of questions. Then, assess the items that seem most promising to you. You may want to assemble them again into a second list in order to streamline your associations, or you may wish to test some ideas against other conclusions that you have reached.

Lists are congenial to a mind prepared to move quickly in scanning mode. When the entries are short, they provide a visual overview of the topic and its main parts. Individual writers or groups of writers can use this way of representing ideas to record the results of other writing process techniques, such as brainstorming, because lists do not require a strictly logical ordering, and each item can trigger associations with succeeding items.

Making Maps

In this context, a "map" is a visual representation of the relationships between ideas—details, arguments, and facts—on a page (or video screen), created by using blank space, circles, various kinds of lines, and other symbols to connect, rank, or separate items. At its least formal, it may be a small step removed from the underrated doodle. At its exalted heights, it may resemble a complex architectural blueprint.

Organizational structures, "flow charts" that represent a chronological sequence of steps, and many conceptual systems are far easier to grasp in this kind of visual form than a sequence of words can be.

Even writers who do not ordinarily think of themselves as having spatial imaginations may find that mapping helps them work out what they want to say and how they want to say it. It is easier to generate relevant ideas when you can see how the ideas you already have about something tend to cluster into certain relationships.

For a rudimentary exploration of your ideas, it is best to start with a very informal kind of map. In the center of a blank page, place a key word or phrase to represent your initial idea of the topic. Circle it, and take several moments to allow this topic to divide into its main parts. Find words or phrases to represent these ideas and jot them down, as if they were points on a circle that use the main idea as its center. Leave room for plenty of other ideas to circle these secondary points, so that your ideas can be developed to whatever level of detail you wish.

Not all maps will have an extended period of usefulness. In many cases, you are simply trying to frame a set of relationships in a way that allows you to think about ideas together instead of one at a time. In fact, the few minutes that it may take to make the map can be more important than any time spent studying it later, and it is not at all unusual to move directly from making the map to making a list, to brainstorming about one of its parts, or to outlining.

Freewriting

Freewriting is a way of thinking on paper about your reader, your material, your general purpose, the tone you want to achieve, or the most effective way to organize your presentation. Normally, you give yourself some initial focus or starting point and then begin writing—without stopping—for ten minutes or so. You do not worry about grammar, spelling, punctuation, paragraphing, or logical ordering. Instead, you write down your thoughts as they occur to you. This technique has the advantages and disadvantages of thinking in sentence form, rather than in the short phrases that are usually a part of a list-making or brainstorming session.

Certainly, you should not be overly concerned about constructing beautiful sentences at this point, and you may not wish to write formally correct and complete sentences on the page in every case. But, when you are writing in this way, your ideas will come to you in something like sentence form, a unit of logical closure that is capable of conveying a much more coherent kind of thought than the successions and groupings of ideas encouraged by invention techniques like making a list or mapping.

Ten minutes may not sound like a very long time, but most people find that the pressure to keep thoughts coming is a little uncomfortable, although the results are often worth the trouble. If you run out of ideas before ten minutes have passed, you might try writing a dialogue.

Writing a Dialogue

Sometimes it is easier to imagine what someone else might say than to put down your own thoughts. When you are writing dialogue, you have a chance to start a conversation between two characters, borrowed or original, one for and one against a position. Your job is to write down what they say to each other and to keep them talking about the topic, just as a good host would. As in freewriting, you should not give either speaker the opportunity to create an embarrassing silence in the conversation, and you should make sure that each speaker has a good chance to respond to the points raised by the other. The dialogue probably should not be a steady succession of declarative sentences. People ask each other questions, and they do not try to talk for exactly the same length of time.

Because ideas have a life and power of their own once they have been unleashed in words, this technique may make it possible to see the attraction of other viewpoints, like those your readers may hold.

A dialogue can be an especially useful preparation for writing a recommendation or a proposal when acceptance is not a foregone conclusion. By setting up a dialogue between you and your reader or a person with opposing ideas, you can isolate issues you will want to address in your document.

Brainstorming

Brainstorming is another technique for getting your mind to move as quickly as possible from idea to idea, using free association to overcome the barriers imposed by ordinary ways of thinking about any subject. To give yourself some initial direction, start by writing down a key word or phrase to investigate. Naturally, this key word could be your central topic, but it could also be a less important area or consideration that you would like to think about more fully. Next, write down every word or phrase that comes to mind.

Logic, neatness, and correctness are of no value to you at this stage; in fact, they may be counterproductive. Try not to evaluate or eliminate any of your ideas, and keep the "storm" brewing as long as you can. If you find yourself temporarily blocked, try writing the key word over and over until you find a new direction. Use drawings, lists, or complete sentences if you want to, but do not rearrange or stop to ponder insights until you have finished writing, usually after ten minutes or so. Then, look over the results, noting the most important or interesting ideas and allowing them to sort themselves into natural groupings. You can expect many of the items you find on the page to be routine and unilluminating. Perhaps only one or two associations will be truly surprising or immediately useful, but these are often the difference between a dull recital of routine facts and an effective presentation of your ideas.

All these techniques of invention may look time-consuming at first, but a few minutes spent looking at a topic from a new perspective may be enough to save you from very costly false starts. To leap into a draft without setting aside any time for invention may be minute-wise and hour-foolish.

The aim of invention is so basic to the writing process that it pervades all stages of writing. The exploration of ideas, begun in the invention stage, should continue until you feel sure that your finished document will achieve the goals you have set for it.

ORGANIZING YOUR MATERIAL

The ideas and information you use in a document should be organized so they are easy to read and understand. For a document to achieve its purpose, the material must be presented in a form that

- ▲ makes your ideas as clear as you can make them
- ▲ emphasizes the ideas you feel are important
- ▲ suggests the relationships these ideas have with each other
- ▲ motivates the reader to respond as you wish.

The more complicated the ideas you are dealing with, the more difficult and the more important this task becomes.

Early Organizational Ideas

Most writers are thinking about the sequence of their ideas almost as soon as they decide on a goal for writing. The subject matter, the requirements of circumstance, the preferences of your readers, and the practices of your institution all influence the organizational form, the order of your ideas, and the length of the document you will write.

As you develop your material, you will begin to envision some sequences of ideas that will serve your purposes better than others, and at this point you may wish to begin constructing a provisional sequence from the material you have gathered through invention.

You may wish to reorganize your lists or construct new ones from key elements. You can underline or highlight main topic areas from freewriting or areas on maps. You may wish to draw arrows that connect sections or represent the flow of ideas. Or you may wish to jot down ideas about some effective ways to organize the material. As long as you can tell later what you meant, it does not matter how you delineate your early, provisional sequences.

But at some point you will want to try a complete succession of ideas and consider the level of development you will give them. Then, you may wish to consider a formal or informal version of outlining.

Outlining

For planning a document with more than one or two main parts, outlining is a convenient, schematic means of representing the sequence of ideas, their relationships to each other, and the level of detail that you require. Occasionally, writers resist using any form of outlining, perhaps because of unpleasant memories of tedious drills inflicted during the seventh grade, but the technique does not need to be contrived, lifeless, and rigid. It can help your writing become more creative and flexible.

The aim of outlining is not to divide your topic into an elegant and symmetrical pattern. Instead, you are using outlining as a tool to discover an order and development of your ideas that is most suited to accomplishing your goal, with a specific situation and reader in mind.

As you experiment with the order and development of ideas, you may find these questions helpful:

- ▲ What are your most important ideas?
- ▲ What is your reader most concerned about?
- ▲ What does your reader need to know first?
- ▲ How much does your reader need to know?
- ▲ What order of ideas will be most effective in this situation?

Types of Outlines

Any sequence of items can serve as an outline, as long as you understand it, but the major types of outlines are discussed below.

Scratch Outline

A scratch outline is a first effort to bring order to the ideas you have collected in the invention stage. It is a preliminary ordering of ideas, and will probably change considerably as you continue to experiment with arranging your material. In a scratch outline, you don't need to be concerned with formal perfection. Your purpose is to develop, from many possibilities, an order that will evolve into the organization of your document.

Formal Outline

A formal outline differs from a scratch outline as an architect's formal plans differ from the rough sketches. The formal plan is certainly not the building nor the reason the building exists, but it is a detailed blueprint for constructing the entire building. A formal outline divides your topic into its major parts, and these, in turn, are subdivided into their supporting elements.

When you are developing the logical progression of ideas for your document, it may be useful to think in terms of four hierarchical levels of specificity. At the broadest level, your document consists of main sections. Each main section consists of main ideas. Together, these main ideas develop the logic of the section. Each of these main ideas is supported with specific detail, information related to the main idea, developing it more fully. A fourth level of specific detail can be provided as a supplement to the main textual argument, either in figures or in attachments to the main document.

Wording the Formal Outline

In formal outlines, entries at the same level of hierarchical importance should be parallel in grammatical form as well as in importance; nouns should be matched with other nouns, phrases with other phrases, and sentences with other sentences.

The topic outline uses brief descriptive phrases for its entries, while the sentence outline has the advantages and disadvantages of being less elliptical. It is usually clearer and more readable, since sentences are less ambiguous, but it is also more cumbersome to create or read.

Formal outlines should be indented, using an alpha-numeric system or decimals to indicate the hierarchical relationships among successive entries.

Traditional Alpha-Numeric Outline Form

The traditional outline is familiar to most people. It starts with a title, followed by a sequence of main points enumerated with roman numerals;

these main points are supported by subordinate entries, preceded by capital letters in sequence. Each successive level of subordination is indicated by further indention, alternating numbers and letters. A typical sequence of numbers and letters appears in the example of traditional outline form in figure 2.

Decimal Outline Form

In the decimal outline, levels of hierarchy are indicated by decimal notation and indention. When decimal notation is used in the actual document, all numbers are sometimes aligned with the left-hand margin, without indention. This common practice eliminates spatial clues about hierarchy and can be confusing to readers who are not completely comfortable with decimals. Figure 3 presents one form of decimal outline. Compare the decimal system with the alpha-numeric one and decide what you feel are the strengths and weaknesses of each.

Developing Outlining Skills

Learning to recognize the hierarchical position of your ideas is invaluable because it allows you to group your ideas in logical order very rapidly. If you feel that you could use practice in this area, you might try developing a formal outline of the next document you write, focusing on developing a logically consistent hierarchy.

Another good exercise involves a technique called reverse outlining, where you develop an outline from a written document. You can apply this technique to any finished piece of writing, whether written by you or by someone else. Trying the technique on a book chapter or journal article is a good way to start. When you outline in reverse, you first identify the main sections in a piece of writing, perhaps by underlining or highlighting. Then, under each main section, you locate what you feel are the main ideas that develop that section. Each main idea will be supported with a variety of narrower ideas or specific facts. As you identify the hierarchical superstructure that supports a finished piece of writing, be sure to critique it as well, noting where its internal logic could be strengthened.

DRAFTING YOUR DOCUMENT

Drafting is the process of giving a narrative shape to the ideas in your outline. The process need not start at the beginning and end at the conclusion, and it may involve only a section of your project at a time; whole sen-

Writing for Publication

(Excerpt from an outline)

I. Reasons for writing for publication
  A. Compulsion to write, having something to say
  B. Need for expression
  C. Pursuit of professional advancement
  D. Desire to contribute to the profession
II. Publication of library and information science literature
  A. Types of publishers
  B. Patterns of editorial staffing
  C. Variety of audiences
  D. Types of articles
III. Publication of articles
  A. Sources of manuscripts
    1. Solicited manuscripts
    2. Staff-written manuscripts
    3. Unsolicited manuscripts
  B. Editorial roles
    1. Determining scope and content
    2. Selecting manuscripts
      a. Criteria for accepting manuscripts
      b. Reasons for rejecting manuscripts
        (1) Substantive weakness in manuscript
          (a) Poor research methodology
          (b) Incomplete coverage of topic
          (c) Faulty logic or reasoning
          (d) Poor organization
          (e) Faulty expression
        (2) Inappropriate submission
          (a) Content not appropriate for audience
          (b) Too long for journal
          (c) Topic covered recently in journal
          (d) All manuscripts staff written
        (3) Problems with form and format
          (a) Failure to follow instructions for submission
          (b) Failure to follow recommended style
          (c) Major inaccuracies in manuscript

Figure 2. **Traditional Outline Form**

tences or paragraphs may be omitted or roughly "sketched" in abbreviated forms, especially in an early draft.

Some writers like to use what they call a "discovery draft" before they have decided what they want to say or how they want to say it. A discovery draft is a first pass at putting down thoughts. It is not even as structured as a

Writing for Publication

(Excerpt from an outline)

1 Reasons for writing for publication
  1.1 Compulsion to write, having something to say
  1.2 Need for expression
  1.3 Pursuit of professional advancement
  1.4 Desire to contribute to the profession
2 Publication of library and information science literature
  2.1 Types of publishers
  2.2 Patterns of editorial staffing
  2.3 Variety of audiences
  2.4 Types of articles
3 Publication of articles
  3.1 Sources of manuscripts
    3.1.1 Solicited manuscripts
    3.1.2 Staff-written manuscripts
    3.1.3 Unsolicited manuscripts
  3.2 Editorial roles
    3.2.1 Determining scope and content
    3.2.2 Selecting manuscripts
      3.2.2.1 Criteria for accepting manuscripts
      3.2.2.2 Reasons for rejecting manuscripts
        3.2.2.2.1 Substantive weakness in manuscript
          3.2.2.2.1.1 Poor research methodology
          3.2.2.2.1.2 Incomplete coverage of topic
          3.2.2.2.1.3 Faulty logic or reasoning
          3.2.2.2.1.4 Poor organization
          3.2.2.2.1.5 Faulty expression
        3.2.2.2.2 Inappropriate submission
          3.2.2.2.2.1 Content not appropriate for audience
          3.2.2.2.2.2 Too long for journal
          3.2.2.2.2.3 Topic covered recently in journal
          3.2.2.2.2.4 All manuscripts staff written
        3.2.2.2.3 Problems with form and format
          3.2.2.2.3.1 Failure to follow instructions for submission
          3.2.2.2.3.2 Failure to follow recommended style
          3.2.2.2.3.3 Major inaccuracies in manuscript

Figure 3. **Decimal Outline Form**

rough draft, but is more like a trial run during which writers experiment with tone and venture into digressions that they may later decide to reject. However, for our purposes, it is more convenient to regard this kind of a draft as a variation of freewriting, with invention as its primary aim.

There are excellent reasons, however, for regarding the first draft you make for any demanding writing project as a discovery draft, even if you have spent considerable time working on invention and organization. The chances are that you will be discovering things that you want to say and ways to say them, and you will probably find that some things need more thought and development than you could detect from even the most detailed outline.

Instead of viewing these common events as unnatural impositions, writers are better off seeing them as useful steps in a process that is followed by virtually everyone who wishes to write well. In addition, thinking of your first draft as a discovery draft may reduce the intimidation that comes with trying to produce error-free, smooth writing when you are still struggling with ideas and organization.

It follows that you can start a draft, discover a problem, "loop" back to an invention strategem for solutions, and start again as often as you need. It is an especially good idea to review, at regular intervals, the material that you have come up with during the invention stage, staying alert for useful details, explanations, organizational strategies, or effective phrasing that you did not appreciate properly at the time. Even if you cannot use all of these things immediately, you can highlight or underscore them for future use.

In particular, you need to keep your overall purpose in mind, as well as the requirements that this purpose imposes. As a technique for keeping your readers' perspective in mind, you may wish to imagine their responses as you write.

Getting Started

Getting the first draft down involves a number of possible blocks, the hardest of which is beginning. If you have difficulty getting started, try beginning at the point in the outline where you feel most comfortable with the material.

Once you have started, keep going, so that you can establish a pace that will keep you from stalling or sliding into distractions. Keep the outline in front of you as a reminder of where you are going and why—but it would be a great mistake to cling to it as more than a momentary stay against confusion. When you are writing well, you can expect to be reorganizing your material as you go. When you find that you are wandering too far afield, use the outline to guide you back to the line of development you have decided upon, unless the digression exerts a power of attraction you find irresistible.

Remember, though, that insertions, revisions, and deletions must meet all the requirements you have set for yourself. So, eventually, you will need to test your results for relevance, completeness, coherence, and effectiveness.

Deciding on a Beginning

The beginning is often the most important part of any document because it shapes the reader's attitude toward what follows. He or she may make instant judgments about the relevance of the content, the ease of assimilating the information, and the credibility of the writer. These judgments can determine whether the message will be read.

Normally, we think of the beginning as the start of the textual narrative, but the true beginning of a document is its title or, in a memo, subject line. Here, readers get their first clue about the subject of the document. Because the title or subject line sets readers up for the rest of the document, we should consider it in more detail.

Title or Subject Designation

The title or subject designation should describe the purpose or nature of your document as specifically as possible. Visualize, for a moment, your reaction when you open your mail and take out a memo. First, you identify the sender and then, unconsciously asking yourself what the memo is about, you look at the title or subject designation. What is written there should answer your question precisely. It should not be so general that it gives almost no information. Compare what you learn from the title "Interlibrary Loans" with what "New Procedures for Handling Interlibrary Loan Requests" tells you. The same principle suggests that you vent your flair for creative metaphors in some more appropriate outlet. Inventing "Libraryland USA" or "Gunfight at the OK Corral" as subjects for memos may relieve the tedium of a gray day, but these fanciful creations may not seem nearly as brilliant to busy readers as they did to you. A precise, descriptive title remains your best chance that the subject will catch your reader's attention and foster a positive attitude as he or she approaches the content.

Summaries as Beginnings

After readers determine the subject from your title, they want more information about the content of the document. Your readers will want to know "what it's all about." Many experts advocate the use of summaries, from one sentence to one page, depending on the length of the document.

These summaries perform the same functions that abstracts serve for journal articles. It is interesting to note that most readers, and especially administrators and managers, like documents that begin with summaries. Although writers occasionally feel that this practice may dampen the reader's enthusiasm for details, the opposite is usually true. If the reader is interested and needs more information, he or she will read on. Using the murder-mystery approach to entice the reader to discover the conclusion works in a novel, but seldom succeeds in on-the-job writing.

Summaries are particularly helpful when your document ends with a recommendation or a request for action or approval. A brief summary, clearly labeled, at the *beginning* of your document alerts readers to your request or recommendation and allows them to test your argument against your conclusion.

Other Beginnings

The principle that professional writing should begin with information that is important to the reader is well established. Formal summaries are a useful way to indicate significance, but other kinds of beginnings can also work well. A good principle is to start your document with significant information that furthers your goals and addresses what you feel will be your readers' concerns after they have seen the title. A number of ways to begin a document are listed below.

- ▲ Summarize the recommendations
- ▲ Summarize the request for action or approval
- ▲ Present the conclusions
- ▲ State the document's purpose or the reason you are writing
- ▲ Describe the content
- ▲ Summarize the main points
- ▲ Address a major concern or anxiety of the reader
- ▲ State an important point of the document.

Constructing "Signposts" for the Reader

Organizing ideas and information is a process of imposing a logical order on a mass of potentially relevant thought. At the beginning of the organizational process, you are concentrating on determining what that logic will be. As the process continues and the logical order of your argument takes shape, you will want to concentrate on making that logic clear to your *reader*. Once you know where you are going, you want to be sure that you leave a clear trail for your reader to follow.

You can help readers follow your argument, instead of wandering off on innumerable side trails, by constructing linguistic signposts along the way.

In addition to making your trail easier for the reader to follow, most writers find that these devices help keep them on track, especially in the early drafts of complicated pieces of writing.

Any language that guides the reader can be considered a signpost. Some of the most helpful are described below.

- ▲ *Title or subject line.* The title or subject line tells the reader what topic the document covers.
- ▲ *Summary.* A summary states the recommendations, conclusions, or major points of a document and tells readers where they are headed.
- ▲ *Headings and subheadings.* These descriptive words or phrases announce the subject of the next group of sentences or paragraphs and prepare the reader for what comes next. When headings and subheadings are placed in a systematic, hierarchical sequence, they provide an easily comprehended structure. They can be genre headings, descriptive of the type of content, such as "Goals" or "Conclusions." They can also be topical and describe the subject of the section, such as "Headings and Subheadings" (used above). Finally, they can be what we might call main-point headings, that describe the content of the section in more detail, such as "Writing Documents That Are Easy to Read."
- ▲ *Topic sentences.* A topic sentence is a general statement of a main idea. Subsequent sentences provide more detail supporting this idea. The topic sentence calls the reader's attention to a main thought in a paragraph or section of your document.
- ▲ *Directional and transitional words.* Words like *therefore, next, so,* and *also* are like roadsigns that tell your readers at a glance what logical, temporal, or spatial relationships they need to recognize to follow you.

Signposts can be powerful tools for directing the reader's attention to main ideas. Because they focus the reader's attention on specific aspects of the document, they must be used in a coordinated and logical way, as reinforcers of your logic and the development of your thought. When used poorly or without adequate thought, they can become distractions. Unless all your signposts lead in the same direction, your reader will have difficulty reaching the right destination.

Signposts can be added during revision, of course, but they are very useful in drafting, too, because they keep you focused on leaving a trail for your reader.

Rewarding Yourself

The tougher the assignment, the better you should be to yourself. Reward yourself for reaching minor goals, as well as the major one of finishing the draft. When it is time to read your draft, give yourself credit for the things you think you have done right. See if you can put the strengths of your draft in words, and use your own highlighting system to single out for special praise words or phrases that you feel work well. Your best chance for writing well, in successive drafts and in the future, is to allow yourself to experience some success and satisfaction. Restricting your attention to problems and mistakes can seriously distort your sense of accomplishment and make good writing harder, not easier, in the future. While you want to retain a realistic notion of what you need to fix during revision, give yourself credit for what you have done well.

Chapter 3

THE PROFESSIONAL WRITING PROCESS: Revising and Editing

CHAPTER OUTLINE

IDENTIFYING PROBLEMS IN YOUR DRAFT
Reading from Your Reader's Perspective
Identifying Your Writing Problems
Using Others to Critique Your Work

A SYSTEMATIC APPROACH TO REVISING AND EDITING

REVISING FOR EFFECTIVENESS
Revising to Accomplish Your Goals
Revising for Your Reader's Reactions
Reviewing Your Communication Strategy
Revising for Organizational Structure
Revising for Personality and Tone
Revising for Effective Sentences
Revising Word Choices

EDITING FOR CORRECTNESS
Detecting Errors
Diagnosing Your Problems of Grammar and Usage
Editing for Accuracy

In most current theories about writing, revision is understood to be more than trying to avoid errors and awkwardness. It is an opportunity to step away from earlier emotions and perspectives and to assess, from a second vantage point, what you have written. Revision gives you the chance to review earlier decisions within the context of a complete document. And if, during the press of original composition, you adopted any aspect of form, approach, content, and organization by habit or because you were unaware of other possibilities, revision gives you a second look and a second chance.

The importance assigned to revision is changing old attitudes, but many writers still have the impression that revision is merely a clean-up operation and so they limit it to cosmetic changes. If they revise at all, they leap from the first draft to what should be the final stages of revision: checking grammar, spelling, and punctuation. These activities are part of a total revision, but making the draft "correct" can easily become the whole definition of revision.

A comprehensive view of revision encompasses reassessment of the major decisions that shaped the document, along with attention to the sentence structure and word choices that gave the ideas substance. As a final step, the smaller details of form are edited for correctness and appearance. Any method that allows you to cover all of these areas is useful; however, it makes sense to approach revision in an orderly progression, starting with the most important decisions and working down to the "fine tuning." This procedure protects you against spending valuable time perfecting sentences that you eventually throw away.

IDENTIFYING PROBLEMS IN YOUR DRAFT

Recognizing problem areas in your writing requires special effort. When writers read their own work, they often "fill in the figure" with meanings that were intended but not expressed. You, as a writer, know *exactly* what you meant, and it is sometimes hard to detect when the document does not convey that meaning to others. To analyze your writing objectively, you may wish to try some of the techniques below.

Reading from Your Reader's Perspective

Modified role playing can be very useful in helping you shed your perspective as the writer and view the document through the eyes of the reader. Picture yourself as the person who will receive the document; try to imagine the circumstance in which you would receive it and how you would react to it. Knowing the attitudes and points of view of your readers will help you "sit behind their desks" in your imagination and judge the document as a piece of writing produced by someone else.

Some very good writers have to take extraordinary steps to achieve objective distance when they are looking at a draft they have written. You may find that you are partial to your own handwriting or to the appearance of an early draft. To counter these biases, it may help to type your working draft on paper of a different color or texture. Also, you can provide yourself a visual cue that you are working on an early draft by using pencil or ink of a different color. You may find it is easier to make changes and additions if you have triple-spaced the draft or written it on only half of a page, leaving room for alternative versions on the other half.

All these techniques are designed to break the mindset you had during the initial composition, encouraging you to establish a fresh perspective from which to assess your document. Whatever method enables you to view your writing objectively is the correct one for you.

Identifying Your Writing Problems

Although the variety of problems that, theoretically, could occur in any draft is dazzling, the problem areas in your writing are neither as random nor as numerous as you might imagine. Difficulties that are the most important—difficulties that interfere substantially with communication of your meaning—often appear in patterns that are recognizable for each writer, although everyone's "error print" is somewhat different. Some writers find that they consistently say too much, providing far more detail than most readers need. Others tend to say too little, to leave out important explanatory information, to sound contentious or apologetic, or to phrase their ideas too starkly or too abruptly. Still others fail to organize their writing, have a chronic problem with parallel sentence construction, or use the nominative case in prepositional phrases ("just between you and I").

Very good writers realize the importance of not making these mistakes, so they pay close attention to the kinds of errors that they are prone to make. Poorer writers not only are much more eager to forget their errors, but are tempted to defend their mistakes when these are noticed. They may deny ambiguities, on the grounds that only one meaning was intended or because, only a few pages later, the meaning becomes obvious.

Since the range of difficulties most writers have is fairly limited, it makes sense to face the reality that no one's initial draft is as good as it could be and to try to identify your areas of vulnerability. These are the problems to look for during revision.

You may know that you have areas of weakness in your writing, but you may have difficulty pinpointing them with enough precision to recognize and fix them consistently. In that case, you might consider asking an editor or an English teacher to help you develop an inventory of your problem areas. Then you can focus on understanding those problems and correcting them.

Using Others to Critique Your Work

The perspective of other people can be very useful in identifying the need for revision. While we all know the value of an outside opinion, accepting criticism gracefully is not easy, and writers frequently ask for comments and then react with annoyance when they get them. Because it is difficult to hear criticisms of your writing, it is important for you, as a writer, to know exactly what you want when you ask for opinions. If you zero in on the areas you want strengthened, you may find constructive criticism more helpful. Knowing the kind of advice you want will also help you select an appropriate critic.

If you are concerned about political overtones in your document, you should choose someone who knows the situation and is astute politically. If you want to reduce your five-page document to one page, you might ask a colleague with strong editorial skills to give you advice. If you know you are weak in certain areas of grammar, an editor or an English teacher can help you spot such problems.

Despite everyone's best intentions, most people feel wounded when weaknesses in their writing are mentioned. One technique for handling criticism is to put time and distance between you and the comments before reacting. An ideal scenario is to accept the criticism graciously, discussing it enough that you understand it thoroughly but avoiding the tendency to argue or defend your point of view. If the criticism is not in writing, you might take notes so that you can review the details later. Then, when you are alone, you can let yourself react. After a little time has passed, you will find it easier to assess the comments more objectively, to see if they are helpful in solving the problems in your draft.

A SYSTEMATIC APPROACH TO REVISING AND EDITING

When you revise and edit your document, you can reassess a wide variety of writing decisions: everything from the main purpose of the document to spelling. In this chapter we have divided this process into two activities: assessing your draft for its effectiveness and editing it for correctness. The same approach works for both activities. As you read your draft, look for problem areas. The checklists in this chapter can help you identify trouble spots. When you find an area that needs improvement, analyze what you think is the problem and devise an alternative. Focusing on one aspect of your document at a time will also help you zero in on difficulties.

The discussion that follows provides advice for diagnosing problems in the following areas: goals, audience, strategy and approach, organization, tone, sentence construction, word choice, correctness, and accuracy.

REVISING FOR EFFECTIVENESS

Once your document has taken shape, you are in a position to evaluate your reasoning about your purpose, approach, readers, and the organiza-

Use these questions to identify areas that need special attention during revision. Each area is discussed in greater detail in the text (as indicated by the topic in parentheses).

1. What do you want to accomplish by writing this document? Will it achieve that goal? (goals)
2. What reaction do you predict your reader will have to the document? What actions will your reader take? What is your reader likely to remember? How will it affect your reader's attitude toward the subject and you? (audience)
3. Is this document, as you have written it, appropriate for the communication channel(s) you have chosen? (communication strategy)
4. Does your purpose stand out clearly? (organizational structure)
5. Have you supported your main points convincingly? (organizational structure)
6. Have you organized your subject logically? Will the logic be apparent to your reader? (organizational structure)
7. Do any paragraphs sound disorganized or confusing? (organizational structure)
8. Do the tone and style seem pleasing and consistent? Have you used language that may cause offense? (tone)
9. Do any sentences sound awkward or confusing? (effective sentences)
10. Will your reader understand specialized terms and abbreviations? Have you avoided unnecessary jargon, wordiness, and awkwardness? Have you avoided clichés and mixed metaphors? (effective sentences and word choice)
11. Does the document contain glaring errors in grammar, punctuation, and spelling? Are all facts, names, and numbers accurate? (correctness)

Figure 4. **Identifying Problem Areas in Your Draft**

tion and expression of your ideas. The checklist in figure 4 provides an overview of the revision process. You can use it, when you begin revision, to pinpoint problem areas in your draft. Each area is discussed in more detail in the rest of the chapter.

Revising to Accomplish Your Goals

As a first step in revision, it is a good idea to review what you wanted to accomplish by writing the document and then to assess whether the draft you have written will do what you had in mind. From this general review, you can identify the areas that need the most revision. The questions below may help you extend your analysis in this area.

▲ Do you predict that your document, as it is now written, will accomplish its intended purpose?

▲ If you are uncertain that the document will be completely successful, can you articulate what obstacles, both in the environment and in the document, may block success in achieving those goals?

▲ How can these obstacles be addressed?—
By using different channels of communication, different media?
By altering content, perspective, or tone?
By altering organization of the document to make your case clearer?
By rethinking your strategy for persuasion or motivation?
By making the document easier to read and understand?
By shortening the document?
By simplifying the language?
By other alterations or revisions?

Revising for Your Reader's Reactions

Trying to predict how successful your document will be with your reader is another way to assess the amount of revision you need. If, for example, you know that your reader prefers summaries to lengthy documents and the one-page document you had planned has expanded to four pages, you can predict that your reader will not read the whole document with complete attention. You then know that you should find some way either to reduce the document to one page or to write a short, introductory summary that could carry your main message to the reader, if that is all he or she elects to read.

The questions below may help you anticipate your reader's reactions to your document.

▲ Do you think your reader will read the document?

▲ If not, what might you do to increase the chances that the document will be read?

▲ Given the level of attention that you predict your reader will give it, is the document structured so that the reader is likely to recognize and retain important information? What can you do to emphasize your main ideas?

▲ What attitudes toward the subject do you predict the reader will have after reading the document? What attitudes toward you?

▲ Is the reader likely to take the action that you desire? If not, what can you do to increase the chances that he or she will do what you seek?

Reviewing Your Communication Strategy

Reviewing the appropriateness of the channels of communication you have chosen, the format you are using, and the approach of your document should help you notice any major shifts in direction that have occurred during drafting. Now that you know the content of your draft, you are in a position to make firm decisions about what additional kinds of communication might be needed to introduce your document, to reinforce its message, and to follow it up at a later time. To reassess your decisions in this area, ask yourself the questions below.

- ▲ Is the channel of communication that you have chosen the best for achieving your purpose?
- ▲ Is the document you have written appropriate for the communication you are using? Are the format, tone, length, and level of detail in your document appropriate? What changes should you make to accomplish what you had in mind?
- ▲ What other channels and communication methods will you use to introduce the topic to your reader?
  reinforce the message in your document?
  follow up your message?

Revising for Organizational Structure

As a first step in revising the organization of your document, you will want to be sure that your purpose is clear to your reader. To do this, read as you expect your reader to read—all at once and quickly, looking for relevance and the main ideas. Then put the draft down, as you can presume your reader will, and think of it as a whole rather than as an assemblage of elaborated parts. Ask yourself these questions:

- ▲ Will the reader understand its purpose and subject quickly?
- ▲ Will the reader understand why he or she is asked to read it?
- ▲ Will the information be useful to the reader? Is it clear why?

If the answer to any of these questions is no, you will want to consider ways to make the purpose of the document more explicit, perhaps by bringing explanatory material nearer the beginning. Look first at your title, making sure that it is a clear, precise statement of the subject of your document. Next, examine the first paragraph. Is the information in that paragraph significant; that is, is it important both to your reader and to furthering your purpose? Do you need a stronger beginning? Review the list of strong beginnings in chapter 2 to be sure that your document opens in a way that states its main concerns.

Checking Main Sections

Long documents, and many shorter ones, can be divided into main sections preceded by section headings. These headings should announce the subject of the section and lead your reader through the document. The main headings you choose will be governed by the type of document you are writing and will be considered further in chapters on types of documents.

Checking the Organization of Paragraphs

Dividing the main sections of your writing into unified and coherent paragraphs can help your readers see where they are going and why, as informational signs provide a traveler with a reassuring sense of progress. Each form of logical closure makes it easier to see the way sections of writing are related to each other and to the purposes of the piece as a whole. Paragraphs are expected to develop points that are clearly related to the central thesis. The sentences within the paragraph need to be related to that point in a logical way, and they need to be connected with each other.

Using Topic Sentences. Paragraph topic sentences can state the unifying topic, suggest its significance in terms of the overall purpose, and signal the major concerns that are taken up by individual sentences in the rest of the paragraph. For these purposes, it is usually a good idea to place topic sentences at or near the beginning of the paragraph, because this position is usually seen by your reader as the most emphatic within the paragraph. The last sentence of the paragraph is the second most emphatic, and it is especially appropriate for paragraphs that move from specific cases to general conclusions.

The goal of good writing is not the "well-formed paragraph" but the paragraph that best serves your goals. If a paragraph works well for you, why change it?

On the other hand, if you discover, when you are revising, that some of your paragraphs are confusing, that they follow too many points for coherence and unity, or that some are too undeveloped and ambiguous to allow your readers to see where they are headed, you will need to address these problems.

Diagnosing Paragraph Problems. Here are some questions to help you diagnose and treat major difficulties in your paragraphs:

▲ Is each paragraph within the problem area clearly related to the main idea in that section?
▲ Are all the details within these paragraphs related to each other and to the main idea of the paragraph?
▲ Are enough details provided in each paragraph to develop its main idea adequately?

▲ Would placing these paragraphs in a different order help the reader see these ideas more clearly?

▲ Would clearer topic sentences help your reader see the logic of your organization more clearly?

Revising for Personality and Tone

Once you have assessed and solidified the organization of your draft and are fairly certain that the content and order of ideas will not change drastically, you can consider the way your ideas are expressed. But before you look at sentence construction and word choice in detail, you may wish to assess the cumulative effect of all these choices.

Problems of Personality and Tone

Here are some questions to guide your examination of the tone and personality of your writing:

▲ Is the level of formality of the document as a whole appropriate to the occasion, your institution and position, and your style?

▲ Do all elements work together to achieve a consistent tone?

▲ Do you detect any hint of pomposity, stiffness, stuffiness, or pedantry in your writing projects? Or any hint of shallowness, insincerity, superficiality, or illogic?

▲ As a reader, what is your reaction to the personality projected by the document?

Recognizing the Potential for Unintended Offense

Despite the importance of avoiding even the appearance of an insult, the unintentional nature of common offenses makes them difficult for a writer to see. Conscious of our own benevolence and purity of motive, we read our drafts in the same spirit with which we wrote them, and if the message goes astray, we may be too ready to assume that the writing was good, our intentions were good, and therefore the fault lies with our oversensitive readers. *We* are insulted if *they* are insulted; our conscience can rest; and our writing continues to blunder on, though perhaps with less good will than in the past.

The task in revision is not assigning blame, but preventing it. You do not need to turn on yourself to anticipate how other people are going to feel about the language you have used, but it is worth your while to try to prevent a destructive misunderstanding about your feelings toward other people.

To revise effectively, you may find it useful to have guidelines that can help you detect potentially offensive language. We may start with the principle that people are offended when they feel that they are diminished in status or value. Since status and value are communicated in almost every human interaction, the number of ways human beings have found to express these ideas about relationships is beyond measure. But it may be useful to classify most of these offenses into three categories:

▲ stereotyping—denying significant individuality to members of a group and significant variation to the group
▲ isolating—addressing, describing, and writing for special groups as if they were essentially different from, and inferior to, other groups that they regard as equal
▲ denying—ignoring the special concerns and significance of a group through overgeneralization or euphemism

From these three categories we can derive questions, presented in figure 5, that can guide the search for language that may sound biased to readers who are unfamiliar with the purity of our hearts.

These questions can be asked to identify language that may be considered offensive:

1. Does language in the document suggest unjustified assumptions about the nationality, economic class, sex, age, or race of the group you are writing about or to?
2. Do you use masculine and feminine pronouns (*he* and *she*) in a way that suggests stereotyping of traits, professions, or opinions?
3. Do you make unflattering assumptions about the knowledge or sensitivities of some of your readers?
4. Do you treat the names of some people differently from the way you treat the names of others?
5. Do you treat the titles of some people differently from the way you treat the titles of others?
6. Do you give information about the age, race, physical appearance, or marital status of some people and not of others?
7. Do you phrase potentially unpleasant statements in language that will sound evasive or deceptive to people concerned about a problem?
8. Are you overgeneralizing about the concerns, attitudes, opinions, or traits of groups of people?
9. Are you using *we* when you mean only *some of us*?
10. Are you using *they* when you should be including some of your readers?
11. Do you use only masculine nouns and pronouns when referring to groups that include both sexes?

Figure 5. **Checking for Unintended Offenses**

Revising for Effective Sentences

Once you have completed a review of your document and are satisfied that approach, tone, length, and organization will remain relatively stable, you can turn to problem sentences with some confidence that your efforts will not be revised out of existence.

The principle that it is best to start with the most disruptive revisions and work progressively toward finer tunings applies in the case of the sentence itself. *The key is to pinpoint sentences that do not communicate your meaning clearly.*

Too many writers not only waste time by trying to "fix" minor parts of their sentences "that ain't broke," they tend to spend more time on these trivialities than on anything else. Perhaps all this practice with fine tuning eventually makes writers better at changing the form of sentences, but it does not make them better at locating the sentences that need changing—and, to make matters worse, these "solutions" often sound worse than the original version.

The best approach is to find those sentences that may sound vague, confusing, or awkward to your reader.

In a surprising number of problem sentences, these difficulties occur because the sentence's main thought has drifted from the grammatical core of the sentence (the subject and verb of the main clause) into modifying clauses, words, and phrases. These subordinate elements are then forced to bear the brunt of meaning, often linked together by vague verbs, like forms of the verb *to be*.

Vague Verbs

Vague verbs have very general or nonspecific meanings. The verb *to be* belongs in this category, not because it lacks a legitimate role but because it has little meaning on its own, beyond denoting identity or existence. It is effective when it connects or links stronger, more substantial elements in a sentence. When you use a vague verb, the sentence must rely on nouns, pronouns, and verbs in subordinate clauses for its specific meaning, so the length and complexity of the sentence increases. Writing that consists primarily of vague verbs becomes longer, more convoluted, and less energetic than writing that relies on strong verbs. Other verbs with general meanings that often act as vague verbs are *exist*, *seem*, and *make*.

Frequently, vague verbs are combined with nouns to take the place of a strong, specific verb. So "make a decision" replaces "decide" and "draw a conclusion" substitutes for "conclude." When these phrases add something specific to the sentence, their use is defensible. If they are merely roundabout, weaker phrases for stronger, more specific verbs, they are diluting sentences without contributing anything in return.

Passive Voice

The passive construction, describing the sentence's subject as acted upon by its verb, is also a perfectly respectable form of the English sentence, though grammarians contradict one another about such basic matters as what kinds of verb can be made passive, what kinds can serve as passive markers, and what effect being made passive has on the transitive nature of the verb. The passive voice is often used as a natural and polite way to keep the "doer" out of the limelight, when identifying the doer is embarrassing or unnecessary. Somehow, it is pleasanter to learn that your bills have not been paid than that *you* have not paid them.

Sometimes, though, this generous, softening impulse turns evasive and dishonest. Then, passives insinuate the implausible suggestion that, because unfortunate things "have been done," no one or nothing has actually done them. Workers "are laid off," civilians "are killed," mistakes "are made"; and the responsible agency is unnamed.

But even when the doer of an action is so obvious or unimportant that it is really not a part of the sentence's main idea, passive constructions can easily become so long and complicated that they end up sounding both vague and wordy. Since this effect tends to be cumulative, you may notice it in your writing only when you use more passive constructions than you have come to expect from the natural flow of thought in English.

Revising Vague or Passive Verbs

Many sentences that sound vague, convoluted, confusing, or awkward have vague or passive verbs. To recognize these problems, look for

▲ a form of the verb *to be* as the main verb in the main clause of an awkward or confusing sentence
▲ a vague verb, like *make*, linked with a noun, like *decision*, to take the place of a strong, efficient verb, like *decide*
▲ a passive construction in the main clause of a sentence that conceals the importance of the doer in the original thought
▲ a passive construction anywhere in a sentence that sounds confusing or overcrowded by other clauses and phrases.

Often you can fix sentences of these kinds just by making the main idea the subject and verb of the main clause. It follows from this that less important ideas in the sentence should be moved out of the subject and verb positions in the main clause and into other grammatical constructions that show their true roles and importance. Once you have placed your main idea in the grammatical core, you may need to rebuild the sentence with subordinate clauses and other modifying elements that complete your meaning. This technique takes a little practice, but the results are usually well worth the trouble. We suggest that you follow these steps:

- ▲ Articulate the main idea of the sentence, the core meaning that the sentence is trying to express. You may not find it word for word in the sentence, and so you may have to struggle to discover the essence of what you want the sentence to say.
- ▲ Phrase that idea with a subject and an action verb, and make them the subject and verb of the main clause.
- ▲ Place modifying ideas in constructions that reflect their importance, starting with independent clauses and descending through dependent clauses, phrases, and words.

You can test your skill at spotting and revising weak verbs with the sentences below. See if you can state the problem in words, as well as fix it, using the suggestions above. More than one kind of error, of course, may be found in each sentence. Compare your analysis and your revisions with the revisions in section A, pages 321–22, of the appendix.

1. Reimbursement for courses in word processing will not be approved unless a recommendation is submitted in writing to the director of Personnel.
2. The necessity for making long-distance calls, especially given the escalating charges for such calls, should be a consideration in requests for changes in telephone service.
3. The fact that the number of requests for this information culminated in an increase from 1976 to 1978 is an indication that additional staffing will be required within the next two years.
4. All employees should be informed that their requests for reimbursement are to be completed in triplicate and sent to the business office as soon as possible.

Other Common Problems with Sentence Structure

Other problems with sentence structure occur frequently enough in professional writing to warrant staying alert for them as possible sources of confusion. These problems are listed below and discussed in detail in section B of the appendix, pages 323–26.

- ▲ Subject separated from its verb
- ▲ Verbs and prepositions separated from their objects
- ▲ Modifiers too far from the words they modify
- ▲ Incorrect or vague referents of relative clauses
- ▲ Inconsistent verb tense
- ▲ Misleading emphasis.

You can use figure 6 to test your skills in revising sentences by identifying the problems that lead to confusion in meaning and by rewriting the sentence to correct the problem. The answers appear in section C of the appendix, page 327.

Answers to the exercises appear in Section C, page 327, of the appendix. Discussion of these issues appears in Section B, pages 323–26.

1. Please make sure that your employees understand the corridor is to be off limits, the main gate will remain open, and the reasoning behind this policy.
2. Having been expanded, I am sure the periodicals room will be a more comfortable place to study.
3. We have placed the sign-up sheet that you gave me Monday in the hall in the library this afternoon.
4. Your report should anticipate the need for additional supplies or personnel that may fluctuate with the level of your department's activity.
5. To determine the amount of charge for lost items, we will use the price shown in *Books in Print* when available; when not available, we will charge $25.
6. We have purchased a number of new books for children that are going out almost as fast as we can place them on the shelves.
7. After reviewing all our applications, some of the candidates were brought in for interviews.
8. An explanation of the arguments for and against our plan to keep the library open during the evening next summer required an extra hour.
9. The number of interlibrary loan requests that we received in the main branch of the library was twice as high as the music library.
10. The conditioner that was shaking severely disturbed the student working next to it.
11. When her daughter was ten years old, she received her doctorate.
12. As long as the no-food rule was observed, students have been allowed to use the lounge area for meetings.
13. Perhaps we welcome this challenge more than other people.
14. The decision to strike was made by us yesterday in a meeting at which coffee, tea, and light snacks were served.
15. She asked the committee, a consultant from Baltimore who had worked on similar projects for two universities and a nonprofit institute and me to come up with a proposal.
16. We have decided to deal with the problem of theft by installing an alarm system, which worries me.

Figure 6. **Test Your Skills: Revising Sentences**

Revising Word Choices

When you are working with problems in your sentences, you will inevitably come up against questions of word choice. Changing the sentences to fix other problems may solve a few of these difficulties, but no amount of shuffling can eliminate all of the basic choices writers face when they select the words they want to use. In this section we will consider some of the reasons individual words and phrases fail to communicate clearly.

When you review word choices from your reader's point of view, you will be in a better position to spot potential problems. An effective way to begin your revision for word choice is to read your entire draft, marking any language that might fit the following descriptions:

- ▲ overly specialized terminology
- ▲ pretentious vocabulary
- ▲ wordy constructions
- ▲ mind-boggling combinations
- ▲ clichés

In the sections that follow, we will discuss each of these areas in greater depth, but the questions below may be enough to point toward a satisfactory solution to your revision problems:

- ▲ Will *everyone* in your intended audience understand the words you have used? If not, "translate" them into plain English.
- ▲ Will these words sound pretentious to your reader? If so, abandon them.
- ▲ Can you say the same idea in fewer words? If so, do it.
- ▲ Will other wording make the idea as clear? If so, use it.
- ▲ Will other wording sound fresher, more alive? If so, consider trying something new.

Specialists' Language

Sometimes called jargon, specialists' language is defined as a vocabulary developed within a profession for concepts relating to its practice. Frequently, no brief, plain English equivalent exists for a specialized concept, spurring adaptation of another word to the specialized use. Consider, for example, the term *wet carrel*. Audiovisual librarians find it useful for describing carrels with electrical outlets. For many librarians and library users, however, the term is baffling.

The specialized vocabulary of a profession often fills a legitimate need. It allows for the precise identification of specialized concepts and provides a shorthand language for rapid communication among professionals. When specialists' language makes communication easier, it is useful, even indispensable.

But specialists' language can also get in the way of communication. When the reader is unsure about the meaning of a term, feels uncomfortable, or does not know what a word means, effective communication is not occurring.

Many specialists do not recognize that others are unfamiliar with the terms they are using. Professional fields have become so diversified that basic preparation may not include the emerging, specialized vocabulary in other branches of a field. Most librarians are now familiar with some computer jargon, but terms familiar to a searching specialist may not be understood by a librarian who has had no experience with computer searching.

Outside the field, the problem becomes acute quickly. For example, users of libraries, while having professional vocabularies of their own, may not understand, or care to understand, the librarian's specialized language. Even when nonspecialists hear specialized terms frequently, they may not understand their full range of meaning. How many people who use your library, for example, would recognize themselves as *end-users*, even if you use the term regularly?

Specialized vocabulary can create a psychological barrier between those who understand the term and those who do not. This separation between the "insiders" and the uninitiated can have effects on both groups, producing elitism and isolation in one and defensiveness or a sense of inferiority in the other. But the greatest cost may be in lost opportunities for real communication, unrecognized by either group through mutual and continued misunderstanding of the words involved.

For example, most people who use libraries frequently identify the term *reference* with the service they receive when they approach a desk that bears that label. But how many users know the levels of training involved in answering different questions or the full range of services available under the term *reference*? Would the public more fully understand what reference people do, and the kinds of services offered by a reference desk, if libraries used plain-English labels or if the term were more self-explanatory?

Jargon

While the term *jargon* is sometimes used as a synonym for specialists' language, we will reserve its use for obscure, vague, or pretentious language, marked by roundabout phrasing and word choices that do not convey clear, specific meanings. Terms that originate in specialists' language can become jargon when they are used in an inappropriate context or when the distinctions they originally marked become blurred or unnecessary. For example, *input* and *interface* have specialized meanings and can be defended in many contexts. These words are also often sprinkled generously about, when their only contribution is to provide a more technical-sounding equivalent of a plain-English concept.

A special form of jargon, known as bureaucratese, sounds to many readers like the buzzing of innumerable bees: "Interactive synthesis may be implemented by enhanced differential clarification." While each of these words has a perfectly appropriate meaning by itself, packing all this unnecessary technical precision into dense phrases creates a kind of verbal pandemonium. The reader has to work too hard to sort out meanings and relationships that often seem perfectly clear to the writer, whose ideas did not happen to come to mind in simple language. Some say that when an idea comes to anyone in language like this, it is really not an idea at all. Certainly, it is true that much bureaucratese clothes a general thought that can be defined more precisely by plain and specific language.

Many, if not most, professionals are aware of jargon, and while they may not avoid writing it, they can recognize it in others. While some readers may be impressed by language that they do not understand, the communication between a writer who uses imprecise, inflated language and a reader who does not recognize the problem is nothing to envy. Further, when readers understand the technical terms, they will detect and resent the mistakes an impressionistic writer is likely to make.

If you feel that your writing may occasionally suffer from this kind of pretentiousness, you may wish to try a word-count test that can be a general indicator of trouble.

Latinate words can be counted by a simple procedure. If a word has a legitimate form ending in *-tion, -sion, -ate, -ative, -atile, -ation, -ite, -ity, -itude,* or *-ition,* it is probably Latinate. Unless you are an expert writer, or writing in Latin, you should try not to use more than twenty-five Latinate words per hundred in successive passages. Such passages are likely to sound pompous. If you find more than eight Latin words in four lines of typed prose (or every thirty-three words), you are in the danger zone.

To address this problem, substitute non-Latinate words for specialized terms that are not critical to your meaning, change idioms where you can, and alter your sentence structure to bring greater variety of language into the passage.

Wordy Construction.

Most writers believe they should use the fewest words necessary to express their meaning. But some ideas require more words than others, and you have the best chance of eliminating wordiness if you look for characteristic symptoms: redundancy, nominalization, and negative constructions.

Redundancies. Redundancies are mindless verbal echoes that have lost their power to emphasize a meaning by repetition. "Each and every" repeats its meaning in an obvious way. A "consensus of opinion" repeats its meaning more subtly, but with the same effect: more words than anyone needs, since a consensus has to be "of opinion." A "general consensus of opinion" repeats both root meanings of *consensus.* What other kinds of consensus could we expect? If the modifier implicitly repeats the meaning of the term it modifies, we can catch these constructions by asking: "What other kind?" or "How, when, or where else?"

Test your reactions to these examples and eliminate the redundancies you find:

repeat again	completely eliminate
true facts	collaborate together
past memories	component part
previous history	both alike
background experience	close proximity
final outcome	plan ahead

Nominalization Nominalization turns ideas expressed directly by other parts of speech into wordy phrases built around a noun, usually one that is overly general or inessential. Identify and correct this kind of wordiness in these examples:

We achieved the task's completion.

The committee reached the conclusion that an increase in the fee for interlibrary loans was a necessity.

We engaged in writing activity for most of the morning.

Test your skills by suggesting alternatives to the constructions below:

exhibit a tendency	in view of the fact that
is found to be in agreement with	with reference to
carries on the work of developing	at the present time
takes cognizance of the fact that	during the time that

Mind-boggling Language

Mind-boggling language baffles your readers by presenting them with constructions resembling unsolvable puzzles. Three types of puzzlers present special problems to writers who may know perfectly well what they mean, but who have lost track of their readers' need to follow them: negative constructions, mixed metaphors, and nouns strung together like boxcars. These constructions are not always dull, but their effect is often numbing.

Negative Constructions. If a sentence sounds a warning bell in your mind and it contains a negative construction, try recasting it in a positive form. Some negative constructions cannot be avoided, but protect your readers from mind-knotting complexities. Remember:

Negatives are not only infrequently less economical, but also less clear. (Rewrite this advice in positive form.)

Mixed Metaphors. Figurative language uses the imagery of a figure of speech, like a simile or metaphor, to clarify an idea or to present it in a certain light, usually through a comparison with something familiar but essentially dissimilar. Most writers try to avoid figurative language in what we are calling professional writing, writing done as part of one's professional responsibility. While the extensive use of figurative language in this context may not be desirable, occasional, careful use of metaphors, similes, and other forms of imagery can reinforce your meaning in memorable ways. As in decisions about other revisions, you will want to judge the appropriateness of each use of figurative language by the effect you predict it will have on the reader.

Staleness, a typical problem when metaphoric language is used, is discussed in the section on clichés below. But even dead metaphors may come to life with a vengeance if they are "mixed" with another, conflicting use of figurative language. A mixed metaphor forces two figures of speech into one ludicrous or impossible combination:

We tested the waters with a trial balloon.

A grateful public flooded the switchboard with plaudits beyond our wildest dreams.

Putting these images together results in a surrealistic vision beyond our wildest dreams.

The simplest and best test for a mixed metaphor is to visualize the images the metaphors invoke. If the imagery conflicts, revise it—before it makes your reader's teeth crawl. And if you find you cannot come up with the literal equivalents of these images, you might ask yourself why you thought you were saying something in the first place.

Strings of Nouns. Nouns that take over the functions that the English language normally allots to adjectives, adverbs, and verbs become mind boggling when there is a good chance that your reader will not recognize their meaning in these new roles. The problem becomes even more acute when a string of nouns assembles, performing different grammatical roles in a sentence. Who can be sure what a "high school teenage sex education course paradigm nuances"? Sometimes the best advice is to reword the sentence, using an adjectival or adverbial construction instead of a noun: not "significance level," but "level of significance"; not "user response" but "users' response" or "responses of users." In fact, some grammarians would insist on rewording, whether it sounds better or worse, clearer or more confusing. Usually, you can come up with a satisfactory alternative, but it must be admitted that our language has always used nouns to express meanings outside any strict definition of their grammatical function, and many of these expressions ("school bus," "ice cream cone," "traffic light," etc.) continue to enrich the language. A dictionary can tell you when a word that is most frequently used as a noun also doubles as an adjective. Trying to eliminate all strings of nouns, even when they are clear, is a task for those who care very much and are willing to spend a great deal of time revising. An alternative is to look for constructions that make your writing sound clogged and unclear, and to revise the offenders. Another tip is to be wary of more than two nouns in a string.

Clichés

The term *cliché* was derived during the last century from the "click" of metal plates used in the process of engraving from metal stereotypes, and some readers may react with a grimace when they encounter an overly familiar phrase. These phrases have been used so often that most of your readers are weary of them. Oddly enough, many of these constructions are far younger than the words and idioms around them, but they still manage to make even the freshest ideas sound mass produced and carelessly constructed. How do these phrases sound to you?

steady as a rock	to stand out like a sore thumb
sharp as a tack	hasty retreat
name of the game	made scramble
the challenge of the future	today's complex society
rich in tradition	old as the hills
to build on our heritage	

To revise the clichés you have spotted in your writing, try to reword your idea as concisely as you can. If you cannot come up with an improved version, you may be better off returning to the original. The fact that your ear has tired of hearing "once upon a time" does not guarantee that you are about to improve on the formula.

Test Your Skills

Figure 7 provides sentences that will give you practice in identifying and solving problems involving appropriate choices of words. This exercise is necessarily artificial, since each sentence is isolated from its context. Nevertheless, these problems are likely to cause difficulty in many situations, especially when they are part of a cumulative pattern of similar usage, and practice in recognizing potential difficulties and identifying alternatives should be useful. Answers appear in section D, page 328, of the appendix.

(Answers appear in Section D, page 328 of the appendix.)

1. We will initiate planning activities in September.
2. I have reached the tentative conclusion, in my opinion, that I am basically in a state of readiness for tackling new horizons.
3. We are not unwilling, at this point in time, to consider paying those expenses that have not been disallowed.
4. Personnel with similar background experience in their past history exhibit a tendency to situate themselves in close proximity to each other.
5. As the old cliché puts it, "Don't cry over spilt milk."
6. Let's collaborate together on this project.
7. All personnel should take cognizance of the fact that we need to form contingency plans like there is no tomorrow.
8. It goes without saying that haste makes waste.
9. The bottom line is that we need feedback about the policy's impact on our work-oriented environment.
10. May we herewith offer you our humble thanks for your very unique assistance?

Figure 7. **Test Your Skills: Word Choice**

EDITING FOR CORRECTNESS

In this text we are advocating that you postpone a thorough search for some kinds of problems in your draft until you have settled the important decisions affecting the overall size and shape of your text. After you have made these major decisions and revisions, you are ready to scrutinize your writing for errors in grammar, usage, spelling, punctuation, format and style. This stage of revision can be thought of as copy editing. Because it is nearly impossible to look for all these errors at once, we are suggesting that you appoint yourself your own copy editor and edit the manuscript for grammatical correctness, punctuation, and accuracy. As a last step, you can look over the final copy, giving all the details a final proofreading.

Many of these details may be small, but they are important in professional writing because such errors often obscure your meaning or distract your readers. Even when readers are able to decipher the intention behind errors, they are very likely to form an unfavorable impression of the writer.

Everyone makes mistakes of one kind or another, especially in early drafts. The first step in correcting them is often the most difficult: recognizing errors for what they are.

Detecting Errors

Errors in grammar, usage, and punctuation present a special problem because some of the most significant errors are made through habit or misunderstandings about the rules. The result, unfortunately, is that if you read your own writing, applying the same habits and rules, you will not find anything that calls attention to the problem, even if the error is a serious one.

To make matters worse, the rules some writers laboriously apply are often based on misunderstandings or misapplications of what they have heard. Surveys have shown that many writers never begin a sentence with *because* in the mistaken belief that such sentences are ungrammatical. Some write interminable sentences because they remember having been told not to start a new sentence until they have a "new thought." Some people always use a comma before quotation marks. Other refuse to use essential commas because they remember having been told not to use "too many commas."

It is not surprising that well-educated people may misunderstand a few issues of grammatical correctness. Many grammatical rules are complex, and even people who feel comfortable with conventions for using commas, for example, may not fully understand restrictive clauses. Regional usage can also blur some writers' sense of grammatical correctness. Probably the biggest source of uncertainty about grammar, however, is the changing nature of language. As language evolves, standards—which are loosely based on the speech of educated users—change. The change often follows a pattern of growing acceptance of the new form. During this period of change, dictionaries, usage books, and grammar texts may disagree.

Even though the complexity and vitality of the English language mean that answers to grammatical questions are sometimes confusing or contradictory, certain errors cause more uncertainty in meaning or more outrage among readers than others. Many readers carry with them the rules they learned during their education, and so they may not be aware that standards have changed, even when those changes have the sanction of language authorities. Because many readers care about what they see as "correct" use of the language, we advise writers to adopt a conservative stance in grammatical matters, if only to ensure their readers' good opinion of their language skills.

Judgment is needed in this area, as in all other areas of writing. Generally, the prudent writer will want to be cautious about matters of grammar and usage in formal English. But in some circumstances, very conservative usage can sound stilted or overly formal to your audience, and more flexibility may be preferable.

No one produces writing that is entirely free from mistakes, in part because of the slippery nature of errors, discussed above. Because some errors are more noticeable than others, the best tack is to identify the highly visible errors that you are prone to make.

Diagnosing Your Problems of Grammar and Usage

Most educated writers make few grammatical mistakes, but almost every writer is uncertain about some aspects of grammar and usage. These uncertainties tend to translate into the same difficulties in document after document. Most writers do not need a complete refresher course in grammar; they merely need some way of identifying the few areas that are unclear.

To help you identify your areas of uncertainty, we have devised a diagnostic test that covers twelve problem areas in grammar and usage. These difficulties are of two kinds. Some are basic errors that can incur the disdain of readers and so should be identified and corrected. Others are errors that appear frequently in the writing of educated professionals. If you tend to make these errors, you may wish to identify the confusion and free yourself from nagging worry about these problems.

We suggest that you use figure 8 to test yourself in two ways: by supplying a correct version in formal English for each problem and by putting in words the reasons behind your choices and rejections.

The answers appear in section E, pages 328–29, of the appendix, and discussion of the problem areas with additional exercises appears in sec-

(Answers appear in Section E, pages 328–29 of the appendix. Discussion of the issues can be found in Section F, pages 330–40.)

1. The (consortia, consortium) (is, are) a valuable resource for libraries in the state.
2. There (is, are) a librarian and a student in the main reading room.
3. The director, along with her staff and an outside consultant, (has, have) considered the proposals carefully.
4. The rotunda was restored by a team of experts (, ; :) many of whom worked on the project for over a year.
5. The terminal has been delivered (, ; :) however, it is not yet installed.
6. At our next meeting, we will vote on the motion that is (laying, lying) on the table.
7. Just between you and (I, me), we may have a surplus in our budget this year.
8. She is an administrator (who, whom) Jim and (I, me) can trust.
9. She is an administrator (who, whom) can trust Jim and (I, me).
10. We talked about forbidding smoking frequently, but never did.
11. Having adjusted the fee scale for next year, the searching budget, plus revenues, should cover our expenses next year.
12. We feel (real, really) (bad, badly) about our mistake.
13. I am not sure which of these two alternatives is (better, best).
14. Our services might improve if we had (less, fewer) people on vacation.
15. Each year seems to bring (its, it's, its') own problems.
16. The total cost will equal two (years, year's, years') rent.
17. It is one of the libraries that (has, have) applied for a grant.
18. Everyone has a chance to voice (their, his or her) own opinions.
19. The report is mainly about the rapidly changing costs of telecommunications and that libraries need to prepare their institutions for major increases in the near future.
20. If I would have been there, the decision would have been different.

Figure 8. **Test Your Skills: A Diagnostic Test for Problems in Grammar and Usage**

tion F, pages 330–40. For convenience, all twelve problem areas are listed in question form in figure 9.

Editing for Accuracy

Good copy editing requires a tolerance for tedium that borders on the heroic. In addition to checking for problems in grammar, punctuation, and usage, you must read your document carefully to ensure its technical accuracy.

When you are editing for problems in grammar, punctuation, and usage, you will want to concentrate on the areas that give you the greatest difficulty, but it may be useful to have a general checklist for all these areas.

1. Do the subject and verb of your sentences agree in number?
2. Are any typographical sentences incomplete, spliced by a comma, or run-on?
3. Does any sentence contain a questionable form of a verb?
4. Are any pronouns in the objective case when they should be in the subjective case, or in the subjective case when they should be in the objective case?
5. Are any modifying words or phrases in a position that suggests they modify a part of the sentence that they shouldn't modify? Would a new position make the meaning clearer?
6. Are adjectives used where adverbs belong? Are adverbs used where adjectives belong?
7. Do adjectives and adverbs have the correct form?
8. Do any of the words you have used present usage problems you are unsure about?
9. Have you checked the spelling of possessives?
10. Do your pronouns agree in number with their referents? Is it clear which words in the sentence they refer to?
11. Do any sentences contain constructions that should be parallel and are not? Are any constructions parallel that should not be?
12. Where you have used the subjunctive, have you used it correctly?

Figure 9. **General Checklist for Grammar and Usage**

The way your writing finally appears is crucial to its chances of success, despite the fact that the changes you should be making at this stage are small and cosmetic. If something major comes to light at this late date, you may find it necessary to "loop" back to an earlier stage, but if you do, try to find time to follow the sequence of steps again for the new sections of your writing.

If you have found techniques that allow you to read for accuracy without succumbing to boredom, there is no reason to change your procedure; on the other hand, if your approach to this task has been unmethodical and less than effective, we recommend that you take on this struggle armed with a checklist of especially important items. That list should include:

▲ careless or distracting punctuation
▲ spelling (including capitalization)
▲ proper names and forms of address
▲ hyphenation
▲ abbreviations and symbols
▲ all facts, especially dates
▲ all numbers, especially decimals

▲ titles and headings
▲ directions (if you are not producing the document) for paging, spacing, underlining, bolding, and margins.

Your first task is to make sure that the punctuation you have used is what you want, and that none has been lost in the shuffle. Many of the mistakes in punctuation that readers report most irritating are those that writers with a cavalier spirit are likely to consider trivial: missing periods, periods where question marks belong, quotation marks at one end of a quotation but not at the other. If mistakes like these distract readers from following your writing, they are no longer trivial.

If you have difficulty with spelling, you may need to read through your last draft and concentrate exclusively on spelling problems. Use a dictionary for every questionable word. Remember that spelling checkers in word processing programs catch only words that have unrecognizable spellings; and many spelling errors consist of a correctly spelled word in the wrong place. At best, your reader will attribute errors to carelessness and, at worst, to ignorance.

Pay special attention to proper names of people and places. You may have to consult sources other than the dictionary for these. Also, notice any hyphenated words and sentences that continue from one page to the next. Typographical errors can compound your problems in these trouble spots.

Look with some suspicion on the abbreviations and symbols that you have used. Other people's writing may give you some help here that dictionaries do not provide, but double-check where you have an opportunity to do so.

If you are guided by a spirit of self-preservation, you already know that you should double-check facts and figures. Bibliographic citations seem especially vulnerable to unpredictable mutations.

Verify the position of decimal points, digits in large numbers, dates, page numbers, and numbers in a table of contents.

Do not forget to check the title, and be sure that any headings you have used for separate sections and subsections are consistent in form and numbering.

Try to imagine the final appearance of the document in the form it is about to take. Make sure that your directions about paging, spacing, underlining, bolding, and margins are clear enough for someone else to follow, if you are not planning to give the document its final shape.

And, of course, proofread your final copy carefully. Errors in proofreading are errors, nevertheless, and will be judged as such by your readers.

The last step in the professional writing process is producing the document. Design and production of documents are the subjects of chapter 4.

Chapter 4

PRODUCING THE DOCUMENT

CHAPTER OUTLINE

WRITING SUPPORT FOR ALL WHO WRITE
  Types of Writing Support
  Choices for Providing Writing Support

PRODUCING THE DOCUMENT

CREATING THE PHYSICAL TEXT
  Writing in Longhand
  Typing
  Word Processing
  Dictating

DESIGNING DOCUMENTS
  Purpose of Document Design
  Principles of Document Design
  Elements of Document Design
  Designing Your Document
  Consistent Design within a Library

PRODUCING THE FINAL COPY
  Revising the Production Draft
  Creating the Text and Graphics in Final Form

A document, to be successful, must be well written, and it must look professional. Whether the document is a memo to all library staff, a report to a department head, or a newsletter for library users, it should be competently written, free from obvious errors and corrections, attractively positioned on the page, and easily readable. It should look as if it is the product of a professionally competent staff.

Although almost all professionals would agree with the preceding paragraph, documents written in libraries, as well as in other organizations, frequently do not look professional. Proof can be found in almost any filing cabinet. Every librarian has come across the following:

▲ documents squashed at the top of a page
▲ documents with typographical errors and other mistakes that are the result of slapdash proofreading
▲ documents containing strikeovers or other visible corrections
▲ documents that are single-spaced, without adequate spacing between paragraphs
▲ documents with faint printing, resulting from faded ribbons or anemic photocopiers.

Librarians who have a heightened sense of professional identity still occasionally produce documents that look less than professional. None of us is immune. And most of us, as readers of communications from others, remember the inaccuracy and sloppy appearance of much that we read.

Problems with the appearance or accuracy of written communication are not unique to libraries, and librarians can learn ways of solving these problems from other organizations. The first approach is to increase the awareness among professional and support staff of the importance of appearance and accuracy in written work. This attitude should be fostered in all areas of the library, especially at the top. If standards for accuracy and appearance are gently but consistently enforced, everyone becomes aware of these issues and realizes that it is necessary to pay extra attention to them. In most cases, problems with appearance and accuracy are not the result of ignorance, but of not taking the time to make revisions and corrections.

The second approach to solving these problems is as important as the first. Everyone who is expected to turn out professional-looking documents should have access to reasonably convenient means for doing so. We must acknowledge that achieving acceptable levels of appearance and accuracy depends upon having the time and the means for correcting drafts and producing an attractive final copy. No matter who produces the final product—the writer or someone who assists the writer—getting good results takes time and attention, and it is made much easier by certain types of equipment.

For these reasons, we strongly recommend that every library analyze the way it provides writing support for all who are expected to write. This kind of support is usually considered part of office activity, but while some libraries have traditional offices with staff that have traditional secretarial job descriptions, many libraries do not, and in those that do, "the office" frequently handles the director's work and work connected with administration. Much writing goes on in all libraries outside the framework of a traditional office.

WRITING SUPPORT FOR ALL WHO WRITE

If we begin with the assumption that anyone who is expected to write should have access to writing support, two questions emerge: What kind of support is needed? And what arrangements for providing it are possible?

Types of Writing Support

Producing professional-looking documents requires staff (a writer and perhaps an assistant), appropriate equipment, and the knowledge to use that equipment.

Staffing

Should professionals produce their own documents or should assistance be available? There is no right answer to this question. Each situation and each library is different. Even businesses where the one-executive/one-secretary model is established are discovering the value of the executive work station: one person can create text and data, manipulate them, edit them, and even produce them. The strongest argument for the do-it-yourself approach is that, with computers, the tasks of creating, editing, and producing text are merging, and it may be more effective for professionals to control all three processes directly. As work stations for text and data merge, this argument will become even more powerful.

Equipment

Once the value of effective, accurate, professional documents is acknowledged, the importance of word processing equipment follows naturally. The ease of editing and revision alone makes word processing worth the investment, and the cost of that investment is decreasing every day. We recommend that libraries try to make word processing capabilities available, either directly or through assistants, to all who are expected to write. These capabilities should include a word processing program and machine, access to printing, and, of course, supplies and maintenance support.

Training to Use the Equipment

Especially when word processing is new, but even after it is a part of library routines, expertise with computers, with the word processing program, and with the printers must reside somewhere, either with one or two resource people or with all who use this electronic equipment. Providing for training, for answering questions, and for troubleshooting is as important as providing the equipment.

Choices for Providing Writing Support

Each library will undoubtedly work out its own patterns for providing all who write with time or assistance, equipment and programs, and the knowledge necessary to use them. Within each library, different patterns are bound to emerge. Library administrators will want to assess each department and determine the pattern that works best and fits the resources available. Below are four models for providing writing support that can serve as a basis for planning.

▲ *One Writer/One Assistant.* This is the classic business model. In libraries, where secretaries are relatively scarce, other types of assistants may learn word processing skills and be paired with one writer.

▲ *One Person/One Station.* In this model, one person, either the writer or the assistant, has all the necessary word processing equipment at his or her work station.

▲ *Shared Assistance.* This model is the updated version of the typing pool, where writers bring their copy to a word processing assistant who produces documents for many people. You can also use this model of shared assistance to provide education, training, and trouble-shooting.

▲ *Shared Equipment.* There are two variations of this model: the independent work station and the network. In the independent work station, a complete word processing station is set up and shared by either writers or assistants. Writers can schedule time at the work station the way time at OCLC terminals is scheduled in many libraries. In the network, writers share various types of equipment or programs through a network. For example, terminals may be placed at work stations, but central processing units are shared. Printers can be included in the network, so that each terminal can order printing at a central location. Programs and files can be shared with appropriate network design and equipment.

Obviously, these patterns can be mixed to form the best arrangement for a given library. Once the patterns are worked out, policies and procedures for providing writing support can be developed and publicized, to assure that everyone who writes has the support to do so effectively.

PRODUCING THE DOCUMENT

Once the document is written, it must be produced in its final form, including text and graphics. Although a few writers may be tempted to think of production as the job of assistants, the preparation of the final copy inevitably involves revision and design of the document, in addition to typing or preparing the text with word processing. In recent years, electronic office equipment, for text and data, has merged the functions of creating and producing, so even writers who turn production over to assistants will want to participate in decisions about production and design.

For the sake of discussion, we will divide the production of text into three activities: creating the physical text, designing the document, and producing the final copy.

CREATING THE PHYSICAL TEXT

Most of this book is devoted to the intellectual process of creating the text; here, we will concentrate on giving the text its physical shape. The relationship between a thought in your mind and in a physical medium (paper, tape, or screen) is intricate, as all writers will testify, and the processes of creation and revision leap back and forth between mental conception and physical manifestation.

An underlying assumption of this book, and of most writing about writing, is that the first appearance of a thought in written form is rarely as good as it can become. Revision is an essential part of writing effectively, even when that revision is accomplished at the same sitting as the creation, an exigency demanded by much professional writing.

The ability to alter your words after they have been written is essential to all effective writing. Each technique for creating drafts involves a different way of making these changes, and your choice of method for producing text will be influenced by the way you prefer to revise. Since common sense tells you that you will be more likely to make changes if it is convenient to do so, convenience of revision should be a major criterion for selecting a method for producing text. Your decision will also be affected by the speed of each method, the cost of equipment, the availability of assistance, and the experience you have had with each alternative.

The four most common methods for creating text are writing it out, typing it on a typewriter, using word processing, and dictating onto audiotape.

Writing in Longhand

Many of us feel very comfortable with writing our thoughts on paper. We have been doing it since the beginning of our formal education, and it is a very familiar process. Moreover, it is almost entirely within our control; there are no ribbons to run out, no machines to stop working for inexplicable reasons; only pencils that can break and pens that can run out of ink, and most of us feel up to coping with these problems. Equipping someone to write with pen and paper costs very little, and writing can be done almost anywhere.

Enumerating the reasons some people prefer writing in longhand is important because the disadvantages are so formidable. Writing by hand is the slowest method of creating text. Revision can be inconvenient, since extensive changes within a sentence require crossouts, interlinear additions, balloons or bubbles with arrows marking the correct path, or other methods. Perhaps the biggest drawback, after the difficulty of revision, is the potential for problems during production, when longhand must be turned into typed or printed characters. Whereas writing by hand is inexpensive in terms of materials, it can be viewed as very costly in terms of the author's time and the time needed to produce final copy from a handwritten draft.

Typing

The typewriter as a means of producing text is well established in libraries. Revision on a typewriter, while possible, seems inconvenient from the perspective of word processing. Electronic typewriters vary in their capabilities for correcting and revising, but most do not offer the flexibility for revision that word processing provides. While typewriters can break down, most library personnel feel comfortable with these machines.

Word Processing

The term *word processing* refers to computer-based systems that permit the entering, editing, and printing of text. As the definition makes clear, word processing is a method for creating drafts and producing final copy.

Of all writing methods, word processing provides the most flexibility for revision. Changes in text, even major changes, are easily made if the person using word processing is comfortable with the procedures. Becoming comfortable with the computer equipment and the word processing program may, for some people, be a major obstacle, but time and use make converts of most people. Disadvantages of word processing include the cost of programs, equipment, and staff time for learning to use and maintain more complex office systems.

Word processing can be provided in different ways, depending on the type of computer and the software program. Most libraries choose to use microcomputers and word processing programs. Microcomputers with hard disks provide many of the conveniences of large computers, since the word processing program can remain in the machine and does not have to be "loaded" each time the machine is turned on. Microcomputers can also be used to run other programs, like database management programs and spreadsheets.

A second method for providing word processing, found more commonly in large office systems, requires a computer that is designed only for word processing. These systems, called dedicated word processors, contain internal word processing software and are limited to word processing; however, they perform this function with great sophistication. A third means of obtaining word processing is the mainframe computer. Some universities, for example, provide a word processing program on a mainframe computer and allow users access to it for word processing as well as other applications.

All three types of systems—dedicated word processors, mainframe computers, and microcomputers (with sufficient power)—can be configured to support more than one work station. Dedicated word processors and mainframe computers are most frequently used for supporting multiple work stations, but clusters of microcomputers, in local area networks, can be designed with appropriate equipment.

The computer is only part of the word processing picture. The word processing program determines the features that are available. Trying to select a word processing program, if you have never used word processing, is a chicken-or-egg dilemma. To select a program, you need to know which features you will want, but it is difficult to understand the range of possibilities until you are familiar with word processing. The novice has several ways of becoming familiar with word processing programs, although none of the methods is entirely satisfactory. Books (several of which appear in the list of selected readings) and numerous articles explain word processing features and evaluate programs. Demonstrations can be useful, but unless you sit down and work with the program, it can be difficult to understand what is happening.

You can attempt to use other people's programs, but, if you are a beginner, you should anticipate that you will need to spend time, and probably need help, just to get started. Frustration in the initial phases of learning a word processing program does not mean that you will be unhappy with the program once you learn it. Programs that are initially easy to use may not be as flexible once you become adept at using them. Finally, you can ask for advice from colleagues inside and outside your institution.

If other word processing systems exist within the institution, it is useful to investigate them first, since you will appreciate having the support of other users. In addition, your institution will probably support only a limited number of machines with supplies and service, and you may find that having them close at hand is very helpful. Our guess would be that most libraries now have some type of word processing available somewhere in the library, and the current challenge is to make that capability available to everyone with writing responsibilities. For libraries that are still considering whether to introduce word processing, books that can help with that decision appear in the list of selected readings.

Dictating

Dictating involves creating the text orally. The spoken text is recorded either by an assistant taking down the text or by a tape recorder transferring the text onto audiotape. The text is then transcribed into typed form, either from shorthand or from the tape.

Dictating as a method of creating text has established its hegemony in the business world, although word processing, in the guise of managerial or executive work stations, is beginning to make inroads. In libraries, dictating has not taken hold to the extent that it has in business, yet some librarians find it useful.

Dictating has clear-cut advantages and disadvantages. Its chief advantage is that it saves the author's time. The author creates, and an assistant turns the creation into typed form. Trained assistants can transcribe from notes or tapes rapidly, so transcribing from dictation is usually no more time-consuming than other methods of producing final copy from an author's draft.

The potential disadvantages of dictation reflect the differences between the spoken and the written word. Although conversational tone can be beneficial in writing, characteristics of spoken language can work against the effectiveness of written communication. Speaking is usually spontaneous, and may not be as well organized as writing can be. Spoken language can be more circuitous than good writing, and a greater latitude in grammar and usage is permitted in speech than in writing. Many of the difficulties in moving from the spoken to the written word can be overcome through planning, revision, and practice. Roughing out the organization of the document in advance, mentally or on paper, provides a sense of direction when you are dictating. Revising the first draft of the written copy as a matter of course, rather than moving routinely from tape to final form, provides an opportunity to adapt the spoken word to its written form. Most people who dictate learn patterns of speaking that translate well into writing.

Effective use of dictation is also dependent on learning techniques for making transcription easier. Tips for effective dictating are summarized below:

- ▲ Organize your ideas before turning on the machine.
- ▲ Provide the transcriber with the following information at the beginning of your session: your name, the date, and the document you are dictating. For example: "This is Susan Smith, July 24, 1988, dictating a letter to Mrs. Nell O'Brien."
- ▲ Provide instructions about the format to be used, or refer to standard instructions that have been agreed on in advance.
- ▲ Dictate word for word, indicating punctuation.

▲ Speak distinctly, pausing slightly at natural breaks within the sentence. Unless you are normally a rapid talker, slow speech is not essential, especially if you divide your sentences into short, natural groupings.

▲ Spell out names and words that are not likely to be found in a standard dictionary.

▲ Edit the first draft of the written copy as a matter of routine. If you *do* move directly from tape to final copy, be willing to have the final draft retyped if in your judgment it can be improved. Use the same criteria for revising and editing the written copy, produced by dictation, that you would use for any drafted document.

▲ Work with your assistant to establish a dictating and transcribing style that works best for both of you.

DESIGNING DOCUMENTS

When you "design" a document, you make the decisions that determine how the final document will look. Designing involves issues about the appearance of the text and graphic material on the page and the choice of the materials, including type, paper, and ink, that will be used. Until recently, production design has been the province of production and public relations professionals, because design options have required special techniques, equipment, and processes; and special effects have required special equipment and personnel. The few design choices that were possible with standard office equipment were submerged as part of general typing, so that the selection of margin width or the placement of headings on a memo or annual report has not been viewed as designing but as part of standard office practice.

Historians of office practice might observe the beginning of changes in this situation as the creative use of photocopying machines and simplified graphic techniques made special production effects possible without special experience in production. Such a historian would see extensive use of "home-grown" newsletters and other promotional documents for library users as prime examples of these do-it-yourself impulses toward design. The dramatic changes in the balance between what can be done "in house" and what has to be sent out to "experts" have occurred recently, with the advent of word processing, computer graphics, and desktop publishing. Whereas variety in spacing, graphics, margins, and columns used to be viewed as more typing trouble than it was worth, these (and other) choices are now easily available, not only for special occasions but for everyday office use. Because writers and their assistants have so many more choices now, design becomes an important feature of every document, from the memo to the annual report.

Purpose of Document Design

Document design can be defined as making choices that determine the visual appearance of your document. Choices in design are possible for all writers with access to a photocopier, an electronic typewriter, or a word processor. Possibilities for production design are limited only by the capabilities of your equipment and the purpose of your document. As a result, the driving question is no longer: Can I conveniently do something more than type a narrative paragraph? Instead, it is: How can I use elements of design to make my documents more effective? This question can be sensibly answered only in the context of what you wish to accomplish through writing. When you have your purpose, your audience, your content, and your approach firmly in mind, you can choose the design options that will be right for your situation.

In general terms, the choices we are calling design choices can assist you as a writer in several ways. Through design, you can reinforce aspects of your message. Using visual principles, you can direct the reader's attention to significant parts of your text. You can also make a text easier to read and, through layout of the text, you can foster comprehension of main ideas. You can attract the reader's attention and create good impressions with a design that is matched to your audience. Finally, you have the ability to increase the professional appearance of your document by using effects that have, in the past, been difficult or expensive to create.

Design choices can affect your message in ways that are as fundamental as choices about content. Almost everyone has seen documents that have used the capabilities of computer graphics programs well—and documents where computer graphics have created baroque effects that are confusing and distracting. Your task, as both writer and document designer, is to make design decisions that will help you achieve what you set out to accomplish with your document. In this chapter, we will review some basics of document design.

Principles of Document Design

The design of printed documents is a special field of its own. The list of selected readings includes several works that treat production design in detail. In this chapter, we will explore what we feel are some important principles for designing documents in professional writing. This treatment is not intended to be an in-depth review of the design of publications. Rather, it aims to orient writers who would like to pay more attention to the elements of design in professional writing.

1. In document design, form furthers function.

    The design of a document should enhance the function or purpose of a document. The design of your library's letterhead, for example, should be consistent with both your library's identity and the way the stationery will be used. Selection of paper provides another example. Bright yellow paper may be appropriate for calling attention to a flyer announcing a library book-sale, but unsuitable for a routine memo.

2. Design is affective, possessing the power to influence feelings or emotions.

Color of ink, weight and color of paper, design of visuals, use of color photographs, and many other elements of design stimulate feelings and create attitudes in readers. Designers must be aware of the effects of these choices, using them to enhance content and function appropriately.

3. In good design, all visual elements are harmonious and balanced.

Harmony and balance are difficult concepts to pin down. Visual harmony and balance can sometimes be assessed by holding a document at arm's length and squinting, so that individual lines lose their distinctness and blocks of text and graphics stand out as shapes.

4. Visual prominence should reinforce content.

Many design decisions determine visual prominence, including size and design of type, use of graphics, position on the page, amount of space surrounding the text, and so forth. In good design, the reader's eye should go immediately to the item of most importance, then to the next item, and so forth. Design is a very important tool for directing the reader's attention, but its very power means that it can interfere with effective communication as well as enhance it.

Elements of Document Design

With the widespread availability of word processing, with graphics programs for microcomputers, and with photocopiers that reduce and enlarge, writers have much more control over the basic elements of production design than ever before. Now the challenge is to use them effectively. In the section below, we review the major elements in production design and the choices that are now available to most writers through word processing, computer graphics, and photocopiers.

Typeface

Typeface refers to the design of type. Typefaces come in different fonts. A *font* is a complete set of characters of the same size in one design. A font usually consists of a number of alphabets, in roman, italic, or boldface type. They can contain all-capital or all-lowercase letters. Typical alphabets, making up a font, include roman lowercase and capitals, and italic lowercase and capitals. Some printers make it possible to have a choice of typefaces, fonts, and alphabets. A boldface alphabet can be created with some word processing software, some printers, and some electronic type-writers.

Page of Type

The appearance of type on a page is affected by the size of the area it occupies in relation to the size of the page. Width is determined by side margins, and length is determined by top and bottom margins. Some word processors simplify the use of columns so that they can be routine. When margins are "justified," they are vertically aligned. Justified left-hand margins are standard. Justified right-hand margins are standard in published books and articles. Right-hand margins that are not justified are termed "ragged." Unjustified or ragged right margins are common in newsletters, and are sometimes used in other publications to create a feeling of informality. Justification of right-hand margins, formerly possible only with typesetting equipment, is now a feature of many word processing programs.

A text is justified by altering spacing between the words. Lines can become very tight, with words extremely close together, or very loose, with words widely spaced. If you are very concerned about the appearance of your justified text, you will want to be certain that these gaps do not form distracting patterns or "rivers" down your text. Holding the text at arm's length and squinting can blur the words and call attention to the patterns these spaces make. Some writers prefer not to use right-hand justification in word processing because of the distracting gaps it sometimes produces between words.

Columns

Many word processing programs make it easy to format text into columns. Columns can be of two types: parallel and newspaper style. In the parallel style, the reader reads across the columns. In newspaper style, the reader reads down one column and then returns to the top of the page to start the next column. Right-hand margins on the columns can be justified or ragged.

Spacing between Lines of Text

In printing, the spacing between lines of text is called "leading" and is adjustable in small increments. Many word processing programs allow you to adjust the number of lines per inch and set the number of blank lines between each line of type.

Proportional Spacing

With proportional spacing, the letters have differing widths. For example, an *m* is wider than an *n*. Typeset text is proportionally spaced. Some word processors have this capability, when combined with an appropriate font and printer.

Spacing around Textual Elements

In production jargon, this design element is called "white space" and is important for making a page look uncluttered and easy to read. White space can be achieved on a typewriter or word processor by a combination of vertical spacing, generous margins, and indentions or tabulations. A more flexible way to work with white space is to cut out blocks of the printed text with a sharp knife and glue them, along with graphic elements, on paper designed for this purpose.

Headings or Headlines

Headings and headlines serve the same purpose, to inform the reader of the subject of the text and to attract his or her attention. Headings are frequently distinguished by effects such as underlining, capital letters, or boldface type. In newsletters and other published material, headlines and headings are frequently set in larger type, a different font, or even a different typeface. When designers use different typefaces for titles, chapter headings, and subheadings, they try to ensure that the text typeface and the *display* typeface work well together.

Without a typesetting machine or desktop publishing software, there are four ways to produce headings and headlines that are distinct from the text:

▲ *Keyboard Effects:* using whatever keyboard techniques are available on your typewriter or word processor, including capital letters, underlining, or bolding
▲ *Different Sizes or Alphabets:* using an italic or a large font, if these options are available for your printer and word processor
▲ *Lettering Systems:* using a number of possible ways to make your own headings and headlines (see below). Usually, you leave space for these in your final copy, paste them in, and then photocopy the composite to produce the copy that you will use for reproduction.

> Rub-on letters. Individual letters come on sheets and may be transferred letter by letter to your text. Effectively using rub-on letters takes manual dexterity, a good eye, and practice.
> Hand-lettering systems. Several hand-lettering systems are available, including stenciling systems. Producing an attractive product takes skill and practice.
> Machine-lettering systems. Several systems (resembling elementary presses) will produce headings in various sizes and typefaces on a clear tape that you place on your text and photocopy to create the final copy for reproduction. These lettering systems are also popular for making transparencies.
> Photocopier headings. Using your ingenuity and the enlarging feature on your photocopier, you can create both large headings and oversize capital letters for the beginnings of words.

▲ *Computer Graphics and Printing Programs:* Until the introduction of graphics programs for microcomputers, the above techniques were about the best that librarians could hope for, without expensive equipment. Now there are inexpensive and sophisticated graphics programs that allow you to generate headings and headlines in a variety of styles. You can use these to print your entire message, varying the size, or you can cut them out and use paste-up techniques to create a composite for photocopying. Because of the wide range of capabilities available, you will need to explore what is practical for your situation.

Graphics

We are using the word *graphics* in its broad sense, to mean symbols or devices relating to the written word. A few graphic elements can be produced as part of the text. Most of them, however, must be added to the text later and then photocopied.

▲ *Keyboard Effects:* these include underlining and use of symbols like asterisks, dashes, and lines. These effects can be produced as an integral part of the text.
▲ *Pictures and Symbols:* symbols, pictures, graphs, and other elements can be pasted onto the final copy of the text and photocopied to produce a composite. Books of symbols and small illustrations, called "clip art," are available and can be used without violating copyright.
▲ *Computer Graphics:* microcomputer programs are available with their own repertoire of clip art. Depending on your program, computer, and printer, you can also construct your own designs. You add these to your text and then photocopy them.
▲ *Illustrations:* you can have graphic material drawn by hand, if talent and supplies are available, and you can add this material to the text.

Paper

Paper is available in various weights, textures, and colors. Books on production of printed documents can provide descriptions of the astounding number of variables. Perhaps a better way to make pragmatic decisions is to browse through a catalog, or better yet, a store with a variety of choices, to see what is available.

Ink

Using ink of any color other than black used to be a special effect, possible primarily through print shops. Now some printers for word processors can provide this feature.

Fastening

You can fasten or bind multipage publications with staples (either at the corner or at the fold), with punched holes and fasteners, with spiral bindings, and by gluing or sewing. Some of these techniques can be done in-house, and others are available from duplicating centers or printers.

Covers

Along with the choice of fastening comes the choice of a cover. Covers can be made of the same stock as the text paper or of heavier paper. Computer graphics programs have greatly enhanced the variety available for covers, as well as for internal graphics.

Designing Your Document

Your decisions about design will be made in the context of the purpose of your document, the reader you are writing for, and the resources you have for production. As a framework for making design decisions, you may wish to decide first on the overall effect you want from the document's design. It can be useful to think of these effects as the "office" look, the "newsletter" look, and the "published" look. Although elements of design could be combined in any way, these three broad groupings, based on familiar documents, can help you organize your choices more systematically.

The Office Look

Design is important in office documents, even though the elements may not be as flashy or as obvious as in the newsletter look. Design elements help reinforce main ideas, make text clear and readable, and create a professional appearance. Below are some guidelines for designing office documents.

- ▲ Take time to plan the layout of the document on the page, noting its length and paying attention to the overall balance of the text on the paper. Let your eye tell you what is pleasing. A short memo or letter, for example, requires spacing adjustment so that it will not look pushed up at the top of the paper.
- ▲ Consider your use of white space surrounding headings, lists, and paragraphs. Looser spacing can highlight text and give the document a more open, accessible look.
- ▲ Review your use of headings and subheadings, considering such keyboard effects as underlining or bolding. Be sure that your use of these headings is consistent at parallel levels, that all first-degree headings are treated the same, all second-degree headings are treated consistently in another way, and so on.

▲ Consider highlighting material by setting it apart from the narrative flow of your paragraphs. You may wish to organize sentences or phrases in outline form, in numbered steps, or in lists of points. You can set material off from the text around it by double- or triple-spacing or by indention. Inserting short tables in the text is useful for focusing the reader's attention on numerical information.

▲ Be sure that the ribbon on the typewriter or printer is new enough to produce letters that are sharp and crisp.

The Newsletter Look

What we are calling the newsletter look is actually a combination of elements from office documents and published documents, with techniques from journalism, advertising, and public relations thrown in, as well. The newsletter look mixes design elements to suit its purpose and its audience. With the increased flexibility offered by word processing and computer graphics, this hybrid style can be used effectively for many library documents, including fact sheets, announcements, bibliographies, and newsletters.

Your design will depend on your purposes, but the following characteristics appear frequently in this approach.

▲ Titles are emphasized by different alphabets, typefaces, or graphic treatments.

▲ A standard logo or design may be used for all library publications.

▲ Headings and headlines receive prominent treatment, with variations of size, typeface, or graphic enhancement. Symbols and small illustrations either identify or supplement textual elements.

▲ The text may be set in columns, either justified or with ragged right margins.

▲ Variety in paper weight, texture, and color is common.

The Published Look

While the newsletter look, as we are defining it, deliberately retains features that mark it as a home-grown product, the published look describes an effect that appears professionally produced. Most libraries that want to achieve this look will have to purchase at least some professional services. Again, there are no firm rules about design to achieve this look, but it is possible to identify some common characteristics of material that looks professionally published.

The variety and size of type fonts are usually different from those in newsletter documents. Using a different typeface for headings and other special purposes is common. Typesetting options such as leading, type size, and design make a difference in the final appearance. Justification and proportional spacing are standard.

In publishing, production professionals pay close attention to the physical appearance of the text. They attempt to eliminate distracting patterns on the page that justification can sometimes cause. They also watch the way the text divides into pages, trying to avoid what are known as "bad breaks," such as a single line carried over from the bottom of one page to the top of another or a heading or subheading alone at the bottom of a page. Publishing professionals value the crisp appearance of letters on the page and look for broken type and spots or other blemishes.

In a published document, illustrations of all kinds can be treated with a sophistication that is virtually impossible to achieve without experience and equipment. For a fuller treatment of the use of graphics and illustrations in printed documents, you will want to consult one of the books on production in the list of selected readings.

Even with sophisticated word processors, achieving a published look requires additional professional experience and equipment for production design, typesetting, and printing. Some desktop publishing software can rival typesetting machines and other printing equipment, but, in general, these programs require considerable computer power, are relatively expensive, and require some expertise. At the present time, a truly professional look still requires special equipment and experience. Large libraries may have some of these production resources available in-house, but they are not difficult to obtain from printing or publishing companies. Desktop publishing programs are developing rapidly and are sure to be within the reach of many libraries in the near future.

Consistent Design within a Library

Institutions and organizations frequently develop policies to establish consistency in design for documents that go beyond the organization's staff. Some organizations also extend that consistency to internal documents. Libraries also can take this approach and develop policies that govern the major design decisions for documents. Standardization of at least some design elements can contribute toward visual consistency and quality and can also, over time, make library publications instantly recognizable. Elements that are typically included in such policies are discussed below.

Logo
A logo is an institutional symbol, frequently used to foster recognition of the institution. The logo is usually an important element in establishing a consistent and recognizable "identity" for an institution, and it is often designed expressly to be a part of the institution's letterhead. Policies governing use of the logo usually define the situations in which it should be used and its position in the document.

Letterhead

Letterhead is stationery printed with the name and address of the institution. Institutions frequently have their letterhead designed to include the logo. Some institutions have a letterhead to use for communication outside the institution, as well as other stationery, sometimes with different imprints, for internal use. A total communications policy coordinates all stationery so that it is consistent in design. Policies for use of the letterhead can define the stationery to be used in specific situations and the extent to which units of the larger institution can vary the letterhead with their own imprint. For instance, libraries that are part of larger institutions might use the general institutional stationery and have the library's name and address printed on it in an appropriate place.

Color of Paper and Ink

Design and communications policies sometimes specify these design decisions for all the institution's publications or for certain types of publications. For example, a library might use a light buff paper for all communications to its clientele. Or it might decide that all fact sheets will be printed on green paper, all newsletters on gold paper, and all informational memos on a light buff. Use of one color for all library publications builds an identity for the entire library. Varying color by type of publication builds an association with a specific kind of communication.

Other Design Elements

Some libraries have chosen to establish a consistent design format for all publications (except, perhaps, internal memos and reports). The simplest implementation of this decision is to adapt the library's logo or letterhead in standard ways for each publication's format. Master sheets can also be prepared and distributed, so that the staff prepares the text and duplicates it onto the master sheet. Professional staff in your institution's public relations or communications department are a valuable source of advice in establishing consistent design policies and procedures.

PRODUCING THE FINAL COPY

The last step in production is preparing the final copy of the text and any graphic elements. Production can mean typing a document, entering it on a word processor, or revising copy that has already been entered and printing it. Production can also mean adding graphic elements to the final copy of the text by pasting them on the copy and photocopying the result. In its most complex library applications, production can mean pasting up a document, using a desktop publishing program to create a document, or coordinating use of outside professionals to obtain a finished product.

Producing the final copy of the document for reproduction involves preparing both the text and graphic elements in final form. The person who produces the document, whether it is an assistant or the author, takes the text on the medium used by the author and turns it into type, arranged in the way it will appear in the final product. Production of the document, as we are defining it, consists of three activities which can occur separately or simultaneously: revising the draft text, designing the document, and preparing the final copy for reproduction. Production is often done by someone who assists the writer, either a secretary or a support staff member with a variety of responsibilities, including writing support. In many libraries, it is routine for the librarians to produce documents themselves, and with the advent of word processing and professional work stations, professional employees in all types of organizations are assuming more responsibility for production. For this discussion, we will assume that the writer will want to oversee production and will probably wish to take an active role, whether or not he or she actually operates the computer and the printer.

Revising the Production Draft

In theory, production involves the physical transformation and arrangement of the text and occurs after the final copy of the text has been created. In practice, writing and production overlap, primarily because the writer, seeing the document in progressive stages of completion, often identifies important revisions that had escaped notice earlier. As production progresses, depending on the process used, revision can cause more and more difficulty and thus can create real dilemmas: situations where changes in the text will disrupt office workflow and yet clearly will improve the document. The most common example occurs when a writer wants to change a document that has just been typed as the final copy.

These difficult situations can occur especially when the so-called final product is the first chance the writer has had to see the document in typewritten form. Another complicating factor is the chronic shortage of time for revision, and the fact that many on-the-job writers do not give sufficient time to revising documents for effectiveness and correctness during the writing stage. Text is created and pushed on its way to the final product before the writer thinks carefully about what should be changed. Then, when the near-final copy is returned to the writer, the necessary revisions are too obvious to ignore. This situation is not necessarily negligence on the writer's part; it is often an unavoidable result of on-the-job authorship.

For this reason, we strongly recommend that the overlap between creation and production be recognized and officially sanctioned. A phase for reviewing the draft should be a routine part of early production, and office procedures should be designed to allow this review to occur as a matter of course, without disruption of routine. Inserting a revision stage into early production can ease tensions between the writer and the person who assists with typing, and it can also increase the quality of the written product.

How the revision phase occurs depends both on the method of writing and the method of production. If word processing is used in either phase, the revision becomes a simple technical matter. The barriers to revision that may remain involve attitudes, perhaps residual assumptions that drafts for review are a waste of time or that the document should have been done right in the first place. If these attitudes exist, they can sometimes be addressed by creating an understanding of the complexity and importance of the writing and revising process, including a recognition of the need for several drafts.

Creating the Text and Graphics in Final Form

The final copy of the document for reproduction or distribution can be created in several ways, depending on the complexity of the document's design. We will call the final copy, from which multiple copies can be reproduced, the original, and discuss four types of originals: all-in-one originals, limited composite originals, composite originals, and professionally produced originals.

Producing All-in-One Originals

This is the traditional type-it-up method, now updated to an enter-it-in-the-word-processor-and-print-it-out method. This method is obviously the simplest, and it is used almost exclusively for documents with the office look. For pragmatic reasons, most people producing office documents limit themselves to the design effects that they can produce on their typewriters or word processors. So, for example, if your machine allowed you to use boldface type, you might choose to use it for main section headings. You would not be likely, however, to use any of the special techniques for creating bold headings that require pasting the heading onto the original document.

Producing Limited Composite Originals

A composite original is one where elements are added to the printed text, and then the composite is photocopied, duplicated, or printed. The most common design elements that are "pasted on" to form a limited composite original are titles in different styles of type, headings (also in different type), graphic symbols, charts, and illustrations. The design elements can be taped on or pasted on the printed text with rubber cement.

Producing Composite Originals

Much newsletter production and printing is done by a technique called "paste-up." Blocks of text, titles, headlines, headings, and all graphic elements are pasted onto specially designed sheets, creating a composite original document for printing or duplicating. Paste-up requires a good eye, basic production supplies, and skill. The easiest way to learn is to watch an experienced person and then try it yourself.

Obtaining Professionally Produced Composites

When you arrange for the printing of a document, a professionally produced composite will be prepared for you. You will need to provide the text, with the exact wording you desire. You will also want to work with the professionals on designing the document, making clear the effects you want. In most cases, you will be asked to proofread either the composite or a first copy printed from it.

Chapter 5

MEMOS

CHAPTER OUTLINE

WHEN TO WRITE A MEMO

CRITERIA FOR EFFECTIVE MEMOS

MAKING MEMOS EASY TO READ
    Summary of Content
    Arrangement of Ideas in Order of Importance
    Headings and Subheadings
    Keyboard Graphics
    Layout

TONE OF MEMOS

ORGANIZATION OF MEMOS
    Direct Approach
    Indirect Approach
    Memo Format

MEMOS FOR SPECIAL PURPOSES
    Transmittal Memos
    Informational Memos: Single Topic
    Update Memos
    Policy and Procedure Memos

CHECKLIST FOR WRITING MEMOS

Memos are the staple of written communication within most libraries. They can be thought of as internal letters, the established format for writing to people within your library. Memos can be defined as short pieces of written communication that can serve a variety of purposes, including providing information or instructions, requesting actions or approvals, or making recommendations.

These same purposes can also be accomplished through more specialized formats, such as reports, policies, and procedures. To muddy the definitional waters even more, these specialized formats frequently use the standard four-part heading we all associate with memos. In this discussion of memos, we will focus on short, multipurpose communications that use the standard four-part memo form. Documents that serve special purposes, such as reports of various types, will be considered in later chapters.

WHEN TO WRITE A MEMO

"Too many memos" is a complaint sometimes heard in libraries. A chorus of "too few memos" rarely rises from the library staff, and yet in almost any library an objective outsider could identify problems that might be clarified, if not resolved, by effective use of written communication. Simply deciding to write fewer memos or to write memos more often is not the answer. A memo is an effective communication tool only if it is used in appropriate situations. Knowing when you should write a memo, rather than pick up the telephone or talk to someone face to face, is the key to preventing an avalanche of paper and still communicating effectively.

A memo is a useful tool for relaying information or making requests when

▲ the information or the request is complex
▲ the recipient of your message is difficult to reach in person
▲ you want to send the same message to more than one person
▲ you want a record of what was said for reference, the historical record, or accountability
▲ you want to be sure that the recipient of the message has the exact details on record for future reference
▲ you want to present your entire message without immediate response from the recipient
▲ you want the recipient to be able to reply at his or her convenience.

Writing down information for people, instead of delivering information to them orally, is often a courtesy. You record the details of the message, rather than place that burden on the recipient of your message. Giving people a written message also minimizes the possibilities for misunderstanding and provides you with recourse in case of difficulties.

The level of formality implied when a memo is used can sometimes be a consideration in choosing whether or not to write a memo. In many libraries and other institutions, memos are the established way of communicating, and therefore using a memo is not considered an unusually formal way to convey a message. In some situations, particularly where written communication is used infrequently or where more personal topics are involved, using a memo may convey a formal tone that you wish to avoid.

Only you can determine when a memo is too formal for either your library or the subject you are addressing. In these cases, a note, a letter, a telephone call, or even a visit may be more appropriate.

You can, of course, modify the formality of your memo by the words you use. A conversational tone and vocabulary can do much to reduce the formal or impersonal effect of the standard memo form.

CRITERIA FOR EFFECTIVE MEMOS

A memo is effective when it achieves the purpose for which it was written. The ultimate test of writing as a professional tool can be summed up by the following question: Did the document do the job it was supposed to do?

Judging the effectiveness of writing by whether it achieves its purpose is useful because it focuses your attention on results and, therefore, on choices you can make that improve your chances of achieving those results. The way a memo is written is, of course, not the only factor determining success. In almost any situation, many elements affect the outcome. However, memos written with as many of these factors in mind as possible are more likely to succeed than those that ignore the complexities of the situation.

From the perspective of professional writing, memos (and other means of communication that you combine with memos) encompass your communication approach to accomplishing a task. The criteria for assessing the success of your communication must include whether or not the task was accomplished as you wished. So, each memo can be assessed by the communication purpose that you, as its writer, have defined for it.

For example, suppose that you are the head of a branch public library and wish to alter the balance of fiction that is routinely sent to your library so that it better matches the tastes of your community. You decide that the best way to accomplish your goal is to send a memo to the head of Adult Services. Your communication is effective if your library begins to receive fiction that suits the needs of your users. To succeed in these terms, the memo must contain a workable solution to the problem and must express it to the head of Adult Services in a way that is clear and acceptable.

Writers can benefit from analyzing memos that they have previously written. Looking back on a situation that has already resolved itself can help you understand how your communication strategy influenced the outcome and how your written communication might have been more effective. Figure 10 provides an exercise in evaluating the effectiveness of a memo. Problems in this memo have been exaggerated to make them more easily recognizable, but they still represent everyday, garden-variety difficulties that appear frequently in memos. Discussion of this exercise appears in sections G and H, pages 341–45.

After practicing on this example, you may wish to subject some of your own memos to the same analytical scrutiny.

MAKING MEMOS EASY TO READ

Good memos are easy to read and assimilate. The significant issues stand out clearly for the reader to comprehend easily.

Business writing experts advocate brevity as essential to readable memos. In libraries and their parent institutions, many administrators want either short documents or executive summaries of longer ones. Short memos are viewed by readers as easier to deal with than long memos, and we suspect that frequently they get attention faster than a document that appears more formidable.

Keeping memos short is obviously important; however, brevity alone ensures neither clarity nor effectiveness. Presenting information so that the important ideas stand out clearly is essential to effective writing. Clear organization serves the cause of brevity, too, since focusing on important ideas helps you eliminate inessential information. Some techniques that can help make memos easier to comprehend are discussed below.

Summary of Content

Summarizing your main points, your recommendations, or your request at the beginning of a memo lets your reader know the essential content of your communication immediately. Many administrators request that a short summary precede anything longer than one page.

Suppose that you, as a subject specialist in a large university library, analyze the effectiveness of memos you have written in the recent past. In that analysis you discover the memo reproduced below (the memo and its contents are entirely fictitious). You recall that your purpose in sending it was to request approval of a complicated transfer of funds to purchase an expensive set of papers on microfilm needed by a professor for the fall semester. There were valid reasons for the rush request, and the funds in question were under your jurisdiction. Your accounting office required that all fund transfers be approved by the heads of Public Services and Technical Services. Once the transfer was approved, the head of Acquisitions would make the formal transfer request to the Accounting department. Since the normal process would take too much time, you knew that the request would have to be handled as an exception to the rules.

You sent the memo to the head of Public Services and followed up once or twice by memo and phone call. Two months later, you received a copy of the transfer request that Acquisitions had sent to Accounting, but by then it was too late to secure the material for the fall semester. You muttered some unkind words about bureaucracies and braced yourself for facing the professor.

Figure 10. **Test Your Skills: Evaluating the Effectiveness of Memos**

DATE: February 1, 1989

TO: Paula Long
               Head of Public Services

FROM: L. A. Jackson
               Subject Bibliographer:
               American History

SUBJECT: Request to Transfer Funds
               to Allow Purchase of Papers of
               Workhorse Press on Microfilm

The complete papers of the Workhorse Press on
microfilm have just become available, at an initial
publication discount of 20% off the regular price of
$10,000. The Workhorse Press, located in Boston, was
in continuous operation from 1804 to 1972. The complete files of the Press were donated to the state historical society, which microfilmed the entire collection and developed a comprehensive index. The microfilmed set became available for purchase last month.
The file represents the longest complete run of publishing documents available and contains much material on New England writers as well as invaluable
material on the history of publishing. In particular, it
contains manuscript revisions for the work of Sarah
Orne Jewett that do not exist in published form anywhere else.

Professor Steven Smith, in the English Department,
will be teaching a graduate seminar on Sarah Orne
Jewett next fall. He teaches this course only once

Figure 10—**Continued**

every three or four years, and he is very eager to have the Workhorse Press papers available for his class. He feels sure that the expense is justified, since faculty and graduate students in American history, English, journalism, business administration, and library science could benefit from having the complete papers of such a distinguished publishing company available, and I completely agree with him. The addition of these papers will enhance our strong collection of primary sources on microfilm in literature, journalism, and history. At this time, none of the universities within driving distance is planning to purchase this collection. The problem in acquiring this material stems from the fact that the bibliographers in these disciplines do not feel that they can fund the entire amount, and Norma Bell, in Periodicals, does not have enough money remaining in the microform budget for a purchase of this size. They all agree that the papers are appropriate for us to buy; it is the size of the expenditure that is the trouble.

After negotiating with all of them, I think I have put together a coalition that will work. The bibliographers responsible for History (account 1407.702), English (account 1411.702), and Business (account 1501.702) have agreed to supply $1,000 each from their budgeted funds; the Library Science account (1709.702) will contribute $500; endowed funds (account 1992.702) for Journalism will supply $2,500; and Special Collections (account 2021.702) and Microforms (account 1298.705) will each supply $2,000.

I know that fund transfers can be very convoluted and time-consuming, and I am still reeling from the difficulties we had getting amounts credited to the right accounts the last time we tried to charge this many accounts for one purchase. An additional complication is that our great and dear friend, the computer, will not process an order unless the account contains enough money to pay for it. To comply with our recent acquisition guidelines, this order should be processed through the microfilm account, but there is not enough unencumbered money there to cover; so, until fund transfers are accomplished, the order can't be processed.

As you can see, it is a very complicated situation, but the result seems worth pursuing. As far as I can tell from Acquisitions, the only workable approach is a fund transfer, but that usually takes more time than we have. I suggest that we request rush handling of the transfer. If we wait until after March 15, the price will go up $2,000, and I don't know whose arm I would twist to get the additional money. I think the well is about dry for this purpose anyway.

All fund transfers need your approval, so I'm passing the problem, and the completed order slip, along to you. Please feel free to call me if I can give you more information. I, and Professor Smith, will greatly appreciate anything you can do to help us get these papers here for the fall.

Thanks for your help.

Since the transfer came through too late to take advantage of the discount, and too late for Professor Smith's seminar, the memo did not achieve its purpose. Analyze the memo and make a list of possible reasons the memo did not succeed.

Discussion of this exercise appears in Sections G and H, pages 341–45 of the appendix.

Figure 10—**Continued**

Arrangement of Ideas in Order of Importance

Organizing your ideas in order of importance is a technique that can make memos easier to read. The main ideas come at the beginning of the memo, thus orienting your reader immediately and providing him or her with a framework for reading the rest of the document. By arranging your ideas in the order that is most important for accomplishing what you want, you are saving your reader's time and also focusing his or her attention on what you want done. The arrangement of ideas in the order of importance is called, in business writing, the direct approach. It and its alternative, the indirect approach, are discussed in detail in the section on the organizational structure of memos.

Headings and Subheadings

Announcing the subject of the upcoming paragraph by heading or subheading prepares the reader for the topic. Headings also reduce the need for lengthy narrative transitions, divide a topic into its significant parts, and display those parts for the reader.

Keyboard Graphics

The graphic capabilities of typewriters and word processors can be used to highlight main ideas and call attention to significant points. Underlining, boldface type, and such symbols as asterisks can be combined with indentions and spacing to guide the reader to main ideas.

Layout

Careful planning of the layout, or the spatial relationships of your sentences and paragraphs, can increase the ease with which a memo is read. You have the entire sheet of paper at your disposal, so instead of letting the words and paragraphs fall where they will, you may want to adjust spacing, indentions, and paragraphing so that the reader's eye is attracted to elements of importance. Making judicious use of spacing, indentions, and graphic elements is an excellent way to increase the ease of reading and, at the same time, reinforce your ideas.

TONE OF MEMOS

Tone is the combined effect of all your writing choices. It encompasses the personality you project and includes your writing style, your attitude toward your subject and your reader, and the effects of all the decisions you have made about sentence structure, length, and word choice. The tone of a memo can be demanding, curt, or peremptory; it can also be casual, relaxed, friendly, or practically any other shade of human feeling.

The tone of a memo affects the reader's reaction to the memo, just as your personality, words, inflections, expressions, and gestures affect the way people react to you when you speak. Readers are extremely sensitive to tone, perhaps because the combined effect we are calling tone represents the writer and his or her relationship with the reader. The literal content of your message is important, of course, but your readers' perceptions of your tone can significantly alter their understanding of your words.

While readers are very sensitive to tone, writers are frequently unaware of the tone they have created in their writing. In the memos we have reviewed, both those written by librarians and by other professionals, problems with tone are common.

Overtones, or suggestions of meaning, created by specific words or phrases, are a problem when their meaning conflicts with the message you wish to send. An overtone is often just a hint of meaning, created by the phrasing of one sentence, or the use of one word rather than another—seemingly a small matter in itself, but a meaning, nevertheless, that your reader will receive. The best means of controlling overtones is to be certain of the precise meaning and current usage of the words you use. This advice is not meant to curtail your efforts to expand your vocabulary. You will want, however, to be certain that you are using all words, especially new acquisitions, in their accepted meanings. When in doubt, consult a dictionary. Controlling overtones, however small, and making sure that they *reinforce* what you are trying to say, rather than undermine it, is important in creating an effective tone.

To be an effective writer, you must become sensitive to the tones and overtones of your writing and alert to the way they might be perceived by your reader. Probably the best way to develop this skill is to read each memo you write as if you were the recipient, trying to hear its overall effect and imagining how your reader will react to specific words and sentences.

ORGANIZATION OF MEMOS

Thoughtful selection of content and careful organization of these ideas are crucial for writing a brief, clear, effective memo. Although you may not care to outline your memo point by point, you will want to make deliberate choices about the information that you should include. Some of the methods for developing your material, discussed in chapter 2, may help you collect preliminary ideas. After you feel you have explored your subject enough to begin to organize your thoughts, you will want to select those that will best accomplish your purpose and to plan the order in which you will present them.

Direct Approach

The organizational pattern known as the direct approach or deductive order is useful in professional writing because it produces a clear, straight-forward document that is focused on the purpose of the writer and the perspective of the reader. In this organizational method, information is arranged in descending order of importance, with the most important information at the beginning of the memo. This lead-off position is usually occupied by a statement of the purpose for writing the memo or a summary of its conclusions or recommendations.

The direct approach, or arranging information in descending order of importance, is an effective technique in memos for the same reasons that it is an established principle in news writing: It attracts the reader's attention with the essence of the communication, provides a framework for reading the rest of the message, and keeps the reader's interest as long as possible by treating the important aspects of the subject first. The more details that readers of direct memos and newspaper articles want, the more text they will read. Memos can also provide additional, in-depth information at the end, in the form of appendixes or attachments, in case the reader wants to delve more deeply into the subject.

A memo using the direct approach begins with the information that answers the two questions that most readers have when they pick up a memo: What does this memo have to do with me, and what am I going to have to do with it?

Introductory paragraphs that address these questions frequently include a statement of the purpose of the document, explaining why the reader is receiving it and what the writer would like the reader to do. Some examples of beginnings that use the direct approach appear below.

Example A

TO: All Agencies
FROM: Circulation Policies Committee
SUBJECT: Agency Review: Draft Revision of Systemwide Circulation
           Policies for Videotapes

Enclosed is a draft of the proposed revision for systemwide policies governing circulation of videotapes. We'd like to ask all branches to review them and send a response to the committee before April 1. The new policies are scheduled to take effect July 1.

. . . .

(Figure 11 shows the completed memo.)

The memo below is organized using the direct approach. The introductory
paragraph begins with the reason for the memo, and the body of the memo
presents information in descending order of importance.

DATE: February 1, 1989

TO: All Agencies

FROM: Circulation Policies Committee

SUBJECT: Agency Review: Draft Revision of
            Systemwide Circulation Policies for
            Videotapes

Enclosed is a draft of the proposed revision for
systemwide policies governing circulation of videotapes. We'd like to ask all branches to review the draft
policy and send a response to the committee before
March 1.

If approved, the new policy will be publicized beginning May 1 and will take effect July 1.

The major changes in the policy are summarized
below:

1. The loan period for videotapes will be 2 days,
   with no renewals.
2. All videotapes are due by closing on the date
   due. Videotapes should not be returned in the
   bookdrop, and tapes found there the morning
   after the due date will be considered a day late.
3. Reservations will be accepted, by phone or in
   person, only on the day of checkout. Reservations will be cancelled at 6 pm. Reserved tapes
   that are not claimed will be available for circulation.

Figure 11. **Organizing Memos: Direct Approach**

Please note that the fine structure and replacement policy, both of which seem to be working well, will remain the same.

These revisions are intended to address the problems, reported by most branches, of high demand on relatively small collections of tapes. If you would like more information about the reasons behind the choice of policies, please feel free to get in touch with a member of the committee (roster attached).

We would like to thank everyone who responded to our earlier call for an analysis of the problem and recommendations for solutions. And special thanks, in advance, to all branch staff for reviewing these draft policies!

Example B

DATE: November 1, 1989
TO: Branch and Department Heads
FROM: Bill North, Dean of Libraries
SUBJECT: New Process for Evaluation of Librarians

All librarians will be receiving the final version of the new evaluation process from the Promotion and Tenure Committee in two weeks. I'd like to ask branch and department heads to take the lead in promoting discussion and understanding of the new process. To help you answer the questions you will get, we've scheduled a discussion with the P and T Committee, on Tuesday, November 7, at 4 pm in the library faculty room.

The new evaluation process is the result of two years of cooperation between our P and T Committee and the university-wide committee on promotion and tenure. As you probably already know, the major issues under discussion were the following:

. . . .

Example C

DATE: September 1, 1989
TO: Corporate Library Users
FROM: Corporate Library
SUBJECT: Schedule for Renovating the Library

The renovation of the Corporate Library will begin August 1 and will be substantially complete by the following June. The proposed temporary locations and the moving schedules for offices, stacks, and services are listed below. Please let me know by October 1 if you foresee any problems or anticipate conflicts with your needs and those of your departments.

The offices below will be moving according to the following schedule:

Office	New Location	Closed for Moving	Reopen
Database			
Searching	106 Dell Bldg.	June 1–4	June 5

. . . .

These examples all contain explicit statements of the action requested and the response time desired by the writer. In some situations, *implicit* statement of the action and response time is preferable. These situations include communication designed to present recommendations or to seek approvals for courses of action, or any communication in which you feel uncomfortable stating your request explicitly.

Frequently, a summary of the purpose of the memo will serve as an implicit statement of the action you desire. Instead of requesting that your recommendation be approved, you as writer assume that the act of submitting the recommendation is, in itself, an implied request for action. Suggestions about *when* you would like an action performed can often be implied, if mentioned at all. Submitting a budget request at the right time for consideration for next year's budget is, again, an implicit statement about the timing. Stating your deadlines for action implicitly or leaving the timetable up to the discretion of the reader are two additional ways for handling the question of when the action needs to be completed.

The examples below show several ways to begin documents with purpose statements that contain implicit requests for action and implicit specifications of response times.

Example D

DATE: February 1, 1989
TO: Jane Smith, Dean of Libraries
FROM: Library Staff Computer Committee
SUBJECT: Adoption of a Word Processing Package for Library Use

The Library Staff Computer Committee would like to recommend that the library adopt GreatWords as the standard for library use and that the library purchase copies of GreatWords for all departments. We also recommend that the staff receive training through (1) a series of workshops organized by this committee, and (2) the establishment of a GreatWords Users Group.

The need for selecting one word processing program as the library standard is critical.

. . . .

Example E

DATE: December 1, 1989
TO: Jane Smith, Library Director
FROM: John Jones, Head, Technical Services
SUBJECT: Request for an Additional Position in Technical Services
SUMMARY: The Technical Services Department would like to request a
            new position, salary grade 8, to supervise our program of
            retrospective conversion. Starting the position in the next
            budget year will coincide with the Halfer grant that sup-
            ports all retrospective conversion costs except staffing.

. . . .

These examples illustrate techniques for putting the purpose and action statements, and sometimes the statements about response time, in the most important position in the memo: the first paragraph. From that lead-in, memos written in the direct approach present ideas in order of importance, from most to least important. The writer must judge which points relate most significantly to what the reader is asked to do in the first paragraph. A major advantage of the direct approach is that it forces you to define what information the reader needs in order to do what you have asked, whether it is reviewing a document or judging the merit of a request for a new staff member.

In the direct approach, closing statements reinforce human relations goals, such as reaffirming positive relationships with the reader, offering to provide more information, or restating aspects of the message that the writer feels are important to the reader's understanding.

Memos written in the direct approach tend to be shorter than memos organized in other ways, perhaps because direct memos are more sharply focused on the problem at hand. For this reason, too, it is often easier to write a one-page document on a complex issue using the direct approach. Administrators also prefer memos written in the direct approach because the central issue appears in the first paragraph, with supporting detail available if they want it. Figure 11 illustrates a memo written in the direct approach.

Writers using the direct approach need to choose their words carefully, aware of the overall tone of the memo. The potential for sounding blunt or peremptory exists in any statement of purpose that contains an explicit request, and the need to find tactful ways to request action arises in any memo, whether the request appears in the first paragraph or the last. Using the direct approach does, however, move the purpose of the memo to center stage and calls attention not only to your request, but also to the tone of that request.

Indirect Approach

In some situations, the direct approach may not be the most effective technique. For example, when you are writing to people you do not know or with whom you have had some conflict, when you are delivering unwelcome news, or when you are attempting to persuade someone whose views differ radically from yours, you may wish to lead into a statement of your purpose. In these cases, you should consider organizing your memo using the indirect approach, or the inductive order.

The indirect or inductive order moves from specific facts or details at the beginning of the document to general conclusions, recommendations, requests, or action statements near the end of the document. The approach corresponds to the process of building a case: starting from details and moving to the general statement, purpose, or conclusion.

Although the inductive method may seem at first to be the most logical way to present information, it has several important drawbacks. First, the information that is most likely to concern the reader comes at the end. After reaching the statement of purpose at the end, the reader frequently finds that he or she must reread the document to understand and evaluate the relationship between the body of the memo and its concluding statements.

Second, documents written using the indirect approach frequently end up longer than documents that start with main points, perhaps because it is very tempting for writers to put in every detail that contributed to the formation of their conclusions. The unconscious assumption is that all the details that the writer considered should be passed on to the reader. In most cases, readers do not need volumes of information to act; they just need the *right* information, information that addresses their concerns and responsibilities. By stating your purpose or conclusion directly, you as writer can see perhaps more clearly what your reader will need to know in the specific situation.

Third, many readers get impatient with the indirect approach and, if they do not find the purpose or the conclusion at the beginning of the document, will turn to the end and read it first anyway.

Finally, in the worst case, readers become bored and stop reading before they reach the main points toward the end.

Although the direct method is effective in most situations, there are times when the gradual building of a case is important, particularly if you feel you can hold your reader's attention while you are presenting your argument. When you do not know the person to whom you are writing, you may wish to build your credibility before you present your conclusion. If you feel that your reader will be resistant to your main idea, you may wish to present your rationale first. And if you are delivering bad news, it is sometimes preferable to present the circumstances and the reasons behind the decisions before stating the negative information.

In almost all cases, however, you will find it worthwhile to try a quick draft of the direct approach before you turn to the indirect method. Your sense of what will be successful in your situation will alert you to cases when the direct method is likely to cause trouble for you.

Many writers use the indirect approach almost unconsciously, without realizing that they have a choice of organizational patterns and that their choice influences the effectiveness of their memos. Training yourself to write memos in the direct approach is one of the quickest ways to sharpen your professional writing skills. To help you become familiar with the effects of these organizational patterns, the memo in figure 11, written in the direct approach, has been rewritten in figure 12 in the indirect approach. As you compare the two memos, observe how the indirect structure of the second version, starting with background and moving through the committee's reasoning, encourages the inclusion of much secondary detail.

The memo in figure 10 is written in vintage indirect style. Rewrite it using the direct approach and then compare your revision to the example in section H, pages 343–45, of the appendix.

DATE: February 1, 1989

TO: All Agencies

FROM: Circulation Policies Committee

SUBJECT: Agency Review: Draft Revision of
           Systemwide Circulation Policies for
           Videotapes

Last fall, Assistant Director John Stone charged the circulation policy committee with revising the systemwide policy on circulation of videotapes. The committee, consisting of representatives from all regions, has spent several months reviewing these policies. We also solicited ideas and suggestions from all the branches and interviewed a representative sample of patrons at libraries with large videotape collections. A literature search and a telephone survey rounded out our study.

We discovered that the major problems with our present policy stem primarily from high demand on our relatively small collection. The current loan period of one week ties up one tape for a week, although users probably view the tape only once during that time. (Note: tapes are being returned more promptly, thanks to the fine and replacement policy implemented last year.) Waiting lists are enormous, and the current procedure of holding the tape for the next person in line, while paralleling our policy for bestsellers, keeps high-demand tapes out of circulation.

Figure 12. **Organizing Memos: Indirect Approach**

Our present policy of accepting reservations also slows down the turnaround time.

As a result of these problems, we have recommended three changes in the policy, summarized below:

1. The loan period for videotapes will be 2 days, with no renewals.
2. All videotapes are due at closing on the date due. Videotapes should not be returned in the bookdrop, and tapes found there the morning after the due date will be considered a day late.
3. Reservations will be accepted by phone or in person only on the day of checkout. Reservations will be cancelled at 6 pm. Reserved tapes that are not claimed will be available for circulation.

Attached is a draft of the full text of the proposed revisions. We'd like to ask all branches to review them and send a response to the committee before March 1. If approved, the new policies will be publicized beginning May 1 and will take effect July 1.

If you would like more information on the reasons behind our policy decisions, please feel free to get in touch with a member of the committee. A roster is enclosed with this mailing.

We would like to thank everyone who responded to our earlier call for an analysis of the problem and recommendations for solutions. And special thanks, in advance, to all branch staff for reviewing these draft policies!

Memo Format

Memos, and also some specialized types of professional writing, begin with a standard four-part heading. The purpose of each line is of course standard, although the precise phrasing varies according to institutional practice and individual preference. A common version of the four-part heading appears in figure 13.

Printed Memo Forms and Letterhead

Many libraries use printed memo forms to save time in creating the standard headings for each memo. Standard forms are useful, for obvious reasons, particularly in a library that depends on typewriters. As library offices switch to word processors, they may elect to use the ability of word processing packages to create a standard format automatically, rather than using a form.

The library's letterhead can be modified to serve as a memo form, whether the headings are typed in from the memory of a typist or a machine. If no organizational or departmental identification appears on the paper used for the memo, the sender's title should be full enough to indicate clearly where he or she can be reached.

Date Line

Dating a memo is essential, and yet it is surprising how many memos have no dates. If you are skeptical, take a look through the files in your library. The placement of the date line varies. Typical positions are (1) as the first heading in the four-part heading structure, (2) as the third heading, between *FROM* and *SUBJECT*, and (3) as the last heading. In another variation, the date appears by itself (not preceded by a label), either as the first element in the four-part structure or flush with the right-hand margin.

Lines Indicating Sender and Recipient

The next two lines in the standard format identify the sender and the recipient. Note that use of the format eliminates the need for a salutation or greeting. The sender writes his or her initials or first name next to the typed name, eliminating the need for a signature at the end of the memo.

The form of names and use of titles are matters of institutional and individual preference. Using titles, along with full names, may make life easier in the future, when the names or positions of the present staff are not known to everyone. For this reason, we recommend first and last names and titles on memos, particularly on those that will be saved and filed; however, this practice creates a more formal tone than names alone or first names only. Signing your first name next to the typed version, rather than using initials, can balance the formality of using your full name and title.

DATE: January 30, 1988

TO: All Library Staff

FROM: Robin Cooper, Chair
           Continuing Education Committee *Robin*

SUBJECT: Workshop on Writing Journal Articles:
           March 15

Ann English, editor of the Bulletin of Librarianship, is coming to give us a workshop on writing journal articles and getting them published. The workshop will be presented on March 15 from 1 pm to 4 pm in the Great Books Room on the second floor of Spenser Library.

Ms. English will focus her presentation on practical suggestions that will help you plan, write, and submit an article for publication. Most of you ranked this topic first in our survey of your preferences for continuing education workshops, conducted this fall.

Ann English is well known as an editor and writer in our field. Her workshops on how to write articles receive rave reviews from the participants, so we feel sure you will find the workshop worth an afternoon of your time.

All library staff with an interest in writing for publication are welcome. Please mark your calendars now. Two weeks before the workshop, we will send out another announcement.

Hope to see you at the workshop!

Figure 13. **Format for Memos**

Choosing whether to use given first names or the names people go by (for example, Robert or Bob), for both you and the recipient, is another decision that depends on institutional practice, the level of formality you choose to establish between yourself and the recipient, and the subject of the communication. Whatever form for names you choose, the level of formality should be the same for both your name and the recipient's. Using your full formal name and title and addressing your reader by a nickname sends a message of inequality.

Subject Line

The subject line of a memo is your reader's first indication of the content of the memo. It should be concise and specific. Achieving both these goals is not always easy, but time spent pinning down a short, specific subject designation will not only benefit your reader, but will be appreciated in the future by anyone looking through the files.

Human Relations Close

The ending statement offers an opportunity to reinforce the human relations dimension of memos. When ending statements that are designed to foster good will represent the writer's sincere feeling, they may establish personality and personal interaction in business writing. Of course, a rote good-will close that is little more than a knee-jerk response to the ending of the memo will not promote genuine good will. Your closing statement should be consistent with both your task-related purposes and your human relations goals. Institutional practice and your personal style should determine how you elect to close your memos.

Distributional Information

Libraries may have their own variations of the standard notation for distribution. Typical symbols are described below; however, observing and following the practice in your institution is probably your best course.

Normally, when you send copies of a memo to someone other than the recipient, you indicate the distribution at the bottom of the memo, using a symbol standing for "copies" and then listing the names of those to whom copies were sent. *CC*, standing for "carbon copy," is still in wide use, although few offices use carbon paper anymore. A plain *c* is the most logical alternative, but it is not widely used. *XC* is another alternative in general use. Again, it is probably best to follow your institution's traditional practice.

The etiquette of sending copies varies from institution to institution, but some general guidelines can be identified. Acknowledging the distribution of copies on the original is a courtesy to the recipient of the message. It also provides an historical record of who received the memo. It is possible, of course, to send copies of memos to people without acknowledging them on the copy of the memo that goes to another recipient. If you do this, you may want to consider noting *bc* (for "blind copy") in pencil on the copy you send to the unacknowledged recipient and on your file copy. In general, we do not recommend sending blind copies, simply because the practice can be misunderstood.

Determining to whom you will send copies is a decision that must be governed by practice in your institution and the requirements of the situation. Some supervisors require copies of communications sent by their subordinates. And frequently writers use the practice of sending copies to their supervisors as a relatively simple way of keeping their supervisors informed. Depending on the content of the memo, the very act of sending a copy to someone else can send a positive or a negative message. Suppose you are the head of Technical Services in a large library. Sending a copy to the library director of a memo commending an employee conveys a very different message to both director and employee than forwarding a copy of a memo documenting a performance problem. To make decisions in individual situations, you as the writer must weight the *reason* you are sending the copy with the *effect* that sending the copy will have on both the recipient of the copy and the recipient of the original memo.

Enclosures

Enclosures or attachments are conventionally noted either by using the entire word or the obvious abbreviations. These documents can be listed or not, at your discretion.

MEMOS FOR SPECIAL PURPOSES

Although the memo format can be used for almost any purpose, several types of memos occur frequently in libraries: transmittal memos, informational memos on a single topic, update memos, and memos announcing policies and procedures. We will consider each briefly.

Transmittal Memos

A memo may accompany a report or other document, informing the reader why the report is being sent and what should be done with it. A transmittal memo may also provide information on the background of the document being transmitted.

The opening statements announce what is being transmitted to the reader and what the reader is expected to do with what is being sent. Many transmittal memos include a short summary of the document. The body of the transmittal memo contains all the facts the reader needs to know about the document, arranged in a systematic order that is suited to what the reader will be expected to do with it. As the writer, you will want to organize the information in the body of the memo in the way that is easiest for the reader to understand and use. If the action statement does not appear in the opening statements, it is usually placed at the end of the body of the memo. The good-will close in a memo is a matter of choice, although we strongly recommend it. The best good-will close is a sincere, specific expression of your appreciation of the reader's part in whatever the memo covers. Figure 14 is an example of a transmittal memo.

Informational Memos: Single Topic

Memos are frequently used to send information on a specific topic. Generally speaking, informational memos are most successful if they treat one topic at a time. (An exception to this principle, the *update* memo, will be discussed below.) If several topics are treated, they should be clearly identified with specific topical headings.

Most librarians who write informational memos want to do more than merely distribute information. Almost always, they have specific ideas about how they would like their readers to react to that information, either by remembering it, acting upon it, or forming certain attitudes toward it. Knowing why you are providing information and how you expect your readers to react is essential to writing an effective informational memo. In an informational memo, the subject line should describe the subject of the memo as precisely as possible. The opening sentence sets the stage for the presentation of information about the subject by establishing the need for the information and motivating the reader to read further in order to learn more. The body of the memo presents your information, organized in a way that will be useful to the reader. The action statement usually recommends ways the information can be used and tries to motivate readers to follow these suggestions. The human relations close, again optional, expresses the writer's thanks to the reader.

Imparting information is one of the most common reasons for writing a memo, and so informational memos are written in a wide variety of styles. Figure 15 is an informational memo written to library users.

Update Memos

The update memo is an informational memo covering several topics rather than just one. An update memo is a useful way to inform library staff or users about a number of smaller items at one time and still focus sufficiently on each item.

DATE: April 23, 1988

TO: Community Librarians

FROM: Jane Smith, Coordinator
            Children's Services Division

SUBJECT: Summer Reading Program Materials

Here are the materials for your summer reading program. We will be discussing the program at the Children's Services meeting, May 20. Please try to take a look at the materials before then and come prepared with your ideas and questions.

Each box should contain the following items:

    posters
    "Let's Read" kits
    instructions for the Summer Reading Program
    evaluation form

If you find anything missing or if you feel you will need more kits, please get in touch with Katherine Jones in my office.

Thanks to the efforts of all of you, the Summer Reading Program consistently gets rave reviews from the public. We're looking forward to kicking off another successful summer program on May 20.

See you then.

Figure 14. **Transmittal Memo**

DATE: July 10, 1989

TO: Users of the Corporate Library

FROM: Ellen Norris   *En*
             Chief Librarian

SUBJECT: New Photocopiers in the Library

New photocopiers will be installed in the library on
August 1. The new machines will have a variety of
features, including enlargement and reduction.

The new machines can be operated in two ways: by
using special cards or by using coins. For business-
related copying, you may request cards from the central supply office. These will be charged to your
departmental photocopying account. For personal
copying, you may purchase a card at the Business Office. The machines can also be operated using coins,
at ten cents a copy. Using the cards gives you a reduced price per copy, depending on the size of card
you purchase. A price list is available from the Business Office.

The new machines have many features, including
reduction and enlargement. After the inevitable
settling-in period, they should give us better copies
than we got from the old machines.

We invite you to stop by the library after August 1
for a demonstration of the new photocopiers.

Figure 15. **Informational Memo**

In an update memo, the subject line identifies the broad subject of the memo, such as UPDATE FROM THE DIRECTOR'S OFFICE or NEWS FROM AUDIOVISUAL SERVICES. An opening statement, introducing the update, is optional. The body of the memo consists of a series of short, single-item minimemos, each preceded by a short, descriptive title. Figure 16 illustrates an update memo.

Policy and Procedure Memos

Memos are often used to announce changes in policies and procedures or to introduce new ones. Chapters 6 and 7 discuss policies and procedures in detail. Here we will cover the use of memos to announce policies and procedures.

The opening statement usually announces the subject of the policy or procedure, and the body of the memo provides the definition and the explanation.

A difficulty in using a memo for distribution of policies and procedures arises when the new policies or procedures need to be incorporated into operational routines and into the compilation of policies and procedures. A memo generally is read once and then thrown away or filed by subject. If the new policy or procedure is to become part of normal operations, it must find its way into the standard documentation of activities. Every library has examples of outdated procedure manuals, and every librarian can also tell tales of updating a procedure by memo and not recording it in the manual. There are several ways around this dilemma. Some libraries file the update memos in the manual, requiring readers to flip through updates if they want to make sure they have consulted the latest procedure. The most reliable solution for the problem of updating policies by memo is to use the memo as the announcement of the policy and then to rewrite the manual, incorporating the change. Another solution is to distribute a new page in the policy manual, using the memo to announce the change.

In order to find the best solution for your situation, ask yourself how the reader would look up the policy if he or she remembered that a change had occurred but did not remember the details. Then, be sure the updated policy appears in that form. Any action that you wish the reader to take, such as filing the memo in a specific place, should be identified in the action statement. Figure 17 illustrates a memo announcing a change in policy.

CHECKLIST FOR WRITING MEMOS

Figure 18 is a checklist that summarizes the process for writing memos. It can be used as a review of the chapter or as a guide when writing memos.

DATE: October 14, 1989

TO: Branch Library Staff

FROM: Larry Whitlock
             Head, Children's Services

SUBJECT: NEWS FROM CHILDREN'S SERVICES

NOVEMBER CHILDREN'S SERVICES MONTHLY MEET-
ING RESCHEDULED
     We have rescheduled our November meeting to
avoid a conflict with the State Library Association's
annual meeting. Our monthly meeting will be held at
the Garcia Community Library on November 19 from
1:30 pm to 3:30 pm. You will be receiving the agenda
around the first of the month, as usual. Please let me
know several days in advance if your library will not
be able to send a representative to the meeting.

STORY-TELLING WORKSHOP PLANNED FOR MAY 20
     The local chapter of the Story-Tellers Guild will be
putting on an all-day workshop for library staff on
May 20. After the tremendous response we received
from last year's workshop on telling folktales, we
have asked the Guild to come back again and focus on
telling contemporary stories. Attendance will be limited to 35, so call our office as soon as your plans are
certain and reserve a place.

VACANCY IN CHILDREN'S SERVICES NOW POSTED
     A vacancy is now posted in the Personnel Office for
Assistant Head of Children's Services at the Main Li-

Figure 16. **Update Memo**

brary. Copy of the position description is attached to this memo. Following our usual practice, applications will be accepted for two weeks. Internal applicants are welcome.

EMERGENCY SUBSTITUTE REGISTER WORKING WELL

The emergency substitute register has been in effect for two months now. Judging from the reports we get from both the substitutes and the branch staff, the program is working well. We now have over twenty trained staff members on the roster, and so far, we have been able to fill all requests for substitute staffing. If you are temporarily unable to cover all service points, particularly on evenings or weekends, call Evelyn Long (652-1254) at least twenty-four hours in advance, and she will provide you with the names of at least two substitutes who are trained and available. You may charge the cost of the substitutes to your part-time staff budget or your contingency budget, depending on the availability of funds. Tell Evelyn which account to use when you phone in your request.

DATE: August 15, 1989

TO: All Circulation Staff

FROM: Wendy Walton   *Wendy*
               Head, Circulation

SUBJECT: Extended Loan Period

The loan period for books will be extended from two weeks to one month, effective September 1. One renewal of four weeks will be granted.

A copy of our Circulation Policy, incorporating the new revision, is attached. On September 1, the revised policy will be available in the Master Manual at the Circulation Desk. Signs are also posted at the desk and throughout the library alerting patrons to the change.

Since we have discussed the proposed revision extensively, this news should not come as a surprise to anyone. We want to be certain, however, that all our desk workers, particularly the part-time students, are aware of the change. Your help in spreading the word will be appreciated.

Figure 17. **Memo Updating Policy**

Use the checklist below to review the process for writing memos.

1. Define your purpose in writing the memo.
   - What do you wish to accomplish by writing this memo?
   - What do you want the reader to do after reading the memo?
   - What human relations issues are involved in writing this memo? What human relations goals can you formulate to address these issues?

2. Understand the perspective that your reader will bring to this memo.
   - What will reader's reaction be to what you are trying to accomplish?
   - Will it be positive, negative, or neutral?
   - What attitudes does your reader have now that will influence his or her reaction to the memo? Are they positive, negative, or neutral?
   - What vested interests does your reader have in the subject, either positive or negative?

3. Plan your communication strategy.
   - What channel of communication is typically used in your library to accomplish purposes similar to the one you have defined? Is the channel effective most of the time? Can you see a better way to get the task done?
   - Is the memo the most appropriate means of communication for accomplishing your purpose? If so, are there constraints on length, level of formality, level of diction, or other aspects of writing imposed by the audience or your institutional environment?
   - Do you anticipate that you will want to use additional methods of communication to introduce, reinforce, or follow up on your memo? How do you plan to communicate, in addition to writing a memo: Schedule a one-to-one meeting? Schedule a small group meeting or a large meeting? Make a telephone call? Write a memo or report? Prepare an abstract or summary? Send further information from published sources? Or something else?

4. Develop alternative ideas until you are comfortable that you have explored the topic sufficiently for your purposes.
   - Have you considered alternative ways of approaching your topic?
   - Do you need to gather any material from published sources? If so, which ones?
   - Do you need to gather any material from inside your institution?
   - How will your reader approach this subject and what will he or she want to know?
   - What information will your reader want or need in order to do what you desire?

5. Organize your ideas in an effective sequence. Use the direct order in most cases.
   - Why are you writing the memo to the reader? What do you want him or her to do—and when? Can you shape your lead paragraph so that it answers those questions, either explicitly or implicitly?

Figure 18. **Writing Memos: A Checklist**

▲ What ideas and information are essential for the reader to know in order to behave in the way you are requesting? Arrange your points in order of importance, from your perspective and the reader's.

▲ Can you identify supporting information that should go in attachments or appendixes, information that may be of interest to the reader who wants to know more, but which is not essential to accomplishing the purpose?

6. Write a draft of your memo, following your organizational plan.
7. Assess the effectiveness of your memo and identify problem areas. Develop and assess solutions to these difficulties.

▲ Do you predict that your memo, as it is now written, will be successful in accomplishing its purpose? Will the reader behave in the way you desire? If not, can you identify the obstacles to success and plan ways to overcome them?

▲ Pretend for a moment that you did not write the memo. What is your impression of the "personality" that is communicated by the memo?

▲ Have you assessed your memo systematically, looking for problems of effectiveness, tone and personality, organizational structure, composition of sentences, and word choice? (Chapter 3 provides checklists to help with this analysis.)

▲ For each problem you find, can you pinpoint the cause and develop alternatives? Which alternative works best in the context of the memo?

8. Edit your memo for correctness.

▲ Have you reviewed your draft for problems of grammar, usage, and punctuation?

▲ Have you used your knowledge of the kinds of mistakes you make to help you find trouble spots? (Chapter 3 provides assistance in identifying and solving these problems.)

▲ Have you checked all matters of fact, including

dates?	raw numbers and computations?
facts?	bibliographic citations?
titles?	proper nouns, especially names?
spelling?	

▲ Have you proofread carefully to ensure accuracy? (Chapter 3 provides a checklist for this activity.)

9. Produce the final copy of your memo.

▲ Have you considered the elements of "design" to achieve an effective, professional office look?

▲ Have you marked the layout for the final copy, noting any special keyboard graphic effects, special spacing, and indentions?

▲ If someone is assisting you by preparing the final copy, have you communicated your instructions clearly, including those about spacing, margins, layout, and special graphic effects?

▲ Have you reviewed a typed draft before preparing the final draft?

▲ After receiving the final copy, have you proofread carefully, for typographical errors and for other difficulties that might have slipped in?

▲ Is the final copy neat and professional looking?

Figure 18—**Continued**

Chapter 6

POLICIES

CHAPTER OUTLINE

CRITERIA FOR EFFECTIVE POLICIES

NEED FOR POLICIES

PUTTING POLICIES IN WRITING

FRAMEWORK FOR POLICIES: A POLICY ON POLICIES
Defining the Process for Developing Policies
Documenting Policies
Distributing Policies and Updates
Evaluating and Updating Policies

WRITING INDIVIDUAL POLICIES
Determining Need and Identifying Results to Be Achieved
Determining the Content of the Policy
Organizing and Writing the Draft Policy
Reviewing the Draft Policy
Writing the Final Draft of the Policy Statement
Planning Your Strategy for Communicating the Policy

TEST YOUR SKILLS

CHECKLIST FOR WRITING POLICIES

Policies are statements that guide decisions and actions. Each policy is intended to produce specific results. A policy encouraging quiet in a university library, for example, is written to produce an atmosphere that is conducive to study.

Policies also are intended to ensure that activities of a similar kind proceed under the same guidelines. For example, a policy defining borrowing districts in an urban public library system attempts to ensure that all decisions about who receives library cards are made following the same rules. Uniform application of policies is important both for achieving the desired result and for providing equitable treatment for all.

CRITERIA FOR EFFECTIVE POLICIES

Policies are effective when they achieve the results intended by their creators. Achieving these results usually requires that all actions taken by the staff and users in the area covered by the policy are shaped by the same considerations. We, therefore, have two criteria for the effectiveness of a policy. The first criterion is that actions shaped by the policy achieve the effects intended by the policymakers. The second criterion is that all decisions covered by the policy be made according to the policy guidelines.

To illustrate these two criteria, suppose that a committee assessing the policy for fines in a large university library system defines the purpose of the policy on charging fines for overdue books as follows: to ensure the timely return of all materials borrowed from the library and to do so in a manner that retains the good will of the library's users. The committee then makes decisions about who will be charged fines, what the fines will be, and the mechanism by which the fines will be collected. Each of these decisions involves developing the specifics that maintain good human relations and that also get the books back on time. After the new policy has been in place for a certain period of time, its effectiveness can be assessed by the two criteria we have suggested, taking them in reverse order. First, are all actions affected by the policy being made according to the guidelines? Is the charging of fines in all the libraries covered by the policy proceeding along the lines defined in the policy? Even during the hectic end-of- the-semester period, when the volume of fines needing to be recorded is overwhelming? Even when an influential person protests? Even late at night, when students are staffing the circulation desk?

Second, is the policy achieving its goals? Is the rate of return for overdue material the best that the policymakers feel they can achieve through regulation of fines? Is the policy on fines straining good human relations with the library's users?

Success in meeting these criteria depends on the content of the policy and on the way the policy is managed. In this chapter on policies, we will consider ways to develop effective policy content and issues affecting the management of written policies, including methods for documenting, disseminating, monitoring, and updating policies. We will also suggest a process for writing policies.

NEED FOR POLICIES

One approach to assessing the need for a policy is to examine practice in the area of your library covered by the policy you are considering. Are you satisfied with the results that you see? Is practice compatible with the library's mission and goals, and with its philosophy of service? For example, if you are contemplating a policy governing staff behavior in public areas, observe long enough to determine whether or not there is a problem. If the staff are mindful of the noise level of their activity, if they do not pursue personal conversations in highly visible areas for long periods of time, if personal telephone calls are not a problem, and if you see nothing that makes you dissatisfied with what is going on, you may conclude that there is no need for a formal policy. Later, if a need develops, your decision may be different.

As you observe practice, you will also question whether or not it is consistent. For example, do library users get the same response to questions concerning library borrowing privileges during all times the library is open? Are there inequities in the way staff matters are handled from department to department? If practice on similar issues differs in significant ways, depending on the department, the staff member, the day of the week, or the work shift, developing policies can be one way to obtain consistency.

In assessing the need for policies, you may also wish to look at how instructions for practice are transmitted to new staff and how changes in policy are passed along. If you observe that too much time is spent on training and explaining, or if you feel that it takes new employees too long to assimilate the basics of library practice, you may wish to consider developing policies as guidelines to ensure that everyone is afforded the same information.

Your observations of practice should alert you to the need for a policy or to a need to make the present policy more effective. Rarely will you find a policy vacuum. Written policies may exist but may not function well, for a variety of reasons. They may not be easily accessible; people may be unaware of their existence; they may be out of date; or supervisors may not use the written policies in training or supervising.

If policies are not written down, some sort of oral tradition almost certainly exists, but understanding of the details may vary from staff member to staff member, or the mechanism for passing it along may be too informal.

What may appear as the need for a policy is often the *need for systematizing some aspect of managing the policy,* such as developing consensus on what the policy really is; reassessing the need for the policy; redefining the details of the policy's content; examining the methods for documentation, distribution, monitoring, and updating; reconsidering how policies are presented in staff training; or deciding to convert unwritten assumptions to written form. Many of these activities rely on written communication.

PUTTING POLICIES IN WRITING

Systematic observation of practice often results in a decision to put policies in writing. Not every principle that guides actions needs to be written down; however, putting policies in writing has certain advantages. Written policies communicate the same content to many people. Written policies can be used to reinforce verbal explanations, and they are available when someone needs to consult them. Having a policy in writing can reduce misunderstandings and can provide clear guidelines for action, and it can provide a means of enforcing accountability. The process of writing policies down can also encourage an examination of important issues, resulting in more precise definitions of expectation and practice.

FRAMEWORK FOR POLICIES: A POLICY ON POLICIES

Individual policies exist in the context of a framework for all library policies. That framework provides the structure under which individual policies are issued, the ways they are distributed and monitored, and the procedure for updating and evaluating them. In some libraries, that framework is very informal and consists largely of patterns of past practice. In other libraries, that structure is formalized and often documented in a policy on policies.

The advantage of having a policy on policies is the advantage of having any policy. It is a vehicle for systematizing practice, defining what you want that practice to be and then providing a tool for obtaining consistent adherence to it. In a policy on policies, you can define the library's philosophy on policies, and you can decide what level of uniformity you would like throughout the library in developing, disseminating, monitoring, and updating library policies. Typically, large libraries and library systems may need more precision in defining practice than smaller units; however, libraries of all sizes can benefit from defining what practice they wish to follow with regard to policies.

A policy on policies, whether it is a general statement of philosophy, a series of specific statements of practice, or a combination, will include decisions about a process for developing policies; decisions about documentation, distribution, and updating of policies; and decisions about evaluating the results. These policy decisions will then guide the writing of individual policies. In the section that follows, general decisions for the policy on policies will be discussed. Following this section, the writing of individual policies will be considered in detail, including developing the content of policies and assessing their effects on users and staff.

Defining the Process for Developing Policies

Although each library will have its own processes for developing contents of policies, all processes will involve some version of the following steps:

▲ assessing the need
▲ developing the content

▲ obtaining a review of the draft from others, particularly those with responsibility for the activities involved, those with relevant experience in the issues, and those affected by the policy

▲ securing the necessary approvals to make the policy official.

Obviously, these activities do not have to be strictly sequential. Review of the draft can occur as the draft is taking shape, and so can obtaining administrative approvals of the directions in the draft. How these activities proceed will vary, depending on the library and on the type of policy. The procedure for developing personnel policies, for example, will obviously include interaction with any larger institution of which the library is a part, like the governmental unit to which a public library is attached, the university that an academic library serves, or the parent organization of a special library. Developing administrative policies for the entire library may be an activity that includes library-wide representation and review, while the process for developing departmental policies may be different.

The value of gaining as much participation as possible in the development of policies is worth stressing. Widespread participation brings out many ideas and alternatives that might be overlooked if only a few people are involved in policy development. The implications in a policy can be ferreted out in advance and reactions can be more accurately anticipated if more people are involved in its development. And the more the affected groups understand the need for the policy and feel they have a part in developing the regulations under which they will function, the more positive their attitudes will be and the easier it will be to achieve their compliance with it.

Participation in the development and review of policies can be of several kinds. *Group development* of policies involves identifying or creating a group that is representative of various constituencies affected by the policy. If your university were developing a policy on quiet study in the library, one group approach would be to convene a committee that included the head of public services for the library, heads of representative branches, public services librarians, and student representatives.

Once a policy is drafted, participation in the reviewing process can be of several kinds. An *organizational review* of a proposed policy usually involves requesting formal review and comment from the heads of the appropriate units or groups in the organization, who in turn can be encouraged to involve their staff or members in developing a response. In our example concerning the policy on quiet study, such a review might entail formal comment by the various student groups, by the heads of public services in each branch library, by the library committee, and by the appropriate administrator of student services. This approach has the advantage of obtaining official stances from various parts of the organization. The extent to which the official stance includes reactions and opinions from the members of the unit depends on the way each group goes about developing its response.

Another approach is to obtain a *review by representative members of all groups involved*, circulating the draft to as many people as possible and asking for their ideas and suggestions. So, our committee on developing the policy on quiet study might circulate drafts to student groups or individual students, as well as to faculty and librarians. This method is particularly effective in obtaining ideas that might have been overlooked or in identifying patterns of reaction that might have escaped the developers of the policy. On the other hand, because each individual represents himself or herself, this approach may not built widespread support for a policy or represent an official stance from any unit or group.

An alternative to asking for representative views is to try to *consult every member of the affected groups, through polls or meetings*. This approach is obviously not feasible in many situations, and it has definite drawbacks, as well as strengths, but it is an alternative that, under certain circumstances, may be warranted. Asking an entire group to review the draft of a policy should be clearly differentiated from sharing the content of a formulated policy with those who will be affected. Do not ask for a *review* of a draft unless worthwhile suggestions can be pursued. When you request a review, you should be sure the reviewers understand what kind of information you want.

Documenting Policies

Ideally, everyone affected by policies should know what they are. In practice, making certain that staff and users are aware of the guidelines under which the library operates is not always simple. Creating awareness of policies can be viewed as two separate activities: (1) distributing the policy to those affected, both users and staff, and (2) documenting the policy by maintaining a permanent collection or display for consultation as needed. Because the method selected for documentation influences distribution, we will discuss documentation first.

Providing a systematic framework for documenting policies requires specifying the ways in which policies will be written, compiled, distributed, and updated. Since policies frequently affect two different audiences, library staff and library users, methods of documentation need to be developed that meet both needs. Many libraries will want to develop one internal system of documentation for all library policies and then select the important policies that affect users and make them available in special ways, such as posting them or printing them in booklets and brochures. Keeping users informed about policies is addressed more thoroughly in the section on distribution of policies.

The method of documentation a library chooses for its policies should encourage the use of policies. First, a system for compiling the policies should be chosen, and then the format for individual policies can be considered. We will discuss these choices in detail because we feel that many potentially good policies are ineffective because of problems with *managing the policy*. These problems can be addressed by thinking through the methods of documentation and choosing those that will make policies convenient to consult and to update.

Compilations of Policies

The ways the policies will be used, distributed, and updated will affect decisions about how to organize or compile them. Figure 19 presents a list of considerations in evaluating systems for organizing policies. Since no one method is best for all, we will discuss the most common approaches and their strengths and limitations.

One of the simplest methods for organizing policies is using a file. In small libraries with few written policies, folders can be grouped under "Policies," with appropriate subheadings, such as "Policies-Administrative," or policies can be filed by subject or department, with the subhead "Policies," such as "Public Services—Policies." Libraries that prefer the convenience of keeping all policies together may consider a separate policy file. Major divisions can be by library unit or department, and within that division, policies can be filed in individual folders or in subject folders. Alternatively, you can arrange policies within groups by number, date, title, or subject.

A file is a relatively simple and familiar method for organizing policies. Routines for distribution and updating are similar to other office routines

Consider the following when choosing an approach to documenting policies.

A. Organization: For the first level of division, will policies be organized by department, by unit, or by subject, or will they all be grouped together under the term *policies*? Within the first level of division, will policies be (1) numbered and filed sequentially as created; (2) filed alphabetically by subject, title, or department; or (3) filed by date of issue?

B. Subject Access: Is it needed? At what level? Will the need to locate policies by subject be addressed only through a table of contents, or will an index be provided?

C. Physical Access: Who needs access to the policies, how often, and at what work locations? How will physical access affect use?

D. Number of Copies of Policy Compilations: Are multiple copies needed? How many? How often are changes needed and how will they be made in multiple copies? What mechanisms will ensure that all multiple copies remain current and identical?

E. Ease of Distribution and Updating: How will policies be distributed? How will new policies and updates be added? Who will be responsible?

Figure 19. **Choosing an Approach to Documenting Policies**

and do not normally require learning new habits. If multiple files are desired, they are relatively easy to set up in several locations. Once set up, they rely on clerical support for maintenance. The policy file lends itself to individual policy sheets, which are easy to circulate when announcing a new policy or updating an old one; substituting new or updated policies in the file presents no difficulty. An intriguing possibility with policy files is that custom-made compilations of policies can be assembled for special uses, like the orientation of new employees.

A major drawback to policy files is the difficulty of consulting the whole body of policies at once. Another difficulty is establishing procedures for removing policies in order to consult them; if procedures are not followed consistently, the integrity of the file is quickly lost. Having one person in charge of supplying photocopies and refiling is an obvious solution. While policy files are not as popular as policy manuals, they are sometimes easier to set up and maintain. And one updated policy file may well be of more use than a raft of out-of-date manuals.

The policy manual is the compilation of policies most familiar to librarians. Policy manuals make good sense; their major drawback is that they require effort of a nonroutine kind to create and maintain. The all-too-frequent result is that complete policy manuals, after taking an inordinate amount of time to produce, become outdated quickly and soon are rarely consulted. Nevertheless, for libraries that are willing to make the effort necessary to maintain current policy manuals, the advantages are numerous.

The term *manual* is applied to two kinds of compilations, one in loose-leaf format, kept in a ring binder, and the other secured in a more permanent way, such as by stapling or binding as a pamphlet. Both types of manuals share many advantages. All policies are available in one portable reference guide; the manual can be divided into units (or "chapters") by department or subject; and a subject and title index is relatively easy to produce. The loose-leaf version can be more easily updated than the other type, although word processing has now made new editions easier to produce.

The major obstacle is establishing a system for updating. A systematic procedure for removing old pages and inserting new ones, or for issuing updated copies, is essential. But even when such a procedure exists, it is often honored more in the breach than the observance, and updates are frequently issued on memos, rather than using the established system to update the manual. At best, the memos are then stuffed into the manual, only to flutter out of place when the manual is consulted. At worst, the memo may not be recognized as a policy communication and so will be lost in a filing cabinet, while the content of the memo becomes a policy to be carried on by an oral tradition, side by side with the written system and weakening its effectiveness.

Format for Individual Policies

Individual policies can be written according to a standard format, or each policymaker can determine the format as he or she writes a policy. Standardizing the format ensures that certain elements will be included in each policy, but standard forms usually mean one policy to a page or group of pages, and so work best in policy files or in loose-leaf policy manuals. Libraries that do not wish to use a standard form, but want to have standard elements in each policy, can specify the core elements that each library policy should contain.

Elements that are often included in the format for individual policies are listed below. Many of these elements are intended to document a formal system for recommendation, review, and approval. In more informal policy systems, some elements may be unnecessary.

department title
policy title
policy number
purpose or rationale
policy statement
implementation or procedure (divided into sections and subsections)
effective date
persons recommending policy, date of recommendation
persons reviewing policy, date of review
persons approving policy, date of approval
distribution
recommended review period
date of revision

Figure 20 illustrates one standard format incorporating these elements.

Distributing Policies and Updates

The distribution of policies and their updates is an important aspect of managing a policy effectively. For this reason, many libraries choose to specify the method of distribution through a policy on policies to ensure uniform practice. How you design a uniform system of policy distribution for your library will depend on the type of system you use for compiling policies. All distribution systems, however, should accomplish three goals:

▲ Inform all who need to know about the policy
▲ Provide convenient access to the policy for all who may need to refresh their memories about the details
▲ Keep all policy sources (whether they are files or manuals) current.

POLICY TITLE: Time away from work for professional activities
ADMINISTRATIVE POLICY NUMBER: 4

PURPOSE: This policy defines the conditions under which librarians will
be granted time away from work in order to participate in professional activities. Its purpose is threefold:

 1. to provide librarians with the opportunity to participate in profes-
     sional activities during time that they would be ordinarily scheduled
     for work
 2. to ensure that the normal activities of the library are not disrupted
     by this participation
 3. to ensure that these opportunities are distributed as equitably as
     possible among those who desire them.

SUMMARY: Librarians are encouraged to participate in professional activities connected with their professional interests as long as such participation
does not interfere with performance of their job responsibilities or with library operations.

IMPLEMENTATION:

 1. Requests for time away from work for professional activities:
    Requests should be submitted to your department head via memo, in-
    cluding a description of the activity and the dates involved, a brief rea-
    son for attendance, and a description of the arrangements you have
    made to cover your responsibilities at work.
 2. Approvals:
    Approval of requests will be at the discretion of the department head,
    who will consider both departmental and individual needs. If more
    requests are received for a given period than can be accommodated
    within the departmental schedule, priority will be given to the librari-
    ans with fewest days away from work for professional activities in the
    preceding twelve-month period.
 3. Funding:
    Each librarian whose request is approved may apply for reimburse-
    ment up to $200 per conference, for a limit of $600 per individual in a
    three-year period. A chart of reimbursable expenses is attached.

POLICY PROPOSED BY: Librarians' Committee 4/85
POLICY REVIEWED BY: Department Heads; Associate Librarians for
                       Public and Technical Services 4/85
POLICY APPROVED BY: Library Director 5/85
                       Revised: 4/87

Figure 20. **Sample Policy**

Informing All Who Need to Know

Everyone who will be affected by the policy should be informed about it in enough detail and in enough time to comply with the policy. All staff who are expected to abide by the policy or enforce compliance with it should understand it thoroughly. All users who are expected to follow a policy should, ideally, know about the policy in advance to avoid major inconvenience. Everyone affected by a policy should be given a chance to understand the reasoning behind the regulations. And, if possible, people who may be affected adversely by the policy should be informed of alternative ways to meet their needs.

These principles are especially important in cases where policies make major changes in current practice. Suppose, for example, that the personnel department of a large public library system changes the way medical insurance claims are handled. Instead of turning claims into the personnel office for processing, employees will have to submit their forms directly to the insurance company.

Imagine that you have just received the news about a change such as this for your own insurance policy; imagine the questions, uncertainties, and hesitations you would have. Also, imagine what you would want to know in advance in order to feel comfortable about such a change. Well before the date the new policy goes into effect, the personnel clerks should feel comfortable with the new policy. They should understand the rationale behind the change so that they can explain it clearly and positively to others. They should also be familiar with the new procedures so that the transition goes smoothly. Library employees should be introduced to the change well in advance, so that they can ask questions and understand the reasons behind such a major change. They should also be given the details of the new procedure, so they feel confident that they can continue to get their insurance claims paid conveniently and promptly.

The library's policy on distribution of policies should pay special attention to the way users of the library are informed about policies. Any change in the rules affects those who use the library, and trying to predict the effects of those changes is important in minimizing the problems caused by the change.

These principles are straightforward, and yet it is often difficult to ensure that each policymaker follows these practices of good policy management. A statement in a policy on policies can encourage such practices if it provides guidelines such as the following:

> Try to involve those affected by the change in the development or the review of the policy so that they can provide their ideas and recognize that change is in the wind.

> Inform staff and users sufficiently in advance for them to understand the change and to prepare for it.

Try to anticipate the effect on the staff and users, and consider methods for minimizing the inconvenience, including providing staff and users with alternatives for meeting their needs.

Providing Permanent and Convenient Access to Policies

Informing everyone affected by a policy about its existence usually involves widespread distribution of the initial policy statement or a narrative explanation. This distribution can be considered distribution for information. After the initial distribution, the policy must continue to be available to those affected by it. Any new or revised policy should also be added to all compilations of policies. Policies affecting users should be displayed or made available in other ways.

Selecting the number and location of policy "sites" where compilations are kept is important because it affects the integrity of the policy system as a whole. If policy sites are started and then not properly maintained, discrepancies will occur in documentation of policies, and these will inevitably lead to discrepancies in implementation and enforcement. One alternative is to have only one official site for the compilation of policies, whether it is a file or a loose-leaf manual. A single site can be monitored easily by one person, who provides others with up-to-date information as requested, and everyone knows where to look for all policies. However, a single site may be inconvenient for library staff, and policies may not be used simply because consulting them is too much trouble.

Multiple sites are more convenient, but systematizing the distribution involves more structure. One response to this problem is to designate official sites for policy compilations, such as one in every department, and to designate persons in charge of maintaining these compilations.

Keeping Policy Compilations Current

Whether policy compilations are kept at one site or several, a system should be designated for incorporating all the updates into the compilations. The procedure for incorporating the revisions into the policy compilation should be clear, so that all revisions find their way into official documents *in the appropriate places.* Separate sheets of paper announcing changes tend to be as useless as errata slips, unless someone takes the time to incorporate the change permanently in the appropriate place. People who consult policies expect to find all applicable information together and will rarely look further. For this reason, the system for updating policy compilations should incorporate the change in its logical place.

The problem of updating policies by memo has already been mentioned. This difficulty alone accounts for the brief shelflife of most policy manuals. If memos are used to update policies, new "official" pages or inserts should be distributed simultaneously to all designated compilation sites. Explaining policies by memo is an excellent way of informing people about changes. The difficulty arises when the memo is asked to do double duty as the official, permanent record of the change. By keeping the distinction clear between the informative distribution and documentation for the permanent record, libraries can avoid undermining their efforts to maintain complete compilations of policies.

Evaluating and Updating Policies

The frequency of evaluations and revisions of policies can itself be a matter of policy and can be accomplished on a regular schedule or tackled as needed. Evaluating the effectiveness of a policy is similar to assessing the need for a new policy, discussed earlier in this chapter. Every evaluation should start with a review of the purpose of the policy and should address the two criteria for the effectiveness of any policy.

- ▲ All decisions and actions covered by the policy should be made according to the guidelines in the policy.
- ▲ The actions guided by the policy should achieve the effects intended by the policymakers.

The evaluators will want to obtain information about the consistency of implementation and about the effectiveness of the policy from both staff and users. In addition, the evaluators will want to examine data and observe the effects of the policy firsthand. The process for developing content for the revisions can be the same as that for developing new individual policies.

WRITING INDIVIDUAL POLICIES

So far, we have been considering elements of the framework that apply to all library policies. We have been implying that the exercise of developing or documenting the practice concerning policies in your library is worthwhile, apart from the development of individual policies. In addition to the reasons we have already discussed, the existence of a well-understood policy on policies makes the writing of individual policies easier because the framework is already there.

Determining Need and Identifying Results to Be Achieved

Determining the need for a policy has been considered at an earlier point in this chapter. Once it has been decided to develop a written policy, the need should be reviewed as a basis for defining the results that you want to achieve. Why is the policy needed? What are the problems with present practice? What is the current policy in this area and what are its strengths and weaknesses?

Frequently, in the process of defining what you want to achieve through a particular policy, you will decide that even the best policy, managed in the most effective way possible, will not completely solve the problem, and you may want to recommend approaches, in addition to the development of policies, to address the issue. For example, the committee on fines (in our earlier example) may decide that the real problem, the high rate of over-due materials, cannot be resolved by restructuring the policy on fines. The committee members might reason that although the purpose of fines is to put some bite into requests to bring materials back, the financial penalty alone may not be enough to produce the desired results. Therefore, the committee might recommend that some means of increasing the university community's awareness of the dimensions of the overdue problem might be developed concurrently with a new fine structure.

Finally, in analyzing the results that you wish to achieve, you will want to consider issues of human relations, as well as the actions that you wish to stimulate. How do the people affected feel about the current policy and how will they react to the change? Our fine committee may decide that it wishes to increase the rate of return of overdue material, but, at the same time, it wants to retain the university community's positive attitude toward the library. By articulating your goals for human relations, you will be able to weigh alternatives in terms of their effect on people's attitudes and per-ceptions, as well as their effectiveness in modifying behavior.

Determining the Content of the Policy

As a developer of policies, you often have reasonably clear ideas about the content your policy should have. You may be strengthening an existing policy and thus building on its directions, or you may be drawing on your experience in other libraries and on the library literature for your models. In any case, it is useful to develop a list of possible policy directions that might achieve the results you want. Casting your net as widely as possible ensures that you will not be overlooking a possible alternative merely be-cause it is different from those you already know. You can gather ideas about alternative policies from many sources, including brainstorming ses-sions with staff, ideas from users, practices in other libraries or in other kinds of institutions, and articles in the library literature.

Choosing between alternative policy directions then becomes a matter of trying to predict the probable effects of each alternative. You will want to look carefully at *who* will be affected by the policy and *how* they will be af-fected. At this stage, you will want to assess thoroughly the effects of each policy choice, considering how it will affect people's behavior and whether it will interfere with their ability to meet legitimate needs. Imagining the effect of the policy from the point of view of those affected by it helps you understand what the policy will mean to others. Looking at it from the staff's or user's perspective can also help you predict whether they will comply voluntarily or whether enforcement will be necessary. You need to assess the impact of any enforcement that will be required: Who will do it, how much time will it take, will it be effective, and what will the consequences be for human relations?

Anticipating the consequences of various alternatives is an essential part of deciding the content of your policy. Even if you decide to go ahead with a policy that will have negative effects, you can plan ways to minimize them if you know what they are likely to be.

Continuing our hypothetical example, the committee assessing a policy on fines might develop the alternatives below:

- ▲ a small fine (perhaps five or ten cents a day) that keeps accruing until the book is returned
- ▲ a large fine (perhaps one dollar a day or five dollars a week) that increases rapidly to a set maximum (perhaps $50)
- ▲ a fine that turns into a bill for the item within a specified period.

Each of these alternatives represents a different approach to the problem; each will have different effects on the users; and each will have adherents who believe that it will be most effective.

Attempting to assess the *effects* of each alternative and matching *them* to your library's philosophy and environment should give you a strong sense of the policy direction you wish to pursue. It may be the one that you have favored initially. On the other hand, the process of gathering information and objectively assessing probable effects will sometimes offer you effective solutions that would otherwise have been overlooked. More discussion on analyzing the effects of potential policies appears in the upcoming section on reviewing draft policies.

Organizing and Writing the Draft Policy

Once you know the rough outlines of the policy you want, you can begin to draft the details of the policy statement. If your institution has a standard format for writing individual policies, you will already have the beginnings of the policy's structure. If you are using a memo format or an open-ended form, you will want to block out an organizational structure for the policy that divides it into its logical components. Most policies begin with a statement describing the purpose or the rationale for the policy. The next statements typically describe the policy in general, followed by further specifics of the policy or by details of implementation arranged under categorical subheadings, if these are appropriate. Many policies conclude with the names of the parties proposing, reviewing, and approving the policy, along with dates for these actions. Dates of any revisions are also noted. The location of filing or documentation can also be included if appropriate. A list of elements commonly included in individual policies appears earlier in this chapter.

Reviewing the Draft Policy

Once you have written a draft of the policy, you will want to subject it to a thorough review to ensure that the content is appropriate for the situation and will produce the effects you intend. It is hard to overemphasize the importance of a thorough review *before* the policy is announced. After a policy is implemented, it takes on a life of its own. Unanticipated consequences can be disruptive, and immediate changes in the policy are difficult and sometimes embarrassing. The method that you use for review will depend on customary practice in your institution and on the nature of the policy. Some alternatives for structuring the review process have been discussed earlier in this chapter.

During your review, you may wish to consider the following issues:

Purpose
Are the results you are trying to achieve clear? Is it clear why you want to achieve these results? Is it clear how the policy will achieve the results and why this particular policy was chosen? Is this policy likely to be an effective way of achieving the results you want?

Comprehensiveness
Is the policy well thought out and complete? Does it cover all aspects of the situation?

Effects on Library Routines and Staff
How will the policy affect current library routines? Are new procedures necessary? Who will develop these? When? What effect will the policy have on the staff's workload? How are staff likely to feel about the policy?

Effects on Users and Their Routines
How will the policy affect users? At what point will they encounter the policy? Will it cause them inconvenience the first time they encounter the policy? Every time they encounter the policy? How will they perceive the policy? If these perceptions are likely to be negative, can anything be done to make them more positive?

Effectiveness
Will the policy achieve the results you want? What measures will you use to assess how effective the policy is? Can you establish criteria for effectiveness at the outset? Do you have data to compare performance under the

new policy with performance under the old way of doing things. What mechanisms do you have for users and staff to give their reactions to the policy? What are the channels to use in changing the policy or asking for an exception? What kinds of exceptions will be allowed and who will decide? At what intervals will you review all indicators of effectiveness and make changes if necessary?

Writing the Final Draft of the Policy Statement

With the final content of the policy determined, you are ready to choose the final wording of the policy. The wording for your policy will depend on its audience and on your plans for distribution. Some policies will be read by staff only, and others will be read by users. Be sure that you know who will be reading the policy and how it will be used before you write the final draft.

Clarity

Policy statements must be unambiguous. Assess your sentences carefully to be sure they mean exactly what you want them to mean. Chapter 3 provides suggestions for detecting and fixing problems with sentence construction and word choice that can interfere with clear communication.

Organization

The format of the policy may be determined by your library's policy on policies or by customary practice. The organization of the policy should foster both clear understanding and quick reference. Visualize for yourself the situations in which people will be consulting the policy and plan an organizational structure that makes important elements stand out clearly. Signposts, like headings and subheadings, topic sentences, and lists of points, are particularly important for leading the reader quickly to the main elements of the policy. Breaking up long narratives into short paragraphs can also encourage quick reading. Figure 20 illustrates one form for a staff policy, and chapter 2 provides further advice on organizing information clearly.

Tone

The tone of policies is particularly important. Many policies are, in effect, regulations governing behavior, and the tone in which those regulations are presented affects people's reactions to them. Most statements of regulations, even prohibitions, can be stated positively, and, in general, a positive tone is preferable to a negative, dictatorial, or admonishing tone. When prohibitions are needed, some indication of the rationale can soften the apparent harshness.

Imagine that you, as a library user, approach the media circulation desk at a public library and encounter the following large sign:

RULES FOR BORROWING VIDEOTAPES

1. No videotapes will be loaned without a valid library card.
2. No more than three videotapes can be checked out at one time.
3. Videotapes are loaned for TWO DAYS ONLY, and no renewals are allowed.
4. Reservations for videotapes will not be accepted prior to the date of use. No reservations will be honored past 6 pm.
5. YOU WILL BE CHARGED $1 A DAY FOR LATE VIDEOTAPES. If your fines are not paid, your borrowing privileges will be revoked.
6. YOU WILL BE CHARGED THE FULL PURCHASE PRICE FOR DAMAGED TAPES!

What effect does the working of this policy have on you? Although there are no firm rules for writing with a positive tone, the following approaches may be useful:

▲ State what the user *can* do, rather than what *cannot* be done.
▲ State what the library *allows*, rather than what it *forbids*.
▲ When describing *negative* actions, soften them with the *passive* voice, as long as important information about the "actor" is not lost.
▲ *Buffer* negative information with an explanatory sentence or clause.
▲ State *restrictions* in moderate, *neutral language*.
▲ Avoid words that have negative meanings or connotations, even when they convey positive information (as illustrated below).

Negative wording for positive information:

Do not hesitate to ask if you have questions.

Positive revision:

Please ask if you have questions.

Using these guidelines, test your skills by revising RULES FOR BORROWING VIDEOTAPES. Compare your revision with the one below. Note that when the overall tone of the policy is positive, mild negatives stand out and have more impact.

POLICIES FOR BORROWING VIDEOTAPES

1. You may borrow up to three videotapes for a period of two days with a valid library card.
2. Our videotape collection is heavily used, so we regret that renewals cannot be granted.
3. Reservations will be accepted by telephone or in person on the day of use only. We will hold the tape for you until 6 pm.

4. Late videotapes will be assessed a fine of $1 per day. Fines must be paid before additional tapes can be checked out.
5. Users are responsible for damage to videotapes.

Specialists' Language and Jargon

Policies should be written in language that is easily understandable to all who will read the policy. Particularly in policies that will be read by library users, you should eliminate library jargon. Assess the potential difficulty with the following statement of policy on circulation, designed for a brochure on library service; then propose alternatives:

CIRCULATION PERIODS

Library materials are circulated for the following periods:

Monographs:	Two weeks
Serials:	One week
Sound recordings:	One week
Audiotapes:	One week
Videotapes:	Two days

Compare your revision with the one below.

LOAN PERIODS

You may borrow library materials for the following periods:

Books:	Two weeks
Magazines:	One week
Records and Tapes:	One week
Videotapes:	Two days

Planning Your Strategy for Communicating the Policy

The success of your policy depends on the way you communicate the policy to those who will be responsible for implementing it and to those who will be affected by it.

You will want to use your predictions about the way the policy will affect users and staff as the basis for deciding how and when it should be announced. As a rule, the more complicated and significant the change, the more comprehensive your communication strategy should be and the more time you should allow between the announcement and the date the policy becomes effective. When a change in policy will have major effects on the budgets of departments or institutions, the change should ideally be announced in time for adjustments in budget requests. Decisions about communication of policies should be based on the impact the change will have and on how much time people need to prepare for the change.

For example, a policy establishing guidelines for the behavior of staff in public areas should be distributed to all staff, but it may need only a short time for general discussion before it is officially implemented. A change in the way medical claims are processed must also reach all staff members. Theoretically, it might not require much time to instruct staff members on handling their own claims; however, because the change itself may be emotionally unsettling, several months for adjusting to the idea of the new system may be desirable. A policy of charging for interlibrary loans, instituted after loans have been free, may need to be announced in advance to prepare users and to allow time for questions and explanations.

After you decide who needs to know what and when, you can choose the best way to reach each group. You will need to decide whether you will distribute the policy in its entirety or whether you will write an informational memo, flyer, or sign describing the main points of the change. You may also want to consider forums, like formal or informal meetings, for comments and explanations. The time spent in planning the way you will communicate the policy change will be amply repaid when the policy slides into place effectively and smoothly.

TEST YOUR SKILLS

Writing policies is an excellent example of the way that good professional writing depends on sound knowledge of library practices, skills for achieving good human relations, and effective writing skills. Figure 21 is a case study for you to test your skills.

> You are the head of Public Services in a college library serving an undergraduate population of 1,000 students and a faculty of 200. At this institution, faculty have virtually unlimited loan periods for books. Loans are stamped for one-year periods, all due on June 1, but renewals are automatic, and, although notices are sent out each year, they are, in effect, requests to return books that are no longer needed. Loans are carried year after year, and, beyond occasional exhortatory letters, no strong efforts are made to call in the loans.
>
> The head of Circulation has analyzed circulation records and has determined that 900 have been checked out to faculty for more than three years. At a librarians' meeting, feeling ran high on the issue. The staff wanted to abolish any sort of special loan privileges for faculty. A few felt uneasy about repercussions from the faculty, but even they felt that having two classes of library citizenship was not fair to the students. One librarian reported an instance where the faculty member put a hold on a book and was surprised to

Figure 21. **Test Your Skills: Writing Policies**

discover that the book was already checked out to him. The suggestion was made that faculty loans be limited to one year, and that books could be renewed for another year if physically returned to the library, but the counter-suggestion, that all loan periods be equal, beginning July 1 of the following year, was eventually approved by a unanimous staff vote. The motion included the recommendation that the decision go to the faculty library committee for approval.

The library committee found the proposal very distressing. They felt that their colleagues considered long-term loans to be a privilege of teaching at this college, one of the advantages they enjoyed over colleagues in other colleges and universities. An opinion was expressed by a senior member of the faculty that in most cases the faculty member who checked out the book had ordered it in the first place and was the only one interested in that subject, and if someone else requested the book, it could always be recalled. After much discussion, the library committee declined to approve or disapprove the proposal. They were clearly uncomfortable with opposing the uniform recommendation of the library staff, but they did not want to support what they felt would be an extremely unpopular decision among the faculty. They decided to share their strong concerns with the library director and left it to him to develop a satisfactory policy on faculty loans.

The director asks you, as the head of Public Services, to do the following:

1. Identify what you feel should be the goals of the policy on faculty loans in your institution. Support those goals with a rationale that makes sense in this environment.
2. Develop two or three policy alternatives and compare them in terms of their ability to meet those goals and their projected effects on the total community of library users and the library staff.
3. On the basis of the comparison, select the policy that you recommend and write a policy statement on faculty loans for inclusion in the printed library handbook under the heading "Library Services for Faculty."
4. Plan a communication strategy for informing faculty of the new policy, recognizing the importance of keeping as much faculty good will as possible. Feel free to include types of oral communication in your strategy.
5. Write the documents that will be a part of your communication campaign, including the memo in which you announce the new policy to the faculty.

For the purposes of this exercise, assume that the library staff will support the policy statement that you derive from your goals, even if it is different from their first recommendation. You may also assume any additional details about the institution, the library, or the circulation policies or statistics that you feel are important. You may wish to involve several others in discussing this exercise and then exchange written documents for review and comment. Discussion of this exercise appears in Section I, pages 346–48 of the appendix.

CHECKLIST FOR WRITING POLICIES

Figure 22 is a checklist that summarizes the process for writing policies. It can be used as a review of the chapter or as a guide when writing policies.

Use the checklist below to review the process for writing policies.
1. State the subject of the policy as specifically as possible and describe the need as you see it.
   ▲ For what activity or action is a policy needed?
   ▲ What written policies exist in this area?
   ▲ What policies exist in the "oral tradition"?
   ▲ What problem needs to be corrected by a policy?
   ▲ What relationship do you see between the current policy and the problem you just described?
       Is the current content of the policy producing the problem or not addressing it effectively? Describe the weaknesses of the current policy.
       Is the problem caused by issues of policy management or by the content of the policy?
       Is documentation of the policy adequate? Are the details of the policy clearly and concisely written?
       Is the policy adequately distributed? Does everyone affected know about the policy? Are there designated sites for the official compilation of policies?
       Has the policy been updated? Was everyone adequately informed about the updates? Were the updates incorporated into the official policy at the appropriate place?
       Has the policy been reevaluated recently? Does it need reevaluation?
2. Articulate what you want to achieve by establishing the policy.
   ▲ What decisions or actions do you wish to regulate through policies?
   ▲ What effects do you wish to achieve by regulating these decisions or actions?
   ▲ What are the human relations dimensions of this issue?
   ▲ What are your human relations goals for this policy?
3. Develop a list of possible alternative policies.
   ▲ What alternative policies will achieve your goals?
   ▲ What do other libraries do?
   ▲ How do other organizations (not libraries) deal with similar problems?
   ▲ What guidance can you find in the literature?

Figure 22. **Writing Policies: A Checklist**

  ▲ What ideas do the people who are affected by the policy have, both staff and library users?
4. Compare the probable effects and effectiveness of each alternative and select the most appropriate for your purposes.
  ▲ What actions will each alternative produce?
  ▲ How will each policy affect the staff?
  ▲ How will each policy affect the users?
  ▲ Will people comply with each alternative voluntarily?
  ▲ How will people feel about each alternative? Is one likely to be more palatable than others?
  ▲ What kind of enforcement is necessary with each? Which policy will be more likely to achieve the behavioral results you desire?
  ▲ Will one be most effective in achieving your human relations goals?
5. Determine the appropriate channels in your library for developing a policy of this kind. Using these channels, decide on the policy content.
  ▲ Does you library have a "policy on policies" that specifies how policies like this should be developed?
  ▲ How have similar policies been developed?
  ▲ What do you think is the appropriate process for developing this policy? Should you consult anyone else, and if so whom, in making this decision?
  ▲ Who in your library should be involved in developing the draft?
  ▲ Have you considered group development of the policy? Who should be in the group?
6. Organize your policy, following your institution's guidelines for writing policies.
  ▲ Does your institution or department have a standard format for policies?
  ▲ How are policies compiled and updated in your library?
  ▲ Which of the standard elements will you include in your policy?
  ▲ How will you organize the presentation of the policy statement? Will it be divided into topical areas?
7. Draft the policy, following your organizational outline.
8. Determine the appropriate process for reviewing and revising a policy of this kind in your library. Using this process, conduct a review of the content of the policy, considering the policy's purpose, comprehensiveness, its effects on staff and library users, and probable effectiveness. Revise as appropriate.
  ▲ What are your library's policies and practices for the review of policies like the one you are writing?
      Does your library have a policy on policies that specifies how policies like this should be reviewed?
      How have similar policies been reviewed in the past? Was that review successful? How could it have been improved?
  ▲ What kind of review process is most appropriate for this situation: organizational review? review by representative individuals? review by group affected?

- ▲ Is the purpose of the policy clear? is the rationale behind its details clear?
- ▲ Is the policy well thought out? Does it cover all aspects of the situation?
- ▲ How will the policy affect library staff?
     How will the policy affect library routines?
     Are new procedures necessary? If so, who will develop them and when?
     What effect will the policy have on staff workloads?
     How are the staff likely to feel about the policy?
- ▲ How will the policy affect users and the way they use the library?
     What groups of users will the policy affect?
     At what point will they encounter the policy?
     Will it cause them inconvenience the first time they encounter the policy? Every time they encounter the policy?
     How are they likely to perceive the policy? If these perceptions are likely to be negative, can anything be done to make them positive?
- ▲ Do you predict that the policy will achieve the results you want?

9. Make decisions about the distribution, implementation, and evaluation of the policy.
    - ▲ How much time should there be between the announcement of the policy change and the date it goes into effect?
    - ▲ When will the policy take effect?
    - ▲ How will you inform people about the policy? By memo? By meetings with those affected? By signs at appropriate places? By other means?
    - ▲ What mechanism do you have for staff and users to react to the policy? What mechanism for response?
    - ▲ Will you have a transition period? What are the guidelines for implementing the policy in the transition period? How will these guidelines be communicated to staff responsible for implementing them?
    - ▲ After the transition period, what exceptions to the policy, if any, will be considered? Who will make these exceptions? How will the guidelines about exceptions be communicated to the staff responsible for implementing the policy?
    - ▲ What measures will you use to assess how effective the policy is?
    - ▲ Can you establish criteria for effectiveness at the outset? Do you have data to measure performance under the new policy against performances under the old way of doing things? What data will you need to collect to measure the effectiveness of the policy?
    - ▲ When should you evaluate the new policy to be sure it is achieving its goals?

10. Revise the draft wording, considering clarity, tone, and style.
    - ▲ Do you predict that your policy, as it is now written, will be successful in accomplishing its purpose? Will people behave in the way you de-

Figure 22—**Continued**

sire? If not, can you identify the obstacles to success and plan ways to overcome them?

▲ Pretending for a moment that you did not write the policy, how do you assess its tone?

▲ Have you assessed your policy systematically, looking for problems of effectiveness, tone and personality, organizational structure, composition of sentences, and word choice? (Chapter 3 provides checklists to help with this analysis.)

▲ For each problem you find, can you pinpoint the cause and develop alternatives? Which alternative works best in the context of the policy?

11. Using the process appropriate in your library, obtain approvals for the new policy. You will probably want to start this process early in the development of the policy.

▲ Who in your library should approve the final policy before it is announced?

▲ Who should approve your plans for distribution and implementation?

12. Edit the policy for correctness.

▲ Have you reviewed your draft for problems of grammar, usage, and punctuation?

▲ Have you used your knowledge of the kinds of mistakes you make to help you find trouble spots? (Chapter 3 provides assistance in identifying and solving these problems.)

▲ Have you checked all matters of fact, including

dates?	raw numbers and computations?
facts?	bibliographic citations?
titles?	proper nouns, especially names?
spelling?	

▲ Have you proofread carefully to ensure accuracy? (Chapter 3 provides a checklist for this activity.)

13. Produce the final copy of your policy.

▲ Have you considered the elements of "design" to achieve an effective, professional office look?

▲ Have you marked the layout for the final copy, noting any special keyboard graphic effects, special spacing, and indentions?

▲ If someone is assisting you by preparing the final copy, have you communicated your instructions clearly, including those for spacing, margins, layout, and special graphic effects?

▲ Have you arranged to review a typed draft before the final is prepared?

▲ After receiving the final copy, have you proofread carefully, for typographical errors and other difficulties that might have slipped in?

▲ Is the final copy neat and professional looking?

14. Plan, write, and produce the supplementary materials that will be needed to announce and explain the policy.

Chapter 7

PROCEDURES

CHAPTER OUTLINE

CRITERIA FOR EFFECTIVE PROCEDURES

NEED FOR WRITTEN PROCEDURES

PROCEDURAL WRITING IN LIBRARIES

DOCUMENTATION OF PROCEDURES

PURPOSE OF PROCEDURES

USES OF PROCEDURES
    General Understanding of a Process
    Understanding and Performing Complex, Interrelated Tasks
    Performing One Task

THE WRITER OF PROCEDURES

CONTENT OF PROCEDURES

ORGANIZATION OF PROCEDURES
    General Information vs. Description of Activities
    Determining a Logical Division of Activities
    Subdividing Sections into Steps
    Choosing Levels of Specificity
    Formats for Presenting Activities or Steps
    Elements of Procedures
    Procedural Style

TEST YOUR SKILLS

CHECKLIST FOR WRITING PROCEDURES

Procedures are sequential descriptions of how things should be accomplished. While policies provide a general framework for decision making and for action, procedures spell out the details of how things should be done. Procedures may supplement policies, describing how they will be implemented, or procedures may exist on their own, describing activities that may not require an enabling policy, like opening the library.

CRITERIA FOR EFFECTIVE PROCEDURES

Procedures, or descriptions of how things are done in an institution, are developed to achieve certain results. Procedures for processing interlibrary loans, for example, are intended to ensure timely, accurate processing of requests. Procedures also try to ensure accurate and uniform performance of library operations by providing a written description of how things are done. The interlibrary loan procedures need to be written and managed in a way that helps the staff to perform tasks as they are described.

The effectiveness of procedures in achieving their purpose, like the effectiveness of policies, must be judged by two criteria. Is everyone who performs the routine following the procedure and performing the activity accurately? And if everyone is performing uniformly and accurately, is the result satisfactory?

For example, suppose that a circulation librarian decides that the purpose of procedures for the circulation desk is to ensure that all desk personnel perform all the required steps in checking materials in and out. The procedure is working effectively, according to the first criterion, if everyone is following the same steps in checking materials in and out. The procedure is working effectively, according to the second criterion, if the checkout system, when followed uniformly and accurately, provides adequate records for materials circulated. If circulation staff are consistently omitting a step in the procedure, the problem may be the result of the way procedures are written, documented, updated, or used in training and evaluation (criterion one). If the procedures result in files that do not allow the staff to determine what books are checked out to a given individual, and if this information is necessary, then the problem is the content of the procedures (criterion two).

NEED FOR WRITTEN PROCEDURES

Procedures, or particular ways of getting things done, can exist without being written down. Both written and unwritten procedures dictate action and, if they are followed regularly, can result in consistent, accurate performance. However, written procedures can achieve that consistency much more effectively than is possible with procedures that are known only to one person or that exist in an oral tradition. Written procedures provide a permanent record, independent of the presence of an individual. With written procedures, differences in understanding of procedures are easier to avoid. Written procedures can serve as a reference tool for staff, and they can be effective in training new staff members. Often, the process of writing down procedures serves as a catalyst for examining the way things are done and for finding better alternatives.

Libraries develop procedures from scratch whenever they begin doing something they have not done before, such as circulating books using an automated system, inaugurating a program to lend microcomputers and software to users, or changing from photocopiers that require change to models that use cards. More frequently, though, librarians who write procedures will be revising an existing procedure or documenting current practice.

PROCEDURAL WRITING IN LIBRARIES

Librarians use the term *procedures* to cover writing that describes how things happen, how something works, or how to do something. Documents that bear the name *procedures* can range from a general explanation of a process, such as the budget process, to a specific description of the way to perform a task, like the procedures for checking in books. In business and technical writing, the most common term for all types of procedural writing is *process analysis*. The term is useful because it emphasizes the purpose behind all procedural writing: to analyze a process or activity.

Types of procedural writing (or process analyses) differ in the reason for which they are used and the level of specificity of analysis and description. For example, the process for borrowing materials from other libraries may be described in a brochure to give users an understanding of the way libraries use a national bibliographic utility to share resources. The way a bibliographic utility, like OCLC, matches borrowers to lenders might be described in a handout for library staff to give them a better understanding of the borrowing process. The processes of the interlibrary loan unit might be documented in a manual for the understanding of departmental staff and for the guidance of staff members in performing their tasks. Finally, the process that a circulation-desk worker should use to check on the status of interlibrary loan requests might be documented in an instruction sheet as a step-by-step guide for part-time employees.

Although it would be ridiculous to insist on new terminology for what librarians have always known as procedures, it is important for librarians to remember that *procedures*, as they use the word, can refer to documents that have varying purposes and differing levels of specificity. The writer designs the procedure to meet the needs of the situation. In this chapter we will look at the choices librarians have in writing procedures.

DOCUMENTATION OF PROCEDURES

Procedures, like policies, have a useful life beyond the moment at which they are distributed, and therefore thought must be given to how they will be compiled and used. The considerations here are similar to those discussed in the chapter on policies, and you may wish to review that section for a more detailed analysis. In summary, procedures, like policies, can be organized in a file by department and subject or in a manual. In choosing a method of documentation, the need for individuals to have convenient access must be balanced by the requirement that all copies of procedures be current. To be effective, a system for documenting procedures should provide easy access to all who need it and should be relatively easy to maintain.

PURPOSE OF PROCEDURES

We have been looking at the purpose of procedures in two ways: (1) to achieve certain results by prescribing steps that must be followed, and (2) to ensure uniform and accurate performance of those steps by providing a document to assist with training, performance, and evaluation.

Writers of procedures need to recognize both purposes. They need to define what results they want in order to design steps that will achieve those results. And they need to consider how the procedures should be used to promote accurate and uniform performance of steps in the procedure. Procedures can be used in a number of ways: to enable new staff to learn routines easily and quickly; to provide all staff with appropriate direction in the ongoing performance of routines; and to serve as a tool for pinpointing areas of difficulty in performance so that additional explanations can be offered.

USES OF PROCEDURES

A procedure is designed to guide a specific audience in understanding and performing a task in order to achieve a desired result. It will work if it is written so the audience will understand it and can use it accurately. The procedure will *not* be effective if it does not make information available when and where people need it and in ways they can understand. For example, the procedure manual for the circulation department may contain much detail about how to do specific tasks. But if this detail is buried in descriptive information, it will be difficult for staff to find and use the directions they need. Similarly, if all the information about how to do one task is scattered throughout a procedure, it will be difficult to follow.

To ensure that procedures are written in ways that will be useful, imagine who will be using a procedure and what level of understanding they are likely to bring to it. You can write for the lowest common denominator and gear explanation to the person with the least background who will have to read the procedure. You might try to imagine why people are reading the procedure, what they will be expected to do with the knowledge, when they are expected to apply it, and how much detail they will need to know.

It may be useful to look at some of the common ways that people use procedures.

General Understanding of a Process

Descriptions of activities can provide a general understanding of a process to many people. A public library might design a bookmark that describes the process through which the library tries to meet the demand for best-sellers. A corporate special library might describe, in its brochure, the process through which books are chosen and the ways that employees can participate. In a handbook for graduate students, a university library might describe the process for obtaining carrels in the stacks.

Understanding and Performing Complex, Interrelated Tasks

Library procedure manuals frequently describe and explain the complex activities of a unit or department. The activities may involve large numbers of people and many different tasks done at different times. A circulation manual will describe many activities, such as checking books in and out, sending notices and invoices, and taking library card applications. Some steps in each activity will be done by full-time assistants with specific responsibilities, such as the circulation assistant; other activities may be done by part-time help, by volunteers, by student workers, and by other library staff who are helping out. Some activities need to be done at specific times, like opening the library in the morning; other activities are done as needed. Some tasks are performed from start to finish at one time, and others are partially completed and left for others.

All the staff who are using procedures that cover multiple activities performed at different times need to understand the interdependence of these activities, and they need to be able to find directions for performing specific tasks.

Procedures are sometimes written for one person or one position and involve many tasks performed at different times. For example, all the procedures that the interlibrary loan assistant performs may be grouped together. Procedures that are organized by position or function need to provide an explanation of the scope and interrelation of tasks, as well as directions on how to perform them.

Performing One Task

Procedures may be written for one task. Often these procedures take the form of instructions, with numbered steps proceeding from the beginning to the end. Such instructions might be written for using the online catalog or for checking in periodicals.

THE WRITER OF PROCEDURES

In general, the best procedures result when one person assumes responsibility for structuring a draft of the procedures and then involves others in testing and reviewing the draft. Writing effective procedures is not a simple task. The writer must have an understanding of the activity and its place in library operations, an ability to analyze situations logically, an understanding of what information people need to know to perform their tasks effectively, and the skill to translate that knowledge into an organized, logical presentation. No rule can be given about who is the best person to develop procedures in a given situation. But it is possible to look at various positions in the library and assess the perspectives from which a person in that position might view the procedures, remembering, of course, that the *person* in the position can bring different kinds of understandings and insights to the position. Each perspective is valuable, and, if it is not represented by the writer of the procedures, it should be provided by the people who review the document. Procedures may be written by those who perform the procedure, by those who supervise it, or by someone from the outside who interviews, observes, and then records the procedure.

The person who performs the procedure obviously has firsthand knowledge of how the routine is being performed. He or she is likely to know a great deal about the immediate consequences of actions, how long activities take, and the levels of difficulty of certain activities. If a "performer" undertakes to write procedures, he or she should have an appreciation of how the activities fit into the larger picture of library operations, an understanding of alternative ways to accomplish each activity, the ability to judge when one alternative is essential or when several approaches might be used equally well, and an ability to explain as well as do.

The supervisor of the activity usually has an understanding of the broader context of the activity and an overview of various approaches to it. If a supervisor undertakes to write procedures, he or she must be familiar with the daily operational details of how activities are done and the difficulties encountered.

An outsider who gathers information from interviews and observation and then records practice can bring an objective perspective to an activity. Asking an outsider to draft procedures occurs more frequently in organizations that have systems or efficiency staff, administrative assistants, or consultative help to provide support in organizing departmental processes and procedures. If an outsider undertakes to draft procedures, he or she must be able to appreciate both the managerial and the operational aspects of an activity, to grasp the essential principles and details of operations quickly, and to organize them effectively for review. To be effective, an outsider almost always needs experience either with the activity being documented or with the process of systems analysis and documentation.

Regardless of the position held by the writer, he or she should try to gain a triple perspective on the procedure: (1) seeing it from above, as it fits into other activities; (2) seeing it from the inside, as it is actually performed; and (3) seeing it from below, as its effects are felt by others. A writer of an effective procedure must also be able to organize complex activities into a systematic description that will serve the purpose of the procedure.

CONTENT OF PROCEDURES

When new procedures are developed or existing ones are revised, you must consider their content. By *content* we mean what happens when a procedure is followed. In other words, developing new content means thinking through the way things should be done and specifying new actions or activities that will be performed as part of the procedure. Even if you are documenting existing procedures, it is a good idea to review how things are being done to determine whether new content is needed.

Developing the content of procedures, or deciding how activities will be done, occurs in different ways in every library. Generally, the best content for procedures emerges when both the perspective of the person who will perform them and the supervisor's perspective are consulted. To develop content, the purpose of the activity should be clearly defined, the results specified, and any limitations on resources recognized. The specific steps of the activity are then decided upon in light of the criteria that you have specified. For example, as a first step in revising the content of a shelf-reading procedure, you might define the purpose as follows: to ensure that the books are in the correct order on the shelf. For results, you might decide that you want to read the entire collection in one year and that you want at least 95 percent accuracy during weekly spot-checks. You might recognize the following limitations: one person cannot read shelves effectively for more than one hour at a time; most staff need training to read shelves effectively; monitoring is necessary to ensure accuracy; and the only labor pool large enough to get the job done within the time allotted is a group of student assistants.

When content is revised, the strengths and weaknesses of the current procedure should be reviewed in light of the purpose, the criteria for effective results, and the limitations of your resources. It takes energy and effort to look at the effects of procedures and to determine and analyze alternative ways of achieving results. The participation of several people in the process not only provides different perspectives but also shares the load.

ORGANIZATION OF PROCEDURES

Organizing a set of procedures, or even one procedure, is often difficult because it imposes a sequential order on activities that are complex and interrelated. The organizational scheme must differentiate between directions for action and general information. In addition, the procedures must always show clearly who is performing the activity described, when it is to be done, and how—all at the level of detail that matches what the reader of the procedure needs to know.

We believe that there are few really useful procedure manuals in libraries precisely because of the difficulty in creating a logical, thorough, and clear manual that meets the needs of those who use it. On the other hand, we believe that the usefulness of well-written procedures in assisting with training, performance, and evaluation can be so significant that the results are worth the agony. We would like to offer some considerations that may be helpful in organizing procedures. Figure 23 presents a hypothetical procedure from a manual for public services. Figure 24 presents a set of instructions for performing one task. Both figures illustrate a variety of approaches to writing procedures, and they will be used as examples in the discussion below.

General Information vs. Description of Activities

Procedures describe how things happen or tell how to do things, so they consist primarily of a description of what happens, a list of activities, or a sequence of steps. Writers of procedures usually find, however, that they want to include general or explanatory information along with the description of the process. The danger in mixing this information with the description is that the instructions will become buried in the explanation and will not be easy to follow.

Several methods can solve this problem. Frequently, you can put explanatory information first, using it to introduce the list of steps. Explanatory information often divides into discrete categories, such as *rationale* or *policy*, and can be labeled as such.

If you want to include explanatory information with each activity, the least confusing technique is to begin with a sentence describing the activity. Then you can provide explanatory detail, making sure that the explanation is necessary to performing the activity. In figure 23, general information appears in several places: under the heading "Rationale," under each activity as "General Information," and as needed after individual steps (for example, "I.A.3").

Step-by-step instructions in business and industry often employ standard notations to indicate types of explanatory information. Although the practice is uncommon in libraries, the idea is promising. The standard notation WARNING is for information that affects human safety. The word CAUTION is used for information about possible damage to equipment. And the word NOTE is used when information necessary to the performance of the procedure is presented.

Public Services Procedure Manual
Procedure Number:

Stacks Maintenance: Shelf-Reading

Definition and Purpose: "Reading the shelves" means
checking the call number of each book on the shelf to
be sure that the book is in its proper place so library
users can find it.

Rationale: Through normal use, books end up out of
place on the shelf. A systematic process is necessary
to check the place of each book. Shelf-reading is an
on-going task involving many people, so a systematic
way of keeping track of progress in shelf-reading and
of spot-checking the results is needed. Because shelf-
reading requires intensive attention to detail, shelf-
reading assignments typically last only an hour.

Overview: Keeping the stacks in accurate call number
order is accomplished through a systematic program
of shelf-reading. The Stacks Assistant is responsible
for overseeing the program for shelf reading, including the following activities: setting up and monitoring the shelf-reading schedule; training shelf-readers;
supervising the shelf-reading; and checking the work
of shelf-readers.

I. Setting Up and Monitoring the Shelf-Reading
    Schedule
    General Information: A complete reading of the
    shelves should be completed once a year, under
    usual circumstances. Student workers read the
    stacks, and library staff check their work on

Figure 23. **Sample Procedure for a Complex Activity**

a regular basis. The Stacks Assistant assigns
each student worker a span of call numbers
for which that person is responsible. The assignment sheets are posted on the Bulletin
Board. The Stacks Assistant also maintains a
shelf-reading sign-in sheet on a clip-board
next to the Bulletin Board. (A sample sign-in
sheet is attached.) The Student Supervisor on
duty makes sure that each student worker
spends at least one hour a week reading in his
or her section. When the student completes
that section, the Stacks Assistant assigns him
or her another span of call numbers. The
Stacks Assistant also monitors students' progress and works out problems with individual
students.

A. Setting Up the Schedule at the Beginning of
the Semester
The Stacks Assistant
   1. Assigns each student worker a range of
      call numbers.
   2. Posts a list of students with their as-
      signments by the bulletin board. (A
      copy of an assignment sheet is at-
      tached.)
   3. Prepares a clip-board with sign-in
      sheets and hangs in next to the Bulletin
      Board. The sign-in sheet has columns
      for the date, student's name, time
      started, starting call number, time fin-
      ished, ending call number, and supervi-
      sor's spot-check.

B. Monitoring the Schedule throughout the Year
    The Stack Assistant
    1. Assigns new call number spans to stu-
        dents when they have finished their in-
        itial assignments.
    2. Checks the clip-board periodically, not-
        ing each student's progress. If a stu-
        dent is not logging in regularly, the
        Stacks Assistant should discuss the
        problem with the Student Supervisor
        and then with the student. If a student
        is progressing very slowly through his
        or her span of call numbers, the Stacks
        Assistant should talk with the student
        to determine the difficulty.

II. Training Shelf-Readers
     General Information: The Stacks Assistant
     trains the shelf-readers at the beginning of the
     semester, generally at the time the student is
     first scheduled to read shelves. Other staff
     members assist with training as needed. Train-
     ing to read shelves covers the following infor-
     mation:

     A. Shelf-Reading Assignments
         1. The student's own range of call numbers
         2. The location of the assignment sheet
         3. The procedure for signing in at the be-
             ginning of his or her shelf-reading
             hour and signing out at the end
         4. The location in the stacks of his or her
             span of call numbers

Figure 23—**Continued**

B. How to Read Shelves
   1. An explanation of parts of the call number
   2. The process of reading call numbers
   3. A practice run—NOTE: Training should include at least two practice runs, in which the student reads a shelf and then has the staff member check the shelves with him or her
   4. What the student should do if he or she is uncertain: turn the book on edge and notify the Stacks Assistant at the end of the shelf-reading shift

C. Spot-Checking
   1. Staff will spot-check shelves from time to time and discuss results with students

D. Importance of Accuracy and Attention to Detail
   1. That a book out of order is a lost book
   2. That shelf-reading requires time and care
   3. That questions or problems should be brought to the Stacks Assistant

III. Supervising the Shelf-Reading
A. The Student Supervisor assigns each student worker in Public Services at least one hour of shelf-reading a week, and no more than one hour a day.

B. Students sign in and out on the clip-board.

C. The Student Supervisor handles all performance problems relating to general behavior, such as excessive chatting with friends.

D. The Stacks Assistant handles all problems relating to the accuracy and speed of reading the shelf.

E. The Assistants confer with each other about problem students.

IV. Spot-Checking

The Stacks Assistant spot-checks each student's work once every week at the beginning of the semester. When the student has read shelves without errors for several weeks in a row, the Assistant will spot-check every three weeks. Checks are marked in the appropriate column of the sign-in sheet. To handle errors found during the spot-check, the Stacks Assistant

A. Writes down the call number of the book that is out of order and the call numbers of the books on either side.

B. Discusses the error with the student, being sure that he or she understands what was wrong and how to fix it.

Figure 23—**Continued**

Determining a Logical Division of Activities

Any process consists of a sequence of activities. Although some processes are simple enough to be described in fewer than ten activities, most processes will need to be divided into a number of main units. In figure 23, the process of maintaining a program of shelf reading is divided into four activities: setting up and monitoring the assignments; training the shelf readers; supervising the shelf reading; and spot-checking. Although the primary person performing the activity is the stacks assistant, a number of other people are involved, and their roles are described. The activities are listed in logical order from a perspective viewing the whole task: first, you set up the system and then you train the shelf readers, supervise the activity, and monitor the results. However, other logical orders are possible. For instance, you could organize the steps based on what the stacks assistant should do every day. To test your skills, you may think about what organization around daily tasks might look like, what its limitations might be, and what circumstances might warrant taking that approach.

Although the main divisions of a process may look inevitable once you have them on paper, working them out can be difficult. Each main section should be roughly equal in importance. Although you will be referring to other tasks, you want each task to be a self-contained and complete unit. You may wish to develop your divisions by listing all the tasks you can think of relating to the process and then sorting them into hierarchies. As you experiment with ways of organizing the steps, the main activities in the process should sort themselves out.

Subdividing Sections into Steps

Once you have determined the main divisions of your process, you will want to subdivide those sections into steps. Here, again, you will be following some logical sequence. Many sequences are possible, and your choice will be based on what works best, given the readers of the procedure, what they are expected to do, and how they will use the procedure. Illustrations of various types of logical sequences appear in figures 23 and 24. Examples are described below.

1. In figure 23, Task I, Setting Up the Schedule, and Task IV, Spot-Checking, follow what one person does in a sequence of steps that occur over time.
2. Task IB, Monitoring the Schedule, lists tasks that one person should perform at irregular intervals, when the need arises.
3. Task II, Training Shelf-Readers, follows a topical rather than a temporal sequence and lists the elements that need to be covered in a training session.

Reading the Shelves: A Procedure
for Student Assistants

Definition and Purpose: Reading the shelves means
checking the call number of each book to be sure that
the book is in its proper place on the shelf so that library users can find it.

Rationale: Through normal use, books end up out of
place on the shelf. A systematic process is necessary
to check the place of each book. Shelf-reading is an
on-going task involving many people, so a systematic
way of keeping track of shelf-reading progress and of
spot-checking the results is needed. Because shelf-
reading requires intensive attention to detail, shelf-
reading assignments typically last only an hour.

Overview: Each student is assigned a span of call
numbers as his or her responsibility. You will be
asked to work in your area at least one hour a week,
but no more than one hour a day. A staff member will
spot-check your work periodically and discuss problems with you.

Procedure:

1. The Student Supervisor will assign you a time
   to work on reading the shelves that have been
   assigned to you.
2. Sign in on the shelf-reading clip-board, entering
   the date, your name, and your starting time.
3. Write the number on which you ended your last
   reading sessions in the beginning column and
   copy that number on a piece of scratch paper.

Figure 24. **Sample Procedure for a Single Task**

(Note: Sheets from previous weeks are kept behind current sheet on the clipboard.)

4. Start reading where you left off last time.
5. Read the call number line by line.
6. If you are not sure whether a book is in the
   right place, tilt it on its side and ask the Stacks
   Assistant or other staff member about it at the
   end of your shelf-reading shift. Or jot down the
   number and ask a staff member later.
7. Please do not carry on social conversations
   while on shelf-reading duty.
8. If a library user asks you for help in using the
   library, refer him or her to the reference desk.
9. Please straighten the shelves as you read them,
   making sure that the books are standing
   straight and that the bookends fit snugly
   against them. If you need to pull a book out to
   see its call number, please put it back.

Date: Nov 19, 1984
Revised: Jan 17, 1987

4. Task III, Supervising the Shelf-Reading, looks at the process as if it were unfolding on a stage and lists all its activities in temporal order, bringing in each player when it comes time for that person's part.
5. Figure 24 illustrates a classic set of instructions, leading one person through one task at one time.

Whatever means you choose to subdivide the main sections, the order must be logical. It should show who performs the step, when the step is performed, and, depending on the level of specificity you want, how the step is performed. Once you have chosen a method of subdivision, all the steps in that logical order must be given. You would not want to leave out an area of training, for example, in Task II of figure 23. It is also confusing to switch methods of subdivision without a logical break.

Choosing Levels of Specificity

When you divide a process into steps or activities, you must choose how general or how specific to make those steps. One of the hardest parts of writing procedures is selecting the level of specificity that suits the complexity of the task. For some tasks, each step needs to be spelled out in exact detail—not only what to do, but how to do it. For other tasks, it is sufficient to indicate what to do, leaving details of how to do the task to the performer.

Task I in figure 23 tells us that the stacks assistant does the following: "Posts a list of students with their assignments by the bulletin board. (A copy of the assignment sheet is attached.)"

This activity could be described in more general terms, providing much less direction, and therefore less control, over the way the schedule is prepared: "Prepares the shelf-reading schedule."

Or this activity could be expanded into additional steps, providing much greater direction:

1. Asks the student supervisor for the names of all students who will be available for shelf-reading duty.
2. Creates a list of students, arranged alphabetically, using the word processor.
3. Lists each student's assignment by his or her name.
4. Posts the schedule on the bulletin board next to the students' sign-in station.

The levels of specificity should suit the task. For practice, comment on the problems with the levels of specificity in the process described below:

1. Take the cash box out from the desk drawer in the back of the Circulation office and open the box, using the combination.

2. Find the blank tally sheets in the assistant's desk drawer, date one with today's date, and tape it to the Circulation desk next to the circulation file.
3. Count the money.
4. Balance the cash box.

Steps one and two provide an inordinate amount of detail for routine activities. Note that variations in these activities are probably not crucial to effective performance of the task. Steps three and four, on the other hand, provide brief summaries of complex activities that leave many procedural questions unanswered. Presumably, variations in these steps could cause significant problems in performance of the procedure.

Formats for Presenting Activities or Steps

Three formats are commonly used for presenting the activities or steps involved in a process. These formats can be used individually or in combination with each other.

Narrative Presentation

The activities or steps in a process can be described in narrative paragraphs. The overview in Task I (figure 23) is written in narrative form. Complete procedures are sometimes attempted in narrative form to provide a general understanding of an activity, rather than to furnish specific directions for performing a task. Usually, the narrative form does not work well for detailed steps that must be followed one at a time.

Lists of Activities or Tasks

Activities or tasks can be set off from the text in a list, as in figure 23. Lists make the individual steps easy to find and allow rapid consultation. If a list stretches beyond ten items, you may wish to subdivide your activities still further. The list is frequently arranged in outline form, using either alpha-numeric or decimal notation.

Instructions

A set of instructions for a task is a special form of list. It provides a sequence of numbered steps to accomplish a task from start to finish. Figure 24 illustrates a set of instructions.

Elements of Procedures

No one organizational structure will work for all types of procedures. Most procedures, however, contain similar information or elements. These are illustrated in figures 23 and 24.

Purpose
A brief statement of the purpose of the procedure tells readers what the procedure is expected to accomplish.

Rationale
If more information is needed, the rationale can discuss the conditions that create the need for the procedure or explain why particular methods were chosen.

Related Policies
If the procedures are related to specific policies, it is sometimes useful to explain those, or to refer readers to a policy manual. Formats that combine policies and procedures present the policies first, followed by procedures.

Overview
Providing an overview of the entire process orients readers and also helps people who are interested in a specific activity find what they need. The overview can be a simple presentation of the main divisions of the activity, either in list form or in a narrative table of contents. A more elaborate overview can be provided by a description of activities or by a flow chart.

General Information
Items of general information can be grouped in an introductory or explanatory section. Clustering general information in one section frees you to list activities in an unbroken sequence.

General information can also be included with each activity, as long as the sequence of steps remains clear.

Activities or Tasks
The description of activities or tasks constitutes the body of the procedure. Techniques for dividing a process into activities and subdividing it into steps, as well as formats for presenting activities and steps, are discussed earlier in this chapter.

Procedural Style

Clear procedures and instructions share certain stylistic characteristics:

Complete Sentences or Phrases
Occasionally, writers of procedures feel they should use elliptical constructions, like "Return books to shelf."

Unless it is necessary to save space (on a small sign, for example), you should write your procedures in grammatically correct phrases or sentences, including their full complement of articles.

Subjects and Verbs First

Start sentences with the subject and the verb to direct the reader's attention to the activity being described. This technique works for narrative instructions as well as for instructions in a list.

Active Voice

Use the active voice to identify the person or thing doing the action. The passive voice allows the doer of the action to "disappear" from the sentence, and frequently the result is confusion, as in the example below:

The wording of the bookplate should be determined when the donation is accepted.

From this sentence, it is not clear who does the determining or the accepting, so essential parts of the procedure are unclear.

Clear Sequence of Steps

Good procedures make the sequence of activities or steps explicit: by chronology in a narrative paragraph, by a sequence in a list, or by numbered steps.

Keyboard Graphics and Layout

Breaking up long narratives with headings and subheadings, short paragraphs, symbols, indentions, and generous spacing can make the logical order of the steps more apparent. Your procedures are then easier to consult.

TEST YOUR SKILLS

Test your skills by writing a procedure for an activity that you know very well. Choose an activity from your current professional responsibilities, such as scheduling public services staff. Or select an activity such as planning a vacation or buying a car. The activity is not as important as the process of describing it clearly and systematically. Figure 25 may help with this exercise.

CHECKLIST FOR WRITING PROCEDURES

Figure 25 is a checklist that summarizes the process for writing procedures. It can be used as a review of the chapter or as a guide when writing procedures.

Use the checklist below to review the process for writing procedures.
1. Define the procedure and describe its purpose.
   ▲ What procedure are you describing?
   ▲ What actions do you want to regulate through the procedure, and why?
   ▲ What purposes do the actions described in the procedure serve?
2. Describe who will read the procedure and under what circumstances.
   ▲ Who will read the procedure?
   ▲ How are people expected to use the procedure and under what circumstances?
   ▲ Are readers of the procedure expected to gain an understanding of the way things are done for their general knowledge? How do you expect them to use the information they get from the procedure?
   ▲ Are readers of the procedure expected to perform specific actions according to steps in the procedure?
   ▲ Will readers need to use the procedure as an on-the-spot aid in performing actions?
3. Decide who will draft the procedure and who will review it.
   ▲ How will the perspective of the person who performs the procedure be considered by the person who writes it?
   ▲ How will the supervisor's perspective be considered by the person who writes it?
   ▲ Would the perspective of a knowledgeable, objective outsider be useful, either in drafting or in review?
   ▲ How will the writer consider the perspectives of all other groups affected by the procedure?
4. Develop the content of the procedure or decide on any changes in an existing procedure.
   ▲ If the procedure is new, consider the following:
       What do you wish to accomplish?
       What limitations of staffing, equipment, time, or resources affect the procedure?
       Are there alternatives? What do similar libraries do? Could similar procedures in your library serve as a model?
       Have you sought the perspective of those who will perform the procedure, those who supervise it, and those who are affected by it?
       Have you tested as many of the steps as possible?
   ▲ If the procedure already exists, consider the following:
       Is this an appropriate time to evaluate and revise the procedure?
       How well is it working? What are its strengths and its limitations? How important are the limitations?
       What are some alternatives for strengthening the weak areas?

Figure 25. **Writing Procedures: A Checklist**

What are the implications of the change for the staff and for others affected by the procedure?

5. Plan the organization of the written procedure.
   ▲ Who will use the procedure and under what circumstances?
   ▲ Should the procedure be primarily a description of a process?
   ▲ Should the procedure be primarily a set of instructions, designed to guide the reader in the immediate performance of the activity?
   ▲ Should the procedure be a combination of description and instruction? If so, how will you ensure that the instructions are clearly separate from the descriptive detail?
   ▲ Is the scope of the procedure such that you can provide a complete description or set of instructions with a reasonable number of steps? Do you need to break the procedure into subroutines, or smaller procedures, to make it more manageable?
   ▲ Have you included the following parts, as needed:
      the name of the procedure and its place in a compilation?
      the purpose of the procedure—what it is designed to do?
      advice to the reader on how to use the procedure?
      an overview of the process or activity?
      a list of equipment or tools needed for the process?
      a division of the process or activity into main sections, if needed?
      a division of the process or activity into steps?
   ▲ How have you treated explanatory material? Does it interfere with the instructional purpose of the procedure?
6. Draft the procedure, following your organizational plan.
7. Review and revise the procedure.
   ▲ Is the description faithful to the process?
   ▲ Have you tried to perform the task, following the instructions, and noted the following:
      Was it easy to use the instructions to perform the task?
      Did the instructions lead you through each step in a logical order? Were steps left out?
      Were the steps overly detailed, describing things that were not necessary?
      Did you have questions that were not answered at a logical place in the instructions?
   ▲ Have you asked someone with the same background as the potential users of the procedure to "test drive" the procedures? (You may wish to discuss the issues above with them, either while they are performing the procedure or afterward.)
   ▲ Have you used good procedural style where appropriate, including the following:
      complete sentences?
      the imperative?
      short sentences that begin with the verb?

▲ Will following the procedures produce the desired results?

▲ Have you assessed your procedures systematically, looking for problems of general effectiveness, tone and personality, organizational structure, composition of sentences, and word choice? (Chapter 3 provides checklists to help with this analysis.)

▲ For each problem you find, can you pinpoint the cause and develop alternatives? Which alternative works best in the context of these procedures?

8. Edit your procedures for correctness.

▲ Have you reviewed your draft for problems of grammar, usage, and punctuation?

▲ Have you used your knowledge of the kinds of mistakes you make to help you find trouble spots? (Chapter 3 provides assistance in identifying and solving these problems.)

▲ Have you checked all matters of fact, including

    dates?   raw numbers and computations?
    facts?   bibliographic citations?
    titles?   proper nouns, especially names?
    spelling?

▲ Have you proofread carefully to ensure accuracy? (Chapter 3 provides a checklist for this activity.)

9. Make decisions about the distribution, implementation, updating, and evaluation of the procedures.

▲ How different are the new procedures from the old ones?

▲ How many people will need to learn the new procedures?

▲ How will you inform those who need to know about the new procedures?

▲ How much explanation, training, or practice will be necessary? Should these activities take place before the procedure takes effect, or can they occur as the new procedures are implemented?

▲ Do users of the library, or others affected by the new procedures, need to know about them in advance? If so, how will you inform them?

▲ How much time will be necessary between the distribution and the date the procedure takes effect?

▲ Who will receive copies of the new procedures?

▲ How will you compile the procedures? How many up-to-date compilations will there be and where will they be?

▲ Is the procedure conveniently located for everyone, in light of the way you wish people to use it?

▲ How will the compilations be updated?

▲ How often should the procedure be evaluated? What kinds of occurrence will signal the need for an evaluation?

Figure 25—**Continued**

10. Produce the final copy of your procedures.
    ▲ Have you considered the elements of "design" to achieve a document that looks professional and is easy to use?
    ▲ Have you marked the layout for the final copy, noting special keyboard graphic effects, special spacing, and indentions?
    ▲ If someone is assisting you by preparing the final copy, have you communicated your instructions clearly, including those about spacing, margins, layout, and special graphic effects?
    ▲ Have you arranged to review a typed draft before the final draft is prepared?
    ▲ After receiving the final copy, have you proofread carefully, both for typographical errors and for other difficulties that might have slipped in?
    ▲ Is the final copy neat and professional looking?
11. Write and distribute supplementary material. Conduct training or informational sessions, according to your plan.

Chapter 8

LETTERS

CHAPTER OUTLINE

CHARACTERISTICS OF LETTERS

EFFECTIVE LETTERS

TONE IN LETTERS

ORGANIZATIONAL PATTERNS FOR LETTERS
Organizing Positive or Neutral Information
Organizing Negative Information
Organizing a Persuasive Letter

FORMAT FOR LETTERS
Parts of a Letter
Layout for Letters
Establishing a Library's Style

CHECKLIST FOR WRITING LETTERS

Just as the memo is the accepted format for sending messages within an institution, the letter is the standard for messages sent to those outside the organization. Of course, there are circumstances when letters are more appropriate than memos for internal communication, particularly when a personal tone is appropriate. And sometimes you may choose to send memos to those outside your organization, especially if you want to send the same message to several people. Memos, for example, often go to members of a committee, even though they work in other libraries. In general, however, letters are used for external and memos for internal communications.

CHARACTERISTICS OF LETTERS

Generally, letters are perceived as more personal than memos. Letters can, of course, be written very formally and impersonally, and the tone of a memo can be adjusted so that it is personal; nevertheless, through a combination of history, usage, and format, letters have a personal "patina" that memos lack.

Letters are primarily a communication from one person to another, and have been so throughout history. The format does not lend itself to addressing many people, the way the memo format does, and therefore many ingenious adaptations have sprung up to adapt the one-to-one letter format, and its personal tone, for multiple readers. Techniques for letters addressed to many people include the inclusive salutation, such as "Ladies and Gentlemen" or "Dear Colleague"; the designation "Open Letter"; the form letter; and now the *merged* letter, made possible by word processing, which combines individualized and standard wording. Even though these letters are sent to many people, their writers have chosen the letter format, presumably because of its characteristically personal flavor. Readers expect a letter to contain a message directly from one person to another, even if they know that a number of people will receive the same message.

EFFECTIVE LETTERS

All professional writing documents, to be effective, need to take into account the perspective and situation of the reader. However, nowhere does a violation of that principle show up more dramatically than in a letter, where the reader *expects* the author to be writing directly to him or her. Many, perhaps most, of the failures in letter writing can be analyzed as a failure to understand the reader's point of view and write from an understanding of this perspective.

For example, suppose that a faculty member writes to you to complain that the policy of not allowing periodicals to circulate compromises students' ability to do research for their classes. An effective response starts from a sympathetic understanding that the policy *does* prevent convenient use of the materials. That inconvenience is the professor's reality at the moment, and that is the issue he or she expects the librarian to address. With that knowledge, the librarian can respond in a way that takes into account several factors: (1) the professor's perspective, (2) the librarian's goals of maintaining and explaining the policy on periodicals, and (3) the goal of promoting good relations with members of the faculty.

Based on this analysis, we can define an effective letter as one that accomplishes the purpose of the writer *and*, at the same time, maintains an appropriate relationship with the reader of the letter. In the example above, an effective response might acknowledge (in some way) the policy's effects, explain the rationale, and preserve mutual respect and cordiality between colleagues. (See figure 29 for a sample response in this situation.)

Suppose, as another example, that you, as director of a corporate library, decide that you cannot accept the gift of old issues of periodicals from the retiring chairman of the board. The success of your letter to him will depend on the extent to which you can determine the chairman's point of view and respond with a rationale that reflects the real situation you are facing, makes sense to him, and maintains appropriate relationships between the retiring head of the organization and one of its administrative staff. (See figure 28 for a sample response in this situation.)

Note that neither of these two suggestions, understanding the reader's point of view and maintaining appropriate relationships, suggests that you should necessarily "give in" to an opposing or conflicting viewpoint. The substance of your response, whether or not you choose to change the policy on periodicals or whether you decide to accept or reject the gift, depends on your analysis of the best way to proceed in that situation. Your letter is your attempt to communicate your decision in a way that reflects the true nature of the situation and, at the same time, makes sense to the reader. Occasionally, it is not possible to bridge your perspective and the reader's while making the response that you feel is required, but the effort to communicate with your reader and to maintain good relationships may still produce positive effects.

TONE IN LETTERS

Tone in letters results from a combination of all the choices you make when writing: the form of names you use, your vocabulary, the length and complexity of your sentences, and even the way you sign your name. Abstract, formal, or jargon-filled language creates a different effect from everyday vocabulary. Long, passive constructions and lengthy clauses can create a ponderous tone. Word choice and sentence construction can combine to achieve a conversational effect or a tone that is neutral and businesslike. A conversational tone is often successful in business writing, because it can be both understandable and pleasing. You will undoubtedly encounter a few situations, however, where you feel a neutral tone suits your purposes better. If you can identify the elements in a document that contribute to its tone, you can make the changes that you feel are necessary.

The "personality" of your letter, or the impression of you that the reader receives from your letter, is an important aspect of tone. Writers sometimes are not aware that their writing style conveys a personality that is different from the personality they imagine for themselves. Objectively reading your letters will help you make certain that the you who writes letters sounds like the real you.

ORGANIZATIONAL PATTERNS FOR LETTERS

The content of letters written in libraries varies widely, but most letters can be classified in one of three ways: as containing positive or neutral information, negative information, or information designed to persuade the reader. Some guidelines exists for organizing each type of information. Like all guidelines of this type, however, they provide only general direction. Each writer must evaluate his or her situation to decide whether the guidelines are applicable, and if they are, how to apply them.

Organizing Positive or Neutral Information

1. *Orient the reader, using the direct approach and a positive tone.* The first sentences orient the reader to the occasion for writing and make the subject of the letter clear. For positive and neutral information, the purpose of the letter may be introduced directly.
2. *State the significant information.* From the opening statement, the letter can move directly to the letter's significant information. That statement should be unambiguous. Because it is a direct statement, the writer will want to pay attention to tone and positive phrasing to avoid sounding blunt or abrupt.
3. *Provide the necessary details.* Decide what the reader needs to know in order to act on the significant information. This section is usually arranged in order of descending importance, starting from the most important supplementary details and working down to the least important. If you wish the reader to do something specific, make this clear.
4. *Close on a positive note.* Your close should be positive and should reaffirm a good relationship with your reader. Some positive letters repeat an aspect of the good news. Others concentrate on reinforcing good personal relations with the reader. If possible, avoid shopworn phrases, like "Thank you for your attention."

Figure 26 illustrates the organization of a letter containing positive information, and figure 27 presents a letter containing neutral information.

Rushmore College
Elton, OR 00000

Governor Library
Office of the Librarian

March 4, 1989

Louis Trent
1234 Center Street
Elmhurst, TX 00000

Dear Mr. Trent:

It was a pleasure to talk to you this morning. This letter confirms our invitation to come to the campus on March 30 to interview for the position of Public Services Librarian at Governor Library.

Generally, it works best for candidates to arrive in the late afternoon or evening of the day before and to plan to fly out no earlier than 7 pm after the interview. We will pick you up at the airport and arrange for your night's lodging. We would prefer that you arrange for your flight and then submit your travel expenses for reimbursement after the interview.

Please let me know your travel plans as soon as possible. When we know your arrival time, we will send you a schedule for the interview.

I am enclosing some information about Rushmore College and our library. If you have any questions or

Figure 26. **Sample Letter Containing Positive Information**

Mr. Louis Trent   –2–   March 4, 1989

would like more information before the interview, let me know.

   We are looking forward to your visit.

                    Sincerely,

                    Patrick Hogan
                    PATRICK HOGAN
                    Librarian of the College

PH:mg
Enclosures (2)

Wellness Memorial Hospital
10 Healthy Springs Boulevard
Seaside City, FL 00000

March 5, 1989

P. J. Knight
Chair, Continuing Education Committee
Medical Library Association
School of Medicine Library
Central State University
Central City, WA 00000

Dear P. J. Knight:

Our hospital library consortium is interested in finding out how medical librarians can become instructors for the Medical Library Association's continuing
education courses.

We frequently see listings for continuing education
courses that interest us, but invariably they are presented at distant locations. We feel that a number of
our local and regional organizations might be able to
sponsor courses if instructors from our area were
available. Our consortium would like to encourage
qualified medical librarians in Florida to become continuing education instructors by publicizing the
qualifications and the process for becoming an in-
structor.

If you have additional ideas for ways that we can encourage our medical librarians to participate in MLA's

Figure 27. **Sample Letter Containing Neutral Information**

P. J. Knight   -2-   March 5, 1989

continuing education programs, both as instructors and as participants, we would love to hear them.

Sincerely,

LISA NORRIS
Librarian

Organizing Negative Information

A letter imparting negative information, or bad news, offers a tougher challenge to the writer than a letter whose content is neutral or positive. As the writer of a "bad news" letter, you want to make sure you convey your message, but at the same time avoid damaging your relationship with the reader. The structure suggested for imparting negative information is designed to buffer the shock of the bad news by providing the rationale first. By preparing the reader to receive the bad news, you are hoping that he or she will at least understand why the decision was made. You are also trying to ease into the bad news more gently than is possible with a direct statement. Here are some guidelines for conveying bad news in a letter:

1. *Orient the reader, using the indirect approach and a neutral tone.* When the reader will not welcome the information in a letter, try the indirect approach, establishing a neutral tone and providing explanations before the bad news is delivered. The opening statement should inform the reader of the topic under discussion, without raising hopes. Then the statement should lead into the explanation of the bad news.

2. *Explain your rationale.* This section should state the reasons that shaped the negative decisions. These reasons should be worded as positively as possible, but they should remain clear. Although you want to phrase your reasons positively, you also want to be careful not to raise false hopes. A well-written explanation of the rationale becomes a harbinger of the negative content, since the reasons should strongly and logically lead to the action that is to come.

3. *Present the negative information as tactfully as possible, while remaining unambiguous.* If your reasons are logical and your explanation is well written, your reader will be anticipating bad news. When it comes, you will want to present it as tactfully as possible, without compromising clarity. When the rationale is strong and compelling, you may find that you can phrase the bad news indirectly. You can soften direct statements of bad news by using the passive rather than the active voice. Your goal is to communicate the negative news clearly, without being unnecessarily blunt or harsh.

4. *End on a positive and sincere note.* After you have presented the bad news, try to reestablish good relations with the reader in a sincere way. If alternatives are available, you can offer them. Letter writers should resist the temptation to compensate for the bad news by unwarranted positive statements. For example, an employer would not want to promise an unsuccessful candidate that his or her application would be kept on file and considered for the next position, unless that were actually the case.

A letter illustrating the organizational structure for a letter containing negative information appears in figure 28.

Organizing a Persuasive Letter

Letters that attempt to persuade readers to take action can be organized along two models. The first model emphasizes an explanation of the stance that the writer wants the reader to take. The second model, widely used in business writing texts, allows for a broad scope of persuasive appeals.

Model I

This organizational structure is an extension of the indirect style used for organizing negative information and attempts to develop a persuasive explanation of the stance you wish the reader to take. It differs from the letter presenting negative information only in the thoroughness with which you build your case and in your assumption that, by the time you present your major point, the reader will be convinced.

1. *Orient the reader, using an indirect approach and finding a common ground.* The opening sentence introduces the reader to the topic under discussion and attempts to find a common ground, an issue on which the writer and the reader can agree. The common ground should be as close as possible to the reader's major interest in the subject.
2. *Develop an explanation that moves from the common ground to the position that you wish the reader to accept or the action you wish the reader to take.* The way you develop your explanation will depend on your assessment of the reader's understanding of the problem. Through that awareness, you can select the facts and ideas that will describe your case in a way that makes sense to your reader.
3. *Present the stance you wish the reader to accept or the action you wish the reader to take, tying it, if possible, to the reader's concerns or interest.* If you are attempting to persuade the reader to accept a stance, you may wish to build a strong case, in step two. Then, in step three, present an indirect statement of the stance that reinforces some aspect of the reader's concern or interest. If you want the reader to take action, state what the action should be. You may also wish to tie the action statement to the central concern of the reader.
4. *Close on a positive note.* The close should reaffirm good relations with the reader.

Figure 29 illustrates a letter that uses explanation as an effective persuasive strategy.

Major Corporation

March 3, 1989

Harrison Styles
90 Skytop Drive
Wilton, CT 00000

Dear Mr. Styles

Thank you for your offer to donate more than fifteen
years of unbound issues of Psychology Today to the
Corporate Library. We appreciate your thinking of us.

A library like ours, which has extremely limited
space for housing information resources, is forced to
weigh very carefully each decision to add books or
magazines to our collection. Deciding whether or not
to buy material, or accept it as a gift, is based on a
number of criteria, including the demand for the
title, its availability at a nearby library, and the ur-
gency of the need for the information.

We subscribe to Psychology Today, and many people
in the corporation enjoy reading each issue as it
comes in. We do not keep issues for more than six
months because we have found that older issues are
rarely used. When someone needs an article, we can
obtain it quickly for them from the public library.

In view of these considerations, we feel that we
should decline your offer with thanks. We have appreciated your support of the library over the years, and

Figure 28. **Sample Letter Containing Negative Information**

Harrison Styles   –2–   March 3, 1989

we hope that you will call on us if we can provide you
with library assistance of any kind.

Yours truly

Lorna Dale

LORNA DALE
Manager, Corporate Information Center

CENTRAL UNIVERSITY
Central City, WA 00000

April 2, 1989

Readmore Library

Dear Professor Jones:

Thank you for your note calling my attention to the
inconvenience students have experienced as a result
of the policy restricting use of periodicals to the library building. I can appreciate the frustration of not
being able to take periodicals home, especially because the periodical literature is so important to research for both students and faculty.

The present policy limiting the circulation of periodicals is an attempt to make them readily available, despite the high use of bound volumes. By restricting
periodical use to the library, we hope that issues will
be available to all library users when they need them.
If checkout were allowed, entire volumes would be
unavailable for several weeks. We recognize that both
alternatives cause some inconvenience, and we hope
that the advantage of having the articles available
when needed will, in some way, reduce the annoyance
at not being able to take them out of the library. As a
compromise, photocopiers are available.

I appreciate your taking the time to write to me about
library issues that concern you and your students. If
you would like to talk further about the periodical

Figure 29. **Organizing a Persuasive Letter: Model I**

Professor Jones   –2–   April 2, 1989

policy, or if you would like me to talk with your students about it, please give me a call.

Thanks again for your concern.

Sincerely,

Edward Madden

EDWARD MADDEN
University Librarian

Model II

This organizational pattern is generally presented in business writing texts as appropriate for messages that attempt to shape the reader's behavior, especially in situations where the reader has, initially, little reason to do or think as you would like. Sales letters are a good example of this type of persuasive letter. We will briefly present this pattern for organization and refer you to the texts on business and persuasive writing in the list of selected readings for a more complete discussion of persuasive messages. In this discussion, we will assume that you are persuading your reader to accept an idea or a product.

1. *Attract the reader's attention.* The first sentence in this type of persuasive message must attract the reader's attention. Many techniques can be used, including presenting an advantage of the idea or product, highlighting a need it meets, stressing a problem that is familiar to your reader, raising an issue that will interest your reader, asking a question that your reader will have about your idea or product, or making an offer that your reader will find attractive.

2. *Keep the reader's interest.* Once the reader's attention is captured, you need to stimulate enough interest to keep him or her reading. You may wish to develop the approach that you took to attract the reader's attention, by providing more details about the problem, the need, or the benefits. In either the attention or the interest statement, you will also want to strengthen your credibility with your reader.

3. *Convince the reader.* The next step in a persuasive letter is to move the reader from an interest in your idea or product to belief in it. Convincing the reader can be accomplished by appeals to emotion, appeals to logic, or a combination of both. Details, including dates, facts, costs, or benefits, are frequently used to convince the reader of the value of your idea or product.

4. *Call for the action you want.* Since the purpose of a persuasive letter is to direct the reader's behavior, your letter should build to an explicit statement of the action you want the reader to take.

5. *Reaffirm the wisdom of a positive decision and close on a positive note.* Many persuasive letters end on a positive note by reaffirming the wisdom of the action that has just been called for. The positive close should preserve the feelings of trust and credibility that have developed throughout the letter.

This discussion of persuasive writing is intended to introduce this technique so that interested librarians can pursue the subject on their own.

FORMAT FOR LETTERS

The format you use for your letters will depend on the style in your library and your personal preference. Secretarial handbooks, like the ones in the list of selected readings, provide detailed information about choices for letter formats. We will present the parts of a standard letter and summarize the most common letter styles. The sample letters in this chapter illustrate different styles. The styles can be used interchangeably, so you should not conclude that use of the modified block style, for example, is necessarily an important part of writing letters containing neutral information.

Parts of a Letter

The letter in figure 30 shows the parts of a standard letter, as well as standard spacing. Since these are self-explanatory, we will not discuss each item in detail. However, a few comments on general usage may be helpful.

Letterhead

Letterhead, or institutional stationery, usually contains your institution's insignia, name, address, and telephone number. In many institutions, department or personal names (and sometimes telephone numbers) are also printed on the letterhead. Every letter you send should contain all the information necessary for the reader to reach you. Therefore, you will want to assess the information on your letterhead and determine if you need to supplement it with more specifics about your address or telephone. A good place to add supplementary information is under your typed name at the end of the letter. You can add it to the letterhead itself, providing you are comfortable with the impression it makes. An alternative to a typed modification is a printed one. Some institutions care about consistent use of the letterhead and some do not, so it is best to check before making printed modifications.

Date Line

The date is usually placed two to six lines below the last line of the letterhead. The horizontal placement of the date varies with letter styles.

When plain paper without a letterhead is used, the sender's address may be placed flush with the right-hand margin. The date appears below the address, flush with the first letter of the address. The recipient's address can occupy the traditional position for the inside address or it can appear flush with the left-hand margin two lines below the signature.

RUNNING BROOK PUBLIC LIBRARY
LETTERHEAD   999 MAIN STREET
                            Upton, MA 00000

          DATE   October 5, 1989

Elena Holton
President
Massachusetts Story-Teller's Guild   **INSIDE**
1111 Central Avenue   **ADDRESS**
Boston, MA 00000

Dear Ms. Holton: **SALUTATION**

The Running Brook Public Library plans to sponsor a
summer of activities centered around the theme "Tell   **OPENING**
Me a Story."

We are planning two kinds of activities: workshops
that will help both adults and children learn more
about how to tell stories, and story-telling programs
where they will have an opportunity to practice what
they have learned. We hope to kick off the summer
program with a weekend "Story-Teller Fest," a com-   **BODY**
munity celebration featuring stories by both profes-   **OF**
sional story-tellers and local residents, and a series **LETTER**
of workshops.

Would the Story-Telling Guild be interested in working with us on this project? We are looking for experienced story-tellers to help us with planning the
"Story-Telling Fest," and we will be selecting leaders

Figure 30. **Parts of a Letter**

Elena Holton   –2–   October 5, 1989

for workshops both at the Fest and throughout the
summer. For leading the workshops, we will be able to
pay a modest honorarium of $100. I am enclosing our
preliminary schedule of events so that you can get an
idea of what we are planning.

Through our summer program, we hope to introduce
our community to the pleasures of both hearing and
telling stories. If you feel that your members might   **CLOSE**
enjoy being a part of our efforts, please get in touch
with me.

COMPLIMENTARY   Sincerely,
CLOSE

Jane Wallen

                                JANE WALLEN   **SIGNATURE**
                                Library Director   **BLOCK**

JW:lc
Enclosure

c: Lois Benson, Children's Librarian   **NOTATIONS**

Subject Designation

A subject line is sometimes used in business letters. Libraries, as a rule, do not follow this pattern, but there is no reason not to if it serves a purpose and if the slightly more businesslike tone it imparts to the letter is acceptable in your situation. If a salutation is used, the subject line, often preceded by the word *subject*, appears two lines below the salutation. If no salutation is used, as in the simplified letter style, the subject line appears three lines below the inside address and is flush with the left-hand margin.

Salutations

As we all know, general practice in salutations has changed considerably in the last two decades. The two major changes are a decline in the use of masculine forms standing for both sexes (Dear Sir, Gentlemen) and a rise in the use of a "generic" form, Ms., for both married and single women. These changes have gained acceptance because of their utility, and substantial numbers of people do not find the former practices acceptable any longer. As with any major shift in language usage, however, there are people who prefer the older usage.

The ideal solution to this dilemma is to discover the preference of the recipient of your letter. When you cannot determine preference or do not know the gender of your reader, you have four choices: guessing and risking a mistake (calling P. J. Smith, who is really Paula Smith, Mr. Smith); using the person's full name (Dear P. J. Smith); using the position title (Dear Head of Technical Services); and using generic salutations. Generic salutations include inclusive nouns (Ladies and Gentlemen, Dear Colleague); Ms. for all women (Dear Ms. Smith); or M. when gender is not known (Dear M. Smith). Another solution gaining ground in business usage is to drop the salutation altogether and use a subject line instead. There is no perfect solution, and you can be sure that there will be readers, somewhere, who take umbrage at every attempt to resolve this troublesome dilemma. If your institution does not have a style that everyone follows, you will want to decide on an approach for yourself based on the people you write to, general practice in your institution, and your own sense of how things should be.

The salutation appears two to four lines beneath the inside address.

Body of Letter

The body of the letter begins two lines below the salutation or the subject line. Letters are usually single-spaced, with double spacing between paragraphs. If possible, the top and bottom margins should be roughly equal, to produce a centered, attractive look.

If the letter extends to two pages, a heading should be typed at the top of the second page, at least an inch from the top. The text begins four lines below the last heading line. Two types of multiple-sheet headings in general use are shown below.

Multiple-Sheet Headings, Sample One:

Page 2
Ms. Jane Smith
December 3, 1988

Multiple-Sheet Headings, Sample Two:

Ms. Jane Smith   -2-   December 3, 1988

Complimentary Close
The complimentary close appears two lines from the end of the body of the letter. Its horizontal placement depends on the style of letter.

Signature Block
The signature block can include a written signature, a typed signature, and the writer's title. Writers may wish to use their signature as a chance to indicate to readers the form of their name that they prefer. The signature block appears two to four lines beneath the complimentary close. Its horizontal placement depends on the style of the letter.

Distribution
For a full discussion of this issue, see chapter 5 (on memos).

Layout for Letters

There are five commonly used forms for physical layout on a page: traditional, block, modified block, simplified, and special. The traditional, block, and modified block styles are illustrated by the sample letters in this chapter. The differences in all five styles are summarized below; for more details, see the secretarial handbook or business writing texts in selected readings.

Traditional
In the traditional style, the date either begins at the center of the page or is aligned with the right-hand margin. The first word of a paragraph is indented, and the complimentary close and signature block are aligned with the date. Figure 26 illustrates the traditional style.

Modified Block
Placement of the date in the modified block style, as well as the complimentary close and the signature block, are the same as in the traditional style. All other elements are aligned along the left-hand margin. Figure 27 illustrates the modified-block style.

Block

All elements are aligned with the left-hand margin, as in figure 28, which illustrates the block style.

Simplified

The simplified style, although used increasingly in business, is not in frequent use in libraries. The simplified style is the same as the block style, but without a salutation or complimentary close.

Special

Writers frequently adapt the letter style to suit special purposes. Although this practice does not represent a style in itself, we feel that it merits a label to call attention to the flexible use of letter styles.

Punctuation

Two styles of punctuation are commonly used in letters: the mixed and the open style. In our observation, the mixed style is more common in libraries. The mixed style uses a colon after the salutation and a comma after the complimentary close. The open style omits punctuation after both.

Establishing a Library's Style

Your library may wish to establish an institutional style for letters. The advantages are consistency and convenience. If everyone follows one model, no one has to guess what to do, and everything has a uniformly professional appearance. A library style can be established by a formal policy; it can also be established informally by providing a copy, marked, for example, "Library's Style for Letters," to all who send letters.

CHECKLIST FOR WRITING LETTERS

Figure 31 summarizes the process for writing letters. It can be used as a review of the chapter or as a guide when writing memos.

Use the checklist below to review the process for writing letters.

1. Define your purpose in writing the letter.
   ▲ What is the subject?
   ▲ What do you wish to accomplish?
   ▲ What human relations issues are involved in the subject of the letter? What human relations goals can you formulate to address these issues?
2. Understand your reader's view of the situation.
   ▲ What does your reader want in relation to this subject?
   ▲ What is your reader's level of knowledge and vested interest in this subject?
   ▲ What do you anticipate your reader's reaction will be to the letter you are proposing to write?
3. Review your approach to accomplishing your purpose by writing this letter.
   ▲ Is a letter the best communication approach for this subject?
   ▲ What characteristics should your letter have? What tone? What length?
   ▲ Will you need other means of communication to introduce, reinforce, or follow up on the subject? If so, what are they?
4. Develop the content for your letter.
   ▲ Have you let your mind roam freely over various aspects of your subject?
   ▲ Have you tried invention techniques, like writing a dialogue, to understand the issue from your reader's point of view?
5. Arrange your ideas in the sequence that best suits your purpose.
   ▲ If your letter contains positive or neutral information, have you presented important information first?
     supported your main point with the details the reader needs to know, arranged in order of importance?
     ended in a way that will further your human relations goals?
   ▲ If your letter contains negative information, have you
     opened with a neutral statement that will orient your reader to the subject of the letter without raising or dashing hopes?
     explained the rationale behind your decision?
     presented the "bad news" in a clear but tactful manner?
     ended in a way that furthers positive human relations and, at the same time, is realistic?
   ▲ If the purpose of your letter is to persuade the reader, have you
     opened with a statement of common ground or interest?
     presented your case in way that responds to the reader's logic or understanding of the situation?
     ended with a statement of what you would like the reader to do or believe?
6. Write a draft of your letter, following your organizational plan.

Figure 31. **Writing Letters: A Checklist**

7. Revise your letter for effectiveness.
   ▲ Do you predict that your letter will accomplish your purpose with your reader? Do you see any obstacles? How can you overcome them?
   ▲ Have your reviewed the tone, organization, sentence construction, and word choice of your letter, looking for problem areas?
   ▲ Have you analyzed each problem area, assessing the problem, developing alternative solutions, and choosing the best alternative in the context of your letter?
8. Edit your letter for correctness.
   ▲ Have you reviewed your draft for problems of grammar, usage, and punctuation?
   ▲ Have you used your knowledge of the kinds of mistakes you make to help you find trouble spots? (Chapter 3 provides assistance in identifying and solving these problems.)
   ▲ Have you checked all matters of fact, including
        raw numbers and computations?
        dates?
        facts?
        bibliographic citations?
        titles?
        spelling?
        proper nouns, especially names?
   ▲ Have you proofread carefully to ensure accuracy? (Chapter 3 provides a checklist for this activity.)
9. Produce the final copy of your letter.
   ▲ Have you considered the elements of "design" to achieve an effective, professional office look?
   ▲ Have you marked the layout for the final copy, noting any special keyboard graphic effects, special spacing, and indentions?
   ▲ If someone is assisting you by preparing the final copy, have you communicated your instructions clearly, including spacing, margins, layout, and special graphic effects?
   ▲ Have you arranged to review a typed draft before the final draft is prepared?
   ▲ After receiving the final copy, have you proofread carefully, both for typographical errors and for other difficulties that might have slipped in?
   ▲ Is the final copy neat and professional looking?

*Figure 31—***Continued**

Chapter 9

ANALYTICAL REPORTS

CHAPTER OUTLINE

PURPOSES FOR ANALYTICAL REPORTS

OBJECTIVITY OF REPORTS

WRITING WITH YOUR READER'S PERSPECTIVE IN MIND

ORGANIZATIONAL STRUCTURE OF ANALYTICAL REPORTS
Format for Analytical Reports
Elements of Analytical Reports

CHECKLIST FOR WRITING ANALYTICAL REPORTS

An analytical report presents the results of an examination or analysis of an issue. Some analytical reports also include recommendations for addressing the issue or solving the problem. Textbooks of business writing sometimes distinguish between analytical reports (those without recommendations) and recommendation reports (those that also contain recommendations). We have chosen to use *analytical report* as the broad term, with the understanding that such reports can have various purposes and will incorporate different levels of analysis and suggestions for action.

PURPOSES FOR ANALYTICAL REPORTS

The blend of information, analysis, and recommendation in each report depends on the purpose of the report. Library administrators frequently request reports from members of the library about issues or problems that need resolution. An administrator may be interested in obtaining systematic information to aid in his or her deliberations or to pass on to others. The head of Media Services, for example, might ask a media specialist to

197

prepare a report for the campus Communications Committee about options concerning wiring the campus for video. The major focus of this report would be *information* about wiring the campus for video.

Although a report will occasionally be requested that contains information only, most requests from administrators will be for a report that analyzes a problem or an issue, with or without recommendations for action. The head of Technical Services might ask the head of Cataloging to prepare a report that analyzes the alternatives for retrospective conversion, preparing for a discussion with the library director. The chief purpose of the report might be to present the pros and cons of various methods, rather than come to an immediate recommendation about which method to use. The focus of this report would be on the *analysis of information*.

Alternatively, an administrator might request a report that recommends a solution to a specific problem. The administrator of a hospital might ask the hospital librarian to study the duplication of resources in departmental libraries and, based on that analysis, to make recommendations for policies. The focus of this report would be a *recommendation*, although the analysis needs to be thorough or it will not adequately support the suggested course of action.

When someone assigns a report to you, your first task is to understand what that person wants from the report. Librarians have an advantage over other professionals in determining what administrators are looking for in reports, since reference interviewing skills are extremely useful in clarifying what is needed. As the person who will prepare the report, you will need to determine what your administrator wants in the way of information, analysis, or recommendations, and in what degree of thoroughness. You will also want to clarify the scope of the report. For instance, the head of Reference in a university library might ask the instruction librarian to analyze the library instruction program and make recommendations for changes. The instruction librarian would need to find out as much as possible about the directions that the head of Reference has in mind, including whether to assess all instructional programs in university libraries or just those in the main library, whether the head has specific areas of concern he or she would like addressed, whether there are suggestions or limits on who should be involved in the review, and what levels of detail and planning are appropriate in the recommendation. The more the instruction librarian knows about what the head of Reference wants in the report, why he or she wants it, and what he or she intends to do with it, the better the chances that the report will succeed.

Not all analytical reports are the result of someone else's request to gather information or study a problem. Librarians frequently prepare analytical reports as vehicles for bringing information, analysis, or recommendations for action to their administrators and colleagues. A children's librarian at a branch public library might prepare a report on the use of microcomputers and software in children's areas of libraries for a systemwide newsletter, in an effort to stimulate discussion of this topic. A reference librarian at a medical school library might analyze the need for consumer health information in the community to present to the local consortium of health science librarians. A library director might analyze the library's space needs in the next decade and recommend to the provost that an addition to the library be built.

When you initiate an analytical report, you will want to clarify your purposes in writing the report, just as you would if someone else had requested it. Why are you writing it? Do you have expectations about the results of the report? Do you have a vested interest in the outcome? If your purpose is to gain acceptance of a solution or a plan, you may decide to write a recommendation, analyzing the alternatives and showing why your suggestions will work better than other solutions. If, on the other hand, your purpose is to call someone's attention to various aspects of a problem or issue, your report may focus on presenting information, using an appropriate level of analysis.

As you write the report, you will constantly be faced with decisions about how far to pursue both the analysis and the recommendations. How many alternatives should you present? How far should you develop each one? How concrete, and how detailed, should the recommendations be? Answers to these questions will come more easily if you have a clear idea of how the report will be used by those who receive it.

OBJECTIVITY OF REPORTS

An analytical report is expected to be an objective analysis of the problem at hand. The credibility of the report stands or falls on the objectivity of your analysis. Especially if you are known to have strong feelings about the problems, you must be certain that you have examined the issue objectively and that the objectivity shows. Strong preferences for recommendations are permissible, but they should be firmly grounded in your analysis, and your discussion of the alternatives should be clear and fair. In other words, the logical, objective reasoning for your preferences must stand out clearly to others. If it does not, you are in danger of having your report dismissed as a biased attempt to secure your own solutions.

WRITING WITH YOUR READER'S PERSPECTIVE IN MIND

An analytical report must be written with the perspective of the readers of the report in mind. If the report is assigned to you by someone, he or she will have expectations about what the report should contain. If you are

writing the report to bring an issue to someone's attention or to make recommendations, you will want that person to understand the logic of your
analysis and your solutions. In most cases, readers of analytical reports will
need to understand your information, analyses, and recommendations *in
their own terms* in order to accept your report.

It is important to note here that writing with the reader's perspective in
mind need not conflict with the objective nature of the analytical report.
The reader's perspective provides guidance in the initial definition of the
task, since the report is prepared for the reader. The reader's perspective
also should guide you to the best way to explain your results to the reader,
the best way to *reach* the reader with your conclusions.

*The analysis you use to solve the problem should be objective; in other words,
you should consider all reasonable alternatives and not come to premature or biased decisions unsupported by facts.* When you present your analysis to the
reader, objectivity requires that you not misrepresent the situation. You
will also select the level of detail required in that situation. In some circumstances, the reader's purpose and his or her understanding will require
much more detail about alternatives than in others.

It is very common for writers of analytical reports to organize their information in the way that they developed their recommendations and to
emphasize the elements of the issue that influenced them.

While this approach is understandable, it frequently results in either
more or less information than the reader needs or wants. The level of detail does not need to include everything you, as writer, discovered or considered in making the decision. The depth of information depends, rather,
on the purpose of the report and on what information the reader needs to
understand the situation.

As you organize your material and then write your draft, you will be
making decisions about the depth of information your reader will need.
Predicting how the reader will use the information or how actively he or
she will want to participate in the analysis of the alternatives can help you
with this decision. Ask yourself whether you think your reader will understand and accept conclusions with minimal explanation and analysis, or
whether your reader wants to bring further analysis to bear on the subject.
To answer these questions, consider your reader's position and sphere of
responsibility, his or her interest in the subject, the importance he or she at-
taches to it, the magnitude of the resources involved, and whether or not
the issue touches on any of his or her pet peeves, vested interests, or
strongly held attitudes. The nature of your working relationship with this
person will also affect your predictions. What level of information has he
or she required in similar situations in the past? Does he or she usually accept your reasoning and recommendations with minimal explanations, or
does he or she want to understand and agree with the basis for every decision?

From this information, you should have a sense of the depth of information and analysis your reader will require in order to understand and accept your report.

ORGANIZATIONAL STRUCTURE OF ANALYTICAL REPORTS

The format and organization of your analytical report will depend on the purpose of the report, the subject, and the audience.

Format for Analytical Reports

Analytical reports generally follow one of three formats: the memo format, a short report format, or a format that accommodates longer reports. Length of the report, institutional practice, and personal preference usually determine what format is appropriate. If you have doubts, find out what formats have been used in your institution for similar reports. The formats are described briefly below.

Memo Format
The memo format uses a standard four-part heading. Subheadings usually set off sections of the text. Attachments may be included at the back, and they can be listed following the text of the memo. Chapter 5 contains more information on memos.

Short Report Format
In the short report format, the title and author are usually centered on the first page of the report. Again, sections of the text may be identified by headings. Attachments can be included after the report, and they may be listed at the end of the report.

Long Report Format
For long reports, you may wish to have a separate title page and a table of contents, including a list of attachments. The report may be divided into chapters, or each section may be started on a new page. For more detail on long reports, consult the specialized books on reports in the selected readings.

Elements of Analytical Reports

The organization of your report will depend on your purpose. The emphasis also varies, depending on whether you are providing information, analysis, or recommendations. Elements that frequently appear in analytical reports are discussed below.

Title, Author, Date, and Front Matter

In memo format, the first three elements are handled in the traditional way, in lines labeled for these purposes. The person identified as the sender is assumed to be the author, unless the report or the transmittal memo identifies someone else. In the short and long report format, these elements also appear, either at the top of the first page or on a separate title page. Precision, completeness, and brevity (that rare trio) are required here. See the chapter on memos for further discussion of transmittal memos and the traditional headings in memo format. *Front matter* refers to the preliminary pages that are sometimes found in long reports, like a table of contents or a list of illustrations.

Opening Summary

The opening statements in an analytical report should provide an overview of the recommendations or conclusions of the report. This summary may be a short paragraph, a list of items, or, for a longer report, a summary called either an executive summary or an abstract. This practice is widely advocated by business writing authorities and by administrators. It provides the important information, the report's major conclusions, first, and it allows the reader to assess the rest of the report in light of the conclusions. The summary or abstract is seen by most busy managers as a time-saver, providing assistance for quickly grasping the main ideas in a report. Occasionally, writers resist revealing their conclusions immediately, preferring to require that the reader follow their logic step by step, leading to what they hope will be seen by the reader as an inevitable conclusion. This writing stratagem, known as the inductive order, is frequently used for persuasive writing, and can be used for report writing, but often it does not work as intended. Most readers of reports do not want to play a guessing game with the writer. They want to know the conclusions first, so that they can evaluate them as they read the report. No matter where the recommendations are located, readers tend to turn to them first anyway.

Origin or Purpose of the Report

Statements about the purpose of the report, who authorized it, who carried it out, and what will now be done with it can appear in a separate section, in the body of the report, or in a covering or transmittal memo. If background statements such as these appear right after the summary, they delay the discussion of the problem and encumber the reader with details less important than the issue itself. On the other hand, the reader *does* need to know who prepared the report and why. One compromise is to include that information in a transmittal or covering memo. Another solution is to present necessary information in short sentences at the beginning, staying

alert to the need to move the reader quickly from the summary of the recommendations to the problem.

Analysis of the Problem or Need

This section presents the problem and lays the groundwork for the information, analysis, or recommendation. This discussion should be based
on your analysis of the issue, but it does not have to include every factor you
considered. *The presentation of the problem should be organized in terms that
make sense to your reader and should be developed in the way that will ensure
that he or she understands the problem.*

To illustrate this fundamental point, let's assume that you, as head of
Cataloging at a large library, have been asked to recommend a method for
converting the library's card catalog records to machine-readable form.
You gather information about various methods of retrospective conversion, study the issues, and decide on the method you will recommend. The
notes you have accumulated during your study will be, no doubt, volumi-
nous and detailed. In your report to the head of Technical Services, your
discussion of the problem may move quickly to a consideration of how each
alternative fits your local situation, since your head of Technical Services is
already well acquainted with the problem of retrospective conversion.
Suppose, then, that later you are asked to write another report on retrospective conversion that will be attached to the dean's proposal for automation, one that goes to the Board of Trustees. Rather than recycle your first
report, you would probably want to write a new report specifically for the
new audience. In this report, you might begin by defining retrospective
conversion and discussing its importance, and then you might deal with
cost, access, and schedules—problems that would be of paramount interest to your audience.

The way you organize your discussion of the problem and the depth of
detail you provide should be directly related to what your audience will
want or need to know. You need to structure your discussion to get your
reader to view the problem in an accurate and appropriate manner. If you
anticipate difficulty in having your reader understand and accept your
conclusions, you will want to analyze your audience's main objections and
try to address them objectively in the presentation of the problem.

For example, suppose you are writing an analytical report on automating a small library in a corporate setting, and you know that your administrator has a preconception that the main purpose of automation is to make
the library staff's technical work more efficient. You also know that this individual feels that staff efficiency alone does not justify the price tag for an
automated system. Your job in the analysis of the problem may be to articulate accurately the functions potentially affected by automation, including
the many services and benefits to users, that the administrator may not
fully recognize.

Characteristics of a Successful Solution

Somewhere in your report, usually following the explanation of the problem, but sometimes developed within it, you will want to define a good solution to the problem in your setting. This definition can be a narrative discussion of what you want to achieve; it can be a more formal list of goals and objectives; or it can be a discussion of specific areas of difficulty and specific types of improvements you feel are important. Often you can identify the characteristics of a successful solution and then use them as points of comparison and contrast when discussing alternatives. If, in your analysis of methods for retrospective conversion, you identified specific goals for the speed, cost, and staffing of the method you would eventually select, you might wish to compare characteristics of the alternative methods in each category.

Discussion of Alternatives

Although not every analytical report includes a formally labeled discussion of alternatives, many will consider more than one possible solution to a problem or way of handling an issue. There are many ways you can organize a discussion of alternatives, and an infinite variety in the kind and depth of information you could provide. From the outset, you will be continually faced with choices: Should you discuss all possible alternatives, even those you feel are not viable? Should you focus on the one choice you feel is possible, presenting its advantages and disadvantages in detail? How much information should you gather on all the alternatives? How far should each alternative be developed?

Only you as writer of the report can make these decisions. You will make them based on your best judgment of the appropriate level of discussion for your purpose and your reader. As an additional aid in making these decisions, we will describe some common methods of treating the discussion of alternatives; however, in the end, you will have to decide which will work best in your situation.

Yea or nay. An analytical report can be structured around a simple yes or no choice. For example, a small public library may be offered the chance to join a grant-funded network for the purpose of providing computer searching. In the report that the librarian prepares for the Board of Trustees, he or she may want to analyze the advantages and disadvantages of joining the network as support for the recommendation he or she wishes to make.

Alternatives: Divided Discussion. When you wish to consider several alternatives, you can take them one at a time, developing your discussion of each around similar points. Treating each alternative in sequence can also lend itself to unequal development of alternatives, since you can dismiss with minimal discussion those alternatives that do not meet basic criteria.

Suppose that you are presenting the results of your analysis of ways to increase the rate of return for overdue books. As part of your study, you have identified four alternatives: sending out collectors, raising fines, instituting telephone renewals, and increasing the loan period. You may wish to discuss each in turn, giving the more feasible alternatives a more lengthy analysis.

Alternatives: Alternating Discussion. Instead of discussing each alternative completely before considering the next, you can organize the discussion around criteria or main points and compare the alternatives with each other, one characteristic at a time. An approach like this might be used in an analysis of periodical vendors, where the desired characteristics of the vendor are listed, perhaps ranked in order, and then the contenders compared with each other, point by point. A concluding section then summarizes the results.

Multiple Possibilities. In situations where several possibilities can be accepted, you may wish to develop a list of suggestions and discuss each one on its merits. For example, if you were asked to study the activities for young adults in a public library system and develop recommendations for expanding the program, you might wish to list five compatible possibilities, all of which would strengthen the program.

Tables and Charts

Tables and charts are useful for summarizing and organizing quantities of information. Charts of various kinds can present main points visually. Further discussion of charts and tables appears in chapter 13.

Presentation of Recommendations

The statement of recommendations can be a formal one, following the presentation of alternatives, and can include a justification. On the other hand, if the discussion of alternatives has been organized so that the clear contenders were the only ones discussed in detail, a simpler statement of recommendation may be all that is necessary. In most cases, though, the explanations of the recommendation will be more extensive than the abbreviated summary that you use at the beginning of the document.

Action Statement

For some reports, you will want to include a description of what happens next or what you would like your reader to do. For informal reports, a sentence inviting the reader to get in touch if more information is wanted, or thanking the reader for his or her help, is appropriate. In all types of reports, tact and control of tone are essential in phrasing the action statement. For more information on phrasing action statements, see chapter 5.

Figure 32 is an example of an analytical report.

DATE: March 17, 1988

TO: Collection Development Committee

FROM: Lee Simmons
             Collection Development Librarian

SUBJECT: DISPOSAL OF WITHDRAWN BOOKS

ISSUE: We need to adopt a new method for disposing
of books that we have withdrawn from the collection.
As a result of our weeding program, we now have
more books to dispose of than our current method
(donation to the library cooperative) can handle.

RECOMMENDATION: I recommend that we sell the
books that we have taken out of the collection to
Books Unlimited, a second-hand book dealer in Central City.

PROBLEM: During the past year, we have begun a
weeding program, and we plan to continue it at least
for the next two years. As a result, we are withdrawing more books from the collection than the library
cooperative, to which we currently give our discarded
books, can handle. We are now out of space for storing
withdrawn materials and need to decide on a new solution as soon as possible.

ALTERNATIVES: After calling other libraries our size
and doing a search of the literature, I have come up
with the following alternatives.

Figure 32. **Analytical Report**

1. Destroying the books. Although this is occasionally done, I do not recommend it. It would be distasteful to staff and users, as well as time-consuming.
2. Having a sale. A few faculty have expressed interest in an annual sale. Although it is a pleasing idea, there are several practical drawbacks for us at this time. We are withdrawing more volumes than we can store for a year. Our previous sales have created good will but have resulted in the disposal of less than half of the material we had on sale. In addition, sales as large as the one we would need are extremely time-consuming. Perhaps in the future we might reconsider the idea of a sale, but now it does not seem practical.
3. Donating to other libraries, locally or beyond. In the past few years, we have explored this issue fully, and the current practice of donating material to the library cooperative is a result. However, the cooperative just cannot take the volume of material that we now have.
4. Selling the books to a used book dealer. Books Unlimited will pick up the books once a month. At that time, they will assess each batch and offer us a price. Although we will not get rich, we will have some money for buying replacement books. I have checked with the Administration, and we are free to sell withdrawn books if that is our decision.

I suggest that we try this plan for a year and then evaluate it.

ACTION: If the committee approves alternative four, using Books Unlimited for a year's trial, I will arrange for our first pick-up as soon as possible.

Figure 32—**Continued**

CHECKLIST FOR WRITING ANALYTICAL REPORTS

Figure 33 is a checklist that summarizes the process for writing analytical reports. It can be used as a review of the chapter or as a guide when writing analytical reports.

Use the checklist below to review the process for writing analytical reports.
1. Define the scope and purpose of the report.
   ▲ What is the subject and purpose of the report?
   ▲ What do you wish to accomplish by writing the report?
   ▲ If someone has asked you to prepare the report, are you clear about what his or her expectations for the report are? Do you feel that he or she has preconceived notions or vested interests in the outcome of the report? What is likely to happen to the report after you have prepared it?
   ▲ If you have initiated the study of the problem, what are your expectations? Do you have preconceived notions or vested interests in the outcome of the report?
   ▲ What do you want the reader to do after reading the report?
   ▲ What human relations issues are involved in the subject of the report and what human relations goals can you formulate to address these issues?
   ▲ What limitations apply to the study? What is their origin? What effects will they have?
2. Understand the perspective of the audience of the report.
   ▲ Who will read the report and what action will be expected of them?
   ▲ What do they know about the problem? What preconceptions or vested interests do they have about the problem?
   ▲ Do they have expectations about the solution?
   ▲ How much will they want to understand about the problem and the alternative solutions?
   ▲ What issues will they want addressed in any consideration of the problem?
   ▲ What will their reaction be to what you are trying to accomplish?
3. Plan your approach to the report.
   ▲ How much analysis of the information will you provide?
   ▲ Will you make recommendations? What are the channels through which the report, and the recommendations, will be approved? Who will make the decisions?
   ▲ How long should the report be?
   ▲ Will you use memo format, short report format, or long report format?

Figure 33. **Writing Analytical Reports: A Checklist**

    ▲ What other supplementary means of communication should you consider to make your analysis and recommendations clear to the readers of the report, those who are affected by the report, and those who will make the final decisions?

4. Study the problem, collect and analyze your information, and formulate your recommendations. Develop the material that you feel will be necessary to include in the report to provide information or support your analysis and recommendations.

    ▲ Have you let your mind roam freely over alternative ways of approaching your topic?

    ▲ Have you systematically gathered information about the problem? From published sources? From knowledgeable people? From institutional records? From your own observations?

    ▲ Have you developed alternatives and assessed the effectiveness of each possibility in solving the problems?

    ▲ Have you developed your recommendations?

    ▲ Have you assessed the level of information, explanation, and analysis that your reader will want?

5. Work out the sequence of ideas and the level of development for your report.

    ▲ Have you made a working decision on the format and approximate length of your report? Two to four pages? Five to ten pages? Longer?

    ▲ Will your report be in memo format, short report format, or long report format?

    ▲ Have you divided your report into logical main sections and chosen the headings for them?

    ▲ Have you chosen the level of development for each section, based on your assessment of what the reader needs and wants to know?

    ▲ Have you considered using attachments and graphics?

    ▲ Will you send a transmittal memo or letter with the report? What information will it include?

6. Write the rough draft of the report, following your organizational plan.

7. Assess the effectiveness of your report and identify problem areas. Develop solutions to these difficulties.

    ▲ Do you see any weakness in the presentation and analysis of information or in your development of recommendations?

    ▲ Will your reader understand and accept your definition of the problem? If not, why not? Will other ways of looking at the issue occur to the reader?

    ▲ Have you provided sufficient alternatives and analysis for your reader?

    ▲ Have your assessed your report systematically, looking for problems of effectiveness, tone and personality, organizational structure, composition of sentences, and word choice? For each problem you find, can you pinpoint the cause and develop alternative solutions? Which

Figure 33—**Continued**

solution works best in the context of the entire report? (Chapter 3 provides help with this analysis.)

8. Edit your report for correctness.
   ▲ Have you reviewed your draft for problems of grammar, usage, and punctuation?
   ▲ Have you used your knowledge of the kinds of mistakes you make to help you find trouble spots? (Chapter 3 provides assistance in identifying and solving these problems.)
   ▲ Have you checked all matters of fact, including
       raw numbers and computations?
       dates?
       facts?
       bibliographic citations?
       titles?
       spelling?
       proper nouns, especially names?
   ▲ Have you proofread carefully to ensure accuracy? (Chapter 3 provides a checklist for this activity.)

9. Produce the final copy of your memo.
   ▲ Have you considered the elements of "design" to achieve an effective, professional office look?
   ▲ Have you marked the layout for the final copy, noting any special keyboard graphic effects, special spacing, and indentions?
   ▲ If someone is assisting you by preparing the final copy, have you communicated your instructions clearly, including spacing, margins, layout, and special graphic effects?
   ▲ Have you arranged to review a typed draft before the final draft is prepared?
   ▲ After receiving the final copy, have you proofread carefully, for typographical errors and for other difficulties that might have slipped in?
   ▲ Is the final copy neat and professional looking?

Chapter 10

MONTHLY REPORTS

CHAPTER OUTLINE

PURPOSES FOR MONTHLY REPORTS
  Information for Your Administrator
  Information for You and Your Staff
  Documentation for the Future
  Communication outside the Reporting Unit

PROBLEMS WITH MONTHLY REPORTS

INCREASING THE CHANCES THAT YOUR REPORT WILL BE READ
  Understanding Your Administrator's Perspective
  Identifying Motivators and Highlighting Them
  Developing a Layout and Style That Encourages Rapid Reading
  Keeping Information Brief, Relevant, and Significant
  Using the Report in Face-to-Face Meetings

DISCUSSING SENSITIVE ISSUES IN MONTHLY REPORTS

DEVELOPING A FORMAT FOR MONTHLY REPORTS
  Choosing an Approach
  Determining the Content
  Selecting the Main Sections
  Designing a Layout for Monthly Reports

EVALUATING THE FORMAT OF MONTHLY REPORTS

TEST YOUR SKILLS

CHECKLIST FOR WRITING MONTHLY REPORTS

In libraries, the monthly report is the most common version of what business writing texts call the periodic report: a report, produced at regular intervals, that summarizes for management the activities of an area or unit during the reporting period. In some libraries, periodic reports are written quarterly rather than monthly. In this chapter we will use the term *monthly report* for convenience; however, the principles we discuss are applicable to periodic reports written at any interval.

Monthly reports are generally written by librarians responsible for an activity, a unit, a department, an agency, or a branch. These reports generally go to the person at the next level of management with overall responsibility for the reporting unit or person.

In many libraries, monthly reports are viewed with distaste, both by those who have to write them and by those who supposedly read them. The writers resent the cyclical return of what sometimes seems like a pointless task, and the intended readers of the reports are often just as negative, with criticisms about lack of meaningful content, poor organization, and excessive length. Even if no one is complaining, reports may be making their periodic journey from writer to administrator to filing cabinet without contributing anything positive to the operation of the library. In this chapter, we will explore ways to convert your monthly report into a communication tool that justifies the time you take to prepare it and the time your administrator devotes to reading it.

PURPOSES FOR MONTHLY REPORTS

The general purpose of a monthly report is implicit in its definition: to summarize the activities of an area of operation during one month. Under that general aim, we can identify several different purposes for providing this summary of activities, depending on who will read the report. The use that you predict different readers will have for information about your activities affects the type of information you should include in the report and shapes the way you can present that information.

Information for Your Administrator

Monthly reports are usually written for your administrator or supervisor. The head of Public Services in a medium-size academic library might write a report to the director of the library; the head of Cataloging in a large university library might write a report for the head of Technical Services; the branch librarian in a public library system might write a report to the district coordinator, or to the head of Adult Services; the head of Library Services in a corporation might report in writing to the vice president for Information and Communication.

To define more precisely your purposes in providing information about your activities to your administrator, let's examine that relationship in some detail. Whatever your position in the library, you have the responsibility for performing or overseeing the performance of specific activities—the provision of reference services, for example. You have detailed knowledge of your area of responsibility and you know what staff, budget, and policies you need to operate effectively. Getting the resources and the support you need, however, often depends on the decisions of someone else, usually your administrator and those above him or her in the hierarchy.

An essential part of your job is to make sure that the people at the next level of management understand your area well enough so that they can make informed decisions affecting your operation and can justify those decisions to the people above them. That understanding does not have to be as detailed as your knowledge. Usually, it is sufficient if your administrator has a *managerial* understanding of what you do, of why it is important to the entire library and the institution, of what resources are necessary, and of the factors that affect performance and productivity. The level of understanding that allows administrators to make good decisions affecting the areas under their control, even though they may not have detailed knowledge of that area, can be called an informed climate for decision making. As part of ongoing interaction with your administrator, you are constantly contributing to this informed climate for decision making using different communication tools. The monthly report can be especially effective in this effort for several reasons.

It presents information in a structured context over a period of time. You define the key elements of operation for your department and organize them in a way that provides a profile of your activity. By using the same structure each month, you can create continuity, foster comparisons, and gradually build understanding of patterns of your activity.

The monthly report can become a source of factual information about your area and can serve as the basis for understanding of your activity. Its purpose is to inform, to report things as they are—not to argue a case or become a partisan document. If your report is a reliable source of data and interpretation, your administration can use it to form his or her own conclusions. These understandings of your activity, based on facts and your interpretations of them, can then become your best ally when the administrator weighs future recommendations.

Using the monthly report as an objective source of information, rather than a partisan document that promotes a specific issue, does not mean that you have to abandon your opinions or interpretations. It *does* mean that you are committed to letting the facts speak for themselves. You can organize them, call attention to certain aspects, repeat them from month to month, and interpret their meaning, as long as the facts of monthly activity are accurate and clear.

An example will illustrate what we mean by the objectivity of a monthly report. Suppose that, as head of a small Technical Services department, you have found that your cataloging staff is simply not large enough to handle the library's volume of cataloging in a timely manner. You have developed cataloging priorities, but a backlog of items is steadily accumulating. One of your management goals is to get another position authorized for cataloging, and you plan to submit a fully documented request at the appropriate time in the budget cycle. Using the monthly report as an objective information tool about the flow of work in your department, you might present statistics showing the size and nature of the backlog. When incidents occur involving users' need for uncataloged material, you can document them in the way you handle other unusual occurrences. You could also comment on the situation, when monthly activity warranted it. In other words, you would present factual information and comment on it as called for by the monthly flow of activities, but you would not treat the report as a forum for arguing your staffing case.

The advantages of this approach should be clear. Throughout the year, you will be providing your administrator with factual documentation of your need, in a neutral and objective atmosphere. In the best outcome, your administrator will "absorb" the situation and become aware of the backlog problem, so that when you present your proposal, with a thorough justification, your administrator will have his or her own knowledge to use in assessing your case. Even if your administrator does not fully recall the situation, the factual data is available in the reports for reference and referral.

The monthly report can be a valuable tool for informing administrators about your operation if it

▲ highlights important information
▲ provides a clear profile of overall activity
▲ fosters understanding of patterns or trends
▲ is an objective source of management data.

With proper organization and structure, the monthly report directs your administrator's attention to major factors, issues, and trends that affect your department.

Information for You and Your Staff

Monthly reports gradually develop a bank of data that you and your staff can use in carrying out your responsibilities. In this sense, you and the departmental staff become the audience for your own report and turn to it for the information you need to report, plan, and manage. Suppose, for example, that you manage the call-in reference center for a major urban public library. Statistics about the time, the duration, and the volume of calls can help you plan the staffing you need at various times during the day.

Monthly reports can also become a valuable source of information about your activities and those of your department. Libraries use monthly reports as sources when they are preparing annual reports. As a matter of course, some supervisors review monthly reports before preparing annual evaluations, in order to refresh their understanding of the scope of the writer's activities.

Documentation for the Future

A third audience for monthly reports is the library staff of the future, the librarians whose job it will be to build on what you leave them and who will no doubt appreciate knowing what was done and why. Documenting activities and leaving a reliable record is a valid and important part of reporting. In most libraries, the annual report carries most of this burden, but monthly reports not only provide material for the annual report, they often document the unfolding of trends and issues in a way not possible in an annual report.

Communication outside the Reporting Unit

Monthly reports can also be a vehicle for communicating information about a department's or a unit's activities to people outside the reporting unit. Distributing departmental reports to staff can be a way of keeping many people aware of the work of the total department. Similarly, distributing departmental reports to other department heads is a way some libraries have chosen to increase awareness of all library activities. When you distribute monthly reports to people other than your administrator, you have added another, more general audience to the list, and you must also consider them when you write.

Monthly reports have multiple uses and multiple audiences, as we have seen. They can provide information for your administration; a management databank and departmental memory for you and your staff; a record for the future; and, if you wish, a source of information about your activity for others outside your department. Although having several purposes means that the monthly report is potentially a very useful document, it also may make it more difficult to write a clear, effective report that accomplishes what you want. Both in designing a monthly report's format and in writing the report each month, it is very easy to lose sight of part of what you wish to accomplish and, as a result, to produce a document that does not address your purposes or readers as well as it might.

PROBLEMS WITH MONTHLY REPORTS

While the concept of receiving a cogent, concise, and relevant summary of activities every month sounds like a manager's dream, in reality, monthly reports can fall considerably short of the ideal, as most library administrators will testify. Poor or ineffective reports show many of the same characteristics, no matter what library service or activity they summarize.

Some of the common problems with monthly reports are presented below.

▲ The information given does not seem to be significant, either to the writer or the reader. Choosing the content of a monthly report is vital to its success. Much insignificant or irrelevant information is preserved for posterity in filing cabinets.

▲ The main ideas do not stand out clearly. It is necessary to pull key points out of long paragraphs.

▲ The narrative rambles. Monthly reports frequently sound like half of a conversation that might take place in the staffroom over coffee. Information is there, but it is buried in an avalanche of irrelevant details.

▲ Information is not presented in the same format each month, so comparisons and trends are hard to see.

▲ The tone is not objective. Often, it seems as if the report is being used as a hobbyhorse for the library's favorite complaint. (Note the potential for adverse reaction to this tone, even when the complaint is valid.)

▲ The tone of the report does not seem appropriate to the purpose. Also, the tone may not contribute to building a positive image of the writer.

▲ A coherent picture of the significant activity of the area does not emerge clearly enough to be effective.

INCREASING THE CHANCES THAT YOUR REPORT WILL BE READ

Monthly reports are easy to ignore. Often, they display many of the problems described above, and so reading them may not be a high priority. They usually do not require any action; normally they are filed to be available if needed. So, if time is limited and the basket of mail is piled high, the reader may send the report on its way, to be filed, without reading or assimilating it.

If you suspect that your monthly report is not getting the attention you would like, you may be tempted to conclude that the Case of the Unread Monthly Report is one of those annoying mysteries that can never be solved. The solution, you may argue, lies with your administrator, who is not interested, and therefore nothing can be done. While there may be a few desperate cases that fit this description, much can be done with most monthly reports that will both solve the typical problems listed above and encourage your administrator to pay at least some attention to your report. Below are a number of ideas about ways to increase the probability that your administrator will actually read your report.

Understanding Your Administrator's Perspective

The most effective way to ensure your administrator's interest is to include information about your area that is important to him or her. Administrators vary widely in what they feel is important to know about operations under them; however, in most cases they will not feel they need to know everything that you know. They will want to focus on certain indicators or measures of activity that represent summaries of the overall situation. For some administrators, measures of library activity or library productivity are important; for others, financial measures are significant; still others are interested in the library's relationship with the user community or to important missions of the parent institution.

From previous interactions, you may have numerous clues about the kinds of information that your administrator considers significant. You may also wish to ask him or her for suggestions about information to include. Having your administrator review a draft of your new monthly report format can be especially helpful.

Identifying Motivators and Highlighting Them

Once you know what information is important to your reader, placing it in a prominent position in the report can provide a reason for your administrator to read the report. You may also be able to create motivators by pointing out key statistical indicators or measures of activity, explaining them, and emphasizing them in other communications.

For example, suppose that you are responsible for circulation and stacks management in a large university library, and your department employs 75 percent of the student workers hired by the library. Suppose, further, that the library's student assistance budget for this year has been cut and that the administration is concerned about whether the library can live within that lower figure. You may want to put a clear summary of the monthly use of student hours in a prominent position in your report. You may also wish to develop a concise measure of the current year's situation, such as the percentage of decrease from the same month last year, or the variance between the amount budgeted for the year to date and the amount used. If the information in your report is important to the head of Public Services in monitoring the budget, he or she will have an incentive for looking at your report.

Developing a Layout and Style That Encourages Rapid Reading

Cultivate a writing style that encourages scanning and combine it with a layout that uses space and graphics effectively. By using hierarchical headings, short paragraphs and sentences, lists, and graphic symbols, you can make your main points stand out for easier reading and quicker comprehension. Express your ideas as concisely and precisely as possible. Using vocabulary that is clear, relevant, and appropriate for your reader also contributes to a readable style. Chapter 2 presents more information on clear organization and style.

Keeping Information Brief, Relevant, and Significant

Make sure that the information you include is relevant to your purposes and to your reader. For each piece of information, ask yourself who needs to have it and why. Be ruthless about removing padding.

As you assess the relevance of information to your readers, you may discover some conflicts among the multiple purposes of your report. You may be attempting, for example, to write a report that your administrator, who is interested only in highlights, will actually read. Yet you also want the report to provide thorough documentation of the department's activities. There are several ways around this classic dilemma. You may wish to start with a summary of highlights, putting in the first section all the important data and conclusions that you want your administrator to know. The rest of the report can then include more detail. Another approach is to use the body of the report for summaries of information and to include detail in attachments. At some point, however, balancing multiple purposes and multiple readers can compromise the success of both goals, and you may need to consider writing two reports.

Using the Report in Face-to-Face Meetings

Refer to the report in meetings with your administrator and bring an extra copy so that he or she will not have to dig through the filing cabinet to find it. If the information in the report is relevant and important, it will form a natural basis for discussion. If your administrator knows that you will be using the report in ongoing discussions, he or she has an additional incentive to read the report in advance.

DISCUSSING SENSITIVE ISSUES IN
MONTHLY REPORTS

The monthly report is a vehicle for ongoing, formally documented communication with your supervisor, and therefore questions about the extent to which you will use it to document departmental problems or raise sensitive issues are bound to arise. How much sensitive material you include in your report depends on your judgment, and your decisions will be made on what you know about your supervisor, the political dynamics of your organization, and the kind of reporting that will actually bring about results. Some general guidelines about sensitive information in monthly reports may be useful.

Since monthly reports often have multiple audiences, you will want to be extremely careful that what you write is appropriate for the various audiences that may have access to it. As an obvious example, comments about personnel situations are inappropriate if the report is likely to be read by the departmental staff. Generally speaking, monthly reports are not considered confidential documents in most libraries, so it is difficult to predict who will be reading your reports in the future. For that reason, confining yourself to objective statements that are suitable for a variety of audiences is probably the wisest course. When you feel that it is appropriate to discuss sensitive problems, pay special attention to tone, objectivity of analysis, and the possible implications of your statements to different audiences. A safer course may be to reserve discussions of such problems for face-to-face meetings. When documentation is necessary, you may wish to use special-purpose reports or memos with controlled distribution.

DEVELOPING A FORMAT FOR MONTHLY REPORTS

Developing a standard format that you can use every month has a number of advantages. You can decide in advance what kinds of information you wish to assemble regularly and how you wish to display it. By collecting the same information systematically every month, you provide continuity and consistency for your readers and, at the same time, develop files of information that may be useful to you. The monthly task of writing the report becomes easier once a standard format has been established. And, finally, the process of designing a format can become an opportunity to discuss with your administrator what he or she wants to know about your area.

Choosing an Approach

To begin with, you will need a clear understanding of which purposes you want your monthly report to serve. Once you have a clear idea of what you wish to accomplish by writing a monthly report and know who will be reading the report, you can make some preliminary decisions about what will make that report most effective. Your ideas will evolve, to be sure, as you develop and organize your material, but the initial collecting of your thoughts about how to accomplish your purpose can guide you as you work through the rest of the process. As you begin to consider what your monthly report format will look like, you will want to envision its ideal length and layout. If you are concerned with producing a report that invites quick reading, you will want to think about headings and sub-headings, graphic means to highlighting information, and charts and other displays, as well as overall length. With your readers in mind, you will consider the tone of the report and the impression you wish the report to leave on the readers. Finally, you will want to consider other means of communication that you plan to use in achieving the goals you have identified for your monthly report.

Suppose you are the director of the technical library for an engineering firm. You have identified as one goal for your monthly report to increase your administrator's awareness of the important role the library's information specialists play in the company's research activities. In your preliminary thinking about your approach to this report, you might decide that since you have had difficulty in the past getting your administrator to read your reports regularly, you want a one-page report that highlights important research projects that your staff has worked on. You may further decide that your tone will be informal, that you will use no library jargon, and that you will highlight main ideas graphically, in attachments, wherever possible. You may also decide to include, as an attachment, a table summarizing all research requests, tabulated by requesting department and including the title of the request, the requestor, and the project. You may further decide to send the report to other department heads within the company to raise awareness of the library. And you may wish to use the report as the basis for your monthly meeting with your administrator, anticipating that conclusions presented in the report can be amplified in person. Finally, you may plan to discuss the approach with your administrator to find out what information he or she would like included and what format he or she prefers.

Determining the Content

Your goal in this step is to identify the generic types of information that you will want to include each month, so that you can develop a format for displaying it concisely and consistently, in a manner that makes comparisons easy. You may wish to approach this step by first listing everything you can think of that you might want to include and then assessing each item individually, asking yourself what your reader, and you, would do with this

information. If you cannot find a clear use for these data, ask yourself why
you are collecting and reporting them. You may wish to include on your list
various levels of detail on the same subject. In the illustration from the
technical library of an engineering company, you might list "research requests" as a type of information you will include, and then list, under that
category, details you might choose to include, like the requestor, title of
project, subject of request, sources consulted, time spent, and so forth.
Thinking through the purposes of including each detail should help you
sort out what information you wish to include.

At this stage in the process, you will want to let your mind roam freely
over many ideas for the content of your monthly report. You may wish to
use some of the techniques in chapter 2 for the invention stage in writing,
since this is the place for the development of new ideas and approaches.

Selecting the Main Sections

When you have reached some conclusions about the types of information you want to include, you can begin to grapple with the best way to organize that information. Your goal is to come up with a structure that
organizes activity into consistent categories and still provides flexibility to
accommodate each month's changing activities.

Your report will, no doubt, be divided into several main sections. In selecting these main categories, you have a choice between two approaches:
organizing by activity or organizing by what we can call, for want of a better word, *genre*. Headings using activities or topics describe something substantive about the specific content of the section. The heading "Information Services" promises information about this topic or activity. When you
use genres, the heading describes a *type* of information, rather than anything specific about the subject of that information. So, for example, "Statistical Review," "Highlights of the Month," "Significant Indicators of
Activity," and "Narrative Summary" are all genres describing a general
characteristic of the information. From the heading "Statistics," for example, you know that you will find numbers in that section, but the topic is not
specified. Figures 34 and 35 illustrate these approaches to the organization of a hypothetical monthly report for a technical services department.

There are no firm rules about when to use topical or generic headings.
Each category organizes information differently, provides different opportunities, and creates different effects. What works for you and your
readers should be the overriding consideration. Within each main section,
you again have the choice of topical or generic subheadings. Because these
two choices are fundamental to the organization of your report, we will discuss each in more detail.

TECHNICAL SERVICES: MONTHLY REPORT
  I. Acquisitions
    A. Acquisitions Statistics
    B. Fund Balances
    C. Vendor Study
    D. Acquisitions Luncheon
    E. Staff Development
  II. Cataloging
    A. Cataloging Statistics
    B. Cataloging Workload
    C. Retrospective Conversion
    D. Training for Student Assistants
    E. Staff Development
  III. Collection Maintenance
    A. Weeding Project
    B. Book Sale
  IV. Automation Project

Figure 34. **Sections for a Monthly Report Using Topical or Activity Headings**

TECHNICAL SERVICES: MONTHLY REPORT
  I. Highlights of the Month
    A. Acquisitions Luncheon
    B. Book Sale
    C. Reduction of Backlog
  II. Departmental Statistical Summary
  III. Fund Report
  IV. Administrative Issues and Exceptional Circumstances
    A. Cataloging Workload
    B. Training for Student Assistants
  V. Special Projects
    A. Automation Project
    B. Retrospective Conversion
    C. Vendor Study
    D. Weeding Project
    E. Book Sale
  VI. Staff Development
    A. Workshops and Meetings
    B. Staff Publications

Figure 35. **Sections for a Monthly Report Using Genre Headings**

Organizing Main Sections with Topical Headings

When you organize by topic or activity, you choose categories that represent a logical division of your department or area. Often, these categories represent the organizational structure of your department, but they need not be limited to administrative divisions. For example, a head of a technical services department in a college library might organize a monthly report first by activity, with each activity divided by topical subheadings. In one possible format, the main headings might be used every month, and the subheadings might vary from month to month.

Organizing by administrative activity or unit ensures that you will report something about that activity every month. Therein lies both its advantage and its disadvantage. If, for your purposes and your audience, you will have significant things to say each month, then choosing activity headings may suit your purposes best. But be aware that once the pattern is established, you may find it difficult to get away from. The disadvantage of using activity headings is that you will feel compelled to fill the section every month and will find yourself including insignificant material, just because you feel you must say something. Organizing the report by department may require that you repeat the same kinds of information under each category. For example, you may find yourself listing professional development activities under each departmental area.

Organizing Main Sections with Generic Headings

When you organize your main sections by genre, you group similar kinds of information together for all areas. Obviously, this organization emphasizes the unity of the reporting unit more than the alternative, organization by activity, does. In most reports that use genre headings for the main sections, subheadings will be primarily topical headings, although a mixture is possible.

Organizing by genre gives you more flexibility to choose activity subheadings each month and reduces the chance that you will be writing useless filler simply to complete the form; however, it dilutes the emphasis on activity. Obviously, there is no one right method. Each one crates a different emphasis and has its own strengths and weaknesses. You, as writer, should choose the combination of headings and subheadings that you feel will be most effective in achieving your purposes with your readers.

Test your skills by designing a format for a monthly report to your administrator or supervisor (figure 36).

Designing a Layout for Monthly Reports

With your main sections identified, you can turn your attention to planning the arrangement and layout of those sections that you can use every month. Establishing a standard format allows your reader to become familiar with the format and what can be found there. The organization and lay-

Design a format for a monthly report to your administrator or supervisor. If you plan to use the report, you may wish to confer with that person as you develop your report. You may also wish to review the process for writing a monthly report that appears later in the chapter.

1. Define the purposes that you want your monthly report to serve. Consider what your administrator will want from your report.
2. Develop a list of the information you will need to report regularly. Use one of the "invention" techniques in chapter 2. Analyze each item on the list in terms of the purpose it will serve.
3. Decide what you feel are the most important concepts or ideas that you want your monthly report to convey. Think about the relative importance of the items on your list for achieving the purposes you have defined.
4. Experiment with outlines for a format that you can use each month. Try both topical and genre outlines and assess the differences that organizational structures will make.

Figure 36. **Test Your Skills: Designing a Format for a Monthly Report**

out that you choose should make reading the report as easy as possible. Outline form, headings and subheadings, lists, graphics, pleasing spatial arrangement on the page, and attachments, all can contribute to creating a monthly report that looks readable. Chapter 4 considers the design of documents in more detail.

EVALUATING THE FORMAT OF MONTHLY REPORTS

You should evaluate the format of monthly reports periodically to be certain that they are accomplishing their purpose and that they are providing relevant, important information. Discuss the report with your administrator and with your staff, determining the usefulness of the format and the information presented. Changing the format of the monthly report too frequently can interfere with year-to-year comparisons; on the other hand, evaluations help ensure that monthly reports record significant information in an effective way.

TEST YOUR SKILLS

Figure 37 is an example of an ineffective monthly report. Test your skills by analyzing the strengths and weaknesses of the report. Then revise the report. Compare your revision with the example in section J of the appendix, pages 349–51.

You are the district coordinator in a large public library system and receive fifteen monthly reports from the branches that report to you. Your monthly report to the assistant director of the library system must summarize operations and issues in your district. You have received the report below from the Western Branch Library.

Western Community Library
July 1988

   July was a very difficult month, with no air condi-
tioning, a small, crowded library, and far too much activity for a staff that is too small to begin with and
that was short this month because of vacations and
lack of a children's librarian. Our children's activities
went on all month, with me trying to run the story
hours, the summer school and camp visits, and the
film programs. Our new children's librarian began
August 1, and I am looking forward to her taking over
the story times and the summer reading club from
me. Participation in the summer reading club is down
this year, with only seventy-five children registered
and fewer than twenty showing up each week. The
ones that come are very enthusiastic, though, and I
don't see how I could handle any more. The story
times had 14 children and 3 adults on July 3; 17 children and 6 adults on July 10; 21 children (would you
believe!) and 10 adults on July 17; 19 children and 7
adults on July 21; and 13 children and 5 adults on
July 28. Summer Thrills Camp asked if they could
come every week, and although at first I thought we
couldn't handle it, everything worked out well.
Twenty-five children and 5 adults came in the morning. They were given a tour, story, and time to browse.
As usual, some of the children became bored with
looking at books. I wonder if we might want to do
what some libraries do and have some blocks or toys
around to play with. The adults from Summer Thrills
Camp supervised the children very well, and they will
come again next week.

Figure 37. **Test Your Skills: Writing Effective Monthly Reports**

Our adult circulation rose again for the fourth consecutive month. July showed an 8% increase over June and a 12% increase over last July. Saturday circulation has doubled since last year, with no declines in other days. Saturday reference questions have almost doubled, and yet I haven't found a way to clone myself or my staff. All other statistics were within 4% of both last month and last year.

We are continuing to have trouble getting enough paging help, and I find myself shelving books at the end of many days. Our high school students are good workers when they are here, but family vacations and activities often take precedence over their jobs. I am sometimes tempted to terminate them when they ask for two weeks off in the middle of the summer, but then it would take me at least two weeks to hire and train new help, so we are faced with coping during the pages' seemingly endless vacations.

Other than that, it was a very busy, normal month. Everyone loved the Summer Travel Series, and more than 100 people attended again this month. The room was so full that it was very stuffy. I took the occasion to sell our last ticket for the Friends of the Library Museum Excursion we are taking on August 5. We have no more tickets left, so since the tickets went for $25 each, I think we will clear at least $500. The Friends asked me for a "wish list" and I gave them one item: a new film projector!

1. From the point of view of the coordinator, what are the strengths and weaknesses of this report?
2. How many ways can you find to improve this report? Rewrite it, considering the purpose of the report, the content, the format of the report, and the organizational structure. Compare your rewritten report with the example in Section J, pages 349–51, of the appendix.

CHECKLIST FOR WRITING MONTHLY REPORTS

Figure 38 is a checklist that can be used as a guide for designing and writing monthly reports. It can also serve as a summary of important considerations in writing monthly reports.

Use the checklist below to review the process for writing monthly reports.
1. Decide on your purposes for writing a monthly report.
   ▲ Will the reports be used to provide information to your administrator? If so,
      what concepts would you like your administrator to have assimilated at the end of one year of receiving the reports?
      what are the primary measures of activity that you want your administrator to understand?
      what does your administrator need and want to know about your area? What does he or she want from a monthly report? What statistical measures is he or she accustomed to getting from units other than the library?
   ▲ Will the report be a management databank and departmental memory? If so,
      what statistics do you and your staff *use* in making decisions about departmental operations?
      what information, other than statistical, do you need, either for other reports or for decision making?
      do you see areas where decision making might be enhanced by the availability of systematically collected information? What are they and what statistics would be useful?
   ▲ How will the report serve your area as a historical record?
      What statistics relating to your department does the library require every year, both for internal and external reports?
      What types of activities and decisions do you think should be documented on a monthly basis for the future? (Be sure to base this judgment on some assessment of the way the information might actually be *used* in the future.)
   ▲ Will the report serve as a source of information for others in or outside the library? If so,
      do you plan to use the monthly report as a way of disseminating information to people other than those mentioned above? If so, who will receive the report and what is your purpose for sending it to them?
   ▲ What human relations goals can you formulate for your monthly report?
2. Understand the perspectives that your readers will bring to your monthly report.

Figure 38. **Writing Monthly Reports: A Checklist**

▲ Can you involve your primary readers in determining both the kind of information that will be included and the organizational structure of the report?

▲ What kinds of information would a person with your reader's responsibilities want to receive on a regular basis?

▲ What can you do to increase the chances that your reader will read your report?

3. Plan your approach to monthly reporting.

▲ Who besides your administrator will receive copies of the report?

▲ What is your administrator likely to do with your report: File It? Send it to someone else? Summarize the information in his or her report?

▲ Are you satisfied with the way your administrator handles your report? What happens to reports from others in your institution? Do you want to try to change the way your administrator deals with your reports?

▲ Ideally, how long should the report be?

▲ How important is it that the report be easy to read quickly?

▲ Can you describe the tone that you would like to achieve?

▲ Do you want to distinguish between levels of detail and put more detailed information in attachments, tables, and charts?

▲ Do you anticipate that you will want to use additional methods of communication to introduce, reinforce, or follow up on your monthly report?

▲ Do you plan to use the report as a basis for discussion in meetings?

4. Plan the types of information that you will want to include each month.

▲ Have you let your mind roam freely over the types of information and analysis that could be included in the monthly report?

▲ What kinds of information will you want to include each month?

▲ What statistics will you want to document, for your administrator, for yourself and your staff, for the historical record (including other reports you may need to write), and for other uses you may have identified?

▲ How will you obtain the types of information you will include?

5. Design an organizational format that you can use each month.

▲ What main sections will give you the flexibility to accommodate information that will arise each month, but will also allow easy comparisons from month to month? Experiment with both topic and genre headings.

▲ How should your statistical information be displayed?

▲ Does the information of most importance to you and your reader stand out clearly?

▲ What attachments will be a regular part of the report and what will their format be?

6. Write your report each month, using your new format.

▲ Have you reminded yourself of *your* goals for monthly reportings?

▲ Have you reminded yourself of what your administrator expects from a monthly report?

▲ Reviewing the monthly activity of your department, what do you see as important? What comparisons and conclusions do you see? What do you want to say about this month's activity?

▲ How will what you want to say about monthly activity fit into your format for a monthly report, so that important information stands out clearly? (If monthly information cannot be accommodated well, you may need to redesign your report.)

7. Revise your monthly report for effectiveness. At regular intervals, assess your format for effectiveness.

▲ Is your report format effective in achieving what you wish to accomplish?

▲ What obstacles or problems do you see that may be interfering with the success of your report?

▲ What do your readers think about the report?

▲ Have you assessed your draft systematically, looking for problems of general characteristics, tone and personality, organizational structure, composition of sentences, and use of words? (Chapter 3 provides checklists to help with this analysis.)

▲ For each problem you find, can you pinpoint the cause and develop alternative solutions? Which solution works best in the context of the document?

8. Edit your report for correctness.

▲ Have you reviewed your draft for grammar, usage, and punctuation?

▲ Have you used your knowledge of the kinds of mistakes you make to help you find trouble spots? (Chapter 3 provides assistance in identifying and solving these problems.)

▲ Have you checked all matters of fact, including

dates?	raw numbers and computations?
facts?	bibliographic citations?
titles?	proper nouns, especially names?
spelling?	

▲ Have you proofread carefully to ensure accuracy? (Chapter 3 provides a checklist for this activity.)

9. Produce the final copy of your monthly report.

▲ Have you considered the elements of "design" to achieve an effective, professional office look?

▲ Have you marked the layout for the final copy, noting any special keyboard graphic effects, special spacing, and indentions?

▲ If someone is assisting you by preparing the final copy, have you communicated your instructions clearly, including spacing, margins, layout, and special graphic effects?

▲ Have you arranged to review a typed draft before the final draft is prepared?

▲ After receiving the final copy, have you proofread carefully, for typographical errors and other difficulties that might have slipped in?

▲ Is the final copy neat and professional looking?

Figure 38—**Continued**

Chapter 11

ANNUAL REPORTS

CHAPTER OUTLINE

PURPOSES FOR ANNUAL REPORTS
Summary of Library Activity for Managerial Purposes
Historical Record
Communication with Administrators
Public Relations

DETERMINING YOUR PURPOSES FOR ANNUAL REPORTING

UNDERSTANDING YOUR AUDIENCE
One Reader or a Larger Audience
Understanding Your Readers' Perspectives

DEVELOPING YOUR APPROACH TO ANNUAL REPORTING
How Many Annual Reports to Write
Characteristics of Your Annual Report

DEVELOPING THE CONTENT OF YOUR ANNUAL REPORT

ORGANIZING YOUR ANNUAL REPORT
Choosing Main Sections and Main Section Headings
Administrative or Organizational Headings
Topical Headings
Genre Headings
"Headline" Headings
Topic Sentences instead of Headings

DESIGNING AND PRODUCING AN ANNUAL REPORT

TEST YOUR SKILLS

CHECKLIST FOR WRITING ANNUAL REPORTS

Annual reports, by definition, review the reporting unit's operation during the year. An annual report may include objectives for the year just completed; statistical and narrative summaries of activities; lists of accomplishments; financial reviews; summaries of staffing or other personnel is-

231

sues; discussions of all problems, issues, or concerns; objectives for the coming year; comparative data with other libraries; and a variety of other possible topics. Annual reports may go beyond statistics and listing of activities to include synthesis, analysis, and conclusions drawn by the writer, but the nature of this information is determined by the individual reporter and what he or she views as the purpose or object of the report.

In some libraries, every professional staff member writes an annual review or report of his or her activities. Departments, like Technical Services, or divisions of departments, like Acquisitions or Cataloging, often prepare their own reports. The director of the library inevitably writes a report summarizing the year's activities for the library as a whole. Then the administrator to whom the director reports usually includes library data with the report of activities in his or her sphere of responsibility.

PURPOSES FOR ANNUAL REPORTS

The annual report is an occasion, as well as a document. It is an opportunity to consolidate information about library activities, to synthesize it and draw conclusions, and to use it in looking ahead to the next year. As summaries of yearly activity, annual reports can serve four broad purposes.

Summary of Library Activity for Managerial Purposes

A major function of the annual report is to bring together data about the year's activities for use in managerial tasks. The report also presents an opportunity to analyze the information and draw conclusions from it. The conclusions can then become the basis for evaluation and planning. Both the writer of the report and the administrator who receives it can use the data and the conclusions for managerial purposes.

Historical Record

The annual report serves as the historical record for the year's activities. Annual reports provide concise, organized information about the reporting unit, and so become an important reference tool for present and future library staffs.

Communication with Administrators

In addition to providing administrators with information for management purposes, the annual report can function as a communication tool, a way for the writer to inform the reader of his or her activities and an opportunity to foster greater understanding of those activities.

Many administrators take what we might call the passive approach to annual reports. They receive them; they may not read them at all or they may read them once, perhaps looking for potential trouble spots or areas that they may need to deal with in the future; and then they file them. In an alternative approach, an administrator may use annual reports for understanding operations, assessing effectiveness, developing solutions to problems, and forming plans for future activities. This active approach can take many forms, from reading the report carefully and asking questions to discussing issues and participating in planning and problem solving. When either the writer or the administrator seeks an active approach to annual reports, the report can serve communication functions.

Public Relations

A fourth use for annual reporting is communication with people outside the library. Public libraries routinely issue annual reports to the public. Such reports can summarize library operations and provide general financial information. In addition, these reports can improve a library's relationship with the public by emphasizing to its users the value and importance of the services it provides. Other kinds of libraries can also benefit from reporting their activities to users, by combining information with good public relations. Finally, libraries frequently share their annual reports with each other.

DETERMINING YOUR PURPOSES FOR ANNUAL REPORTING

Understanding clearly what you, as writer, and your administrator, as reader, expect annual reporting to do is essential to writing an effective report. You can no doubt articulate these goals to yourself with a little introspection. You may wish to discuss with your administrator what he or she expects from an annual report, although administrators differ in their ability or desire to articulate what they want from annual reporting. From your experience in your institution, you will undoubtedly have ideas about what your administrator wants and needs to know about your operation, and you will also have ideas about what you want to communicate to him or her.

Goals for an annual report can be very general and relatively modest, or they can aim at achieving a specific communication goal. Your goals can also change from year to year. One year you may be content with using the report to describe and document the year's operation, and the next year you may wish to make readers aware of the many ways the library contributes to the mission of the organization. The more specific you can be about your goals, the easier it will be to determine what information you need and how best to collect and present it.

UNDERSTANDING YOUR AUDIENCE

The purposes that you have articulated for writing an annual report will usually define at least one audience. In fact, most writers start out thinking about their annual reports in terms of an audience: writing an annual report to your director, for example, or to the community at large. By defining what you wish to accomplish through annual reporting, you focus your thinking on why you want to write an annual report, on what you hope to achieve by sending a summary of library activity to specific people. The definition of your audience, the people who will be reading the report, should arise naturally from your goals.

One Reader or a Larger Audience

Some reports are written for one person and others address a larger audience. Even those that are addressed to an individual may be passed along to other people. Many annual reports become quasi-public documents, and some actually are public documents, so you will need to be sure about who will read your report and how it will be used. This decision may not be entirely within your control, depending instead on your administrator's preferences and your institution's practices.

For example, suppose that you have just completed your first year as the director of a special library in a law firm. When you were hired by the senior partner to whom you report, he or she made it clear that you were to address specific issues and problems of information service in the library, and now you wish to write an annual report, describing the progress made so far and outlining your plans for next year. For an assessment of this kind, you will require a level of confidentiality appropriate to the sensitive managerial information you are reporting. You are also aware that, historically, the library's annual report has been a one-page memo that served both informational and public relations purposes, and that it was sent to all the partners, who then shared it with others. The obvious solution here is two "annual reports," each with a different purpose: one memo report to the senior partner, assessing the year's progress and presenting plans for next year, and a public report to make the library visible throughout the firm.

Most annual reports are not considered confidential documents. You should assume that, in addition to the readers you have in mind when you write the report, others may read it, even if the only unanticipated reader is the next person who holds your job. Our recommendation is to use the formal annual report for information of record. If you would like to use the year's end as an occasion to discuss less public matters, do so in a memo or another report reviewing the year's progress or addressing the issues you have in mind.

Because of the quasi-public or outright public nature of annual reports and their potential use by various audiences, many institutions prefer that annual reports have a positive or neutral tone, saving the analysis and discussion of problems for other memos or reports. As a writer of an annual report, you should determine what the practice and expectation is in your department and in your institution.

Understanding Your Readers' Perspectives

If your primary audience is your administrator, you can use your knowledge of that person's perspective to help you determine how you will select and present information. For example, if you know from experience that your administrator reads executive summaries of long reports carefully and then skims the report, you will want to present all your main points in the initial summary.

When you are writing for many readers, you will have to rely on general characteristics of your audience to guide the shape of your report. Even though generalizing about a large group of people is difficult, you may be able to come up with some ideas about what would interest your audience. For example, an annual report sent from Special Collections to the Friends of the Library might highlight recent acquisitions and the Friends' activities. Directors of public libraries will need to make assumptions about what will interest their communities when they prepare their annual reports. They may decide that their audience will not be fully comfortable with library jargon, including even such common terms as *reference* and *circulation*, and so they may make an effort to use less specialized vocabulary.

DEVELOPING YOUR APPROACH TO ANNUAL REPORTING

When you have identified your goals for annual reporting and the audience you will be reaching, you can plan your approach to reporting. At this stage in the process, you will want to decide several things: how many reports to write, the general characteristics of these reports, and perhaps some supplemental ways of achieving your reporting goals.

How Many Annual Reports to Write

Your answer to the question of how many annual reports to write depends entirely on what you wish to achieve through reporting and whether you think that you can accomplish everything in one document. Several examples may illustrate the decisions involved here.

Suppose that you are a director of a hospital library in an urban medical center, affiliated with a university. Your library is a branch of the university's medical library, twenty miles away. You report to the director of the Medical Library, but you also work closely with the director of Medical Education at the hospital. Instead of sending the same report to these two people, you might want to create two reports, each tailored for a different purpose. If you decide to write a one-page summary of library activities for the director of Medical Education, you would focus that report on demonstrating the importance of the library's information service to patient care and medical education. Then, you might want to write a more detailed report about the library's activities to the director of the medical school library.

As another example, the head of Adult Services for a large public library system might have annual reporting goals that called for separate approaches. For discussion's sake, assume that you are the head, and, as an objective for this year, you want to focus on the systemwide process for the selection of books. You may wish to provide extensive analysis of annual selection data in an annual report to the director as an addendum to the standard annual report data that he or she requests for compiling that library's public annual report. In addition, you might decide that you wish to use annual reporting time as an occasion to publicize the adult services programs and accomplishments throughout the system. You might develop a short, breezy, newsletter-style annual report to circulate to all branches, designed to share information, promote a sense of accomplishment, and generate new enthusiasm.

As a third example, suppose you are the head of reference in an academic library, reporting to the associate director for Public Services. Your annual report will serve as the primary source of information about reference services during the past year. You know that the associate director will read it carefully and will use it for preparing his or her report. You also know that the three associate directors share reports from their departments with each other and that the dean of libraries occasionally asks to read departmental reports. You also wish to use annual reporting time as an opportunity to assess the year's activity and block out plans for next year.

After collecting your data and analyzing it, you come to conclusions about the progress you have made this year, the problems that still need to be addressed, and the goals that you wish to achieve next year. You decide to include among the sections in your annual report these three sections:

▲ *Goals for the Completed Year.* In this section, you provide a short analysis of your progress toward objectives, noting briefly what was not accomplished and why.

▲ *Issues Facing the Department.* Here you decide to list (briefly) the significant management issues that you feel remain unsolved.

▲ *Goals for the Upcoming Year.* Here you list (briefly) the areas you wish to concentrate on during the next year.

When you have written your draft, you assess the tone and content in light of the use that your administrators will make of the document. You may feel that you wish to go into more detailed analysis of several goals, discussing the obstacles that will be encountered, so you decide either to discuss that goal face to face with the associate director or to put it in a follow-up memo.

As a final example, let's assume that you are the head of the Rare Books department in a university library that has a very active program. The department collects at a brisk rate, and you and your staff are active among groups in your geographical area that are interested in antiquarian books. The Rare Books department sponsors lectures and fellowships, and it also operates a consulting service for other institutions about the collection, preservation, and use of rare books and manuscripts. The university library also has a very active Friends Group that works primarily with the rare books and special collections program. When it is time to write an annual report, you may elect to produce an impressive catalog report, highlighting new acquisitions, outstanding lectures, and consulting activities.

The report may also present a complete statistical review of financial data, acquisitions, and services. Since you feel you need to report a wide variety of activities and services to many different types of bibliophiles, you may decide to include all significant information about the year's activities in the one booklet, finding ways to highlight what may be of interest to different groups. In this way, you can avoid the expense of separate reports to the Friends, to the library director, and to the general community of bibliophiles, while still communicating effectively to groups with varying interests. Diverse goals are not easy to accommodate effectively in one production, but careful planning can produce effective results.

Characteristics of Your Annual Report

As you begin to develop your material, you will want to make some preliminary decisions about the way you want your report to look. You can always change your mind, but these considerations have an effect on how you select, organize, and phrase your material.

Length

Too frequently, the length of an annual report is determined by how much the writer ends up saying in the rough draft. If you wish to take a more planned approach to length, and especially if you are concerned about motivating people to *read* the report, you may wish to make some preliminary choices about ideal length for your purposes, taking into account your preliminary assessment of what you will have to cover to achieve your goals. Your tentative choice might include the options below:

1 page (short)
2–4 pages (moderate)
5–9 pages (long)
10 pages and more (tomelike)

Making this choice at the beginning, based on what length you feel will be most effective, can encourage you to discover creative ways to achieve your goals within that constraint. For example, suppose you decide that a one-page summary of statistical and service highlights is the only way to ensure that the busy vice president for Marketing will even look at the report from the Research Library; however, you are uncomfortable about writing an annual report and omitting detailed information about the operation of the library during the year. To solve this problem, you might prepare a one-page summary of highlights and conclusions, supplemented by a page or two of tables and graphics as attachments. You may also decide to enlist the help of the corporation's production department to design a visually appealing report.

By using summaries, highlights, tables, and charts, you may find that you can convey a quantity of information compactly and effectively.

Tone and Style

Important here is the extent of your commitment to clear, jargon-free prose. First drafts of annual reports frequently contain jargon and complex constructions that cry out to be rephrased in plain English. You should use your assessment of your audience to decide on levels of diction, complexity, and specialized vocabulary, but *all* readers will appreciate readable, straightforward prose.

Distribution

Deciding who will receive copies is important at this stage, not only because you need to know who will be reading the report in order to develop, organize, and phrase your material, but also because the number of copies you need many influence decisions about the length and type of production.

Design and Production Decisions

Annual reports, as finished products, range all the way from ordinary, typed reports in memo format to professionally printed brochures or booklets. At this stage in the writing process, you will want to decide tentatively what you want the report to look like and to reconcile these decisions with the available equipment, staff, and money. A fundamental choice is whether you want your report to have an "office" or a "printed/published" look. An "office look" resembles the style used in memos and reports, with some attention to what we are calling keyboard graphics and layout. A "printed/published" look can include any combination of design features generally associated with production and public relations, such as paper in a variety of colors, varying sizes of type, graphics, and illustrations, justified text or text in columns, use of photographs, or use of ink in colors other than black. You can see from this list that the capabilities of microcomputer programs for word processing and graphics, and sophisticated copying machines make various parts of the "printed/published" look possible. You have so many choices now that the most sensible strategy is to decide what you would like the report to look like and then to assess the resources for production available to you. Chapter 4 summarizes some of the choices you may wish to consider.

DEVELOPING THE CONTENT OF
YOUR ANNUAL REPORT

In writing an annual report, you will want to leave yourself plenty of time to develop your material, to think through what you want to say about the year's activities. You will undoubtedly start with your source material: statistics collected by you or the people who report to you; annual reports from people who report to you; filing cabinets full of monthly reports, special reports, and memos on significant activities; printouts with financial information; statistics from other libraries; and perhaps even a sample or two of annual reports that you admire. Many professionals who write annual reports year after year keep "tickle files" of facts, ideas, or important information for use at annual reporting time. The most basic of these systems consists of notes on the calendar. Another easy way to accomplish the same thing is to jot down notes to yourself and collect them in a file folder. Other people routinely use their monthly reports to record issues or to keep track of the kinds of information that they will need at annual report time. Once you have standardized your annual report format and you know what information you will need, you can set up systems to collect that information during the year and minimize the time you need to spend gathering your material.

For example, if, as an academic librarian, you knew that you would like to append to your annual report a list of faculty for whom you have taught classes in bibliographic instruction, you might choose to record all the pertinent information on the calendar entries for appointments during the year. Alternatively, you might devise a short form for yourself to provide a structure for recording all the information you will need. Organizing systems so that data is collected regularly and is conveniently available at the end of the year can save much more time than you spend setting them up; however, you want to be sure that the time and trouble involved in keeping the records does not outweigh the benefits of having the information.

Once you have gathered your source material, your task is to review, analyze, select, and summarize the data that you wish to include, and to develop the themes, ideas, and conclusions that you will use to accompany your statistics. The extent to which you use this step to analyze past activity depends on you, your administrator, and your goals in reporting. Some annual reports are occasions for thorough analysis, and others are vehicles for summarizing the facts and drawing attention to highlights. The more analytical your approach, the more time and care you will need to take in developing your ideas.

Failure to take sufficient time to think through what you want to say about the year can be obvious in your final report. The most common sign is a vague, weak, and virtually meaningless statement. "This has been a busy year" is probably the most frequently used phrase in annual reports, but does it say much? Does it mean busier than last year? More patrons? More circulation? More programs? Would you ever expect to see the opposite in a report: "We've really not been very busy around here this year"?

Often a general statement, like "It was a busy year," is the starting point for a more concrete thought that will take shape as you work with it: Are you busier than last year? In what ways? Why? What does it mean? What do you want to say about it? The specific facts and ideas underlying "It was a busy year" might develop into any of the hypothetical forms below, as well as an infinite variety of other possibilities.

Possibility One:
"The total number of service transactions increased 20 percent last year, making itself felt in virtually every department from interlibrary loan to stacks maintenance."

Possibility Two:
"The temporary freeze on hiring in effect this year reduced our staff by one professional, thus producing a net increase in the workload of the entire staff."

Possibility Three:
"Both the number of high school students studying in the library and the number of reference questions they asked doubled this year, a result, we speculate, of the inauguration of the new 'Back to Basics' curriculum in the city's high schools."

Many specific thoughts or ideas have their beginnings in generalities. Unnecessary generalities in finished prose usually mean that the writer has prematurely stopped the development of his or her thought.

ORGANIZING YOUR ANNUAL REPORT

Throughout this book, we have urged you to think of the task of organizing your writing as a conceptual one, considering the relationship of ideas to each other, and as a visual one, considering how the graphic presentation and layout on the page contribute to meaning and comprehension. Final decisions on layout do not have to be made until directions are given to the typist, but many writers find it useful to think about layout when they are developing the organizational structure of their writing. Thinking about headings in advance, for example, makes more explicit the organizational structure that the reader will see and often helps you, as writer, keep the overall picture in mind. As part of your organizational planning, you can consider graphics and spacing when you decide whether to display information in a table in the text or in a list introduced by a colon. Writers vary in the thoroughness with which they develop their organizational structure before they begin drafting, and even those who outline rigorously, tinker with organizational structure during writing and revising. In fact, organizing your ideas is a task that should continue until the time you decide that your document is finished.

Choosing Main Sections and Main Section Headings

Annual reports invariably cover a number of major topics. Some report writers will elect to cover these in one flowing narrative, but most will divide their report into main sections. Even those who do not use formal markers for sections will organize the flow of their ideas and will mark that organization with topic sentences, transitional phrases, and all the traditional narrative tools for orienting the reader. For some situations, the annual report as essay is effective, and librarians who are persuasive and eloquent writers may choose to use flowing, formal prose. If it works, it is effective.

Most writers, however, will want to divide their report into main sections and decide how to mark those sections for the reader. Selecting these sections is a major organizational decision because it affects the focus, emphasis, and detail of the discussion. Since these sections are usually preceded by headings, a quick look at the headings should give the reader an overview of what the report covers. That overview in itself can be an important part of the message of the report.

No paradigms can determine the most effective sections and their headings for a specific report. But in the discussion below, we will highlight several major patterns of subject organization that are frequently used in annual reports. We will discuss headings as a descriptive shorthand for the content of each section. The discussion is intended to stimulate thinking about the division of annual library activities into descriptive sections and about the effect of these choices on the organization and content of the report. You, as writer, will develop the organizational structure that best suits your goals, your readers, and your institution.

In selecting content and headings for main sections, you have a number of choices: headings corresponding to administrative units; topical or activity headings; genre headings; and mainpoint headings. Or you can forgo all headings and rely on topic sentences to alert your reader to the subject under discussion. You have the same range of choices with subheadings as with main-section headings. It is possible to mix types of headings and subheadings, as long as the logical organization of the whole report remains coherent.

The wording of headings is more than cosmetic. Not only does it alert the reader to the organizational structure, but it often defines the focus of the section. Parallelism in content and in phrasing is important for consistent logic and for style.

Administrative or Organizational Headings

A common organizational pattern uses headings that reflect the library's administrative or departmental organization. Each section reports on a specific administrative or activity. The annual report of a medical school library might have the following structure of main headings:

    I. Administration
        A. Financial summary
        B. Personnel summary
        C. Administrative summary
    II. User Services
        A. Information Service
        B. Database Searching
        C. Interlibrary Loan
   III. Technical Services
        A. Acquisitions
        B. Cataloging
        C. Serials

Alternatively, each unit, such as Acquisitions, could become a main section, reflecting the library's organizational chart less accurately, but creating a simpler structure for the sections. Under Administration, the subheadings might reflect topics of importance, rather than the units within Administration. This scheme of organization focuses your report on each unit and allows full development of each unit's activities. Statistical information may be treated under each unit. Alternatively, a section labeled

"Statistical Summary" could bring together all statistics, either at the beginning or the end of the report.

Departmental reports that are organized around administrative units use those units as section headings. The disadvantages of organizing by departmental or unit structure include the need to focus on all units individually, the inevitable length of such a report, the fact that much of the information may already be in other reports issued by staff in the unit, and the inherent difficulty of achieving an integrated overview of library activity. If you use the departmental model of organization, you may wish to combine it with other techniques that stress overall library activity and issues, such as including a section highlighting facts and issues or using a section of statistical summaries. You can also use the administrative section for issues of general importance.

Topical Headings

A second, and less obviously structured, organizational model groups your information by topical subject headings that you select. These subject headings can be descriptive of the contents, like "Use of the Library." They can also be terms that are synonymous with library departments, such as "Information Services." Departmental and unit reports are frequently organized around topical headings that represent the main activities or concerns of the unit. The topics that you select determine the focus for your report. This flexibility can be an advantage; it can also mean that the report does not follow the same pattern year after year. An annual report outline, using topical headings, is presented below:

    I. Summary of Library Activity
    II. Financial Summary
   III. Use of the Library
   IV. Library Collection
    V. Library Services
   VI. Library Programs
  VII. Staffing

Genre Headings

Genre headings describe the type of information rather than the specific content. "Highlights of the Year's Activity" is a genre heading. When you use genre headings for main sections, the subheadings in each category frequently include topical headings. An example of an outline using genre headings for the main sections and a mixture for subheadings is presented below:

    I. Highlights of the Year
   II. Review of Objectives
  III. Review of the Year's Operations
        A. Library Collection
        B. Information Services
        C. Document Delivery Services
        D. Audiovisual Services
        E. Technical Services
   IV. Statistical Summary of Operations
    V. Administrative Review
        A. Summary
        B. Assessment of Needs for Library Services
        C. New Services
        D. Policy Changes
        E. Changes in Operations
        F. Staffing Changes
   VI. Budgetary Review
        A. Summary
        B. Budget and Expenditures
        C. Grant Funding
        D. Revenues: Users
        E. Revenues: Departmental Charge Backs
  VII. Staff Development
 VIII. Cooperative Services and Activities
   IX. Objectives for the Upcoming Year

Note that genre headings, illustrated above, can be adapted for reports covering the entire library or for reports covering specific departments or activities.

"Headline" Headings

Headings that resemble titles or headlines can be used effectively in annual reports. This approach is found frequently in reports aimed at the public, but we have seen creative uses of the technique in all types of annual reports. Its chief aim is to attract the reader's attention. "Headline" headings are topical headings that resemble newspaper headlines. Some examples appear below:

What Happened in Our Library Last Year?
Do You Know What Goes on in Your Library?
Library Service: The Best Bargain in Town
Book Circulation Rises Dramatically
Library Resources Meet Community Needs
Who Uses Our Library?
Films, Films, Films

Topic Sentences instead of Headings

Establishing an organizational pattern by topic sentences depends on dividing your content by subject focus, without using headings. In this model, the first sentence of the paragraph is a clear, topic sentence that alerts the reader to the subject of the paragraph. Each paragraph becomes a new subject, without section headings to tie them together. Graphic techniques, like capitalizing the first few words, italicizing the main sentence, or using small illustrations, can give the reader clues about subject matter. This narrative approach, even when clearly divided by short, subject-oriented paragraphs, offers the reader minimal guidance about the organization of the report.

None of these patterns should be considered mutually exclusive. The creative writer will "carve up" his or her subject in the way that best suits the report's purpose and readers. The models and the specific headings presented here are reminders of the variety of choices you have.

DESIGNING AND PRODUCING AN ANNUAL REPORT

The design and production techniques you use for your annual report will depend on the way you wish it to look, on the staff and equipment you have within the library, and on your resources to pay for outside production. As part of planning your approach, you have selected the look you want for your annual report: an office look or a printed/published look. Within the printed/published category, annual reports can resemble flyers, newsletters, pamphlets, broadsides, or booklets. Chapter 4 discusses a wide range of design and production alternatives.

TEST YOUR SKILLS

Figure 39 presents you with an opportunity to test your skills by writing a short annual report. Discussion of this exercise appears on page 352 of the appendix, section K.

CHECKLIST FOR WRITING ANNUAL REPORTS

Figure 40 is a checklist that summarizes the process for writing annual reports. It can be used as a review of the chapter or as a guide when writing annual reports.

Assume that you, as head of Public Relations in a public library system, are in charge of designing and writing the library's one-page annual report that will be mailed to everyone in the county. You have interviewed the director of the library and the associate director of User Services. Notes from each interview are summarized below. Feel free to invent details and statistics if what you need is not provided.

The report will be printed, front and back, on one sheet of paper, 8½ by 11 inches, and it will be folded in thirds to form a brochure. For simplicity, let's assume that the three outside panels of the brochure (one side of the single sheet of paper) will contain the mailing address and the library logo, the hours of service for all the libraries, and the list of trustees, county officials, and library administrative staff. That leaves one side of the sheet for the report itself.

Information from the Interview with Director

Goals for the annual report:

▲ To provide the basic facts of library operation
▲ To create a positive impression of the library as a busy, friendly agency that provides many kinds of services to many kinds of people
▲ To show the wide variety of services and resources available
▲ To make people feel they get a good bargain for their library tax dollars

Audience: One pamphlet will be mailed to every household and business that pays taxes. Copies will be distributed to city agencies and not-for-profit organizations and institutions.

Statistics from the Director's Office

County population		272,473
Library Income:		$2,049,042
County Appropriation	$1,627,697	
State Grants	174,754	
Federal Grants	47,734	
Endowment (Income)	23,070	
Miscellaneous	85,322	
Fund Balance	90,465	
	$2,049,042	
Library Expenses:		$2,049,042
Personnel	$1,224,827	
Materials	437,729	
Operations	386,486	
	$2,049,042	

Figure 39. **Test Your Skills: Writing an Annual Report**

Visits to the Library	573,742
New Registrations	23,410
Reference Questions Answered	241,956
Library Exhibits	83
Story Hour Attendance	2,406
Summer Reading Club Membership	3,902
Childrens' Program Attendance (excluding Story Hours and Summer Reading Club)	917
Film Program Attendance: Young Adult Series	509
Film Program Attendance: Adult Series	1,516
Lectures and Concerts Sponsored	27
Voters Registered	12,104
Tax Forms Distributed	423
Interlibrary Loans Obtained for Our Users	2,102
Interlibrary Loans Lent to Other Libraries	1,989
Circulation: Total	980,902
Circulation: Main Library	342,960
Circulation: Branches:	637,942
Elm Street	159,485
Locust Street	105,691
Oak Street	127,588
Poplar Street	108,450
Aspen Street	136,728
In-House Utilization of Library Materials	624,802
New Acquisitions, Systemwide (Books)	21,756
Total Collection (Books)	472,961

Notes from Your Interview with the Associate Director of User Services

▲ Big emphasis on use of nonprint materials this year

▲ Added significantly to collections of video cassettes, audio cassettes, records, and films

▲ Started a compact disc collection

▲ Publicized our services for visually impaired citizens, including large print and "talking books"

▲ Maintained roster of volunteer readers for the blind and provided referral services

▲ Lending program for special equipment very popular; equipment included personal computers, video players, and cameras

▲ Started "Welcome to the World of Reading" collection of high-interest books for adults who have just learned to read

▲ Continued high use of popular paperback collection

▲ Started "Great Romances" discussion group, reading and talking about love stories from literature and popular fiction; big success

▲ Sponsored seminars on fashionable dressing on a budget, health and beauty tips, controlling stress, financial management, and other popular topics

▲ Continued popular travelogue film and lecture series

▲ Wide range of children's programming, including storytelling fest, puppet shows, morning and bedtime story hours, summer reading club, and craft activities

▲ Emphasized information resources and the library as a place to find out what you need to know

▲ Special displays on quilting, the Constitution, and Black History Week

▲ Heavy use of auditorium and meeting rooms for community meetings

▲ Friends of the Library sponsored annual used book sale and donated the proceeds for refurbishing the local history room

▲ Increased user services staff by three professional positions and two support staff positions

▲ Held staff training sessions for online circulation system

▲ Sponsored successful seminar (also sponsored by Strong and Strong, business consultants) on applying consumer-oriented service attitudes and practices to public services

A discussion of this exercise appears in Section K, page 352, of the appendix.

Figure 39—**Continued**

Use the checklist below to review the process for writing annual reports.
1. Define your purposes for annual reporting.
   ▲ Do you plan to use the annual report as a management tool for yourself and your staff? Will your administrator use the report for management purposes? If so, consider the following questions.
     What data about library operation are currently collected by you and your staff? How are the statistics used? Do you need additional data?
     What kind of analysis do you want to make routinely at the end of each year? Comparisons with last year? Percent increases or decreases? Trends?
     Do you want to define measures of activity and performance that will serve as benchmarks from year to year and aid in analysis? What will these be?
     Do you want to include evaluating and planning as part of annual report activity, either formally or informally?

Figure 40. **Writing Annual Reports: A Checklist**

▲ Will your report serve as the historical record of the year's activity?

What statistics and other facts are needed for the permanent record of department or library activity?

What statistics are needed for the national reporting of data?

Will your report provide information for a report that your administrator will prepare? If so, what would he or she like for that report?

To what extent will your administrator expect you to use the annual report as an occasion for analysis? Evaluation? Identification of problems? Planning?

How have annual reports have been used in your library or institution in the past, especially by the other departments that report to your administrator?

▲ To what extent do you wish to use your annual report as a communication tool with your administrator?

What are your goals in communicating through your annual report? What "messages" do you wish to send?

How do you assess the effectiveness of your current report as a communication tool? What are the obstacles? How can they be overcome?

Has your report been read by your administrator in the past? If not, do you want to make that one of your goals?

Do you want to increase the interaction between you and your administrator over the content of your report?

▲ Do you wish to send an annual report to others, such as library users, community members, or other libraries?

To whom will you send the annual report? Users of the library? Members of the community? Other libraries?

What do you wish to achieve by sending a report to your target audience?

What information do you wish to communicate to each audience?

▲ What human relations goals can you formulate for your annual report?

2. Understand the perspective your readers will bring to your annual report.

▲ To whom have annual reports been addressed in the past?

▲ Who will be the primary reader(s) of your report, the person or people to whom you will address the report? Who else might read the report?

▲ Do the primary readers have expectations for annual reports? What have they received in the past from others or from you?

▲ What interests your primary readers about the library? What do you think they would like to read about in your annual report?

3. Plan your approach to annual reporting.

▲ Do you have several, and possibly conflicting, goals for your annual report?

▲ Will you try to accomplish everything in one report or will you write more than one report?

▲ What do you envision as the ideal length for your report?

▲ Do you plan to use attachments?

▲ Can you articulate the tone you wish to achieve in the report? Businesslike? Casual? Approachable? How would you describe the tone of reports that you admire?

▲ What "look" do you want for the report: an "office," "newsletter," or "published" look?

▲ What production resources do you have in your library: typewriter? photocopier with reduction and enlargement equipment? word processor? do-it-yourself graphics supplies and talent? desktop publishing software? (For more information on this topic, see chapter 4.)

▲ What production functions will be done outside the library and what will they cost: typesetting? layout? printing or duplicating? collating, fastening or binding? addressing? mailing?

4. Work out the facts, statistics, information, and conclusions that you want to present in your report.

▲ Have you used formal or informal "invention" techniques (see chapter 2) to gather ideas for what you want in your annual report?

What have past reports included?

What do reports that you admire include?

What kinds of information will support achieving your goals?

What content will your administrator or other readers expect?

What content will interest your readers?

What do you want to say about the year?

▲ Have you collected statistical data and other factual information?

▲ Have you analyzed factual data and speculated about its meaning?

What trends do you see?

What conclusions can you draw about the year?

What kinds of statistical analysis and comparisons would be useful?

Comparison with past years? With other libraries?

▲ Have you narrowed your list of ideas, bringing it into line with your goals, your readers, and the characteristics you have chosen for your report, including length, tone and style, and production?

5. Determine the sequence, level of development, and rough spatial layout of your ideas.

▲ Have you decided on the main sections of your report and chosen tentative section headings?

Will you use administrative headings, topical headings, genre headings, headline headings, or no headings at all?

What impact will your choice of main sections and headings have on the whole document? (Write the headings in outline form to help in this assessment.) Does the overall impact fit with your

Figure 40—**Continued**

goals? Is the logic clear to readers? Will it be of interest to them? Will you use any special graphic treatment for the headings of your main sections: capital letters, boldface printing, underlining, graphic symbols, ornate first letter, different typeface? (See chapter 4 on design.)

▲ Have you assessed whether you have a conflict between the ideal length that will best achieve your goals and the amount of information you wish to convey?

Is the length of the report critical to achieving your goals? Do you foresee a conflict between the amount and depth of information that you wish to present and the length that is ideal to achieving your goal?

What solutions will you pursue to resolve this classic problem in a way that is consistent with your goals? Introductory summary of important information? One-page report with detailed attachments? Short report with attachments? Selective subject coverage?

Can you narrow down the material that you will cover in the report by focusing on what the readers want, or expect, to learn from it?

What do *you* want the readers to know? If they will not have intrinsic interest in this information, and if this information is creating a lengthy report, what solutions do you see? Create an interest in the information? Summarize it and put details in attachments? Other solutions?

▲ Have you assessed the importance to your goals of a report that can be quickly understood?

Is ease of reading an important characteristic for your report?

If so, what techniques will you use to ensure that the report can be quickly read and is easy to comprehend: headings and subheadings; short paragraphs; layout with generous spacing; outline form, indentions, or graphics to highlight and indicate relative importance of ideas; short sentences; everyday vocabulary (no library jargon)?

▲ In view of your decisions (above), have you decided on the content, organization, and method of presentation of the main sections?

What will each main section contain and how will it be organized?

Will you use subheadings? What kind and what wording?

Will you use narrative form, outline form, or a combination of both?

Will you use variations on layout, other than standard paragraphing? If so, what will they be?

Will you use "graphic" effects: typewriter/word processor graphics? newsletter graphics? published graphics?

▲ Have you planned and designed your attachments?

What information will you put in your attachments?

Which of the following forms will you use for the information in your attachments: copies or summaries of other reports; narrative summaries or discussions of issues; tables; bar charts; pie charts; line graphs; other statistical analyses; copies of published articles? (Chapter 13 provides information on using charts and tables.)

6. Write a draft of your report, following your organizational plan.
7. Revise your report for effectiveness.
   ▲ Have you predicted the reactions of your readers and pinpointed areas for revision if you anticipate any discrepancy between their reactions and your goals?
     Will your readers read the report?
     Will they react in a way that is consistent with your goals?
     What obstacles do you see to effective communication with your reader? What ways do you see of overcoming these obstacles?
   ▲ Have you assessed your report systematically, looking for problems of effectiveness, tone and personality, organizational structure, composition of sentences, and use of words? Look for problem area or trouble spots, analyze the difficulty, develop alternative solutions, and choose the best one. Chapter 3 provides checklists that can help with these activities.)
8. Edit your annual report for correctness.
   ▲ Have you reviewed your draft for problems of grammar, usage, and punctuation?
   ▲ Have you used your knowledge of the kinds of mistakes you make to help you find trouble spots? (Chapter 3 provides assistance in identifying and solving these problems.)
   ▲ Have you checked all matters of fact, including
     dates?   raw numbers and computations?
     facts?   bibliographic citations?
     titles?   proper nouns, especially names?
     spelling?
   ▲ Have you proofread carefully to ensure accuracy? Chapter 3 provides a checklist for this activity.)
9. Produce the final copy of your annual report.
   ▲ Have you considered the elements of "design" to help you in achieving your goals?
   ▲ Have you marked the layout for the final copy, noting any special keyboard graphic effects, special spacing, and indentions?
   ▲ If someone is assisting you by preparing the final copy, have you communicated your instructions clearly, including spacing, margins, layout, and special graphic effects?
   ▲ Have you arranged to review a typed draft before the final draft is prepared?
   ▲ After receiving the final copy, have you proofread carefully, for typographical errors and other difficulties that might have slipped in?
   ▲ Is the final copy neat and professional looking?

Figure 40—**Continued**

Chapter 12

MISCELLANEOUS FORMATS

CHAPTER OUTLINE

INFORMATIONAL REPORTS
Purposes for Informational Reports
Understanding Your Reader's Perspective
Developing Content and Organizing Informational Reports

PROPOSALS

AGENDAS AND MINUTES
Agendas
Minutes

ABSTRACTS AND SUMMARIES
Organization of Summaries
Techniques for Writing Summaries

JOB DESCRIPTIONS

RESUMES
Content of Resumes
Organization of Resumes
Assessing Your Resume from Your Reader's Perspective
Writing the Letter of Application

In libraries, as in other organizations, a number of special writing formats are used for specific purposes. Among the most common are informational reports, internal proposals, agendas and minutes, abstracts and executive summaries, job descriptions, and resumes. We will consider each one separately, discussing issues unique to that document. Because of the number of documents involved, we will depart from our usual practice of summarizing the writing process for each format and refer readers who want a step-by-step summary to the process for writing memos in chapter 5. That process, along with the discussions and guidelines provided in this chapter, should provide sufficient direction for these special formats.

INFORMATIONAL REPORTS

Reports, as their name implies, are documents that present information on a specific subject. Reports can be classified according to the writer's purpose: (1) to present information, (2) to present information and interpretation or analysis, or (3) to make recommendations based on the analysis of information. In this section, we will consider reports whose primary purpose is to present information. Chapter 9 focuses on analytical reports, or reports whose primary purpose is to provide interpretation and recommendations.

Purposes for Informational Reports

The impetus for writing an informational report can come either from the writer or from someone other than the writer, usually the administrator to whom the librarian reports. When someone asks you to gather information, the written document in which you respond to that request is an informational report.

Before beginning to gather your information, you will want to know from the requestor as much as possible about how he or she intends to use the information, so you can make sound judgments about what to include. This process can be considered a reference interview, and the request for an informational report is basically an expanded reference request. For an informational report, you will generally select from a variety of facts the information that will meet the requestor's specific need and organize it in a way that responds to what the requestor asked. The tailoring of information to the exact need of the requestor and the organizing of data in a format that makes the data accessible may go beyond the usual response to reference requests; however, this reporting approach is sometimes used by reference librarians in special libraries and in other libraries that provide in-depth reference service for clients.

Suppose that you are the head of the Information and Media Services department of a corporation that has recently expanded and reorganized its international operations. The vice president for Communications, to whom you report, has asked you to get him "all you can find" about international standards for color television. Using your reference interviewing skills, you learn that education, training, and development (ETD) activities for all operations, including those in fourteen foreign countries, have been centralized under the administration of the headquarters office and your administrator. He is planning to develop a series of training videotapes to be used in any corporate office, and he expects to establish a tape library in every national corporate headquarters. These offices would then supply tapes to their field operations. As you talk with him, you realize that although he expects these videotapes to be produced at first in the United

States, he is hoping that the foreign offices will eventually participate in making tapes for their own use and for sharing.

Based on your discussion with him, you write the informational report in figure 41.

You, as writer, can also initiate informational reports when you wish to provide others with information. You will want to understand your own purposes in sending the information, being particularly alert to what you are expecting the reader to do with the information.

Understanding Your Reader's Perspective

If someone else requested the report from you, that person's purpose in asking for the information shapes your report. In addition to knowing why the person needs the information and what he or she wants to do with it, you will need to take into account that person's general concerns so you can determine what information to include. The report in figure 41, for example, includes information on converting videotapes that goes beyond the initial request. This hypothetical writer chose to include brief information on this subject because she had concluded that her administrator was really interested in how countries might share videotapes. She directed him to further information about conversion because she anticipated that his concerns would lead him to want to investigate the most cost-effective alternatives for sharing.

When you initiate informational reports on your own, you will want to give your reader's perspective the same analysis that you would for any memo or report. Since your reader did not request the report himself or herself, you will want to consider why he or she should be interested in the information. You will also want to find a way to make that reason clear in your opening sentences. Readers may be annoyed if they receive an informational report, especially a lengthy one, and do not know why they received it or what they are expected to do with it.

Developing Content and Organizing Informational Reports

Developing the content of your report consists of gathering information and then choosing what is relevant, based on the needs of the person requesting the report. If you are the initiator, your purpose in sending the report and the perspective of your reader will help you select the appropriate information. Chapter 2 provides more detail on gathering information.

The topic of the report and the needs of the reader of the report will dictate the organizational approach. The combination of the subject line of the memo and the opening statements should make clear the subject of the report and its purpose. Headings and subheadings are useful in informational reports, as in memos, to orient the reader to the subject under discussion.

DATE: September 21, 1989

TO: Walter Knowles,
             Vice President for Communications

FROM: Ellen Morton,
             Director, Information and Media Services   *EM*

SUBJECT: International Television Standards

Color TV broadcasting signals around the world differ considerably. The three signals used in most of the
world are

    NTSC (used in U.S. and 18 other countries)
    PAL (48 countries)
    SECAM (26 countries)

I am attaching a list of the countries that use each
signal.

These signals differ in the lines per inch and in the
field frequency. NTSC uses 525 lines per inch and a
field frequency of 60 Hz, while PAL and SECAM use
625 lines per inch and 50 Hz. These signals are not
compatible with each other, so that American NTSC
televisions will not receive PAL or SECAM signals.
American video recorder/playback units and monitors will not play back PAL or SECAM prerecorded
videotapes, and tapes recorded on American equipment cannot be played on PAL or SECAM equipment.
Nor are PAL and SECAM interchangeable.

Figure 41. **Informational Report**

Multistandard televisions/monitors and video playback/recorders that alleviate the standards problem are available. A tri-standard television/monitor (110–220 v. and 50–60 cycle) can receive television signals on all three standards and, with a tri-standard video player, can play back videotapes produced in any country that has PAL, SECAM, or NTSC.

Recording videotapes must be done with equipment that is compatible with the country's scanning system. Those tapes can be played back on video equipment that receives the appropriate signal or on tri-standard equipment.

Two methods are thus available to exchange videotapes between countries using different signals. All offices can be equipped with tri-standard equipment. Alternatively, all tapes that are sent to countries with noncompatible systems can be converted to the appropriate system, either where they originate or where they are received. I have not investigated conversion methods extensively, but initial investigation shows that converting is done by video companies that primarily convert foreign tapes to their own signal. I also have not investigated the feasibility of purchasing conversion equipment and converting at corporate locations. A complicating factor with conversion is that it is impossible to tell from the tape itself what signal has been used to produce it. Unless the person who records the tape writes the signal on the tape label, you don't know that the tape is incompatible until you try to play it and it doesn't work.

Even then, you don't know which of the other two
systems was used.

I am attaching the names of several companies that
specialize in conversion, as well as the names of some
media consultants that might be able to advise on the
feasibility of in-house conversion.

If I can provide any further information, please let
me know.

Figure 41—**Continued**

PROPOSALS

In professional writing, the term *proposal* can refer to three types of documents with distinct characteristics. All have as their purpose "proposing" a course of action, but they are used in different circumstances.

In business and industry, companies prepare proposals outlining the services and equipment they can provide and what they will cost. Librarians are becoming familiar with proposals of this kind as they deal with vendors of library automation systems.

Proposals are also written by libraries to public and private funding agencies, in order to propose projects and request funds. Writing grant proposals is an extensive subject in itself, and many excellent books and articles are available. To get you started, several appear in the list of selected readings.

A proposal can also be written as an internal document, from a librarian to his or her administrator or to other people responsible for approving courses of action. Internal proposals suggest a course of action, and their primary purpose is to receive approval for the action indicated. Memos and analytical reports can also be used to propose projects or courses of action. Identifying your document as a proposal and using some of the standard elements in the proposal format can make your request more formal.

Proposals have much in common with both memos and analytical reports, and both chapter 5 and chapter 9 should be useful for writing proposals. Both proposals and reports that include recommendations suggest courses of action. Generally, a recommendation report focuses on selecting a course of action, based on an examination of the problem and the alternative solutions. Proposals concentrate on one course of action and provide enough details about it to allow the appropriate people to decide whether or not to proceed.

Internal proposals do not need to follow a rigid format, and can be tailored to the situation. Writers may want to consider the standard list of elements for proposals when they decide how to structure their document. Typical elements in a proposal are listed below:

Title
Summary
Statement of the Problem or Need
Goals and Objectives
Project or Action Plan (the specifics of the proposal)
Projected Impact
Costs
Methods of Evaluation

Figures 42 and 43 are examples of internal proposals.

DATE: April 7, 1988

TO: Alice Newton,
             Head, Adult Services

FROM: Irene Altman,   *Irene*
             Head, Reference, Main Library

SUBJECT: PROPOSAL: DO-IT-YOURSELF SEARCHING
             ROOM

SUMMARY:

   A do-it-yourself searching room providing microcomputer access to menu-driven databases will give
users a chance to learn to search databases themselves. Costs would be shared by the user and the library (from the Library Computer Literacy Endow-
ment). The searching room can be considered a pilot
project designed to test the feasibility of having
users perform searches. The project will also provide
information about the use and costs of various databases.

NEED FOR DO-IT-YOURSELF SEARCHING:

   Currently, librarians do searches for users. The
popularity of this service has increased so much that
there is often a week's wait for an appointment.
Users, especially those who have watched us do
searches for them, have repeatedly asked if they can
search for themselves. We also have had numerous requests for classes in how to search the more popular

Figure 42. **Proposal (1)**

consumer databases with microcomputers. Since more and more information sources are appearing in online format, the library needs to take an active role in teaching people the techniques for finding information in online sources.

GOALS:

We have the following goals for the do-it-yourself project.
1. To train users to do their own searching, with assistance when needed from a library staff member
2. To provide classes in searching online databases, with emphasis on search strategy
3. To test the interest in this service and obtain experience about the costs and staff time involved
4. To evaluate various software, hardware, technology (e.g., compact discs), and products for their suitability in a do-it-yourself area.

PROJECT PLAN:

1. After receiving approval, the reference committee will continue as a steering committee for the project.
2. Tentative plans include using two micros with modems and several compact disc players, depending on the reference tools selected.
3. The committee is now determining which databases should be available through which vendors for the trial project. The criteria are popu-

larity with the public, cost, and ease of do-it-
yourself access. We are also attempting to provide a variety of online sources for public use.
4. The classes in searching will be developed by
the reference committee. These are envisioned
as one-hour classes offered at various times.
5. Draft procedures for using the room are attached.

COSTS:

The costs for the project are summarized below.
Complete breakdowns in each category are attached.

Start-up costs (first year's operation)
Hardware	$8,000
Software	6,000
Database charges	10,000
Instructional and publicity materials	1,000
	$25,000

Ongoing yearly costs
Software	$10,000
Database charges	10,000
Instructional and publicity materials	1,000
	$21,000

REVENUES:

For the first year, we will charge patrons $3.00 per
search. We will then evaluate this fee in light of use
and costs.

*Figure 42—***Continued**

EVALUATION:

The project is intended to test the feasibility of providing the public with the opportunity to search databases themselves. A list of the issues the committee will be evaluating and the criteria they will use is attached.

DATE: October 14, 1989

TO: Ronald Loring, Hospital Administrator

FROM: John Adams,
             Director of Libraries

SUBJECT: THREE-YEAR PLAN TO UPGRADE THE
             LIBRARY'S JOURNAL COLLECTION

  I would like to propose a plan to upgrade the
library's journal holdings. This plan will enable us to
meet approximately 80% of the physicians' needs for
current medical information without the delay of interlibrary loan.

NEED: Last year, the library was able to fill from our
own collection only 24% of the requests for articles
by physicians. Obtaining the rest took an average of
eight days per article. The chiefs of all clinical departments feel that they need more immediate access to
essential clinical medical information and have written the attached letters requesting that the library
increase its holdings.

PLAN: We propose that the library subscribe to a core
list of clinical journals (see attached). This list was
developed by asking each clinical department to rank
its needs. The resulting list closely matches the standard core list of clinical titles used by many hospital
libraries.

COST: Purchase of the titles on the core list that we

Figure 43. **Proposal (2)**

currently do not have will cost approximately
$10,000. Phasing the subscriptions in over three
years results in the following projected costs for each
year:

	1989	1990	1991
Previous Year's Subscriptions	$19,213	$24,134	$29,547
10% increase for inflation	1,921	2,413	2,954
Increase for new subscriptions	3,000	3,000	3,000
TOTAL COST EACH YEAR	$24,134	$29,547	$35,501

Please let me know if you would like more documentation.

AGENDAS AND MINUTES

Librarians are familiar with agendas and minutes as standard tools for meetings. Groups of people meeting and working together can accomplish a great deal; however, in any meeting it is easy to waste time, get off the track, and fail to reach conclusions or to decide on the next step. In addition, much good thinking can be lost if no official "group memory" of what has been accomplished is solidified in a permanent record to inform others and to serve as the basis for future actions. The meeting's leaders and active participants can do much to ameliorate these persistent problems by providing effective direction and leadership for the group. References to books on making meetings work can be found in the list of selected readings. Effective use of both agendas and minutes also can aid meeting leaders and members in getting the most out of meetings.

Agendas

Agendas are formal lists of topics that will be covered in a meeting. Although many meetings are planned and conducted without agendas, agendas serve two important functions that can make meetings more productive. First, agendas are planning tools. Meetings work better when the leader has considered what needs to be accomplished in the meeting and then provides a level of structure appropriate to whatever he or she wishes to accomplish. Second, agendas are communication tools, letting the participants know enough about the meeting to allow them to come prepared to discuss the topics at hand.

Purpose of the Meeting

Before an agenda can be structured, the meeting's planner must decide what the purpose of the meeting is and what he or she wishes to accomplish. These purposes can be very broadly defined, such as providing an opportunity for participants to report on departmental activity, to make announcements, or to discuss issues of common concern. Meetings can also be focused on accomplishing a specific task, like developing a policy. In formulating your purpose for the meeting, you may find it helpful to consider what you would like as the meeting's result. A simple role-playing exercise can be quite useful. Imagine yourself coming out of the meeting with a tremendous sense of accomplishment. A trusted colleague happens to come into your office and says, "You certainly look pleased. What happened at your meeting?" You smile, letting all your satisfaction show, and say, "Well, the meeting was terrific! We. . . ." Then describe the best possible outcome. You might want to inject a little realism into your fantasy and choose a gratifying outcome that is within reach, given your situation.

This combination of fantasy and realism can help you clarify what you expect from the meeting. It should also give you a clue about the amount of preparation you will need if you are to achieve your goals. If your ideal scenario is in reality a very long shot, you will want to think carefully about what you can do to create a more promising climate for discussion in the meeting.

Once you know what you feel the meeting should accomplish, you can plan the agenda—the topics that you will consider—in the way that provides the best chances for achieving that purpose.

Planning the Meeting's Agenda

Planning the meeting's content and developing the written agenda are two activities that are almost impossible to separate. The agenda provides initial direction for the meeting, and it is the tool for communicating the topics of discussion to the participants, so it strongly influences the shape of the meeting. When you decide on what the agenda will say, you are, to a great extent, planning how the meeting will proceed. The detail provided in the agenda can affect the direction of the discussion. Agenda items that are phrased in a general way will tend to encourage general, wide-ranging discussion. Agenda items that are phrased specifically or that are subdivided into narrower topics will tend to be more focused.

The purpose of the meeting should be clear to the participants from the agenda. The meeting's purpose can be communicated in several ways. The title of the meeting or past practice often announces the purpose. A "purpose statement" can introduce the agenda, or a memo explaining the purpose of the meeting can accompany the agenda. And sometimes the agenda itself, with a clear phrasing of the task at hand, is sufficient to communicate the purpose of the meeting to the participants.

The agenda proper, at its simplest, is a list of topics that need to be covered. The topics for discussion at a meeting can range from very general to very specific, even when dealing with one subject. For that reason, the level of specificity of the topical description you select should match the issues you wish to discuss as precisely as possible.

Choosing the level of specificity for your agenda item is a substantive decision that can affect the direction and success of your meeting. Choosing a topic that is too broad can result in a diffuse discussion that may never fully center on what you want to accomplish. Choosing a topic that is too narrow can cut off ideas and possibilities that might be useful.

For example, the topic "library security" on an agenda could signal discussions of many issues, including personal safety in the library, issues of the theft of books and materials, and all the various subsets of topics that these subjects imply. If you wish to discuss the procedures the staff should follow when the alarm on the book-detection system sounds, or alternatives for improving exit control in the library, or ways to respond to situations that have the potential for threatening personal safety, these topics can be clearly and explicitly stated on the agenda.

On the other hand, using a very explicit topic can result in a focus that is too narrow. For example, an agenda item described as "Alarms for the basement exit doors" would provide an obvious and explicit focus for discussion and could serve your purposes excellently. If, however, the real purpose of your meeting is to discuss exit control and to determine if using alarms at the doors is the most feasible solution, then "Improving Exit Control for the Basement Doors" allows room for the discussion of other solutions, even if the discussion eventually focuses on alarms.

Open-ended topics are also useful, especially when you want the subjects of discussion to come from the meeting's participants. Topics such as "New Business," "Departmental Reports," or "Announcements" work best when the participants know about them in advance and are not under pressure to think of relevant items on the spot.

Agendas, at their simplest, are lists of topics. The listing approach can be amplified in several ways to provide more structure for the discussion and to give the participants additional information in advance. Again, the amount of detail you provide, either on the agenda or in a supplemental memo, directly affects how your meeting will proceed. Suppose that you, as chair of the Collection Development Committee, are scheduling a meeting to review the library's current procedures for disposing of withdrawn books and to discuss alternative approaches. The heading "Alternative Approaches for Disposing of Withdrawn Books" is very specific and describes the topic under discussion exactly, but it does not provide any direction about what kind of alternatives might be discussed. You, as chair, can always rely on yourself (or others) to come up with alternatives. On the other hand, listing in advance some of the possible ideas that are bound to surface can be helpful in focusing people's thinking. The danger of this approach is that additional ideas will not be encouraged or discussed, but you, as chair, can overcome this possible disadvantage by including open-ended items with your suggested subdivisions, by allowing some time for brainstorming and discussion of additional ideas during the meeting, and by using your subdivisions as thought-provoking ideas and not as a confining order for discussion. A subdivided agenda item for the example concerning disposing of withdrawn books might appear like this:

Alternatives for Disposing of Withdrawn Books

Distribution to other libraries
    through state library?
    through local cooperative?
    international distribution? how?
    by other means?
Book sale to library users
    periodic sale: yearly? monthly? weekly?

sale shelf or table available on ongoing basis?
other?
Selling to used-book dealers
Other methods?

The purpose of a subdivided agenda is to stimulate thinking about specific aspects of the agenda item, both in advance of the meeting and during the meeting itself. Its advantage is that it provides extra background and content without narrowing the focus too exclusively. A subdivided agenda is not intended as a straitjacket for discussion during the meeting. Its disadvantage is that it may be used as an order of business and stifle, rather than promote, discussion. Your choice about whether or not to use a subdivided agenda depends on your purposes, the meeting's participants, and your style as the meeting's leader.

An additional method for amplifying an agenda is to provide a supplementary memo providing background on the purpose for the meeting and explanation of the content of the agenda items. A simple list as an agenda can be included as part of the content of the memo, or the agenda can be attached as a separate sheet. Additional supplementary information can also be attached to the memo.

Minutes

While agendas describe the topical content of a proposed meeting and serve as a guide to discussion during the meeting, minutes report what actually did take place during the meeting. What we call minutes of a meeting are seldom verbatim accounts but are, instead, summaries written after the meeting, from notes taken at the time, sometimes supplemented by taped recordings of the actual meeting.

Functions of Minutes

Minutes serve as the official record of the meeting, and many groups determine at the outset that minutes of their meetings are part of their official operating procedure. Minutes document when and where the meeting took place, who attended, and what action was taken. Formal meetings, run by Robert's Rules of Order, require minutes. These minutes document what was done, and also document that these rules were followed. So, for example, if you adopt formal meeting procedures that include reading and approving of the previous meeting's minutes, your minutes indicate this. When meetings are less formal, minutes still perform a valuable service in documenting who attended, what was discussed, and what action was taken.

Whether minutes are formal or informal, they provide a permanent record of the meeting; they can inform others about what took place; and they can become a means of organizing the group's work. Minutes can re-cord actions taken; they can document assignments for the meeting; and they can serve as the "collective memory" for the participants, allowing them to pick up their work where they left it at the last meeting, despite any lapse of time that has occurred.

Theoretically, minutes function as a permanent record, a tool for com-munication, and an organizer of a group's workflow, but the extent to which they effectively do one or all of those jobs depends on how they are planned, written, and organized. Minutes are more useful when the plan-ners of the meeting, both chair and secretary, decide in advance how the minutes will be used and make conscious decisions about the kind of min-utes that will work best in a specific situation.

Responsibility for Minutes

It is useful to look at responsibility for the minutes in three ways: respon-sibility for planning the minutes, responsibility for taking notes and pre-paring the minutes, and responsibility for the accuracy of the record of the meeting. At first reading, the idea of responsibility for planning minutes may seem a bit unusual. It may seem that what happens in a meeting *hap-pens*, and the function of the secretary is just to write it down. The appar-ent simplicity of that task is deceiving. The kinds of information recorded, the level of detail, and the organization of the material not only affect the usefulness of the minutes but determine their character as well. With the passage of time and the fading of memory, what is written down about the meeting *becomes* the meeting. The minutes contain what the committee members read about their actions, what others read about the committee's activity, and what is preserved for the record. Yet, despite the fact that most chairs and participants devote tremendous energy to the actual meet-ing, the documentation of that meeting, the minutes, sometimes receives little meaningful attention. Much valuable thought can be wasted if it is not adequately and appropriately recorded in the minutes.

In most meetings, two people have official responsibility for the meet-ing's activities: the chair and the secretary. Traditionally, the chair con-ducts the meeting and the secretary records what takes place. If the written record is viewed as another version of the meeting, the permanent one, then both officers should work together to decide how the minutes will be used, what kinds of information they should contain, and how they should be organized. And both officers should also be involved in verifying the ac-curacy of the minutes before they are submitted to the group for approval.

Determining the Approach to the Minutes

The chair and the secretary should work together as a team to deter-mine the approach to minute-taking that is most appropriate for the partic-ular meeting. This task does not have to be difficult or time-consuming, and can usually be accomplished in a short conference before the meeting.

The structural elements of most minutes are standard and generally will not need to be reviewed, unless either person is approaching this responsibility for the first time. These standard elements are presented in the upcoming section on organization. The chair and the secretary will want to review how they wish the minutes to be used. Will the committee members use them to review the issues and their assignments for the next meeting? Will the minutes be sent to anyone other than the committee? What will these people need to know? What future uses are anticipated? Will next year's committee review the work of this year's group to set future courses of action? What decisions will be made? How important is it to have the rationale for decisions on official record?

Once the chair and the secretary reach a common understanding of the purposes the minutes will be expected to serve, they can agree on an appropriate level of documentation. For purposes of illustration, we can consider the level of detail describing a discussion as existing on a continuum from a verbatim record (the most specific) to a descriptive statement that a discussion took place (the most general). We might identify four points on that continuum as follows:

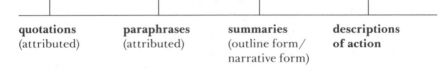

quotations	paraphrases	summaries	descriptions
(attributed)	(attributed)	(outline form/ narrative form)	of action

As an example, let's look at an excerpt from the hypothetical set of minutes concerning alternatives for disposing of withdrawn books. We will look at part of the section documenting the discussion of the advantages and disadvantages of book sales.

Verbatim Transcript. . . . "We used to have an annual book sale, years ago. After a while, we just stopped. The patrons liked them, as I recall." (J. Evans)

"Book sales are fine, but you have to remember that when you sell the books in the community, you're never quite rid of them. People forget they bought them and years later they show up back in the library, 'withdrawn' stamp or not." (H. Green)

"They're a lot of work, but people do like them. They're good P.R., too. I don't think Mrs. Jones will feel so bad about our taking out the eleventh copy of *Pride and Prejudice* if we offer to sell it to her." (Laughter) (P. Wright)

"A book sale might bring in a little bit of money, too. That would be nice." (L. Archer)

"Don't count on it! Not if you think about all the time that goes into it." (H. Green)

Paraphrased Discussion. . . . The possibility of having a book sale was explored. It was mentioned that a lot of work was involved. Linda suggested using volunteers. Pat brought up the P.R. value of a sale, but Harriet thought there might be negative consequences, too. Handling any complaints by taking the book back was suggested. Linda thought a sale might bring in a little revenue. Harriet was concerned that the books would find their way back to the library. At the end of the discussion, John suggested that we pursue the idea a little further, and Pat and Lance agreed to call other libraries and to rough out an outline of what a small summer sale might involve. Harriet volunteered to work on it with them.

Summary of Main Ideas: Outline Form. During the discussion of the possibility of having a book sale, the following points were raised:

Advantages:
A. Good public relations value
B. Possibility of some income
C. Project for the volunteers

Disadvantages:
A. Time-consuming
B. Books may be returned to the library someday
C. Calls attention to weeding

Action:
A. John will check to be sure we're authorized to sell books. (Completion date: next week)
B. Pat, Lance, and Harriet will investigate how successful sales at other libraries have been. They will also draw up a brief projection of how much time a sale would involve and what the revenue would be. (Completion date: next meeting)
C. We'll discuss having a sale at the next meeting.

Summary of Main Ideas: Narrative Form. The advantages and disadvantages of having a book sale were discussed. The advantages include disposing of the books in a way that has good public relations value, the possibility of some income, and providing a project for the volunteers. The disadvantages include the time it takes, the fact that some books may find their way back to the library, and the attention the sale brings to the weeding process.

The question of having a sale will be pursued further. John will check to be sure we're authorized to sell books and let Pat know next week. Pat, Lance, and Harriet will investigate how successful sales at other libraries have been. They will also draw up a brief projection of how much time a sale would involve and what the revenue would be and bring it to the next meeting.

Description of the Discussion and Action. The advantages and disadvantages of having a sale were discussed. John will check on whether or not a sale is possible. If it is, then Pat, Lance, and Harriet will investigate further by calling other libraries and by estimating what is involved. Further discussion was postponed until the next meeting.

The examples above illustrate different levels of detail that can be recorded in the minutes. A verbatim record of a meeting, provided by either taping the meeting and transcribing the tape or using the services of a court reporter, is appropriate when a complete record may be necessary for legal reasons or when the organizers of the meeting feel that a verbatim account would be useful. It is ethical and courteous to inform the participants in a meeting that a verbatim account is being taken.

Paraphrased discussion, although seen occasionally, is generally not considered useful in minutes. If a record of who said what is necessary, a verbatim one is usually preferred. Otherwise, minutes generally concentrate on what was done rather than what individuals said. Paraphrasing ideas, however, is a possibility, and so we include it among the alternatives.

When it may be useful to have a record of the main topics or ideas of a discussion, a summary, either in outline or narrative form, can be used, varying the level of detail to suit the purpose of the minutes. In some discussions, only the resulting action needs to be preserved in the official record. In other situations, it may be very useful to have a permanent account of the issues that were considered.

In all types of minutes, the action taken should be stated explicitly, as should any assignments for the next meeting.

Organizational Structure

The organizational form of minutes varies, depending on the purpose of the meeting and the level of formality. Common elements appear below.

Name of institution and group.

Date, time, and place of meeting.

Attendance. A list of those present and of those absent (frequently).

Presiding officer. Standard for formal minutes and useful for informal ones.

Approval of minutes of the last meeting. Standard for meetings following formal procedures.

Body of minutes. Minutes are usually organized following the meeting's agenda. Two types of organization are common: by topic and by what we are calling genre. Topical organization describes the substance of the topic discussed, such as "Disposing of Withdrawn Books." Organization by genre uses headings that frequently carry over from meeting to meeting. Such headings can be names of committees, names of departments or other administrative units, or headings such as "Reports," "Old Business," "New Business," "Announcements," and so forth. These headings are frequently subdivided by substantive topics.

Each item includes a summary of that item and of the action taken. Motions are given verbatim, with the name of the maker and the person seconding the motion. If future action is agreed upon or assigned, that is also stated.

Adjournment. The motion for adjournment and the time of adjournment are traditionally noted.

Verifying Accuracy

Most minutes are circulated to the group, and opportunities for corrections are presented at the next meeting. In addition to that, the chair and the secretary may confer to be certain that the minutes represent their recollections of the meeting. When other people are quoted verbatim, it is both wise and courteous to check with them to be sure they are correctly represented. Wording of motions should also be verified. Since minutes become the permanent record of the meeting, great care should be taken to ensure that they are accurate.

ABSTRACTS AND SUMMARIES

Abstracts and summaries are documents that are short representations of longer documents. Typically, they summarize accurately the main points of a longer document. Their purpose is to allow readers to review the substance of a long document quickly. After reading the overview, they can read the entire document more efficiently or read only those parts that provide the information they seek. Abstracts and summaries save time by distilling a piece of writing to its essence.

Librarians write several kinds of abstracts and summaries. The abstract that appears at the beginning of a journal article is the most familiar. Usually around 250 words, and rarely over 500 words, this abstract is a miniature version of the entire article. Summaries of various lengths can introduce a wide variety of professional documents. Long reports traditionally begin with a summary of one page or less. In businesses, this summary is usually called an executive summary. While librarians may or may not wish to adopt this standard business term, they will find the form extremely useful for overcoming the reluctance of some readers to tackle long reports. Shorter summaries, from one sentence to one paragraph, can be used effectively in many kinds of documents.

Abstracts and summaries of various kinds, while representing different kinds of documents, share the same characteristics. For simplicity's sake, we will use the term summary as the general term covering all kinds of abstracts and summaries.

Summaries, as representations of documents, must accurately reflect the content of the parent document, both in meaning and in emphasis. As miniature documents of their own, however, they also must be coherent by themselves, with the same standards of logic, complete sentences, and clear wording that you would apply to any other piece of writing.

Organization of Summaries

Summaries begin with a topic sentence that states the organizing idea (also called the theme or central thesis) of the parent document. Subsequent sentences present the parent document's main points, frequently paraphrasing or recasting topic sentences from the document's main sections. For example, an abstract of a research article would contain sentences that summarize the article's thesis, the methodology, the results, and the conclusions. A summary of a budget request might present the total budgetary figure, the total percentage of increase from the previous year's budget, and then a summary of the major requests for increased funding. A summary of a study comparing your library with other, similar libraries might begin with your conclusion, based on the comparison, and then might summarize your major findings.

Summaries benefit from the techniques of good writing that make other professional documents effective: short, clear sentences, and vocabulary that is free from any distracting jargon or cryptic abbreviations. Many professional writers pay extra attention to the writing in their summaries, knowing that the readers will form their first impressions of the document's ideas and style from the summary paragraphs.

Techniques for Writing Summaries

When writing summaries of finished documents, read the document through several times to become thoroughly familiar with the content. Identify the central thesis of the document, and experiment with writing a lead sentence that sums up the main idea. Then identify, perhaps by underlining, the main points in the document as a whole. Look for topic sentences that begin sections and paragraphs. Develop your paragraph by shaping these ideas into a flowing narrative. As you write, keep to summary statements of main ideas, trying to resist the temptation to add explanation or background.

A sample executive summary from a longer report describing a media services department appears in figure 44. Abstracts are considered in more detail in chapter 13.

JOB DESCRIPTIONS

Job descriptions are documents that define the positions within the library. Typical job descriptions include the name of the position, a general description of responsibilities, and a general listing of duties. Also, job descriptions commonly include the qualifications needed to fill the position.

The document below is a summary of a hypothetical 15-page report for the
dean of the college about the status of a three-year-old program of instructional media administered as part of the library system.

Instructional Media Services: A Three-Year Report
Executive Summary

This report documents in detail the planning that
went into the formation of the Instructional Media
Services (IMS) Department, its growth during the past
three years, and the new five-year plan that is being
proposed to meet the needs of the campus for Instructional Media Services.

At the end of its third year, the consolidated Instructional Media Services Department is experienc-
ing the successes and frustrations caused by demand
for services that is outstripping our resources and
our ability to respond effectively. The consolidation
of five media units (the Curriculum Center, Instructional Television, the Library Audio-Visual Department, the Language Laboratory, and the Film Library)
has achieved the short-term goals formulated in the
planning process four years ago. All services are now
provided during all hours the library is open; full-
time adult staff is available to assist with all media;
processes and procedures have been systematized; a
central equipment pool has been established, as well
as centralized service to provide projection; and a
complete catalog of all media has been produced and
is updated each semester.

Use of IMS has increased significantly each year.
Use of programs and equipment was nine time greater
this year than the year we opened (from 1,996 to
17,964). Use of all other services has tripled in three
years. Complaints from faculty and students have

Figure 44. **Executive Summary**

dropped dramatically, and now arise primarily from the delays caused by lack of resources for production.

Our progress toward the long-range objectives identified four years ago has been understandably slow since we concentrated first on issues of basic services. As we approach our fourth year, we should focus our attention on plans for achieving our long-range goals. These goals include establishing teaching support services for faculty, like the production of instructional aids; providing consultative assistance with the use of media in the classroom; and offering instructional design services. To meet the college's projected needs in these areas for the next five years, the Instructional Media Services Department will need an additional media production specialist, an increase in the student assistant budget, and additional video production equipment.

Job descriptions serve several functions. They outline the responsibilities of each job and its relationship to other jobs in the organization. They form the basis for the system of compensation. In some institutions, job descriptions are used as a basis for training and for evaluation.

The major variant among job descriptions is the level of detail describing responsibilities. Some job descriptions are very general, and some are very specific. The level of detail you choose depends on how you will use the job description. If you plan to use the job description to orient and train new employees, you will need more detail than if you are using it as a general definition of areas of responsibility.

Figure 45 is a typical job description. Note the following stylistic characteristics: use of headings, numbering of responsibilities, parallel construction of elements, word choice, and level of detail in description of the duties.

RESUMES

Resumes can be viewed as special-purpose reports about your qualifications and work experience. The art of writing resumes has received much attention recently, along with various strategies for securing jobs. In this section, we will provide a quick overview of the issues involved in writing an effective resume. Readers who are interested in more detail should check the list of selected readings.

Resumes are summaries of your professional qualifications and experience. The most typical use for a resume is as part of an application for a position or promotion. In books about job seeking and resume writing, job seekers are advised to tailor their resume to a specific position, so that the aspects of their background that apply most directly to the position can be highlighted. If, for example, you have been both a librarian and a teacher, and you are now applying for a librarian's job, you might wish to describe your work as a librarian in greater detail than your work as a teacher. If you were applying for a position as a children's librarian, your resume might highlight both kinds of experience. Fortunately, word processors make it easy to revise resumes, so organizing your resume to meet the needs of the position you are applying for is much less trouble now than when it meant retyping a new document for each job.

Content of Resumes

Resumes can contain any information that you believe qualifies you for the position you seek. Listed below are the kinds of information that typically appear on resumes.

Personal Data

You should include your name, address, and telephone numbers where you can be reached when people wish to call you. If you do not list a daytime telephone number, you are making it difficult for people to reach you during working hours. Legally, employment decisions cannot be based on personal data such as age, race, sex, or marital status, unless it can be proven that these are legitimate job qualifications. Whether or not to include these details on your resume is a personal decision. Employers are interested in the applicants who apply for their positions, and frequently like to have that information, but you are under no obligation to provide it.

Career Objective

Many books for job seekers advise that you identify on your resume the type of position for which you are looking. If you choose to do this, be certain that the objective matches the job for which you are applying.

Education

This section should list the institutions you have attended from high school on, beginning with the most recent. Include dates of attendance, degrees granted, dates of graduation, and your major courses of study. Although listing continuing education on your resume is becoming more common, it is frequently listed in a separate section.

Library Experience

You will want to include the names and addresses of the organizations, the names of the libraries, the dates you were employed, and the titles of your positions. Most librarians also like to provide some details about their responsibilities and their accomplishments. Positions are normally listed in chronological order, with the most recent first.

Other Work Experience

This section can include other positions you have held. Typically, you do not need to list jobs such as summer positions while in school, but you *do* want to account for large blocks of time and, also, demonstrate other kinds of experience and skills that you may have. An alternative approach is to list all work experience together; however, most employers and search committees appreciate having library experience separated from other types of work experience.

Professional Activities

This section typically includes memberships in professional associations, offices and committee appointments held, and other professional activities. You may wish to list continuing education courses or workshops here. Alternatively, you may wish to give "Professional Development" or "Continuing Education" its own section.

Reference Librarian: Job Description

GENERAL DESCRIPTION:
  The Reference librarian works with other members
of the Reference department to provide reference and
information services to students, faculty, and city
residents. Duties include staffing the reference desk,
planning and teaching classes in bibliographic instruction, searching online databases, and working
with selected academic departments in collection development. In addition, this position is responsible
for coordinating the development of the reference collection.

SPECIFIC DUTIES:
  1. Staffs the reference desk approximately 20
     hours a week, providing reference service di-
     rectly to library users and supervising student
     staff
  2. Searches online databases in response to re-
     quests from students and faculty
  3. Prepares and teaches classes in bibliographic
     instruction
  4. Serves as a liaison to academic departments in
     the Social Sciences
  5. Coordinates selection of resources for the Refer-
     ence collection
  6. Participates in departmental and library man-
     agement
  7. Performs other duties as assigned

Figure 45. **Job Description: Reference Librarian**

REPORTS TO: Head, Reference Department

QUALIFICATIONS:
   Required: Master's degree in library science from
an ALA-accredited program; two years' experience in
a library reference department. Desired: A second
Master's degree and experience with online searching
and bibliographic instruction

Publications

You may wish to expand this section by entitling it "Publications, Papers, and Presentations," to include professional work that has been presented but not published.

Honors and Awards

If you have only one honor, you may wish to list it in a larger section entitled "Achievements," rather than list just one item. As your resume fills up with details of your work life, you may wish to drop high school and college honors, unless they indicate unusual academic excellence or skills that relate directly to your present activities. For example, an experienced librarian applying for a position as an editor of a library journal may elect to retain on his resume the honor he received for editing the best college newspaper in the state. On the other hand, a librarian who has long since shown herself active in professional associations might not choose to include her election as college class president on her resume. But both these honors might be appropriately included on the resume of a recent graduate looking for a first library job.

References

Listing references on your resume is preferable, in our opinion, to stating that they are available on request. Withholding names may ensure that no one will be consulted without your knowledge, but you cannot anticipate how searches will proceed, and your lack of listed references could cause delays. A better approach is to identify several people who are willing to respond to calls or letters requesting information about you and to include their names on your resume. Since many reference checks are done by telephone, you will want to include telephone numbers, if your references are willing to respond to telephone calls.

Every employer and every search committee reads many, many recommendations. The ones that are most meaningful are those that relate your skills and qualifications to the position that is open. For that reason, it is generally worth your while to tell your references something about the positions for which you are applying. That is also the reason that letters from placement files, although acceptable in searches, do not have the same impact as a letter written specifically for the position at hand. Letters from placement files also age rapidly. A letter assessing your performance in a class five years ago will not be as effective as a letter describing your skill at the reference desk last year.

These categories, with variations in wording, are the ones librarians most frequently use on their resumes. The categories are weighted toward people with several years of professional experience. Other types of information can be useful, both for entry-level professionals and for individuals in special circumstances or with special qualifications. Examples of additional categories include achievements, special skills, activities, military service, and interests.

Organization of Resumes

Resumes are typically divided into sections, each with a clear heading describing the content of the section. When you are organizing your resume, you will first decide on the main sections that you will use and the order in which you will present them. Then you will need to plan the arrangement, sequence, and level of detail of the information within each section. In making these decisions you can follow the traditional *chronological* approach or the *functional* approach.

Chronological Approach

The chronological format is the traditional format known to us all. It is ideally suited for applicants whose education and work experience match the position they seek. It focuses on work experience and begins with your most recent job. Frequently, librarians choose to place the section on education first and then move to library experience.

There are many alternatives for arranging the information within each section. When you are designing your resume, you may wish to pay special attention to the impact of the spatial arrangement that you choose. What elements hit the reader first? What elements stand out clearly? Can the reader skim the resume and still retain main points? One entry from a typical section on library experience is presented in three different styles below. Test your skills by assessing the strengths and weaknesses of each.

Example A

EXPERIENCE

Reference Librarian   June, 1984–August, 1987
Central City Public Library, Central City, Iowa

Provided reference service to adults in the Main Library; gave library tours and demonstrations of the online catalog; participated in selection for the Social Sciences; organized adult lecture series.

Example B

EXPERIENCE: Reference Librarian, Central City Public Library, Central City, Iowa. Provided reference service to adults in the Main Library; gave library tours and demonstrations of the online catalog; participated in selection for the Social Sciences; organized adult lecture series. June 1984–August 1987.

Example C

LIBRARY EXPERIENCE:

Reference Librarian
    Central City Public Library, Central City, Iowa
    June, 1984–August, 1987
    Duties:
        Provided reference service to adults in the Main Library
        Gave library tours and demonstrations of the online catalog
        Participated in selection for the Social Sciences
        Organized adult lecture series

Figure 46 is an example of one of the many possible formats for a chronological resume. Test your skills by analyzing what you feel are its strengths and weaknesses.

Functional or Skills Approach

Recently, an alternative approach in choosing main sections has become popular, particularly in situations where many different types of training or experience could equip an applicant for a particular job. Called the functional approach, this technique stresses the responsibilities candidates have had or the skills they have acquired, rather than the positions they have held. This approach may work particularly well for candidates looking for their first library jobs, when most of their skills have come from experiences outside libraries. Skills resumes can be particularly helpful for people seeking support staff positions in libraries, since those positions require certain kinds of skills that can come from previous experience in libraries, but can also be acquired in other ways. The skills approach always includes a chronological listing of positions, labeled Work History. No matter how you choose to organize the presentation of your work experience, employers will want to have a chronological list of your employment. If you do not provide it conveniently for them, they will construct it for themselves, and the extra effort that this takes will probably not awaken positive feelings toward your candidacy. Functional resumes are not commonly used by professional librarians seeking positions beyond the entry level, but since they are used outside libraries, we have included them here. Figure 47 is an example of a functional resume.

Combination of Approaches

Thinking of your experience in terms of the skills you have acquired and reviewing the responsibilities that either created or honed those skills may help you assess your strengths objectively. You may find it useful to experiment with ways to combine information about your skills and related accomplishments with the traditional chronological approach.

Assessing Your Resume from Your Reader's Perspective

When you have completed a draft of your resume, take an objective look at it, from the perspective of your prospective employer. A simplified form of role playing may be useful. After learning all you can about the library and the job for which you are applying, imagine that you are the person with responsibility for filling this position. Try to analyze what your prospective employer is looking for in a candidate. You may even want to jot down a list that includes experience and specific skills, such as knowledge of business reference tools, supervisory skills, or communication skills. Then read your resume from the point of view of the person doing the hiring. What information stands out? What questions remain unanswered? In terms of this employment opportunity, what are the strengths and the weaknesses of your resume? Obviously, the point is not to manufacture skills and abilities that you don't have, but rather to be sure that you have put forth your qualifications for that job in the clearest possible way. You also want to identify points that you may wish to clarify or amplify in your cover letter.

You may want to pay special attention to the questions that reading your resume may raise in a prospective employer's mind. For example, if you have changed jobs frequently, you may wish to find a way to address this issue, either in the resume or the cover letter. Similarly, if you have had a period of unemployment, you can expect your reader to wonder why. In general, we feel it is better to anticipate questions employers will have and to find unobtrusive ways to answer them than to run the risk that employers will make unfounded assumptions from the data you have given them.

If you have participated in hiring at some point in your career, you will have a feel for the kinds of questions and considerations employers have. If you have *not* been involved in hiring, you may wish to discuss the process with someone who has.

Writing the Letter of Application

Chapter 8 discusses letters in detail, including the importance of understanding your reader's perspective and writing a letter that addresses your reader's concerns. This advice is crucial in writing a letter applying for a job. In the section above, we advocated trying to understand as much as possible about the way an employer will look at your resume. The letter of application gives you an opportunity to highlight the parts of your background that will be of interest to your employer and to answer, in an unobtrusive way, any questions that you feel might arise from your resume. The letter is also your opportunity to match your qualifications with the position. While you do not want to repeat every detail in your resume, you may wish to isolate several strong points and elaborate on them.

The sample resume below illustrates the traditional approach to organizing resumes. Within these sections, many different formats for presenting the information may be used. The sample below indicates one such format; others are suggested in the text. The chronological style is much more common in libraries than the functional style (illustrated in figure 47).

Paula West

Resume

Paula West   Home Telephone: (000) 000-0000
000 Central Street   Work Telephone: (000) 000-0000
Western City, CA 00000

EDUCATION

M.L.S. Meridian University, Meridian City, CA
        00000, 1980
B.A.   Quality College, Heath, IA 00000, 1978
        (Physics)

EXPERIENCE

Science Librarian   Quality College, Heath, IA 00000
1985–

                    Duties: Reference work, book se-
                    lection, bibliographic instruc-
                    tion, and database searching in
                    the sciences; general reference
                    work; supervision of student
                    workers; and participation on li-
                    brary and university
                    committees.

Reference Librarian Central Public Library, Heath, IA
1980–1985

                    Duties: Reference work with em-
                    phasis in the sciences; book se-

Figure 46. **Chronological Resume**

The sections below are intended as illustrations. Other sections are often included in traditional resumes. Please see the discussion in the text for a list of commonly used sections.

Alternatively, the names and addresses of references can be listed. See the text for further discussion.

lection for fiction and the sciences; planning programs for young adults; and participation on library committees.

PROFESSIONAL ACTIVITIES

Member, American Library Association, 1978–

Member, Iowa Library Association, 1981–
Chair, State Conference Committee, 1987
State Conference Committee, 1984–87
Continuing Education Committee, 1982–84

PUBLICATIONS

"Planning programs that appeal to young adults," Iowa Librarian, v. 5, July, 1984.

"Convincing science departments that librarians can select science books," Academic Library World, v. 25, October, 1987.

REFERENCES

References are available upon request.

The sections below are intended as illustrations of typical sections in a functional resume. Please see the discussion in the text for a list of other commonly used sections.

RESUME

Jan Jones   Home Telephone: 000-000-0000
1234 Main Street
University City, Washington 00000

EMPLOYMENT OBJECTIVE: Support Staff Position in a
    Public or University Library

EDUCATION:

    B.S.   1980 State University, Major City,
              Nebraska
              Major: History
    Diploma   1976 Central City HIgh School, Major
              City, Nebraska

LIBRARY SKILLS:

    Staffed circulation desk, using automated circula-
        tion system
    Processed interlibrary loans, using OCLC
    Shelved books, read stacks, participated in
        inventory

OTHER SKILLS:

Working with People:
                Handled customer complaints in two types
                    of businesses
                Staffed service and sales counters in two
                    types of businesses

Figure 47. **Functional Resume**

Alternatively, the names and addresses of references can be listed. See the text for further discussion.

Supervisory Skills:
    Supervised counter personnel, including training, scheduling, and evaluation
    Supervised two clerks in customer service department

Office Skills:
    Familiar with general secretarial and office routines
    Familiar with two word processing systems and able to learn others quickly
    Familiar with simple accounting; maintained accounts for two offices, using microcomputer-based systems

WORK HISTORY:

1986–88	Customer Service Representative	Town Dept Store, Omaha
1983–86	Salesperson (20 hrs/week)	Town Dept Store, Omaha
1983–86	Office Assistant (20 hrs/week)	A-1 Insurance Agency, Omaha
1980–83	Assistant Manager	Fine Fast Foods, Omaha
1976–80	Counter Assistant (summers)	Fine Fast Foods, Omaha
1976–80	Circulation Student Asst. (10 hrs/week)	University Library, Major City
1974–76	Page (10 hrs/week)	Major City Public Library Major City

REFERENCES

References are available on request.

Applicants for positions frequently send bare-bones letters of application, merely asking to be considered for the position and announcing that they have enclosed a resume. The major argument against this approach is that you are forfeiting an opportunity to give the employer additional information about yourself. This additional information is not limited to extra factual details but also includes clues about your communication skills, your interest in the position, and the type of person you are. While bare-bones letters tell too little, garrulous letters can convey too much. Be sure to use your skills in professional writing to shape a cogent, reader-oriented letter.

The tone of your letter is of crucial importance. One of the strongest arguments against a bare-bones application letter is that it shows little enthusiasm for the job and little initiative on your part. It also contains nothing to encourage the employer to look seriously at your application, and nothing to make you stand out from other applicants.

After you have written a draft of your letter, analyze its tone carefully, and then be certain that it is appropriate for the situation. Librarians who are experienced in hiring have read colorless letters, letters that are aggressive, and letters that convey a sense of the uniqueness of the person behind the letter. Again, talking to librarians who have had extensive hiring experience can alert you to the many ways employers can react to letters. Unless you have specific information about a given situation, the wisest course is usually a letter that matches your background with the position, answers questions left unaddressed by the resume, demonstrates your communication skills, and conveys something of your personality in a pleasant, conversational way.

It seems unnecessary to say that letters of application for employment should be accurate and professional in appearance. Yet almost every search calls forth letters that are crowded at the top of the page, single-spaced without an extra line between paragraphs, typed with worn ribbons, and sprinkled with inaccuracies, whether from inattention or ignorance. Your letter and your resume represent *you* to potential employers, and employers *do* form impressions about applicants from these documents.

Chapter 13

WRITING ARTICLES FOR PUBLICATION

CHAPTER OUTLINE

WHY WRITE FOR PUBLICATION?

PUBLICATION OF ARTICLES
Sources of Manuscripts
Editorial Roles
Review of Manuscripts
Conditions of Publication

WRITING AN ARTICLE
Choosing a Subject
Reviewing the Literature
Identifying Target Periodicals
Developing Your Ideas
Developing an Organizational Plan
Writing a Rough Draft
Developing Graphics
Revising Your Article
Writing the Abstract
Preparing the Manuscript for Submission

TYPES OF ARTICLES
Report of Research
Report of Experience
Analytical Article
Procedural Article

Almost everyone who has published enjoys having written, but not everyone considers the activity itself pure pleasure. Most people, including experienced writers, find that writing is hard work. Even those writers who say that they *like* to write will admit to frustration, annoyance, and even despair at some time between the beginning of an idea and its final appearance in print. Writing for publication also takes a great deal of time, whether you are a novice or an experienced writer, time that could be spent in a thousand other personal or professional endeavors. Because writing publishable material is difficult, time-consuming, and not always immediately rewarding, we should begin by considering what motivates people to write for publication.

WHY WRITE FOR PUBLICATION?

The most fundamental motivation for writing is probably the most elusive. Many people say that they want to write, or claim that, for professional advancement, they *should* write, but those who actually stick with it until they succeed seem to have an inner drive to communicate their particular way of looking at things to others. Perhaps it is a variation of the desire to shape or order our environment; perhaps it reflects social needs for recognition, or an elemental search for self-expression. However you choose to define it, the push to write is a compulsion that some people have and others do not. If you, as a potential writer, do not feel some inner force that nudges you on, despite the difficulties, anxieties, and insecurities that plague all writers, you may find yourself unwilling to put forth the effort to write publishable material. This observation is not intended to be discouraging. If anything, it should reassure those writers who find themselves continuing to pursue their dream of writing for publication, while alleviating the guilt of those people who feel they ought to write, but always seem to find something else to do instead.

In addition to the amorphous urge that we are calling the drive to write, there are many other reasons to write for publication. Perhaps the most obvious is having something that you feel you must say. In fact, many readers of the library literature, and most editors, would rather call this a requirement for publication than a motivating force. Our published literature is the written record of the concepts, theories, facts, procedures, and assumptions of our profession. Working with the ideas that form the body of our professional practice, testing them, challenging them, and then testing *your* ideas in a wider community through the printed word contributes to your professional growth and to the growth of the profession.

Professional advancement is frequently cited, with varying degrees of cynicism, as a primary motivator for writing for publication. It is undoubtedly true that publications can make the writer known beyond his or her local area, that a list of publications enhances a resume, and that publications are important in the promotion and tenure process in academic libraries. Certainly, publishing can benefit the librarian who writes. Some view this possibility as affecting the quality of the library literature, resulting in the publication of material that does not deserve to be in print.

Librarians who wish to write are naive indeed if they think that only the fact of publication is important, and not the quality of what they publish. Shoddy thinking and poor writing *are* noticed and *do* affect one's professional reputation, even though all the rewards of publication may not be meted out along a qualitative scale. Unless librarians who read the literature, employers who evaluate resumes, and committees and administrators who make tenure decisions abandon critical judgment entirely, mere publication should not ensure positive response or positive effects. Desire for career advancement as the *only* reason for writing, divorced from other motivations, is probably as futile as (we hope) it is rare.

The view that career survival or professional aggrandizement dominates publishing patterns introduces the issue of quality in the literature and raises the question: Who should, and who can, serve effectively as a watchdog of quality in the professional literature?

In a broad sense, all librarians, as consumers of the literature, can help to maintain its quality. We can be critical readers, analyzing, questioning, debating what we read, keeping ourselves open to new ideas, and subjecting the new and the old to rigorous inspection. We can resist any tendency we may have to revere what appears in print, and we can replace automatic admiration with critical judgment.

Editors and reviewers can also affect the quality of the literature by insisting on high standards in research methods, in logical thought, and in use of language. But even editors are limited in what they can do to uphold quality. They can select the best from what they receive; they can write material themselves or cajole proven writers into submitting material; they can revise manuscripts as time and the author's receptivity allow. But, in the end, they must have something to publish.

Ultimately, the individual writer must be the guardian of the quality of his or her published thought. Collectively, writers are the arbiters of our professional literature. The audience, the reviewers, even the editors, are spectators; they can observe and protest when they feel the ship of quality listing in the water, but they are not sailing the boat. It is the individual writer who must care about the meticulousness of research methods, the veracity of ideas, the logic of argument, and the precision of expression.

And that brings us back to the motivation to write and, even more significantly, to write well. Writers must care—care about the ideas they work with, the language they use, their responsibility as writers and thinkers, and the health of the profession's body of knowledge. These writers stick with it when the words will not come; they are willing to stand up to critical examination of their thoughts; they deserve the rewards of publication. For writers like these, knowing that they have written well is a most satisfying reward.

The purpose of this chapter is to encourage librarians to write for publication and to encourage them to care about doing it well.

PUBLICATION OF ARTICLES

Librarians who have not written for publication are usually eager to learn as much as they can about how manuscripts are selected and what writers can do to increase their chances of being published. As we all realize, the best formula for getting published is to write a worthwhile manuscript of publishable quality on a subject of importance to the profession. Writing an excellent article is still the best guarantee of success in publishing, despite the occasional mutterings of cynics. It is also helpful to understand something about publishing, in general, and the publishing practices of the periodicals that interest you, in particular. A systematic approach to choosing your publishers and to writing your manuscript will improve the chances that your work will be accepted for publication.

Every publishing operation is its own unique business, so the generalizations that follow should be seen as practical guidelines for understanding, and not as a definitive categorization of publishers' practice. For almost every statement of common practice that we make, there is undoubtedly a publisher or editor somewhere who is doing it differently, and succeeding.

Sources of Manuscripts

Editors of professional periodicals generally obtain articles in three ways. The most frequently used method is the acceptance of unsolicited manuscripts, completed manuscripts that are offered for publication to the editor by the author. The editor then decides whether or not to accept the manuscript.

Editors can also obtain manuscripts by inviting an author to write a specific article. This practice, called soliciting articles, usually occurs when editors are seeking contributions on specific subjects or articles from well-known authorities. If an editor plans to have an issue devoted exclusively to one topic, formal or informal solicitation is almost always necessary. Sometimes a satisfactory alternative is to announce the topic well in advance and hope that enough publishable articles are submitted to cover the subject adequately. When manuscripts are solicited, the subject and deadlines for submission are agreed on before the article is written, and an honorarium may be involved.

A third way for an editor to obtain publishable material can be described as the journalistic approach. The editor either writes the material or assigns the task to a member of the editorial staff. The staff often obtains ideas and information from members of the profession, either through interviews or from written material. Some staff-written articles carry bylines and others do not. Frequently, contributing editors are named who then write regular columns within a broad subject area.

Editorial Roles

Editor is the title usually given to the people to whom the publisher delegates the responsibility for producing the periodical. The editor's responsibilities include determining the mechanisms for selecting manuscripts, making the final selections, overseeing preparation of the copy for the printer, and performing or delegating a wide variety of business tasks. Two patterns of editorial staffing predominate in the publishing of periodicals directed at members of a profession. It is difficult to find appropriate labels for these two patterns, for reasons that soon will emerge. Perhaps the best way to classify them is to distinguish between those for whom editing the periodical is their one full-time job and those who edit the periodical in addition to holding another position in the profession. Beyond that distinction, it is risky to generalize. Both types of editors may have experience in the profession and as professional editors. Both types may be chosen through competitive processes. There may be little difference in the amount of time both types devote to working directly on the periodical. And both types may edit "refereed" journals, where reviewers recommend the selection of manuscripts. In our experience, any attempt to draw firm lines between those periodicals that have full-time staffs and those that use practicing members of the profession as editors encounters too many exceptions to be useful.

Since both types of editors do a variety of jobs, the best approach is to describe various editorial functions, acknowledging that different organizations will have different structures for seeing that these tasks are done.

Determining Scope and Content

Probably the most basic editorial task involves determining the scope of the periodical as a whole and then the content of each issue. An editor's job is to know both the subject field and the markets well enough to know what is needed by the target audience and what will be well received by it. The matching of material with the audience's needs is the editor's task, no matter what sources for manuscripts are used.

Earlier we discussed three sources for manuscripts: solicited manuscripts, material written by salaried or volunteer staff, and unsolicited manuscripts. It is true that many periodicals combine several methods. Still, the last method, using unsolicited manuscripts, is fundamentally different in editorial approach from using solicited material or from having a staff member write what is needed. The underlying assumptions governing the use of unsolicited material are that the profession will produce what it needs, and that the profession will determine what it reads by what it writes. The editor and the reviewers control quality by selecting the best from the material that the profession submits, but they do not influence, except indirectly, what the profession writes. They respond to the written product.

Editorial control over the content and quality, in this approach, can be described as passive rather than active, since the editor's choices are limited by what authors submit. A particular issue of a periodical may represent the best of whatever was submitted and still not be what the editor would, ideally, like to publish—in content or in style. Any editor who has worked entirely with unsolicited material can describe the strengths, and also the editorial frustrations, inherent in this approach. When a reader complains that the content of an issue was "not up to the journal's usual standard," the editor may have to shrug and say, "It was the best I had."

The inherent problem of quality control in professional journals that depend on unsolicited submissions argues for improving writing skills within the profession.

Underlying the use of solicited and staff-written articles is the assumption that the editor has the responsibility for determining the coverage of the periodical. An editor's attempt to retain active control over the content of each issue does not mean that he or she is indifferent to the wishes or the prevailing trends of the profession. An argument can be made that such an editor can be very responsive to the needs of the profession because he or she can anticipate needs for material and seek it out, rather than having to wait until it happens to come in the mail.

Most professional periodicals reflect one predominant approach or the other, although almost all publications include both types of articles. Publications whose major articles are unsolicited may have regular features written by paid or volunteer "staff" editors. And publications that use predominantly staff-written or solicited material may publish, either occasionally or on a regular basis, unsolicited material from the profession.

Selecting Manuscripts

Whether the editor selects from unsolicited submissions or solicits and assigns articles, he or she usually makes the decisions about final selections, using the periodical's guidelines on scope and audience and considering recommendations from reviewers and editorial assistants.

All editors have their own criteria for selecting manuscripts for their publications. Some typical considerations are listed below:

- ▲ soundness of content, including knowledge of field, methodology, statistical analysis, and logic
- ▲ logic and organizational clarity
- ▲ clarity, precision, and conciseness
- ▲ relation of subject to scope of periodical
- ▲ importance of subject to primary audience
- ▲ frequency of treatment of similar subjects (in this periodical or others)
- ▲ appropriateness of approach, length, tone, and treatment

- ▲ extent to which article conforms to accepted standards of grammar and usage
- ▲ "authority" of author
- ▲ extent to which manuscript conforms to periodical's style and requirements
- ▲ accuracy of the manuscript

Problems with manuscripts can be divided into three general groupings: substantive weaknesses in the manuscript, problems with the appropriateness of the article for the periodical, and problems with the form of the manuscript. Not all objections carry equal weight in the selection decision, obviously, but all affect editors' and reviewers' opinions of the manuscript and, therefore, play some role in the outcome.

Substantive Weakness in the Manuscript. Most manuscripts are rejected because they are not of publishable quality: they contain substantive weaknesses in content, logic, organization, or expression of ideas. Editors differ in the amount of help and advice they are willing to give in overcoming these difficulties. If the problems are relatively minor, and the editor feels the author is capable of revising them successfully, he or she will frequently return the manuscript with suggestions for revision.

Inappropriate Submissions. A manuscript without major substantive weaknesses may be rejected because it is not, in the eyes of the editor, appropriate for the periodical. Some of these difficulties—for example, a mismatch between the subject of an article and the scope of the journal—might have been anticipated by the author if he or she had taken the time to assess the kinds of manuscripts that the periodical had previously published. Other difficulties—like the recent appearance of several articles on similar topics—might have been anticipated by a review of the literature. Only a few problems, such as scheduling a similar article in a future issue or the editor's feeling that the audience is no longer interested in a particular topic, are difficult for the author to spot in advance of submission.

You can avoid most inappropriate submissions by taking the time to analyze the characteristics of the periodicals in which you would like to publish and by making certain that your article matches what they tend to publish. We will discuss a method to select these periodicals later in the chapter.

Problems with Form and Format. The final category of manuscript problems concerns difficulties with the form and accuracy of the manuscript. These include poor proofreading, typographical errors, incorrect footnote form, errors in bibliographic references, failure to conform to the periodical's stylistic requirements, and other shortcomings that might seem of less importance than substantive errors. Problems with form, by themselves, may not result in rejection of a manuscript, but they can make an editor uneasy. An editor worries that errors like these may signal a lack of rigor and attention to detail that could affect more important areas of the article. And such errors almost always increase the amount of time that the editorial staff must spend preparing the manuscript for publication. Matters of form and format may not seem earthshaking to a beginning author, but they contribute to the impression the manuscript makes on an editor. Complaints about these problems occur consistently in editors' writing, and so writers wishing to be published would do well to listen.

Editing

In our discussion of editorial roles, we now come to editing, or preparing the manuscript for publication. Three levels of editing can be identified: copy editing, substantive editing, and rewriting. Editors have differing terms and definitions for these levels of what they refer to as "fixing" the manuscripts and what authors sometimes consider "meddling" with their work. We offer our definitions not as the final word but as operational categories.

Copy Editing. The lightest level of editing focuses on bringing the manuscript in line with accepted grammatical standards and with the periodical's style. Copy editing can include cosmetic changes in language, if the reworking leaves the ideas and the organization intact. Copy editing can include marking the manuscript in standard editorial symbols.

Substantive Editing. Editing at this level often involves some reorganization of ideas and restructuring of sentences. Paragraphs may be moved around to strengthen the flow of thought, but, though organization and expression are improved, the basic ideas and argument of the original remain intact.

Rewriting. Rewriting involves rethinking and reorganizing of the original. New or reorganized concepts distinguish the rewritten article.

Authors are usually concerned about the amount and type of editing that will befall their manuscripts. Editors, and publishing houses, vary in the level of editing they do, and in the way that they interact with the author about revisions. In the case of substantive editing or rewriting, most editors consult with the author.

Overseeing Production

After manuscripts are selected and edited, the issue goes into production. These activities are typically done outside the editorial offices, although, in some cases, staff editors and artists are responsible for preparing copy for printing. Editors are also involved in "proofing" the copy at various stages in the process of production.

Review of Manuscripts

Editors frequently seek recommendations from others about whether or not a manuscript should be accepted. If the editorial staff includes assistant or associate editors, they may be involved in reviewing manuscripts. Editors often use members of the profession to review manuscripts, either as part of a structured process or on an *ad hoc* basis, when an opinion is needed in a particular case. Periodicals that use reviewers from the profession on a regular basis are called "refereed" periodicals. As unlovely as this bit of jargon may be, it is used frequently. Whether or not a periodical uses practicing professionals as reviewers is sometimes seen as an indicator of its quality.

Reviewers can be part of an official editorial board or panel, appointed for fixed periods of time, or they can be selected on a one-time basis, depending on the topic covered by an article. When an extremely technical subject is involved, an editor may seek out professionals experienced in that field. Reviewers who regularly review manuscripts grow in their knowledge of the needs of the periodical and in their ability to assess and describe weaknesses of manuscripts. On the other hand, they are not necessarily experts in all the subjects covered by the manuscripts they review. An expert in a specific field may review manuscripts very infrequently and therefore may not have the chance to strengthen his or her editorial skills, but he or she will know the specialized field very well.

Editors of refereed journals rely heavily on reviewers' recommendations, but most editors make the final selection themselves. They assign the reviews, weigh the evidence, and then decide which manuscripts will be published in which issues. The "balance of content" in a given issue is often important in deciding when a manuscript will appear.

Authors sometimes wish to know the process that a specific periodical uses to review manuscripts. Many describe their reviewing practices in information near the front of the periodical, along with instructions on how to submit an article and how long the reviewing process should take. Some periodicals publish guidelines that they send to prospective contributors. If an official statement about the selection process is not easily available, clues can sometimes be found by looking at the masthead and the by-lines on articles. If the authors of a substantial number of articles are also listed as editorial staff members, much of the periodical is probably written by the staff and, therefore, fewer articles may be selected from unsolicited contributions. If the authors' names are different from the editors', it is likely that unsolicited manuscripts are published, unless there are other clues that publication is by invitation only. If an editorial panel or contributing editors are listed by name on the masthead, you can probably assume that "referees" are consistently involved in the reviewing process. The absence of named reviewers does not necessarily mean the absence of an outside review, however, since the editors may choose reviewers from the community of known experts on the subject of a specific article.

The statements above are intended as guidelines, though many arrangements for selecting and reviewing exist. If it is important to you to know the process of selection for a particular publication, you can call the editorial offices.

Virtually all periodicals will return unsolicited manuscripts to the authors if the manuscripts are accompanied by a self-addressed stamped envelope (a phrase abbreviated in some publications as SASE). There, however, similarities end.

Although most periodicals that use reviewers have some sort of form for reviews, not all of them share the reviews with the authors. When reviewers' comments *are* sent to the author, they may be forwarded verbatim or summarized by the editor. Frequently, reviews are anonymous, and the author does not know the name of the reviewer. Anonymity in the other direction—withholding the names of authors from reviewers—is less frequent, although it does occur.

Some periodicals use printed forms to indicate their reasons for rejection. However, a quick glance at some of these explanations is enough to tell the author that the response is *pro forma*. Receiving a reply like "The manuscript does not meet our needs at the present time" does not necessarily mean that the manuscript was considered less thoroughly than if a detailed response had been written. Formulaic responses usually reflect an editorial policy against providing specific reasons for rejection, not the amount of time spent in considering the manuscript.

Some editors are very willing to discuss editorial decisions with authors. This tends to happen when publications are affiliated with professional associations or when the editorial staff has a commitment to developing the writing talents of members of the profession. Other editors prefer reply forms for explaining selection decisions and evade attempts by authors to pin down reasons for rejection.

The time that it takes for a periodical to review a manuscript and respond to the author varies considerably. Guidelines for average response time are often published in the periodical's guides to authors, but these times can be affected by workloads, vacations, and slow responses from reviewers. Authors often want advice on when to inquire about a manuscript. Manuscripts occasionally get lost; on the other hand, the editorial process can be quite slow, particularly if it depends on volunteer reviewers. It is best to wait at least as long as the announced review period, and even longer—if you can stand it.

Conditions of Publication

Most periodicals offer to publish an author's unsolicited manuscript under standard conditions. Those conditions are usually printed in the front pages of the periodical or in the guidelines for authors available from the publisher. Negotiating agreements for the publication of an article in the same way you might attempt to negotiate a book contract may result in a withdrawal of the publication offer. On the other hand, if you care very much about a particular issue, you may wish to inquire about the options you have.

Most periodicals in library and information science do not pay for manuscripts. A few give an honorarium for major articles. As yet, most periodicals in our field do not charge the author for reviewing or publishing articles.

Most periodicals ask authors to assign their copyright to the periodical before the article is published. The rationale behind this practice involves the difficulties of granting and obtaining permission to republish articles if each author controls this permission. Although some authors feel strongly about this issue, the practice is not likely to affect the author's ability to reuse his or her manuscript. When the need for reuse arises, authors should write to the periodical, stating what they would like to do and requesting permission to do it.

Some periodicals ask authors to read proofs to catch typesetting errors that only they could identify, since either the printer or editor also reads the proofs. Every editor hopes that the author has *carefully* reviewed the article before submission to be sure that everything is the way he or she wants to see it in print. Making changes at the proof stage is costly. Most periodicals will make changes requested by the author, although somewhat reluctantly if the changes are numerous and if they could have been avoided by more care on the author's part. Rewriting the article at the proof stage to improve meaning or expression is strongly discouraged by almost all editors. Publishers sometimes charge authors for corrections that exceed a fixed limit.

WRITING AN ARTICLE

So far, we have been looking at mechanisms through which manuscripts are selected for publication. Now we will turn our attention to writing the article itself.

There is no one correct method for writing a periodical article, but a number of activities need to occur during the writing of an article. These activities can be organized into a series of steps, from choosing a topic to submitting a manuscript. This process can be a useful guide for writers, especially as a reminder that attention must be paid to a number of activities. The order of these activities is not sacrosanct, and, in fact, most writers move back and forth, from step to step, during the writing process.

A process for writing an article is presented in figure 48. Each activity is considered below.

1. Choose your subject area and narrow it into a topic for research or for an article.*
2. Review the literature on your subject.
3. Identify several periodicals that are good "matches" for your article.
4. Develop your ideas, using techniques that allow you to explore a variety of possibilities.
5. Develop a working organizational plan.
6. Write the rough draft.
7. Develop the graphics.
8. Revise your rough draft.
9. Write the abstract.
10. Prepare the manuscript for submission.
    *If you choose to explore your subject area by conducting research, research becomes your first focus, and of course the article reporting your results comes after you have concluded your research.

Figure 48. **Writing Articles: A Process**

Choosing a Subject

Before you write an article, you must have a subject about which you have something to say. Most good articles spring from the author's relationship with a given subject, a complex blend that may include extensive experience, observation of a variety of circumstances over time, reading, perhaps formal or informal investigation, and considerable thought and analysis. At some time, perhaps early in your thought on a particular subject, you may feel that, if all goes well, you will write an article, just as researchers assume that if their results are worthwhile, they will publish them. In cases like this, you are thinking about writing an article before you have begun to explore your subject. On the other hand, you might suddenly realize that your experiences over the last few years with a particular subject (such as teaching online searching workshops to library users) have provided knowledge and a perspective that you wish to communicate to others. Or, you might finish a project and decide to write up the results. There are no rules about when you should begin to think about writing an article. At some point during your exploration of a subject, your thoughts will begin to focus on specific topics, and possible approaches and ideas will begin to take shape.

Nevertheless, potential writers frequently ask for advice about how to choose a topic for an article. Since articles spring from knowledge and experience with a subject, would-be authors should identify the subjects that they know about and the areas in librarianship that matter to them. From there, they should begin the process of exploring these subjects or areas in the ways that seem most logical to them. They should read the literature, discuss the subject with colleagues, try out various new ideas, analyze what they already know, ponder the unanswered questions, and dream about how they would solve significant problems. For some, this exploration may lead into formal or informal research. For others, exploration will take the shape of reading, thought, discussion, and observation. As their relationship with the subject deepens, seeds of ideas that can be cultivated into articles will inevitably appear, but the growth of an individual's thought cannot be forced. It must come as the natural fruit of an exploration and examination of a subject.

Once you start to consider writing an article, the writing process has already begun. Now you need to narrow your *subject* of interest down to the *topic* that you will treat in your article. You will make tentative decisions about the approach you will take to the topic, the type of article you will write, and the audience you want to reach. Ideas about the scope of what you will consider and, therefore, about the probable length of your article will emerge, as will ideas about tone and treatment.

In one sense, the entire process can be viewed as progressively narrowing your focus; each successive decision that you make about content, approach, audience, organization, and language moves you from the general subject to the specific topic and gets you closer to the unique treatment of ideas that will become your article.

Reviewing the Literature

It is hard to imagine reaching the stage of writing an article without being familiar with what else has been written on the subject. Knowledge of the literature should be a part of the process of exploring ideas to write about. Certainly, once you begin the formal process of planning your article, it is worthwhile to review the literature on your subject, perhaps in ways that you have not done previously.

Since you are now looking at the literature from a writer's point of view, you will want to notice the types of articles that have been written and the periodicals in which they have appeared, as well as approaches to content that writers have taken. Being familiar with what others have said recently is invaluable as you plan your approach.

At some point in your review of the literature, you may wish to extend your scope and look at relevant literature in other fields, if for no other reason than to give yourself a sense of how others approach topics similar to yours. For example, librarians writing articles on management topics may find it useful to be familiar not only with library literature on management, but also with business literature in their area of interest.

Identifying Target Periodicals

Once you have made preliminary decisions about your topic, type of article, audience, and general tone, you can consider where you would like to have your article published. Making a tentative decision at this time about your targeted publication is useful because you can then become familiar with that periodical from a writer's perspective and keep its style and requirements in mind as you write.

Many writers immediately decide to try to publish in the periodical that they read the most. Although that publication may well end up being your first choice, a more analytical approach might increase your chances of being published, as well as ensure that your ideas reach the most appropriate audience.

Deciding on the purpose and audience of your article is the first step toward systematically selecting a market for it. An example will illustrate this process of matching your goals in writing with your topic and the audience you wish to reach.

Suppose you have completed a research study on the problems users have in searching an automated catalog, and your purpose in designing this study was to use this information in developing instructional techniques and materials for automated catalogs. You will want to decide, first, what segment of librarians would benefit most from this knowledge. Usually, you will come down to the following choices: all types of librarians, librarians in one type of library, librarians responsible for one type of activity, or persons in other fields. In this example, you could make any of these choices, depending on how you saw the purpose of your article. You might wish to alert all librarians to users' problems in approaching automated catalogs; you might wish to focus on academic or public libraries; you might prefer, instead, to try to reach those librarians who design and develop instructional materials, or those librarians who work primarily with online systems; or, alternatively, you might dream of influencing the design of online catalogs and, therefore, want to reach the developers of systems for information access, whoever they may be.

When you have selected the audience for your ideas, you can try to determine what publications are most likely to reach it. Once you have identified several target periodicals, you will want to examine a volume or two from a writer's perspective. It is tempting to skip this step, but first-time writers can benefit greatly from analyzing how others have written articles in their periodical of choice. Figure 49 presents an approach to examining a periodical from a writer's perspective.

You can, of course, always change your mind about where you submit your manuscript, but having a goal in mind during the writing process is useful for providing models and for focusing your efforts.

Looking at these characteristics of a specific periodical can provide potential authors with useful background for writing articles for that publication.
1. Periodical's title
2. Affiliation with a professional association
3. Target audience
4. Scope of subject coverage
5. Policies and procedures for manuscript selection and review
6. Authors who write for the periodical
7. Types of articles typically published: reports of research, reports of
   experience, procedural articles, news, reviews of the literature,
   book reviews
8. Structure and style of individual articles: Look at major headings
   and subheadings; follow the main line of reasoning though the article; form your own judgments about strengths and weaknesses
9. Tone of articles
10. Target audience for advertisements

Figure 49. **Analyzing a Periodical from a Writer's Perspective**

Developing Your Ideas

By the time you begin collecting your ideas for an article, you should already have a broad understanding of your subject. During this stage, you
will be exploring the specific topic for your article and experimenting with
ideas that will gradually narrow to what you wish to say in the article.

If you are writing an article based on a research project, you will be analyzing your results, pondering their meaning, and thinking through what
you want to say about them. If you are writing other types of articles, you
will be collecting ideas, exploring their relationships to one another, and
testing possible avenues of thought.

The developmental phase is an excellent time to go back over the literature, update your searches, and perhaps expand your searching into pe-
ripheral fields. The more ideas you bring into your field of vision at this
point, the better. As you work through the developmental phase, you will
concentrate on certain lines of thought and begin to narrow these down
into the ideas that will form the basis of your organizational plan.

Developing an Organizational Plan

Most topics may be treated in many different ways. A fundamental
choice for any potential author, after the subject has been decided upon, is

the approach to the topic that his or her exploration will take. That approach will largely determine the type of article that will result.

A list of the major types of articles in library literature appears below.

▲ research articles   ▲ reviews of the literature
▲ reports of experience   ▲ book reviews
▲ procedural articles   ▲ brief communications
▲ analytical reports   ▲ news articles
▲ historical articles

Each type has characteristic organizational features. The first four types are discussed in more detail later in the chapter.

Good articles of all types have an inherent logic; they proceed according to an organizational plan, either overtly visible or covertly directing the flow of ideas. Almost all experienced writers follow some sort of organizational notion, whether it exists in detailed form on paper or in conceptual form in their imaginations. This notion usually changes and shifts as the article matures, but—at almost all stages—it is useful to have an overview of the way your topic will proceed.

Chapter 2 discusses a variety of methods for developing an organizational plan. Whatever technique is used, it should allow you to develop a sequential and hierarchical ordering of ideas. A formal outline is the most highly structured tool for accomplishing this task, but many people find that lists and other groupings serve just as well.

Most articles divide into main sections. Typically, an article will have from three to six major topical divisions. Since the choice of these sections imposes an order on your ideas, you may wish to experiment with several ways of dividing your topic. Different topical organizations make sense for different types of articles, so it is useful to notice the way other writers organize reports of research or reviews of the literature.

When you have determined the main sections, you can develop each individually, focusing on the main ideas that comprise that section and supporting them with details. You will want to think about what information is best conveyed narratively and what material is most effective in graphic form (such as tables and charts). Most writers find that if they can "block out" the order of their ideas in advance, writing the rough draft is significantly easier.

Writing a Rough Draft

The purpose of a rough draft is to get your ideas on paper. Although you will probably be following a topical outline of some sort, your ideas will begin to take shape in earnest as you write the rough draft. Most people experience writing the rough draft as a bumpy process, like learning to drive a car with a manual transmission. Abrupt stops, jerky shifts from one gear to another, stretches of smooth going punctuated by long waits and a seeming inability to get in gear, all are familiar to the writer of rough drafts. These discomforts are natural when you consider that writing the rough draft is an extremely difficult endeavor. After all the preparation, you are finally at the point where your ideas must take concrete form. When you write the rough draft, you must decide exactly what you want to say.

That pressure can paralyze even experienced writers. One approach to keeping your rough draft flowing is to commit yourself at the outset to rigorous revision. If you know that you will go over what you have done with a critical eye, you can give yourself the freedom to experiment, to follow ideas to their conclusions, to write sentences the way they come to you, and not to worry (at this stage) about wordy constructions or punctuation. During the writing of the rough draft, content is your major concern.

Some writers choose a special symbol that indicates the need for revision or further refinement of thought. Then, if they find themselves stuck on a particular idea, they do the best they can with it, mark it for further attention, and keep going. This method takes advantage of momentum. It works as long as you are faithful about returning to solve whatever difficulties you left behind.

The only danger inherent in writing a rough draft is that you will not return to revise it—that once the draft is finished, it will suddenly acquire a new status simply by virtue of being done, and that all the blemishes you had worried about during drafting will suddenly seem inevitable or inconsequential. Rough drafts, when printed on a word processor, provide an even greater temptation because their appearance makes them *look* finished, even though they are not. These problems occur less frequently with experienced writers and others who know the difference that revision makes in the quality of writing. Writing the rough draft is only the beginning, the time to put the shape of your thoughts on paper. Working with those thoughts until you are *satisfied* is still to come.

Developing Graphics

Choosing and designing the graphic material that will accompany your text is similar to writing. You are conveying ideas and information by numbers and graphic symbols—in much the same way that you have been using words. The meaning of your illustrative material will be clear to your readers only if it is clear to you, as creator of your graphics.

A common problem in periodical articles is poor display of data. This problem is integrally connected to problems with the collection and analysis of data, both of which are researching and statistical concerns and are beyond our scope here. We can caution potential writers and researchers about the importance of careful design of research and of thinking through what data you will collect, how this data will shed light on the questions you are asking, and what you will do with the answers once you have them. But these are complex concerns, and all we can do here is refer readers to the list of selected readings. In this discussion, we will be considering only the *display* of data—how you, as author, can present to your audience the data that you have systematically gathered and analyzed.

From the concerns that many beginning writers express about designing their graphics and from the poor quality of graphic material often accompanying manuscripts, it is clear that this is an area of difficulty for a number of librarians and authors. For that reason, we present a basic approach to simple graphics display. For more detail, consult Edward Tufte, *The Visual Display of Quantitative Information*.

In our basic approach, graphic design is a four-step process:

1. *Define the purpose of the graphic: the concept, idea, or relationship that you wish to convey.*

   In general, graphics can serve two purposes. They can *make data available* in an organized and systematic format, and they can *depict relationships* among data in visual terms. The first step in designing effective graphics is conceptual: thinking through what data you want to make available, what relationships you want to emphasize visually, and what relationship your pictorial ideas will have to your narrative text.

   Graphics are intended to supplement written explanations. They are useful when they organize, summarize, or synthesize data more effectively than is possible with words. Graphics and narrative should not merely present the same information; their contributions should be complementary. As a writer, you will want to consider the relationship between your text and your graphics.

2. *Select the graphic form that is best suited to show what you wish to convey.*

   As mentioned previously, graphics serve two purposes: making data available and depicting relationships visually among data. Although both purposes can be served (in one way or another) by most graphics, each type of table or graph serves some purposes better than others.

   Tables are usually the most efficient way to make quantities of data available in an organized fashion. Relationships among data can be determined by comparing values in the table, but frequently such comparison requires initiative and effort on the part of the reader. In general, the tables do not display the *relationships* among data with the same visual impact as charts and graphs.

   Charts and graphs, in general, are suited to displaying relationships among data. Different charts and graphs are suited to different relationships. Pie charts emphasize the relationship of the parts to the whole. Bar charts, on the other hand, display the relationship of quantities to each other. Graphs, or line charts, show changes over time. Charts and graphs focus attention on the visual impact of the relationships among data. Depending on the type of chart, the actual values for the data may be more or less difficult to ascertain.

3. *Develop rough drafts of the graphic, experimenting with different ways of presenting your main idea. Choose the graphic that most clearly depicts the relationships you are trying to communicate.*

Roughing out several drafts for your charts is an essential step in producing a sharp, clean visual that communicates your idea clearly. Using graph paper makes it easier to draw scratch drafts that will give you a feel for the impact of a well-drawn graphic.

Computer graphics packages allow much more freedom for experimentation with graphics than was previously available to writers. As in all graphic design, more choices means the writer must exercise more judgment to ensure that the graphic elements support communication of the main idea. The ease of creating complex graphics with the computer often obscures the difficulty in designing a chart that communicates clearly. (See Edward Tufte for an interesting discussion of this problem, which he dubs "chartjunk.")

At this point, you will also want to choose the title and labels for your graphic. The title should be precise and exact, without becoming a narrative in itself. The labels you choose for your graphic will be influenced by the amount of space that you have. Use only standard or very clear abbreviations. Legends can be used to identify graphic symbols or shadings, and footnotes can provide further information.

Here are some questions you may want to ask yourself as you assess your draft:

What is the immediate visual impact of the graphic?
Is the visual impact consistent with the depicted factual data?
What relationship stands out most clearly?
Is the general impression clear, or cluttered?
Can everyone tell immediately what each symbol represents?
Is the notation in the legend visually distinct?
Is it easy to determine the numerical values?
Is the labeling clear and concise?
Will the graphic reproduce clearly?

4. *Secure a professional-looking copy of your final figure.*

Most periodicals require that copy for graphics be submitted in what they call camera-ready form, meaning that all they have to do is reproduce it. In addition, most publications adhere to professional standards for their graphic materials. Therefore, you as a writer may have to submit graphic material of professional quality with your manuscript.

For some types of graphs, a T-square, blue-line graph paper, and a drafting-quality pen (as well as much patience) can produce a satisfactory product. If you feel uncertain about producing the graphic yourself, you can usually find people with artistic or drafting talent to help you. Sometimes art or drafting students in high schools or community colleges are eager for projects that might result in publication. And you can always purchase professional assistance, if necessary.

If you have used a computer to help you draft your graphics, you may wish to inquire about submitting computer-generated material. Generally, computer-generated material is acceptable when it is indistinguishable from hand-drawn graphics.

Revising Your Article

During revision, you examine your rough draft and determine what it needs to bring it up to publishable standards. In a sense, you are functioning as your own editor.

Your role as your own editor is doubly important because periodical editors normally do not expect to do much editorial repair on a manuscript. They almost always judge it as they receive it. If it needs too much editorial work, it will usually be rejected. So, being your own editor and solving your own problems before the manuscript is sent off will increase your chances for publication.

If the editor finds your manuscript passable, it may be accepted, perhaps on the condition of some revision from you. However, acceptance is not a judgment of editorial perfection. The editorial staff may correct some minor difficulties, but, by and large, your manuscript will be published as it is when accepted, in all its glory and with all its weaknesses. Therefore, it is very much in your best professional interest to edit your manuscript as thoroughly as possible before you submit it.

Learning to think like an editor will also improve your writing. By assessing technical strengths and weaknesses after the fact, you will improve your ability to write better first-draft prose.

The following checklists are designed to help you improve your editorial skills by focusing on common difficulties. The questions won't always help you solve the difficulty, but they will call your attention to technical issues. The checklists have been divided into categories to help you concentrate on one aspect of revision at a time. Chapters 2 and 3 provide detailed discussion of these issues.

Revising for Logical Organization
▲ Is the title clear and descriptive of the content?
▲ Is the abstract substantive?

- Can you find one or two sentences, near the beginning, that inform the reader of the purpose of the article or the study?
- Is the article clearly divided into main sections, and are these preceded by clear, descriptive headings?
- As a group, do the first-level headings provide a logical, comprehensive division of the subject of the article, and are they roughly parallel in content and phrasing?
- Can you identify the main points in each section?
- Do these main points lead the reader logically through the section, like stepping stones?
- Is each main point logically supported with detail? Is each sufficiently established, without overkill?
- Is the main purpose of each chart or graph clear? Is the visual impact consistent with the facts?

Revising for Language and Style

Before proceeding to the checklist for problems of language and style, we would like to consider an issue that arises frequently in the writing of periodical articles: appropriate use of the passive voice.

Passive voice. Use of the passive in scientific or social scientific writing is a subject of some debate, primarily because it is a complex issue that can't be resolved by simple rules. The reason most frequently given for avoiding the active voice is to eliminate the subjectivity implicit in the use of *I* or *We*. It is important to note that using the passive voice merely takes the actor out of the *sentence*, not out of the reality behind the sentence. In other words, the passive voice does not make the content more or less subjective; it merely makes it *sound* less personal.

For example, in the sentence below, who has identified the reasons for failure?

Three major reasons for the failure of innovative projects were identified.

It is probably the writer who has made the analysis of the causes of failure, even though he or she is not the subject of the sentence. If so, this sentence represents a subjective statement of the writer's opinions or conclusions, even though it is in the passive voice.

Recognizing that the passive voice does not intrinsically make *ideas* more objective leaves the writer free to decide when the passive best clarifies content and when it obscures it.

Using the passive voice is preferable when the focus is on the action, rather than on the actor. The focus on actions in research writing accounts for a legitimate use of the passive in many sentences. For example, the section on methods in research articles describes what *was done*, and so is often a natural habitat for the passive voice.

The passive voice may obscure meaning by allowing the actor to remain unclear. In many cases, as in statements about methodology, the actor is unimportant, and so it doesn't matter that the reader cannot identify the person responsible for the action. "The questionnaire was mailed"—and no one needs to know who mailed it to understand the important idea behind the sentence.

In some cases, however, knowing *who* performed the action is important to understanding the full meaning. In these cases, using the passive may interfere with clear communication. Such cases tend to arise in expository writing, including research articles, when the writer presents the results of his or her own thought, such as opinions or analysis, using the passive voice. As in the previous example concerning reasons for innovation, the passive sentence does not clearly identify whose thoughts are being presented. Are they common opinions that everyone accepts? Are they the consensus of the literature? Are they the result of the writer's analysis or research? The use of the active voice attributes responsibility for the pronouncements of the action verb, as in this revision of the sentence concerning innovation:

Our analysis shows that innovations fail for three reasons.

Another revision of the same sentence uses the first person:

We found that innovations fail for three reasons.

When the actor is the writer, use of the active voice can result in a plethora of first-person pronouns. If the use of the first person creates an author-centered tone that is not appropriate, several solutions are possible. Sentences can be reworded so that the active voice does not require a first-person pronoun. In addition to the revisions previously suggested, the innovation sentence could be reworded as follows:

Innovative projects fail for three major reasons.

If rewording is not possible, writers can identify those sentences where attribution of thought, using personal pronouns, is important to meaning, and they can use the active voice in those cases only. Most editors do not object to the first person when it is used to identify responsibility for opinions and actions.

Writers overuse passives when they do not use them appropriately or, of course, when they use too many of them. In quantity, passives clog up prose with overly long sentences and vague constructions. Much writing in periodical articles suffers from this sluggishness, and attention to appropriate use of the passive is one remedy.

Our advice on passive and active verbs in articles parallels our approach to the problem of voice in all writing. We suggest that writers cultivate a style that uses the active voice wherever possible. Using verbs in the active voice tightens sentences almost automatically. Then, during revision, writers should look for sentences that sound long, convoluted, vague, or unclear. When problem sentences are identified, check the voice of the verb as a possible source of trouble. In addition, writers of articles may wish to scan their passive constructions, looking for those that obscure important elements of meaning, especially the appropriate acknowledgment of actions, opinions, and analysis.

Checklist for language and style. Chapter 3 provides advice on detecting problems in your manuscript. Here are some questions that may be useful when revising articles.

- ▲ Do you use action verbs wherever appropriate?
- ▲ Do you use passive constructions for a specific reason?
- ▲ Have you identified wordy constructions, and tightened them where it makes sense?
- ▲ Have you examined sentences with multiple clauses to see if a more concise structure, using phrases or single words, would do as well?
- ▲ Have you assessed your use of specialists' language to be certain that everyone in your target audience will understand your vocabulary? When you are in doubt, have you included an unobtrusive definition in the sentence?
- ▲ Are all abbreviations (except the most obvious) defined the first time they are used? Are they used so that your reader will recognize the meaning without having to flip back through many pages to the first use?
- ▲ Do you use so many abbreviations, defined or not, that your manuscript resembles alphabet soup?
- ▲ Have you checked your word choice to weed out vague, pretentious, or inflated vocabulary?
- ▲ Listening as objectively as you can to the "voice" of the person speaking in your article, do you sound like a reasonable human being? Do you sound pompous, pretentious, dogmatic?
- ▲ Have you examined your manuscript for standard grammar and usage? If you do not feel confident of your ability to recognize such mistakes, have you asked someone with these skills to review the manuscript for you?

Revising for Accuracy

- ▲ Are all the words spelled correctly?
- ▲ Have you checked all the facts that can be verified?
- ▲ Are the spellings of all personal and institutional names accurate?
- ▲ When you quote others or refer to the work of others, are the quotations and references accurate and true to the spirit of the original?
- ▲ Have you double-checked the bibliographic information in the original work?
- ▲ Do all your sentences mean precisely what you intended?
- ▲ Have you proofread the document carefully?

Using the Opinions of Others

At various stages in the writing process, you may want to use the opinions of others to help you assess areas for improvement. You may request the help of colleagues or others with editorial skills. As a result of submitting your manuscript, you may receive comments from reviewers, or even the editors.

Comments from others are valuable because they represent a reader's response to what you have written. As readers, the people who provide the comments may have varying levels of editorial ability, but if even one has difficulties understanding what you have written, you have a problem communicating with at least one reader—and, more than likely, with other readers.

The best way to respond to criticism is to take it as an indication of a trouble spot. Your critic may have provided you with an explanation of what he or she thought the problem is. Evaluate that advice when you make your assessment of the difficulty and then develop your own solution. No critic can solve a writing problem for you unless he or she rewrites your work. Critics are superb at indicating where problems exist, but they have varying abilities to articulate the true nature of the problem. You are the one who must fix the difficulty, and therefore both the problem and the corrective measures should make sense to you.

Writing the Abstract

Many periodicals require that you submit an abstract of 100 to 300 words with your manuscript. An abstract provides a summary of the article for potential readers. In addition, abstracts are frequently included in secondary sources, such as online databases, and can therefore serve either as a preview or a surrogate for the article itself.

Abstracts are frequently classified as either indicative or informative. Sometimes the terms descriptive and substantive are used instead. An indicative, or descriptive, abstract describes the contents of the article, including the purpose, the scope of coverage, and the methods used. It can be thought of as a representation of the document that is more detailed than the title or the subject terms assigned to the document. Figure 50 provides a sample of an indicative abstract for a hypothetical article.

An informative, or substantive, abstract summarizes the contents of the document. It presents the purpose, scope, and methods of the article but also summarizes the major findings or conclusions. The informative abstract can be thought of as a miniature version of the article itself. A sample of an informative abstract appears in figure 51.

As a miniature version of the document, the informative abstract provides more information to the user than the indicative abstract does, and a good informative abstract can sometimes be sufficient for the user's needs. The indicative abstract usually functions as little more than an elaborate

The purpose of this study is to identify the reasons that editors of journals in the health sciences give for rejecting manuscripts. Articles written during a 10-year period by editors of fifty journals were surveyed, and the reasons they gave for rejecting manuscript were recorded. Reasons for rejection were coded as "primary reason" or "secondary reason." Responses were then sorted by topic. From this analysis, three topical categories emerged, two with more than 80% primary reasons, and one with 90% secondary reasons. Some tentative conclusions about the reasons editors give for rejecting manuscripts were drawn, and suggestions for a more detailed study were made.

Figure 50. **Indicative Abstract**

The purpose of this study is to identify the reasons that editors of journals in the health sciences give for rejecting manuscripts. Articles written during a 10-year period by editors of fifty journals were surveyed, and the reasons they gave for rejecting manuscript were recorded. Reasons for rejection were coded as "primary reason" or "contributing reason." Editors, when writing about their selection processes, gave reasons for rejection that fell into three broad categories: (1) rejection because of perceived substantive flaws in the research or in the presentation of the research in the article; (2) rejection because, in the editor's opinion, the article was not appropriate in some way for the journal; and (3) rejection because of failure to conform in some way with the journal's expectations for style, format or submission procedures. Rejection because of substantive flaws and because of inappropriate submission were termed "primary" causes for rejection, since 80% of the responses in these categories received primary codes, based on the context in the articles. Rejection for failure to conform to expectations was labelled a "contributing factor," since 90% of the responses in this category received "secondary codes," based on context. The article includes the specific reasons for rejection included in each category. The authors conclude with recommendations for the design of a more detailed study of the reasons editors reject manuscripts.

Figure 51. **Informative Abstract**

table of contents, indicating the kind of information the user would find in the article. Nevertheless, the indicative abstract does provide additional information and is useful as a more thorough representation of the document's subject than the title.

In spite of the fact that informative abstracts are frequently more useful to readers, indicative abstracts are more common, probably because they are shorter and easier to prepare. Some kinds of articles, such as philosophical pieces, are difficult to summarize adequately in a few words. Writing a good informative abstract of any article is difficult, but, in our opinion, the benefits to the user are worth the effort.

Writing abstracts is a little like outlining in reverse. You pull from the article the purpose, the scope, the thesis, and the main ideas. Below are some guidelines for writing abstracts.

▲ Be sure you are familiar with the article. (If you did not write it, read it several times.)

▲ Identify the thesis or purpose of the article and shape that into a summary sentence.

▲ Underline or highlight the sentences in the article that present the major points.

▲ Using the thesis or purpose statement as a topic sentence and the main ideas as supporting points, develop a coherent and readable paragraph.

▲ Revise your abstract, adding details if you feel they are necessary (and if you will not exceed your word limit).

▲ Be sure that the balance of ideas in your abstract accurately reflects the balance of ideas in your article.

▲ Revise your abstract as you would any other paragraph, assessing overall content, organization, and style.

Preparing the Manuscript for Submission

Almost every periodical has guidelines for submitting manuscripts. These guidelines are sometimes printed near the masthead or in one issue a year. They are often available on request from the publisher. Reference books can also provide information on the requirements of various periodicals, although this information can be out of date. Titles of some reference tools appear in the list of selected readings.

Every editor has a fund of stories about how would-be authors send in manuscripts without bothering to look at the periodical's requirements. These stories run the gamut from submitting children's poetry to a scientific journal to sending a copy of a single-spaced manuscript, without an abstract, to a periodical that requires double-spaced submissions in triplicate, with an abstract on a separate page. Failure to proofread manuscripts carefully is another common fault of would-be authors.

Editors differ in their reactions to these practices, from amused toleration to anger at an implied discourtesy. At the very least, submissions that do not follow the rules cause the editors more work. They also cast doubt on the thoroughness of the author. For these reasons and more, it makes sense to take the time to discover the periodical's requirements for submission, and follow them.

Typically, a periodical's information for authors will advise you on the style to follow in preparing your manuscript, including the form for footnotes and references. The requirements will also tell you whether the manuscript should be single or double spaced, how many copies to submit, whether or not an abstract is required, and more.

TYPES OF ARTICLES

So far, we have talked about articles in general. In this section, we will consider several types of articles that librarians are likely to write.

Report of Research

A fundamental approach to a subject is to attempt to establish new information about that subject—to discover, to prove, or to confirm facts and theories. Definitions of research and classifications of types of research have been formulated, ranging from very narrow to very broad. These definitions, and arguments over what is and is not research, vary within and between disciplines. We are not interested so much in defining the methods that constitute research as in identifying what we call a research approach to a subject. For our purposes, we can define the research approach as *following a systematic method to develop new information that answers a question, tests a hypothesis, or sheds light on a subject.* When a librarian takes this approach to investigating a topic, an identifiable type of article can result, which we will call the report of research.

The design and the conduct of research are complex subjects, treated extensively in other publications, and are beyond the scope of this book. Although performing research and describing the results are independent activities, they are mutually dependent. Reporting the results of research is essential to the research process. Once researchers have obtained data, established facts, or tested relationships, their results should be made available to the professional community for discussion, debate, and testing. The analysis and validation of research results through publication is an important part of establishing factual knowledge.

Looking at a research article as a piece of writing shows another vital connection between the process of research and the process of reporting the results. Frequently, what looks at first glance like a poorly written research article turns out to be, in fact, a poorly conceived or badly executed piece of research. For example, vague, general, or unsubstantiated conclusions may seem at first to be a writing problem; but on further analysis they may turn out to be a problem with content, resulting from the lack of focused or concrete research or inconclusive results. A poor article can follow adequate research, but it is very difficult to get a good article from poor research. As obvious as this may seem, it is worth stating that the quality of the research article depends on the quality of the research itself.

In some disciplines, particularly in the sciences, articles reporting the results of research are expected to follow a prescribed organizational pattern:

(Introduction)
Methods
Findings
Discussion (Analysis, Recommendations)

We can surmise that this pattern has endured because it is a logical way to present the results of inquiry. Each section presents a different type of information, and the seemingly rigid separation of sections serves to isolate what was done, what was found, and what the researcher thinks it means. For this reason, the logic underlying this formal structure provides a good organizational model for reports of research, even when authors choose to vary wording or make other modifications in the heading structure.

As a mnemonic device, we suggest this paradigm for the structure of a research report:

why?	(introduction)
how?	(methods)
what?	(findings)
so what?	(discussion or analysis)
now what?	(recommendations)

Failure to keep the content of these sections discrete is one of the most common problems in poorly written research articles. When this happens, writers fail to distinguish the methods they used from the results they obtained, or they do not differentiate between their results and their ideas about those results. These difficulties are more than problems in organization; they infringe on the basic notion of the investigative procedure. And from a pragmatic standpoint, problems with maintaining these distinctions in a research report almost always result in a manuscript that is difficult to follow.

Report of Experience

Another basic approach is to describe, discuss, and evaluate your experience with a subject. A report of experience can be defined as the description of a project, procedure, or solution to a problem.

In some ways, a report of research is the easiest type of article to write, because it has the clearest organizational pattern. Within the types of articles that we are labeling reports of experience, no clear-cut organizational pattern exists. Many articles that report the experience of the author consist of sections with purposes that could be broadly defined as similar. Typical sections used in reports of experience are listed below. The phrases below describe the purposes of each section. They do not represent the actual phrasing of headings used in the articles.

- ▲ statement of general problem
- ▲ statement of local problem
- ▲ analysis of problem
- ▲ criteria for a successful solution
- ▲ topical division into main sections
- ▲ discussion of strengths and weaknesses

Although articles describing practices in libraries can be extremely useful, they can also be little more than glowing reports of a library's inspired decision to use red instead of yellow flags in the card catalog. Some typical pitfalls in articles describing practices in libraries are:

- ▲ The topic is not significant to the general library community.
- ▲ The practice is too local; generalized applications to other situations are not readily apparent.
- ▲ The approach is not objective or analytical; no attempt is made to discuss weaknesses of the approach as well as strengths; the article is gleaming with "project glow," an enthusiasm about new approaches that does not provide realistic analysis.
- ▲ The article focuses inordinately on procedural details, obscuring or ignoring basic principles.

Analytical Article

In analytical articles, authors bring their research, experience, observation, and thought to bear on a topic. Here, the author is speaking from an authority that transcends a specific research project or experience. Several types of informed analysis are quite common in our literature:

- ▲ *State-of-the-art article:* This type of article could more accurately be called state-of-the-technology, since it frequently summarizes new developments in technology. Updates in all fields, technological or not, can be grouped here.
- ▲ *Presentations of techniques from another field:* Articles that explain the basics of another field or discipline; anything from marketing to machine repair is included here.
- ▲ *Predictions and philosophy:* Articles looking backward to our roots, forward to our future, or inward to our essence fall here.

Analytical articles are almost always organized topically, using main sections that represent the broad division of the subject into its parts.

Procedural Article

Articles that describe procedures can be very useful in a practitioner's field. Their major purpose is to present a procedure that can be used by others. It may well be that the procedure is not exactly the way you do it at your shop; instead, it may represent steps that can be generalized and applied anywhere. The writing checklists in this book are generalized examples of processes that are intended to raise awareness of important steps, rather than dictate rigid sequences.

Procedural articles can be organized by following the guidelines for writing procedures and instructions. Chapter 7 provides specific advice on writing procedures.

Appendix

TEST YOUR SKILLS
Discussion and Answers

A. REVISING WEAK AND PASSIVE VERBS
(Chapter 3)

1. Problem sentence: *Reimbursement for courses in word processing will not be approved unless a recommendation is submitted in writing to the director of Personnel.*

   Notice that this sentence contains many ambiguities in meaning: approval of or for what? What is being requested? By whom? What should be recommended? By whom? In a real situation, some of these questions may be answered from the context of the sentence, but frequently the context does not make the meaning clear. The sentence contains two passives (will not be approved) (is submitted). While it would be unfair to say that the passive *causes* ambiguity in meaning, it allows the writer to leave out potentially important information. Notice, too, that as you attempt to recast the sentence in the active voice, you are forced to confront the ambiguities and decide *who* is the important actor, and *what* is the important action. Although a number of revisions of this sentence might be effective in specific contexts, the one below illustrates how the search for an active verb can trigger a more precise formulation of the idea behind the sentence.

   > Employees seeking reimbursement for courses in word processing should submit a note from their supervisors to the Director of Personnel, indicating that word processing is important to performance of their jobs.

   Additional revision of this sentence might result in creating more than one sentence to include all the detail necessary for clarity, further illustrating how the search for an active verb acts as a catalyst in revision.

2. Problem sentence: *The necessity for making long-distance calls, especially given the escalating charges for such calls, should be a consideration in requests for changes in telephone service.*

   The main idea in this sentence is obscured by subordinate elements. By identifying who should do what and why, the sentence regains focus and strength. Note, again, that the search for the significant action verb calls your attention to a variety of possible meanings and forces you to choose exactly what you wish to say. Your search for the verb *triggers* the revision process, which can continue through several steps and frequently ends with an entirely new configuration of the sentence:

> Before requesting changes in departmental telephone service, depart-ment heads should review needs for long-distance calls carefully. The following guidelines should help in selecting the level of long-distance service available from each phone.

3. Problem sentence: *The fact that the number of requests for this information culminated in an increase from 1976 to 1978 is an indication that addi-tional staffing will be required within the next two years.*

This sentence contains a weak verb plus a noun (is an indication) and an ineffective passive (will be required), as well as numerous other difficulties. Moving the main action to the verb and changing the passive to active cuts through the verbiage:

> The increase in requests for this information from 1976 to 1978 indi-cates that we will need additional staffing within the next two years.

4. Problem sentence: *All employees should be informed that their requests for reimbursement are to be completed in triplicate and sent to the business office as soon as possible.*

This sentence contains two passives that obscure the meaning. Who should inform the employees? Who should do what?

> Department heads should inform all employees to send three copies of their request for reimbursement to the business office as soon as possi-ble.

After completing this revision, you might decide that the emphasis you want is not on "informing," but on the information itself, so you might re-vise as follows:

> Please send three copies of your request for reimbursement to the busi-ness office within one month of completing the course.

Vague, convoluted sentences frequently contain ambiguities. Searching for a specific action verb that embodies the main idea of your thought ena-bles you to consider several possibilities and narrow your meaning to pre-cisely what you wish to say.

B. COMMON PROBLEMS WITH SENTENCE STRUCTURE
(Chapter 3)

In the discussion below, we cover sentence problems that occur frequently in professional writing. We suggest that you use this discussion like a reference book, turning to the appropriate discussion when you think you have encountered a problem in that area. The sections may also be useful as a reminder of the variety of problems with sentences. Exercises testing your skills in these areas appear in figure 6, page 61. Answers appear in section C of this appendix, below.

Subject Separated from Its Verb. In modern English, the position of a finite verb is a crucial clue to its subject. As phrases and clauses attach themselves to the sentence's subject or predicate, the *temptation* (subject) that every writer feels to push the verb back to make room for the newcomers *becomes* (verb) stronger (as in this example). Separations of subjects and verbs are natural and inevitable, but the greater the separation, the greater the chance for confusion.

To fix these problem sentences, move the verbs closer to their subjects by moving some of the modifying phrases or clauses out of the way: "As phrases and clauses attach themselves to the sentence's subject or predicate, every writer feels a growing temptation to push the verb back to make room for the newcomers."

Verbs and Prepositions Separated from Their Objects. Again, this problem tends to occur in professional writing with heavily "embedded" sentences that often sound clear when writers are composing the sentences. Not only do they already know what they are trying to say, but they "hear" clues, like rhythm and pitch, that are not available to their readers. Even during revision, a writer may find it necessary to examine the structure of a sentence to locate this kind of problem, rather than rely on how a sentence sounds.

Once you have located the problem sentence, of course, the solution is to move the verb or preposition nearer to its object, eliminating as many chances for confusion as possible. Diagnose and fix the problems in the following sentences.

1. Please return by campus mail or in person any books that are overdue.

The direct object, "books," is too far from its verb, but if you place "by campus mail or in person" after "overdue," the prepositional phrases seem to modify "overdue." The solution is to simplify "books that are overdue" to "overdue books" and then to move "books" next to its verb:

Please return any overdue books by campus mail or in person.

2. The computer furnishes valuable information, which is used for decisions about the purchase of new and replacement materials, and the capability for performing a greater range of tasks.

In sentence two, the direct object, "capability," is so far from its verb, "furnishes," that it appears to be one of the objects of the preposition "about," which is closer to it. The simplest solution is to reword the sentence with two subjects and two verbs, keeping the complex phrases intact:

> The computer furnishes valuable information, which can be used for decisions about the purchase of new and replacement material; it also allows us to perform a greater range of tasks.

Modifiers Too Far from the Words They Modify. Place individual words, phrases, and clauses near the words they modify to avoid the confusion caused by dangling or "floating" constructions. Find the problem in this sentence with a floating adverb:

> I thought of coming here often but never did.

This sentence is not correct unless my thought was that I would come to this place many times. If "often" should modify "thought," it should be moved closer to that word:

> Often, I thought of coming here but never did.
> (Or) I often thought of coming here but never did.

Identify the dangling modifier in this sentence:

> Leaving the lounge, the reference desk is on your right.

In this construction, the reference desk seems to be leaving the lounge. To correct the problem, you can give "leaving the lounge" something more probable to modify:

> Leaving the lounge, you will find the reference desk on your right.

Or convert the participial phrase into a clause, so that "leave" has a subject:

> As you leave the lounge, the reference desk is on your right.

Problems with dangling modifiers seem simple to detect when isolated in single sentences. However, they occur frequently in early drafts, and all writers need to be on the lookout for them during revision.

Incorrect or Vague Referents of Relative Clauses. Relative clauses use pronouns like *who, which,* and *that* to allow a clause to attach itself to the pronoun's referent, normally an antecedent noun or pronoun, as in the sentence:

> He is the *man* (antecedent) *who* (relative pronoun) *said* (relative pronoun's predicate in relative clause) so.

Relative pronouns must agree in number (singular or plural) with their antecedents, but their grammatical function in their own clause determines their case (nominative, possessive, or objective). Problems with the pronoun's number can occur, though they are seldom as confusing or irritating for your reader as using the wrong case. If your grasp on the grammatical rule is not very firm, the vague sense of the antecedent's power over the form of the pronoun may cause considerable trouble. The antecedent has no influence over the pronoun's case, but keeping these two rules separate may require special attention during your revision. See if you can spot the problem with this sentence:

She was the director *who* we noticed in Chicago.

"Director" is the antecedent for the relative pronoun "who," but it has no influence over the relative pronoun's case. The pronoun's case is determined by its use in its own clause. In that clause, it is the object of "noticed" and so it must be in the objective case:

She was the director *whom* we noticed in Chicago.

For the same reason, you can create a syntactical tangle by using the objective case immediately after a preposition that has the entire relative clause as its object. See if you would spot this error:

I hope they will award the grant to *whomever* needs it.

As always, the pronoun should take its case from its use in its own clause, where it is employed as the subject of "needs." The sentence should be corrected by putting the relative pronoun into the subjective case:

I hope they will award the grant to *whoever* needs it.

In addition, relative pronouns are responsible for another frequent and noticeable error in the sentences of many writers: the use of *which* to refer to hopelessly complex units of thought—sometimes a preceding clause, sometimes whole paragraphs. Writers who write complicated sentences are especially prone to this error, but it can be easily detected and corrected during revision.

In speech, you can usually make someone understand whether you want *which* to refer to a whole clause or an individual antecedent by verbal pace, pitch, and emphasis. Unfortunately, when you try the same trick in writing, the reader is deprived of all these clues. Since you will probably hear the sentence the way you heard it when you wrote it originally, your best chance of catching this awkwardness is to get in the habit of going on a "which" hunt. Some stylists advocate burning all *which*'s at the stake, but the word can still be useful when it refers to something definite near it in the sentence.

Describe the problem in this sentence:

I forgot the title of the book, which embarrassed me.

What does "which" refer to? The book? The title? Forgetting the title? If "which" refers to a clause or might refer to several things in the sentence, you are better off rewriting the sentence:

Forgetting the title of the book embarrassed me.
(Or) I forgot the title of the book that embarrassed me.

Inconsistent Verb Tense. Consistent verb tense is not the same as uniform verb tense. When events occur at different times, writers shift the tense of the verb to show the sequence of events. Earliest events are placed in the past perfect tense: "He had arrived ten minutes before I did." The present tense and present tense perfect would then indicate actions after the past tense action: "We closed at midnight last summer, but we have closed at 2 a.m. since September."

Inconsistent verb tense occurs when you shift from one tense to another although you are referring to events that occur at approximately the same time. Verb tense is also inconsistent when you use the same tense for events that occur at distinctly different times. Such inconsistencies are common in first drafts, especially when a narrative of events is recalled.

Verb tense is one of the few devices a writer can use to keep the sequence ,of events clear in the reader's mind, so an alert reviser will be sensitive to any deviation from the operating principle: events that occur at approximately the same time should be in the same tense, and earlier events should use an anterior tense in the sequence of verb tenses.

Consider the way using the sequence of verb tenses could eliminate this ambiguity:

He asked for the report earlier than I intended to give it to him.

What sequence of events does this statement indicate: Did I first intend to give it to him next week and then hear from him that he wanted it tomorrow? Or had he already asked me to give him the report tomorrow, and the sentence informs us that I have defiantly decided to turn it in later?

We can indicate the first situation by placing "intended" in the past perfect tense, showing that action as coming first:

He asked for the report earlier than I had intended to give it to him.

Or indicate the second sequence of events by placing "asked" in the past perfect tense, showing that the "asking" came before the "intending":

He had asked for the report earlier than I intended to give it to him.

Misleading Emphasis. A main clause at the end of a sentence should contain the information you want to stress. If your important ideas are not placed in independent clauses, and unimportant information appears in the main clause or in a position of emphasis, like the end of the sentence, readers may misread your emphasis or feel vaguely puzzled. If several sentences nearby contain the same problem, the entirely unpredictable rise and fall of the sentence may prove distracting, if not disorienting.

What does the writer seem to be emphasizing in each of these sentences?

1. He failed to show up, thus losing his job. (Try rewriting this sentence by using the modifying phrase as the main clause and compare the result with the original.)

2. She has prepared an excellent report, in my judgment. (Rewrite the sentence to lessen the emphasis on the writer's judgment.)

3. When he fell down the stairs, we were at the water fountain. (What do you feel is the main thought here? Experiment with revisions that alter the emphasis.)

4. The fire began at 3 p.m., destroying the Whitman collection. (Rewrite the sentence to emphasize what you feel is significant.)

C. REVISING SENTENCES
(Figure 6, Chapter 3)

These answers represent one way of revising. Other effective revisions are also possible. Discussion of the grammatical issues illustrated here appears in section B, above.

1. Please make sure that your employees understand that the corridor is off limits and that the main gate will remain open. Please also make sure that they understand the reasons behind this policy.
2. Since the periodicals room has been expanded, I am sure that it will be a more comfortable place to study.
3. This afternoon, we placed in the library the sign-up sheet that you gave me on Monday.
4. Your report should anticipate the need for additional supplies and personnel. This need may fluctuate with the level of your department's activity.
5. To determine the amount to charge for lost items, we will use the price in the current *Books in Print*; when no price can be found there, we will charge $25.
6. We have purchased a number of new children's books that are going out almost as fast as we can place them on the shelves.
7. After we had reviewed all the applications, some of the candidates were brought in for interviews.
8. We needed an extra hour to explain the arguments for and against our plan to keep the library open during the evening in the summer.
9. The number of interlibrary loan requests that we received in the main branch of the library was twice as high as the number received in the music library.
10. The air conditioner shook so severely that it disturbed the student working next to it.
11. She received her doctorate when her daughter was ten years old.
12. Students are allowed to use the lounge for meetings as long as they observe the no-food rule.
13. Perhaps we welcome this challenge more than other people do.
14. In a meeting yesterday, we decided to strike. (You might describe the bill of fare in another sentence, if you think this is a good time to be thinking about food.)
15. She asked the committee, a consultant from Baltimore, and me to come up with a proposal. The consultant had worked on similar projects for two universities and a nonprofit institute.
16. We have decided to deal with the problem of theft, which has worried me greatly, by installing an alarm system.

D. WORD CHOICE
(Figure 7, Chapter 3)

1. We will begin planning in September.
2. I think I am ready to do something new.
3. We are considering paying allowed expenses.
4. People with similar backgrounds tend to get together.
5. Don't cry over spilt milk. (Can you improve on it?)
6. Let's collaborate on this project.
7. All personnel should recognize the urgent need to plan for contingencies. (Alternative: All employees need to plan for contingencies immediately.)
8. Haste makes waste. (Did you improve on it?)
9. We need to know how the policy affects our work.
10. Thank you for your help.

E. DIAGNOSTIC TEST FOR PROBLEMS IN GRAMMAR AND USAGE
(Figure 8, Chapter 3)

Discussion of the problem areas appears in the pages given below.

1. The *consortia are* a valuable resource for libraries in the state. (Alternatively: The consortium is a valuable resource for libraries in the state.) (subject-predicate disagreement, page 330)
2. There *are* a librarian and a student in the main reading room. (subject-predicate disagreement, page 330)
3. The director, along with her staff and an outside consultant, *has* considered the proposals carefully. (subject-predicate disagreement, page 330)
4. The rotunda was restored by a team of experts, many of whom worked on the project for over a year. (punctuation error, page 331)
5. The terminal has been delivered; however, it is not yet installed. (punctuation error, page 331)
6. At our next meeting, we will vote on the motion that is *lying* on the table. (incorrect form of verb, page 331)
7. Just between you and *me*, we may have a surplus in our budget this year. (incorrect form of pronoun, page 332)
8. She is an administrator *whom* Jim and *I* can trust. (incorrect form of pronoun, page 332)
9. She is an administrator *who* can trust Jim and *me*. (incorrect form of pronoun, page 332)
10. Frequently, we talked about forbidding smoking, but never did. (misplaced modifiers, page 333)

11. Having adjusted the fee scale for next year, we expect that the searching budget, plus revenues, should cover our expenses next year. (misplaced modifiers, page 333)
12. We feel *really bad* about our mistake. (adjective and adverb confusion, page 333)
13. I am not sure which of these two alternatives is *better*. (incorrect form of adjective or adverb, page 334)
14. Our services might improve if we had *fewer* people on vacation. (problem in usage, page 334)
15. Each year seems to bring *its* own problems. (incorrect form of the possessive, page 336)
16. The total cost will equal two *years'* rent. (incorrect form of the possessive, page 336)
17. It is one of the libraries that *have* applied for a grant. (ambiguous or incorrect pronoun reference, page 337)
18. Everyone has a chance to voice *his or her* opinions. (Alternatively, although with a slightly different meaning: Everyone has a chance to voice opinions.) (ambiguous or vague pronoun reference, page 337)
19. The report is mainly about the rapidly changing costs of telecommunications and the need for libraries to prepare their institutions for major increases in the near future. (unparallel construction, page 338)
20. If I *had* been there, the decision would have been different. (misuse of subjunctive, page 339)

F. DIAGNOSTIC TEST FOR PROBLEMS IN
GRAMMAR AND USAGE
(Chapter 3)

Here is a discussion of problem areas in figure 8, chapter 3.

Subject-Predicate Disagreement (1, 2, 3)

Confusion or irritation is likely when you match a singular subject with a plural form of the verb or a plural subject with a singular form of the verb. If you missed problem 1, test yourself again:

The data (is/are) now conclusive.

In problem 1, you had to watch out for a plural subject that did not end in *s*. Words like *media* and *data* are derived from Latin neuter plurals, and they still require plural verbs.

Correct: The data are now conclusive.

If you missed problem 2, test yourself again:

There (are/is) a letter and a speech on the desk.

Watch out for false subjects, like *here* and *there*, followed by the verb. In these sentences, the real subject follows the verb, but it still determines whether the verb is singular or plural:

Correct: There *are* a letter and a speech on the desk.

If you missed problem 3, test yourself again:

The speech, along with his letters, (was/were) in the desk.

Watch out for subjects and verbs that are separated by prepositional phrases. Whether the verb should be singular or plural depends upon its subject, not upon the nearer noun or pronoun. The object of a preposition is never the subject of a verb.

Correct: The speech, along with his letters, was in the desk.

A less frequent and less noticeable problem in subject-predicate agreement, but one that troubles many educated writers is how to treat collective nouns, like *jury* or *committee*. The rule is that they are plural when they are thought of as a collection of individuals, and singular when they are thought of as a group.

Plural meaning: The committee *do* not agree (among themselves) about the policy.
Singular meaning: The committee (as a whole) *does* recommend the new policy.

Punctuation Errors (4, 5)

If you missed problem 4 or 5, test yourself again:

We are anticipating another successful fund-raising campaign, therefore, we plan to begin several important, new programs next September.

If a sentence contains two or more complete thoughts, be sure these independent constructions are properly joined. A subordinating conjunction can properly join the two clauses, making one of them dependent. Except when independent clauses are joined by coordinating conjunctions (*and, but, for, or, nor, yet,*), commas are not enough. Watch out, especially, for words like *therefore, however, thus, consequently,* and *nevertheless.* They may look like conjunctions, but they are adverbs, and they have not been deputized to link independent clauses together by themselves.

Correct: We are anticipating another successful fund-raising campaign; therefore, we plan to begin several important, new programs next September.

Test yourself again in this example:

The auction of withdrawn books; however, has become an annual event.

The rule about the semicolon is very simple in these situations. If you cannot use a period at that spot, you cannot use a semicolon. Do not use semicolons to separate dependent clauses or modifying phrases from the parts of the sentence that they need in order to make sense.

Correct: The auction of withdrawn books, however, has become an annual event.

The semicolon is used properly as a more powerful comma only to separate the major units in a series of clauses or phrases, some of which contain at least one comma:

Present were Greg Noyse, our representative from Public Relations; Margery Butterworth, from Personnel; and Hillary South, from Purchasing.

Normally, of course, the elements of a series like this one would be separated only by commas, but if you replace the semicolons with commas here, your readers will not be able to tell who came from where. Semicolons are not used because this is a series; they are used because your reader needs them to understand you.

Incorrect Form of Verb (6)

If you missed problem 6, test yourself again:

I *laid* down for a nap.

The chair *sets* in the lobby.
A significant problem *has arose*.
The report *was laying* on your desk.
The fountain *was broke* by vandals.

Readers seem to look at verbs harder than they look at anything else in a sentence, and if you have chosen the wrong form of the verb (*broke* for *broken*, *ain't* or *isn't* for *am not*, *if I would have* for *if I had*, etc.), the result is righteous indignation more often than confusion.

If you aren't sure of the meaning or correct form of any verb, look it up in a dictionary under its present tense form to be sure it is acceptable. If you are still not sure, avoid it in your final draft.

Correct: I *lay* down for a nap (yesterday).
The chair *sits* in the lobby.
A significant problem *has arisen*.
The report *was lying* on your desk.
The fountain *was broken* by vandals.

Incorrect Form of Pronoun (7, 8, 9)

If you were not sure about problem 7, test yourself again:

Give Jim and (I, me) a chance to solve the problem.
For (he, him) and for many other people, grammar was difficult.

The use of the nominative form of a pronoun instead of the objective in compound indirect objects and in prepositional phrases is one of the most frequent and glaring mistakes made by educated professionals.

I and *he* are the nominative forms of the pronoun, so they cannot be used as an indirect object, a direct object, or the object of a preposition.

Correct: Give Jim and *me* a chance to solve the problem.
For *him* and for many other people, grammar was difficult.

If you do not see the structural principle involved in these examples or in problems 7, 8, or 9 on the diagnostic test, we advise you sit down with a grammar book or an English teacher and work on these problems until you are satisfied you understand them. Readers notice these errors, and they count against you.

If you missed problem 8 or 9, test yourself again:

Give it to (whoever/whomever) wants it.
Give it to (whoever/whomever) he chooses.

Look carefully at the way *who(-ever)* and *whom(-ever)* is used *within its own clause*. *Who* and other personal pronouns in the nominative form, like *I*, *he*, *she*, *we*, and *they*, also have an objective form. Whenever one of these pronouns is an object of a preposition or an object of a verb *in its own clause*, it should be put in the objective case, no matter what happens in the rest of the sentence.

The relative pronoun "whoever" is the *subject* of the dependent clause, "whoever wants it," and so must be in the nominative case:

Give it to whoever wants it.

In the second example, the relative pronoun "whomever" is the *object* of "chooses" in the dependent clause, "whomever he chooses"; therefore, despite the same beginning of the sentence, the correct form is:

Give it to whomever he chooses.

Misplaced Modifiers (10, 11)

If you missed problem 10 or 11, test yourself again:

We *only* requested that she appear in person.
Having been warned about the danger well in advance,
his arrival was handled very carefully.

Readers use the location of modifiers as an indication of what the modifier is supposed to modify. Unfortunately, these modifying words and phrases do not always occur to writers in the order that is most convenient for the reader, and since writers already know what their modifiers modify, they do not always see the need to change the sentence in order to prevent confusion.

If prepositional phrases and adverbs look as if they could modify something they do not, move them as close to the words they modify as you can. If you cannot move them without making the sentence sound awkward or ambiguous, however, leave them where they are.

Correct: We requested *only* that she appear in person (unless, of course, we really only requested it).

Watch out for introductory phrases of every kind, but especially participial phrases followed by passive constructions. If they look as if they could modify something else in the sentence, reword the sentence, rather than take the chance you will be misunderstood.

Correct: Having been warned about the danger well in advance, we handled his arrival very carefully.

Adjective and Adverb Confusion (12)

If you had trouble with problem 12, test yourself again:

We had to wait for a *real* long time.

When an adjective is used in place of an adverb, or an adverb is used when an adjective should be used, the reader is not given the right clue about the part of the sentence the word should be modifying. Adjectives modify nouns and pronouns. Adverbs modify verbs, adjectives, and other adverbs. So watch out for the adjective *real*. It is not supposed to modify an adjective or an adverb, and so *real long* is ungrammatical.

Correct: We had to wait for a *really* long time.

Watch out, also, for adverbs misused after verbs like *appear, feel, look, seem*, and *sound*. Modifiers that follow these verbs normally describe the subject of the verb, not the action being performed. In "He looks tall," "tall" does not describe the action of the verb; it describes the subject of the verb. When you feel well, "well" is an adjective—just as you feel healthy, not healthily. On the other hand, if you feel badly, your sense of feeling does not perform well. Since people seldom write about their numbness, we can elevate this special case to a general rule: Feel bad, if you must; but never *feel badly*, if you want your writing to look good.
Test yourself:

I believe the exhibit looks (well, good) where it is.

"Looks" requires an adjective, not an adverb, so, in this sentence, "well" is correct only if the exhibit happens to look *healthy*.

Correct: I believe the exhibit looks *good* there.

Incorrect Form of Adjective or Adverb (13)

If you had trouble with problem 13, test yourself again:

She is the (taller/tallest) of the two students.

Don't use the superlative form when only two things or people are compared. Use the comparative:

She is the taller of the two students.

Some errors in this category are judged very severely, primarily as evidence of ignorance; others are rarely noticed by most readers.
    The most serious problems arise with an inappropriate application of comparative and superlative endings to adjectives that change their root form when they change degree. *Bad*, for example, should become *worse* or *worst*. *Worser, badder*, and *baddest* are incorrect.
    Some modifiers can form their comparative and superlative degrees using either *more* and *most* or the *-er* and *-est* endings, but no form should use both (not *more quieter, most quietest*).
    Dictionaries are your most reliable guide when you are not sure of the correct form for an adjective or adverb.

Problems in Usage (14)

Usage errors turn perfectly acceptable words into offenders by using the wrong word for the job. The number of possible mistakes is very large, of course, but examples of ten very frequent and blatant errors are listed below. The handbooks listed in the selected readings contain extensive lists of frequent usage problems.

Affect/Effect. Choose the correct form in the sentence below:

The criticism did not seem to (affect, effect) him at all.

Use *effect* as a verb only when you mean accomplish or produce (as a result): He *effected* the settlement by himself. Use *affect* as a verb when you mean influence:

The criticism did not seem to *affect* him at all.

Amount/Number. Choose the correct form in the sentence below:

We didn't know the (amount, number) of sources he needed to cite.

Use *amount* only when the quantity is not being thought of in terms of countable units: We didn't know the *amount* of material he needed to cite.
Use *number* when the quantity is being thought of in terms of countable units:

We didn't know the *number* of sources he needed to cite.

Lie/Lay. Choose the correct form in the sentence below:

Yesterday he (lay, laid) down for a moment to rest.

Use *laid* as the past tense form of the transitive verb *lay*, meaning "put": He *laid* it on the table. The past tense of *lie*, meaning "recline," is *lay*:

Yesterday, he *lay* down for a moment to rest.

Due to/Because. Choose the correct form in the sentence below:

Costs skyrocketed (due to, because of) overruns.

Use *due to* only if you mean "owed to": More praise was *due to* him. Use *because of* when you mean "caused by":

Costs skyrocketed *because of* overruns.

Equally as . . . as. Choose the correct form in the sentence below:

She is (equally as qualified as, as qualified as) the male candidate.

Equally as is never used correctly, because it is always redundant. Use *equally* by itself or *as . . . as* by itself:

She and the male candidate are *equally qualified*.
She is *as qualified as* the male candidate.

Fewer/Less. Choose the correct form in the sentence below:

It cost (less, fewer) dollars than we had feared.

Use *less* when the quantity is not thought of in terms of countable units:

It cost *less* money than we had feared.

Use *fewer* when the quantity is thought of in terms of countable units:

It cost *fewer* dollars than we had feared.

Principal/Principle. Choose the correct form in the sentence below:

You should list four (principle, principal) accomplishments.

Use *principle* as a noun meaning "rule" or "law": a basic *principle*.
Use *principal* as a noun meaning "main" or "chief one," and as an adjective meaning "chief" or "most important":

You should list four *principal* accomplishments.

Hopefully/(We) Hope. Are both sentences below correct? If not, which is the correct one?

Hopefully, our problems are behind us.
We hope our problems are behind us.

Use *hopefully* only as an adverb modifying the nearest noun or pronoun, and meaning "with hope":

Hopefully, we watched the sky for signs of clearing.

Use *(we) hope* when that is what you mean:

We hope our problems are behind us.

Most unique/Unique. Choose the correct form in the sentence below:

The building's architectural style is (most unique, unique).

Unique mean "unequalled." If the building's style is *unique*, it cannot get any "uniquer," much less, "most unique":

The building's architectural style is *unique*.

Infer/Imply. Choose the correct form in the sentence below:

His manner (infers, implies) that he is confident.

Use *infer* to mean "interpret":

I *infer* from his manner that he is confident.

Use *imply* to mean "assert indirectly":

His manner *implies* that he is confident.

Incorrect Form of Possessive (15)

If you had difficulty with problem 15, test yourself again with these sentences:

We discussed the (childrens, children's, childrens') rights.
You can't tell a book by (its, it's, its') cover.

The rule that you should use *'s* for singular possessives and *s'* for plural possessives has one serious drawback: it isn't always true. Some pronouns, like *his, hers, ours, yours,* and *its,* form their possessives without an apostrophe. *It's* is the contraction of "it is," and that is all it can mean.

Correct: You can't tell a book by its cover.

When a noun does not add an *s* to form its plural, its plural possessive is formed by adding *'s* to the plural form: the media's responsibilities, the oxen's diet, the women's movement.

Correct: We discussed the children's rights.

In every case, you can be sure the apostrophe is in the right place if you place it after you have spelled the noun, singular or plural, that does the possessing:

Mr. Jones + *'s* car = Mr. Jones's car
the Joneses + ' = the Joneses' car

Then, let your ear tell you whether you need to add an *s* after the apostrophe. If you would add an *s* sound saying the word, add it when you write it: Keats's (or Keats') ode—but not Keat's.

Ambiguous or Incorrect Pronoun Reference (17, 18)

If you were unsure about problem 17, test yourself again:

He is the only one of all those participants who (is, are) prepared for the meeting.

He is one of the few participants who (is, are) prepared for the meeting.

Watch out for *that, which,* and *who* when they are the subject of a verb in their own clause. Whether they are singular or plural depends upon the pronoun, noun, or noun phrase that they refer to, called the antecedent. You cannot tell what this antecedent is from its role or position in the sentence.

The only test is to ask yourself what the pronoun means in your sentence—how many things or people are being said to perform an action (or to be something)?

In "He is the only one of all those participants who (is, are) prepared for the meeting," "who" means the same thing as "one" and "He." Of all those participants, he is the only one who *is* prepared for the meeting.

Correct: He is the only one of all those participants who *is* prepared for the meeting.

In "He is one of the few participants who (is, are) prepared for the meeting," "who" means the same thing as "participants." A few participants are prepared for the meeting, and he is one of those participants who are prepared.

Correct: He is one of the few participants who *are* prepared for the meeting.

Clearly, when you use a singular pronoun to refer to something plural or a plural pronoun to refer to something singular, you are depriving your readers of one of the few clues they have to tell them what the pronoun means.

If you were unsure of problem 18, test yourself again:

Anybody in that group who (thinks, think) you are wrong must be unsure of (himself or herself, themselves).
Watch out for pronouns like *anyone, anybody, each, every, everyone*, and *everybody*. They are singular in meaning, and they require a singular verb. *Who* refers to *anybody*, and so it is singular.

Correct: Anybody in that group *who thinks* you are wrong. . .

When other pronouns in the sentence refer to singular pronouns like these, they too should be singular:

. . . must be unsure of *himself or herself.*

Unparallel Construction (19)

If you were unsure of problem 19, test yourself again:

The job description for circulation assistant includes the following duties: staff circulation desk, answer telephone, type overdue notices, and mail clerk.

When two or more items are linked by coordinating conjunctions, such as *and* and *or*, the reader expects them to be similar in importance and grammatical structure. Verbs are linked with verbs, things with things, modifiers with modifiers, and clauses with clauses. Within a sentence or paragraph, any departure from this rule and any unnecessary shifting of voice, tense, number, or person can sound inconsistent and confusing.

Parallel clauses: The search could take several weeks, or it could take several months.

Parallel verbs: The search could take several weeks or could take several months.

Parallel objects: The search could take several weeks or several months.

A clearer job description (and one much easier on the clerk!) appears below:

The job description for circulation assistant includes the following duties: staff circulation desk, answer telephone, type overdue notices, and serve as mail clerk.

Misuse of Subjunctive (20)

If you were unsure of problem 20, test yourself again:

If I (was, were) in Chicago then, I don't remember it.

If I (was, were) you, right now, I would do it.

In modern English, the subjunctive mood often gives good writers a bad case of insecurity. It is not used often enough to become familiar, but it is required often enough to create strange-sounding mistakes, especially in the *if* clause: "if I would have done it"—or even "would of done it." To express a meaning with the verb that is "contrary to fact," even the youngest speakers of English feel the need to change the verb's form, and the frequency of *would* in the main clause of such constructions tends to bring it to mind, despite the fact that it does not sound quite right either.

So, if you spot a "would have" or "would of" in an *if* clause, you can almost be sure that you want to use the subjunctive form of the verb and that the form you have used is wrong.

In the first example above, the *if* clause does not imply that the speaker was or wasn't in Chicago in the past, only that *if* the speaker was, *then* something follows as a consequence. So, this verb should be in the much more familiar indicative mood.

Correct: If I *was* in Chicago then, I do not remember it.

If you want to imply that you are *not* in Chicago (that is, assert that something is contrary to fact), then the verb in the *if* clause has to change, and as soon as you have made that change, your ear will tell you—unfailingly—how to change the verb in the main clause. To express the subjunctive meaning in the present tense, change the verb in the *if* clause to the plural, past tense form: *am* becomes *were*, *knows* becomes *knew*, *helps* becomes *helped*, regardless of the subject.

The sentence above becomes: "If I *were* in Chicago now (but I'm not), I would remember it."

Correct: If I *were* you, right now (but I'm not), I would do it.

If you want to use a past tense meaning of the subjunctive—that is, to imply (for example) that you *were* not in Chicago then, but that if you had been in Chicago, something would have followed as a consequence—you have to change the verbs in both clauses in order to express a past tense meaning:

If I *had been* in Chicago then (but I *wasn't*), I *would have remembered* it.

The subjunctive expresses this past tense meaning by using the past perfect tense in the *if* clause (*had* plus the past participle for active verbs, or *had* plus *been* plus the past participle for passive verbs), and the *would* clause (or main clause) will automatically change to the correct (present perfect) form.

Spot the problem and provide the correct form for this past tense, passive subjunctive:

If I *would have been told*, I'd have known his name.

For the past tense subjunctive, in the *if* clause you need to follow "I" with *had*, plus *been*, plus the past participle *told*:

Correct: If I *had been told*, I'd have known his name.

G. EVALUATING THE EFFECTIVENESS OF MEMOS
(Chapter 5)

The purpose of this exercise is to provide practice in identifying, within a specific context, factors that influence the success of written communication. This is a hypothetical situation, and so there is no definitive list of reasons for failure.

For additional practice, imagine how different circumstances might affect your decisions. The questions below may help direct your analysis.

1. Comment on the purpose for the memo, considering the following:

    What did the writer wish to accomplish by writing the memo?

    What precise statement of purpose fits this situation?

    What are the human relations goals in this situation?

2. Comment on the audience for the memo, and the perspective of that person or persons, considering the following:

    Given the purpose, is the memo addressed to the right person or persons?

    Did the writer know clearly what he or she wanted the reader to do? Was that communicated clearly?

    What did the reader need to know in order to agree to do what the writer wanted?

    Can you divide the information that might be useful to the reader into two categories: (1) information that is essential to the requested action and (2) additional information that may be of interest to the reader but is not vital to the decision?

    What are the potential concerns or vested interests of the reader? Does the memo address these concerns?

3. Comment on the communication strategy and the approach that the writer selected to accomplish his or her purpose, considering the channels that were used, the characteristics of the memo, and the means of communication that the writer might use to introduce, reinforce, or follow up on the memo.

    What seem to be the normal channels for getting a transfer of funds in this institution?

    Given the nature of the purpose of the memo (a rush transfer of funds), are there variations on the use of these channels that the writer might have explored?

    Does the memo make clear how the writer thinks the rush transfer can be accomplished?

    Is the memo tailored to work within the channels that the writer wants to use?

    What other means of communication might be used, depending on the situation, to introduce, reinforce, or follow up on the memo?

4. Comment on the development and selection of content for the memo, considering the following:

    What were the key elements of the situation that the reader needed to grasp? Base your analysis on the purpose of the writer and the perspective of the reader.

Does the memo include all the information immediately relevant to the action that the writer is requesting from the reader?

Is some of the information unnecessary, and, if so, does it impede understanding of the memo?

Are there gaps in the information? Should content be included that is not there?

5. Comment on the organization of ideas and information in the memo, considering the following:

Locate the place where the writer makes clear the reason for writing the memo. What effect might the placement of this information have on the reader's response?

Locate the place where the writer makes clear what he or she wants the reader to do. What effect might the placement of this information have on the reader's response?

Which pattern of organization is used:

Direct order—moving from general to specific, from most important to least important?

Indirect order—moving from specific to general, from details to conclusions?

Are there organizational ways to provide hierarchies of information, highlighting the most important and making additional information available?

Consider the relationship of length to effectiveness. Is the memo too long, given the situation and the content? Too short? What are some organizational ways to approach the problem of length?

6. Comment on the language skills used in the memo, considering the following:

Is the tone appropriate to the purpose and the reader?

Do you see problems with sentence length and construction that would interfere with the effectiveness of the memo?

Do you see problems with word choice that would reduce the effectiveness of the memo?

In what ways did the memo motivate the reader to cooperate with the writer? How could the motivation be strengthened?

H. USING THE DIRECT APPROACH
(Figure 10, Chapter 5)

Here is an illustration of one way to rewrite the memo about the transfer of funds to purchase the microfilm of the Workhorse Press papers.

DATE: February 1, 1987

TO: Paula Long, Head, Public Services

FROM: L. A. Jackson

SUBJECT: Request for Transfer of Funds to Purchase the Papers of the Workhorse Press on Microfilm

I would like to ask for your approval of a rapid transfer of funds from several subject accounts to the microform account.

This transfer will allow us to order the papers of the Workhorse Press on microfilm for $10,000. The rush request is necessary in order to receive a $2,000 discount and to have the papers available for Steven Smith's seminar this fall. (See attached.)

No procedure exists for a rush request, so Betty Lee in Acquisitions and I have come up with a rush process that would meet Acquisitions' guidelines. If you approve of the transfer, the next step is to forward this memo to Linda Dawn for her approval. From her, this memo can go directly to Betty Lee, who will process the request for the transfer and the order simultaneously. If Betty has this memo, with the necessary approvals, by February 10, we should be able to order the papers within the deadline.

The papers will be purchased from several funds.

The other subject specialists and I have agreed that
the purchase is important and worth the effort to
fund it jointly. Their authorizations appear by each
request.

REQUEST TO TRANSFER FUNDS
Please transfer the following amounts as indicated.

Amount	Transfer from	Transfer to	Authorization
$1,000	History (1407.702)	Microforms (1298.705)	*L. Held*
$1,000	English (1411.702)	Microforms (1298.705)	*C. Baker*
$1,000	Business (1501.702)	Microforms (1298.705)	*R. Rawlins*
$ 500	Lib. Sci (1709.702)	Microforms (1298.705)	*T. Carter*
$2,500	Jrnlism (1992.702)	Microforms (1298.705)	*J. Jorden*
$2,000	Spec. Col (2021.702)	Microforms (1298.705)	*F. Barton*

The completed order slip is attached.

I am also attaching a description of the Workhorse
papers. Their acquisition will enhance our extensive
collection of primary materials in business, literature, and journalism. No university within driving
distance contemplates purchasing these papers at
this time.

Thanks for helping with this rush request.

```
            Attachments:   Justification for the rush request
                              from Steven Smith
                           Description of the Workhorse Press
                              Papers
                           Completed Order Slip for the Work-
                              horse Papers

            c:   (List of subject specialists)
                 Steven Smith
                 Betty Less, Acquisitions

            ADMINISTRATIVE APPROVALS:


            _____      _____
            (Head, Public Services)          (Date)


            _____      _____
            (Head, Technical Services)       (Date)


            _____      _____
            (Head, Acquisitions)             (Date)
```

This revision assumes, for illustrative purposes, an environment that requires all the details in writing. The revision also combines an explanation of the request with a form that can be forwarded, documenting authorizations. An alternative method for revising would be to use two documents, one as an explanation and the other as a transmittal form. For additional practice, consider the pros and cons of the two approaches.

I. WRITING POLICIES
(Figure 21, Chapter 6)

This exercise provides an opportunity to make policy decisions in the context of a specific situation. The goals you choose will shape your responses to the questions. Identifying goals first, rather than taking sides with either the librarians or the faculty, will help you focus on what you are trying to accomplish. In deciding on goals, you will want to consider the limitations imposed by the situation as well as your ideal goals.

The variety of possible goals in this situation forms a continuum, from the hard-line purpose of establishing one loan period for all users to maintaining the faculty's prerogative of unlimited loans. Human relations goals might include statements about retaining positive relations with both faculty and students.

Once you have defined what you wish to accomplish, you should be able to identify alternatives and choose the one that will best accomplish those goals. You may wish to think specifically about trade-offs between human relations goals and other goals. Try to predict the possible effects of the alternative you choose. The policy you write for the library handbook should include the rationale, along with the statement of policy. Write it in a positive tone, with the assumption that faculty, students, and library staff will read it.

The communication strategy that you follow to inform the faculty will depend on your policy statements. If you have written a policy that you know will be unpopular, you will want to consider how best to communicate the rationale to the faculty, including means of communication in addition to writing.

Below is one version of a letter announcing a policy that is a compromise. Compare it with your policy and assess the strengths and weaknesses of both. Then experiment with planning the communication strategy for a policy that makes all loan periods uniform. Be sure to write out all the documents, since this policy will test your skill in handling difficult policy situations.

DATE: March 12, 1989

TO: College Faculty

FROM: L. K. Franklin, Library Director   *LKF*

SUBJECT: Policy on Faculty Loans

   Under the present policy, faculty can check out books on virtually unlimited loans. The purpose of this policy was to provide materials for extended projects. However, a recent check of our files showed that more than 900 titles have been checked out for at least three years. Many of these titles were checked out when the book first arrived, and consequently the book has never been available for use by students and other faculty.

   The goal of an equitable lending policy should be to meet the needs of the individual user while not compromising the good of the whole user community. We understand the faculty's need to extended access to materials, and we are also committed to the principle of providing access to these materials to our entire user community, including students.

   We have come up with a revised policy that, while admittedly a compromise, will meet both needs with only slight inconvenience, we hope, on both sides. Material will be checked out to faculty for one semester. If, at the end of the semester, you are still using a particular book, you may renew it for another semes-

ter. If the book is not returned, it will be overdue, and
we ask that you return it for others to use.

We hope that this policy will encourage the return
of books that are not being used, so that they will be
available for others.

J. WRITING EFFECTIVE MONTHLY REPORTS
(Figure 37, Chapter 10)

There are many ways to rewrite the monthly report from figure 37. One possibility appears below. You may wish to analyze it, as well as your own version, examining the effects of each organizational alternative.

August 15, 1985

Western Branch Library
Monthly Report: July 1985
Submitted by Toni Ellis

I. Statistical Highlights

Adult circulation rose again for the fourth consecutive month. July showed an 8% increase over June and a 12% increase over last July.

For the third month in a row, Saturday circulation has been twice that of the same month last year. Saturday reference requests have almost doubled.

All other statistics were within 4% of both last month and last year.

II. Staffing

Short Staffing: With one staff member on vacation and another position vacant until the end of the month, we sometimes had only one adult staff member in the library. July is one of our busiest months.

Children's Librarian Position Filled: Dera East began on August 1 as our new children's librarian.

III.   Adult Programming (See attached table for attendance)

Summer Travel Series: This series continues to be well attended, with over 100 adults per session.

Friends of the Library Museum Excursion: The trip to Chicago's Art Institute, August 5, is now sold out. At $25 a ticket, the Friends expect to clear $500 and purchase a new slide projector for the library.

IV.   Children's Programming (See attached table for attendance)

Camp Visit: Summer Thrills Camp has requested a weekly visit in July and August. The group of 35 children was well monitored by the 5 adults who accompanied them.

Summer Reading Club: We have 75 children enrolled, compared with about 100 last year. Weekly participation averages fewer than 20, although those who come are enthusiastic. Since our programming is essentially the same as in other years, I am not certain what accounts for the lower enrollment.

V.   Activities, Issues, and Concerns

Our program schedule continues to tax a staff of our size. Having a children's librarian

We continue to have problems with pages wanting unscheduled vacations, despite our stern warnings at the beginning of the summer. I suggest that we hire an extra page next year so that we can cover these unexpected requests more easily. I'll have my plan ready for our next meeting.

K. WRITING AN ANNUAL REPORT
(Figure 39, Chapter 11)

Obviously, you have much more information than you can use, so you will
have to select the content for the report. The information you select and
the way you present it will be based on what you feel will achieve the director's goals for the report. Many different, and very good, reports can be
designed around this basic information. When you are assessing your report, and the reports of others, consider the following:

What is the overall impression given by our report?
What information stands out clearly?
What were your main sections? What types of headings did you use?
Did you make use of tables and graphics? What points do they make? Are
they clear and easy to read?
What is the tone of your report?
Is the information of general interest?
What motivates the readers to read the report?
Do you use library jargon or a plain-English vocabulary?

SELECTED READINGS

The number of books and articles on the subjects touched on in this book is staggering. For that reason, the list below is limited to books that provide good introductions to their topics. Journal articles were excluded because of their numbers and their relatively narrow focus. We felt, too, that they were easily accessible through various indexes and from the bibliographies in the works below. More specialized texts will also be listed in the appropriate general works below. Finally, we included some textbooks because of the overview they provide.

Alley, Brian, and Jennifer Cargill. *Librarian in Search of a Publisher: How to Get Published*. Phoenix: Oryx, 1986.

Aschman, Catherine. *The Word Processing Handbook: A Step-by-Step Guide to Automating Your Office*. Seattle: Self-Counsel Pr., 1981.

Baker, Sheridan. *The Complete Stylist*. New York: Thomas Y. Caswell, 1966.

Balkin, Richard. *A Writer's Guide to Book Publishing*. New York: Hawthorne, 1977.

Beach, Mark. *Editing Your Newsletter: A Guide to Writing, Design and Production Editing*. 2nd ed. Portland, Oreg.: Coast to Coast Books, 1982.

Belkin, Gary S. *Getting Published: A Guide for Businesspeople and Other Professionals*. New York: Wiley, 1984.

Bolles, Richard. *Tea Leaves: A New Look at Resumes*. Berkeley: Ten Speed Pr., 1976.

Bostwick, Burdette E. *Resume Writing: A Comprehensive How-to-Do-It Guide*. 3rd ed. New York: Wiley, 1985.

Bradford, Leland P. *Making Meetings Work*. La Jolla, Calif.: University Assoc., 1976.

Bryant, Margaret M. *Current American Usage: How Americans Say It and Write It*. New York: Funk & Wagnall, 1962.

———. *A Functional English Grammar*. Boston: Heath, 1945.

Butcher, Judith. *Copy Editing: The Cambridge Handbook*. New York: Cambridge Univ. Pr., 1975.

———. *Typescripts, Proofs and Indexes*. New York: Cambridge Univ. Pr., 1980.

Campbell, Jeremy. *Grammatical Man*. New York: Simon & Schuster, 1982.

Cappon, Rene J. *Associated Press Guide to Good Writing*. Reading, Mass.: Addison-Wesley, 1982.

Cassata, Mary B., and Roger Cain Palmer, eds. *Reader in Library Communication.* Englewood, Colo.: Information Handling Services, 1976.

Clark, Ruth Anne. *Persuasive Messages.* New York: Harper & Row, 1981.

Conway, Barbara, and Barbara Schindler Jones. *Improving Communication in the Library.* Phoenix: Oryx, 1986.

Copperud, Roy H. *American Usage: The Consensus.* New York: Van Nostrand Reinhold, 1970.

Corry, Emmett. *Grants for Libraries: A Guide to Public and Private Funding Programs and Proposal Writing Techniques.* 2nd ed. Littleton, Colo.: Libraries Unlimited, 1986.

Cortez, Edwin M. *Proposals and Contracts for Library Automation: Guidelines for Preparing RFP's.* Chicago: ALA, 1987.

Cross, Mary. *Persuasive Business Writing: Creating Better Memos, Letters, Reports, and More.* New York: American Management Assn., 1987.

Day, Robert A. *How to Write and Publish a Scientific Paper.* 2nd ed. Philadelphia: ISI Pr., 1983.

Emery, Richard. *Staff Communication in Libraries.* London: Clive Bingley, 1975.

Evans, Bergen, and Cornelia Evans. *A Dictionary of Contemporary American Usage.* New York: Random House, 1957.

Farace, Richard V., Peter Monge, and Hamish Russell. *Communicating and Organizing.* Reading, Mass.: Addison-Wesley, 1977.

Flores, Ivan. *Word Processing Handbook.* New York: Van Nostrand Reinhold, 1983.

Flugelman, Andrew. *Writing in the Computer Age: Word Processing Skills and Style for Every Writer.* Garden City, N.Y.: Anchor, 1983.

Follett, Wilson. *Modern American Usage: A Guide.* Ed. and completed by Jacques Barzun et al. 1966. Repr. New York: Grosset and Dunlap, 1970.

Fowler, Henry W. *A Dictionary of Modern English Usage.* 2nd ed. Rev. by Sir Ernest Gowers. London: Oxford Univ. Pr., 1965.

Frost, Joyce H., and William Wilmot. *Interpersonal Conflict.* Dubuque, Ia.: William C. Brown, 1978.

Goldhaber, Gerald M. *Organizational Communication.* 3rd ed. Dubuque, Ia.: William C. Brown, 1979.

Grossman, Lee. *Fat Paper: Diets for Trimming Paperwork.* New York: McGraw-Hill, 1976.

Guth, Hans P. *The New English Handbook.* Belmont, Calif.: Wadsworth, 1982.

Halcombe, Marya. *Presentations for Decision-Makers: Strategies for Structuring and Presenting Your Ideas.* Belmont, Calif.: Lifetime Learning Publications, 1983.

Hall, Donald. *Writing Well.* 5th ed. Boston: Little, Brown, 1985.

Hall, Mary J. *Developing Skills in Proposal Writing.* 2nd ed. Portland, Oreg.: Continuing Education Publications, 1977.

Hunt, Gary. *Communication Skills in the Organization.* Englewood Cliffs, N.J.: Prentice-Hall, 1980.

International Paper Company. *Pocket Pal.* 13th ed. New York: International Paper Company, 1983.

Jefferies, James. *The Executive's Guide to Meetings, Conferences, and Audiovisual Presentations.* New York: McGraw-Hill, 1983.

Johnson, Richard D. *Written Communications in Libraries.* Chicago: Assn. of College and Research Libraries, 1986.

Jones, Barbara S. *Written Communication for Today's Manager.* New York: Lebhar-Friedman, 1980.

Kett, Merrilyn, and Virginia Underwood. *How to Avoid Sexism: A Guide for Writers, Editors, and Publishers.* Chicago: Lawrence Ragan, 1978.

Knapp, Mark L. *Nonverbal Communication in Human Interaction.* 2nd ed. New York: Holt, Rinehart & Winston, 1978.

Laborde, Genie. *Influencing with Integrity: Management Skills for Communication and Negotiation.* Palo Alto, Calif.: Syntony, 1983.

Lambert, J. J. *A Short Introduction to English Usage.* New York: McGraw-Hill, 1972.

Larsen, Michael. *How to Write a Book Proposal.* Cincinnati: Writer's Digest, 1985.

Leathers, Dale G. *Nonverbal Communication Systems.* Boston: Allyn & Bacon, 1976.

Lewis, Phillip. *Organizational Communications: The Essence of Effective Management.* Columbus: Grid, 1975.

Line, W. C. *News Writing for Non-Professionals.* Chicago: Nelson-Hall, 1976.

Malandro, Loretta A., and Larry Barker. *Nonverbal Communication.* Reading, Mass.: Addison-Wesley, 1983.

Marins, Richard, and Harvey S. Weiner. *The McGraw-Hill College Handbook.* New York: McGraw-Hill, 1985.

Marsh, Patrick O. *Messages That Work: A Guide to Communication Design.* Englewood Cliffs, N.J.: Educational Technology, 1983.

McCrimmon, James A. *Writing with a Purpose.* 8th ed. Eds. Joseph F. Trimmer and Nancy I. Sommers. Boston: Houghton Mifflin, 1984.

McKenzie, Alan T. *A Grin on the Interface: Word Processing for the Academic Humanist.* New York: MLA, 1984.

McWilliams, Peter. *The Word Processing Book: A Short Course in Computer Literacy.* Los Angeles: Prelude, 1982.

Miletich, John J. *Writing, Editing and Distributing News Releases: A Bibliography of Information in Books.* Monticello, Ill.: 1981.

Miller, Casey, and Kate Swift. *The Handbook of Non-Sexist Writing.* New York: Lippincott and Crowell, 1980.

Mullins, Carolyn J. *A Guide to Writing and Publishing in the Social and Behavioral Sciences.* New York: Wiley-Interscience, 1977.

Pease, Allan. *Signals.* New York: Bantam, 1984.

Pence, R. W., and D. W. Emery. *A Grammar of Present-Day English.* 2nd ed. New York: Macmillan, 1963.

Plotnik, Arthur. *Elements of Editing: A Modern Guide for Editors and Journalists.* New York: Macmillan, 1982.

Polking, Kirk, and Leonard Meranus. *Law and the Writer.* Cincinnati: Writer's Digest, 1978.

Powell, Judith W., and Robert B. LeLieuvre. *Peoplework: Communication Dynamics for Librarians.* Chicago: ALA, 1979.

Powell, Walter W. *Getting into Print: The Decision-Making Process in Scholarly Publishing.* Chicago: Univ. of Chicago Pr., 1985.

Price, Jonathan. *The Definitive Word Processing Book.* New York: Penguin, 1984.

Renton, Michael. *Getting Better Results from the Meetings You Run.* Champaign, Ill.: Research Pr., 1980.

Ross-Larson, Bruce. *Edit Yourself: A Manual for Everyone Who Works with Words.* New York: Norton, 1982.

Sellen, Betty-Carol, ed. *Librarian/Author: A Practical Guide on How to Get Published.* New York: Neal-Schuman, 1985.

Shores, David L., ed. *Contemporary English: Change and Variation.* Philadelphia: Lippincott, 1972.

Sides, Charles H. *How to Write Papers and Reports about Computer Technology.* Philadelphia: ISI Pr., 1984.

Sigband, Norman. *Communication for Management and Business.* 2nd ed. Glenview, Ill.: Scott, Foresman, 1976.

Steiner, Dale R. *Historical Journals: A Handbook for Writers and Reviewers.* Santa Barbara, Calif.: ABC-Clio, 1981.

Stevens, Norman, and Nora B. Stevens. *Author's Guide to Journals in Library and Information Science.* New York: Haworth Pr., 1982.

Stevens, Norman D. *Communication throughout Libraries.* Metuchen, N.J.: Scarecrow Pr., 1983.

Stratton, John, and Dorothy Stratton. *Magic Writing: A Writer's Guide to Word Processing.* New York: New American Library, 1984.

Strunk, William Jr., and E. B. White. *The Elements of Style.* 3rd ed. New York: Macmillan, 1979.

Stultz, Russell. *Writing and Publishing on Your Microcomputer.* Plano, Tex.: Wordware, 1984.

Tropman, John. *The Essentials of Committee Management.* Chicago: Nelson-Hall, 1979.

Tufte, Edward. *The Visual Display of Quantitative Information.* Cheshire, Conn.: Graphics Press, 1983.

Van Leunen, Marie-Claire. *A Handbook for Scholars.* New York: Knopf, 1979.

Visco, Louis. *The Manager as Editor.* Boston: CBI, 1981.

Weaver, Patricia. *Persuasive Writing: A Manager's Guide.* New York: Free Press, 1977.

Whalen, Doris. *The Secretary's Handbook.* Rev. ed. New York: Harcourt Brace Jovanovich, 1973.

White, Jan. *Mastering Graphics: Design and Production Made Easy.* New York: Bowker, 1983.

Zinsser, William. *On Writing Well.* 2nd ed. New York: Harper & Row, 1980.

Zinsser, William. *Writing with a Word Processor.* New York: Harper & Row, 1983.

INDEX

Abstracts: discussion of, 274, 314–16; example of, 315; guidelines for, 316. *See also* Summaries

Accuracy, editing for: discussion, 70–72; in analytical reports, 211; in annual reports, 252; in letters, 196; in memos, 124; in monthly reports, 230; in policies, 149; in procedures, 172–73

Action statements. *See* Requests for action

Adjectives and adverbs: confusion of, 333–34; incorrect form, 334

Agendas: definition of, 266; organization of, 267–69; planning of, 267–69; purpose of, 266–67; subdivided, 268–69

Analytical articles, 319

Analytical reports: checklist for, 209–11; definition of, 197; elements of, 201–5; example of, 206–8; format for, 201; objectivity of, 199–201; organization of, 201–5; purposes of, 197–99

Annual reports: approaches to, 235–39; audience for, 234–35; checklist for, 245, 248–52; content of, 239–40; definition of, 231–32; designing and producing, 245; organization of, 241–45; purposes of, 232–34; test your skills, 245, 248

Appearance of documents. *See* Professional appearance of documents

Approach, development of: in analytical reports, 199–201; in annual reports, 235, 252; in letters, 175–77, 195; in minutes, 270–73; in monthly reports, 220–21, 229–30; in policies, 137–39, 146–47

Assistance with production: revision during production, 91–92; staffing,
75,76; training in use of equipment, 75, 76

Attachments, 115, 251–52

Beginnings: importance of, 44; in informational memos, 116; in policy and procedure memos, 119; in transmittal memos, 115; in update memos, 119; summaries as beginnings, 44–45; title or subject line, 44; types of, 45

Blind copies, 114–15

Block style for letters, 194

Brainstorming, 36–37

Brevity: conciseness, 7; in memos, 97; in monthly reports, 219; revising for, 58–60, 62, 64–65

Channels of communication: analysis of, 15–17; downward, 16; for analytical reports, 209–10; for memos, 123; institutional practice, 16–17; lateral, 16; upward, 16

Charts. *See* Tables and charts

Checklists: for analyzing communication channels, 17; for analyzing communication preferences of individuals, 27; for analyzing periodicals from a writer's perspective, 305; for choosing an approach to documenting policies, 131; for deciding when to write, 10, 95; for dictating, 80–81; for grammar and usage, 71; for identifying problems in your draft, 52; for organizing negative information in letters, 182; for organizing persuasive letters, 183, 188; for organizing positive information in letters, 177; for planning communication strategy, 29; for reviewing your communication strategy, 54; for revising for reader's reactions, 53; for revising to accomplish your goals, 52–53; for unintended offenses, 57; for writing analytical reports, 209–11; for writing annual reports, 245, 248–52; for writing articles for publication, 302; for writing letters, 194–96; for writing memos, 123–24; for writing monthly reports, 228–30; for writing policies, 146–49; for writing procedures, 169–73; for writing to a specific reader, 29; of beginnings of documents, 45; of communication formats, 8; of signposts, 46; of the professional writing process, 23. *See also* Professional writing process

Choice of words: ethics of, 18; exercise for revision of, 67; revision of, 61–67

Chronological organization of resumes: discussion of, 283, 284; example of, 286–87

Clarity: of policies, 141; principle of professional writing, 7; revising for, 58–67

Cliches: discussion of, 66–67; exercise, 67

Columns, 84

Communication policy: for channels of communication, 15–17; for consistency, 89–90; for policies, 128, 135–37

Communication preferences: analysis of, 26–27

Communication strategy: choice of channels and format, 30–31; for analytical reports, 209–11; for annual reports, 249–52; for letters, 195–96; for memos, 123–24; for monthly reports, 229–30; for policies, 143–44, 147–49; for procedures, 170–73; planning of, 29–31; reviewing of, 54

Communication systems. *See* Channels of communication

Complimentary close in letters, 193

Conciseness. *See* Brevity

Confidentiality of written documents: in annual reports, 234–35; in monthly reports, 220

Consistency: in design, 89–90; in letter styles, 194

Content, development of: general discussion of, 31–37; of analytical reports,

210; of annual reports, 239–40; of informational reports, 255; of letters, 195; of memos, 123–24; of monthly reports, 221–22; of periodical articles, 295–96, 305, 317–20; of policies, 138–39, 140–41, 146–48; of procedures, 156, 170–71

Context of professional writing, 3–4

Copies: distribution of, 114; etiquette of, 114–15

Corporate identity. *See* Consistency

Covers, 87

Criteria for effective writing: general discussion, 2–3; letters, 175–76; memos, 96, 341–42, 343–45; policies, 126; procedures, 151

Critiques of writing by others: 50–51, 313–14

Date line: in letters, 189; in memos, 112

Deductive order. *See* Direct approach

Description as a technique in minutes, 272–73

Design: consistency, 89–90; elements of, 83–87; general discussion, 81–90; newsletter look, 88; of annual reports, 245; office look, 87–88; principles of, 82–83; published look, 88–89; purpose of, 82

Desk-top publishing, 81, 89

Development of content. *See* Content, development of

Dialogues, 36

Dictating, 80–81

Direct approach: examples of, 103–7, 243–45; exercise in, 97–100, 109; in organization, 103–8; to make memos easy to read, 101

Direct order. *See* Direct approach

Distribution: notation for, 114–15; of annual reports, 238; of policies, 133–37

Document design. *See* Design

Document production. *See* Production of documents

Documentation: of policies, 130–33; of procedures, 152–53; use in administration, 213–15, 218; use of annual reports for, 232–33; use of monthly reports for, 213–17

Documents. *See* Sample documents

Downward communication, 16

Drafts: general discussion, 40–41, 43–46;

of analytical reports, 210; of annual reports, 252; of letters, 195; of memos, 124; of monthly reports, 229–30; of periodical articles, 306–7; of policies, 147–48; of procedures, 171; revision of, 48–67, 77

Easy-to-read documents: memos, 97, 101; monthly reports, 217–19

Editing: being your own editor, 310–14; copy editing, 298; editorial roles, 295–301; rewriting, 298; substantive editing, 298

Editing for correctness: general discussion, 68–72; in analytical reports, 211; in annual reports, 252; in letters, 196; in memos, 124; in monthly reports, 230; in policies, 149; in procedures, 172

Effective writing: achieving goals, 2–3; failures in writing, 4–5; in letters, 175–76; in memos, 96, 341–42, 343–45; in policies, 126; in procedures, 151; principles of, 6–7. *See also* Revision

Effective writing, criteria. *See* Criteria for effective writing

Emphasis: exercise in, 61; problems of, 60

Enclosures, 115

Ethics: in choice of words, 18; in organization of content, 18; in professional writing, 17–19; in selection of content, 18; of ends, 17–19; of means, 17–19

Examples of documents. *See* Sample documents

Evaluation of documents: assessing effectiveness, 96–100; exercise, 97–100; of policies, 137, 147; of procedures, 156, 170–72

Executive summaries. *See* Summaries

Exercises: designing a monthly report format, 225; diagnostic test of problems in grammar and usage, 69–70; evaluating the effectiveness of memos, 98; revising sentences, 61; revising weak and passive verbs, 60; word choice, 67; wordy constructions, 65; writing annual reports, 245, 246–48; writing monthly reports, 225–27; writing policies, 144–45; writing procedures, 169

Failures of professional writing: document not read, 5; document not understood, 5; general discussion, 4–6; goals not reached, 6; reader antagonized, 6; reader not convinced, 5; relevance misunderstood, 5; responsibility for, 6

Fastening of document, 87

Figures. *See* Tables and charts

Form of name. *See* Signatures

Formality: of memos, 95–96; revising for, 56. *See also* Tone

Format: for agendas, 268–69; for analytical reports, 201; for annual reports, 241–45; for informational reports, 255; for letters, 189–93; for memos, 112–15; for minutes, 271–74; for monthly reports, 220–25; for periodical articles, 297–98, 316–19; for policies, 133; for procedures, 167; for proposals, 259; for resumes, 283–84; for summaries, 275

Freewriting, 35–36

Front matter for reports, 202

Functional organization in resumes: discussion, 284; example, 288–89

Gathering material: institutional information, 34; published information, 33; unpublished information, 33–34

Generalizations, 240

Genre headings: in annual reports, 243–44; in monthly reports, 222–24

Goals of professional writing, 2–3, 6–7. *See also* Purposes for professional writing

Grammar and usage: adjectives and adverbs, 333–34; checklist, 71; diagnosing problems, 68–70; diagnostic exercise, 61, 70; exercise in revising sentences, 61; exercise in revising word choices, 67; misplaced modifiers, 60, 324, 333; possessives, 336–37; prepositional phrases, 60, 323–24; pronouns, 332–33, 337–38; punctuation, 331; relative clauses, 60, 324–25; sentence structure, 60, 323–40; subject-verb problems, 60, 323, 325–26, 330, 331–32; subjunctives, 339–40; usage problems, 334–36

Graphics, 86

Graphs. *See* Tables and charts

Headings: as signposts, 46; computer graphics for, 86; different fonts, 85; genre headings, 243–44; headline

headings, 244; in annual reports, 241–
    45; in memos, 101; in monthly re-
    ports, 222–24; keyboard effects, 85;
    lettering systems for, 85; purpose of,
    85; reflecting organizational struc-
    ture, 242–43; topic sentences as head-
    ings, 245; topical headings, 243; ways
    to produce, 85–86
Headline headings in annual reports, 244
Historical record. *See* Documentation
Human relations: goals in writing, 24–25;
    in informational memos, 116; in let-
    ters, 175–76; in memos, 114; in trans-
    mittal memos, 116; unintended of-
    fenses, 56–57

Indention: as technique for making memos
    easy to read, 101; in outlines, 40, 41
Indirect approach: as organizational pat-
    tern, 108–11; examples of, 98–100,
    110–11; exercise, 109; unconscious
    use of, 109; use in organizing negative
    information, 182, 184–85; use in or-
    ganizing persuasive information, 183,
    186–87
Indirect order. *See* Indirect approach
Inductive order. *See* Indirect approach
Information for administration: in analyti-
    cal reports, 197–99; in annual reports,
    232; in informational reports, 254–
    58; in monthly reports, 213–16
Informational memos: discussion, 116; ex-
    ample of, 118
Informational reports: content of, 255;
    definition of, 254; example of, 256–
    58; organization of, 255; purpose of,
    254–55; reader's perspective in, 255
Informed climate for decision-making,
    214–15
Ink: choice of, 86; consistency in use of, 90
Institutional practice: analyzing channels
    of communication, 15–17; sending
    copies, 114–15; style for letters, 194;
    use of formats, 30–31; use of names
    and titles, 112, 114
Instructions. *See* Procedures
Invention: brainstorming, 36–37; free-
    writing, 35–36; gathering material,
    33–34; general discussion, 31–33;
    making lists, 34–35; making maps, 35;
    writing a dialogue, 36

Jargon: discussion of, 62–64; exercise, 67;
    in annual reports, 238; in policies, 143
Job descriptions: definition of, 275; exam-
    ple of, 280–81; organization
    of, 278
Justified line, 84

Keyboard graphics: as technique for mak-
    ing memos easy to read, 101; defini-
    tion of, 86; use in the office look, 87–88

Lateral communication, 16
Layout: as a technique for making memos
    easy to read, 101; for letters, 193–94;
    for monthly reports, 219, 224–25; fos-
    tering comprehension, 82–83; in rou-
    tine library documents, 87–88. *See also*
    Design
Letterhead: general discussion, 90; use for
    letters, 189; use for memos, 112
Letters: characteristics of, 175; checklist,
    194–96; definition of, 174–75; effec-
    tiveness in, 175–76; examples of, 178–
    79, 180–81, 184–85, 186–87, 190–
    91; formats for, 189–93; layout for,
    193–94; of application for jobs, 285,
    290; organization of negative informa-
    tion, 182, 184–85; organization of
    persuasive letters, 183, 186–87; or-
    ganization of positive information,
    177, 178–79; tone in, 176–77
Levels of formality. *See* Formality
Library identity. *See* Consistency: in design
Lists, 32, 34–35
Literature review as a step in writing arti-
    cles, 303
Logo, 89, 112. *See also* Letterhead

Manuscripts (periodical articles): condi-
    tions of publication, 300–1; inappro-
    priate submissions, 297; problems
    with format, 297–98; reasons for re-
    jection of, 296–98; review of, 298–
    300; selection of, 296–98; sources of,
    294; substantive weaknesses in, 297
Maps as visual representation of ideas, 35
Media for communication: planning com-
    munication strategy, 29–31; prefer-
    ences of communication media, 26–
    27; use of other media to augment
    writing, 29–30

Meetings: agendas, 266–69; as a communication tool, 27; minutes, 269–74
Memos: checklist for, 119, 123–24; criteria for effective memos, 96; definition of, 94–95; direct approach in, 103–8; examples, 98–100, 104–5, 106–7, 110–11, 113, 117, 118, 120–22; format of, 112–15; indirect approach, 108–11; informational memos, 116; making memos easy to read, 97–101; organization of, 102–11; policy and procedure memos, 119; transmittal memos, 115–16; update memos, 116, 119; when to write, 95–96
Mind-boggling language: discussion of, 62, 65–66; exercise, 67
Minutes: definition of, 269; function of, 269–70; organizational structure, 273–74; responsibility for, 270; types of, 270–73; verifying accuracy, 274
Misplaced modifiers. *See* Modifiers
Mixed metaphors: discussion of, 65–66; exercise, 67
Modified block style for letters, 193
Modifiers: exercise, 61; problems with, 60, 333
Monthly reports: checklist for, 228–30; definition of, 212–13; evaluation of, 225; exercise, 222–25; format for, 220–25; layout for, 224; organization of, 222–25; problems with, 216–17; purposes for, 213–16; sensitive issues in, 220; writing reports that will be read, 217–19
Motivation: for writing articles, 291–93; in monthly reports, 218–19; to act, 12–14; to read document, 12–13. *See also* Persuasion
Multiple-sheet headings for letters, 193

Names, form of. *See* Signatures
Needs assessment: for analytical reports, 197–99, 209; for policies, 126–27, 137–39, 146; for procedures, 151–52, 170–73
Negative constructions in syntax: discussion of, 65; exercise, 67
Negative information: discussion of, 182–83; example of, 184–85. *See also* Indirect approach
Negative tone, 141–43

Neutral information. *See* Positive information
Newsletter look in document design, 88
Nominalization: discussion of, 65; exercise, 67. *See also* Strings of nouns
Nonverbal communication, 9

Objectives for writing. *See* Purposes for professional writing
Objectivity in reports: in analytical reports, 199–200; in monthly reports, 214–15, 217
Offensive language: checklist, 57; discussion of, 56–57
Office look in document design, 87–88
Opening statements. *See* Beginnings
Oral communication: characteristics of, 9; combined with written, 11, 29–30; types of, 8
Organization: of agendas, 267–69; of analytical reports, 201–5, 210; of annual reports, 241–45, 250–51; of content, 37–40; of informational memos, 116; of informational reports, 255; of job descriptions, 278, 280–81; of letters, 177–94, 195; of memos, 102–15, 123–24; of minutes, 273–74; of monthly reports, 222–24, 225, 229; of periodical articles, 305–6, 317–20; of policies, 133, 139–40, 141, 147; of procedures, 156–69, 171; of proposals, 259; of reports of experience in periodicals, 318–19; of reports of research in periodicals, 317–18; of resumes, 283–84; of summaries, 275; outlining, 38–40; revising paragraphs for, 54–56; to reinforce meaning, 241–42
Outlines: alpha-numeric (traditional), 39–40; decimal, 40; examples of, 41, 42; types of, 38–40
Overtones in memos, 102

Paper, 86, 90
Paragraphs, 55–56, 101
Paraphrased discussion in minutes, 271–73
Participation in development of policies: group development, 129; organizational review, 128–29; review by entire group, 130; review by representative group members, 130
Parts of a letter, 189–93

Passive voice: discussion of, 59–60, 311–13; exercise in revision, 60
Periodic reports. *See* Monthly reports
Periodical articles (manuscripts). *See* Manuscripts (periodical articles)
Periodicals, types of, 305–6
Personality in writing. *See* Tone
Persuasion: ethics of, 18–19; letters of, 183, 186–88; logical persuasion, 12–14; reasons for action, 13–14
Persuasive writing. *See* Persuasion
Policies: checklist, 146–49; content of, 128–30, 137–39; criteria for effectiveness, 126; definition of, 125; distribution of, 133–37; evaluating and updating, 137; example of, 134; exercise, 144–45; format for, 133; importance of, 127–28; informing people about, 133, 135; keeping policies current, 136–37; need for, 126–27, 137–38; organization of, 139–40; planning communication strategy for, 143–44; policy on policies, 128–37; providing access to, 136; reviewing draft policies, 129–30, 140–41; writing policies, 133, 137–43
Policy and procedure memos: discussion of, 119; example of, 122
Policy files, 131–32
Policy manuals, 132
Policy on policies, 128–37
Policy on written communication in libraries. *See* Communication policy
Positive information: discussion of, 177; example of, 178–79. *See also* Direct approach
Positive tone, 141–43
Possessives, incorrect form of, 336–37
Prepositional phrases: exercise, 61; problems with, 60
Principles of professional writing: clarity, 7; conciseness, 7; consumer-orientation, 7; goal-orientation, 6–7
Procedural articles, 320
Procedure files, 152–53
Procedure manuals, 152–53
Procedures: checklist, 169–73; content of, 156; criteria for, 151; definition of, 150–51; documentation of, 152–53; elements of, 167–68; example, 158–62; exercise, 169; formats for, 167;

need for, 151–52; organization of, 156–57, 163, 166–67; purpose of, 153–54; style of, 168–69; users of, 153–54; who should write, 155–56
Process analysis. *See* Procedures
Process approach. *See* Professional writing process
Production of documents: composite originals, 92–93; discussion of, 73–81; of analytical reports, 211; of annual reports, 252; of letters, 196; of memos, 124; of monthly reports, 230; of policies, 149; of procedures, 173; preparing final copy, 90–93. *See also* Design
Professional appearance of documents, 73–74
Professional writing: definition of, 1–2, 21; purpose of, 2–3; skill in, 2, 21–23
Professional writing process: checklist for analytical reports, 209–11; checklist for annual reports, 245, 248–52; checklist for letters, 194–96; checklist for memos, 123–24; checklist for monthly reports, 228–30; checklist for periodical articles, 301–2; checklist for policies, 146–49; checklist for procedures, 169–73; definition of, 21–23; importance of, 21–22; outline of, 23
Pronouns: ambiguous reference, 337–38; incorrect form of, 332–33
Proofreading, 70–72, 316–17
Proportional spacing, 84
Proposals: definition of, 259; examples, 260–63, 264–65; organization, 259
Public relations: uses for annual reports, 233
Published look in document design, 88–89
Punctuation: errors, 331; in letters, 194
Purposes for professional writing: action goals, 24; of agendas, 266–67; of analytical reports, 197–99, 209; of annual reports, 232–34, 236, 248–49; human relations goals, 24–25; information goals, 24; of informational reports, 254–55; of memos, 94–96, 115–23; of monthly reports, 213–17, 228–30; of policies, 125–28; 137–38, 146; of procedures, 150–54, 170; revising documents to achieve purpose, 52–53

Quality in periodical articles, 293

Quarterly reports. *See* Monthly reports

Reader-orientation as principle of professional writing, 7
Reader's perspective: checklist, 29; discussion of, 25–28; in analytical reports, 199–201, 209; in annual reports, 234–35, 249; in informational reports, 255; in letters, 175, 176, 195; in memos, 123; in monthly reports, 218, 228–29; in policies, 147–48; in procedures, 170–71; in resumes, 285; revising for, 53
Recommendations in analytical reports, 197–99, 205
Redundancies: discussion of, 64; exercise, 67
Refereed periodicals, 298–300
Referees. *See* Reviewing of manuscripts
Relative clauses: exercise, 61; problems with, 60
Reports. *See* Analytical reports, Monthly reports, Annual reports
Reports of experience in periodicals, 318–19
Reports of research in periodicals, 317–18
Requests for action: explicit in the direct approach, 103–5; implicit in the direct approach, 106–8; in analytical reports, 205
Research. *See* Reports of research in periodicals, Gathering material
Research articles. *See* Reports of research in periodicals
Response times: explicit requests in the direct approach, 103–6; implicit requests in the direct approach, 106–8
Resumes: content of, 278–79, 282–83; definition of, 278; example of, 283–84, 286–87, 288–89; organization, 283–84; reader's perspective, 285; with letters of application, 285, 290
Review process. *See* Reviewing of manuscripts
Reviewing of manuscripts, 298–300
Revision: checklist for grammar and usage, 71; checklist for problem areas, 52; checklist for unintended offenses, 57; definition of, 48–49; during production, 77, 91–92; for accuracy in periodical articles, 313; for language and style in periodical articles, 311–13; for

logical organization in periodical articles, 310–11; identifying problems, 49–51; of analytical reports, 210–11; of annual reports, 252; of letters, 196; of memos, 124; of monthly reports, 230; of policies, 140–43, 148–49; of procedures, 171–72; systematic approach, 51–67; using opinions of others in, 50–51, 314
Rough drafts, 40–44, 306–7

Salutation: elimination in memos, 112; in letters, 192
Sample documents: abstract, indicative, 315; abstract, informative, 315; analytical report, 206–8; executive summary, 276–77; format for letters, 190–91; format for memos, 113; informational memo, 118; informational report, 256–58; job description, 280–81; letter containing negative information, 184–85; letter containing neutral information, 180–81; letter containing positive information, 178–79; letter illustrating block letter style, 186–87; letter illustrating modified block letter style, 180–81; letter illustrating traditional letter style, 184–85; memo updating policy, 122, 347–48; memo using the direct approach, 104–5; memo using the indirect approach, 110–11; minutes, description of activity, 272; minutes, paraphrased discussion, 271–72; minutes, summary of main ideas in narrative form, 272; minutes, summary of main ideas in outline form, 272; minutes, verbatim transcript, 271; monthly report, 349–51; policies illustrating negative and positive wording, 142–43; policies illustrating specialists' language, 143; policy, 134; procedures for a complex activity, 158–62; procedures for a single task, 164–65; proposals, 260–63, 264–65; resume, chronological style, 286–87; resume, functional style, 288–89; transmittal memo, 117; update memo, 120–21
Scope of periodicals, 295–96
Sections. *See* Headings
Sections in periodical articles, 306, 317–20

Sentence structure: exercise, 61; problems with, 60; revising for effective sentences, 58–60
Sexist language. *See* Offensive language
Signatures: in letters, 193; in memos, 112
Signposts: definition of, 45–46; directional words as, 46; headings as, 46; summaries as, 46; title or subject line as, 46; topic sentences as, 46
Simplified style for letters, 194
Solicited manuscripts, 294
Spacing: as technique for making memos easy to read, 101; in design, 84–85
Specialists' language: discussion, 62–63; exercise, 67; in policies, 143
Specificity. *See* Generalizations
Strategy. *See* Communication strategy
Strings of nouns: discussion of, 66; exercise, 67. *See also* Nominalization
Subheadings. *See* Headings
Subject line: in letters, 192; in memos, 114
Subject-predicate disagreement. *See* subject-verb problems
Subject-verb problems: discussion of, 58–60, 330, 331–32; exercise, 61
Subjunctive, misuse of, 339–40
Submission of manuscripts: preparing manuscripts, 316–17; selecting target periodicals, 304–5
Summaries: as beginnings of documents, 44–45; as signposts, 46; as technique for making memos easy to read, 97; definition of, 274; example of, 276–77; in minutes, 271–72; organization of, 275. *See also* Abstracts

Table of contents in reports. *See* Front matter for reports
Tables and charts: in analytical reports, 205; in periodical articles, 307–10
Telephone as a communication tool, 27
Test your skills. *See* Exercises
Titles: as beginnings of documents, 44; as signposts, 46; of analytical reports, 202
Tone: discussion of, 14–15; of annual reports, 238; of letters, 176–77; of

memos, 101–2; of policies, 141–43; revising for, 56–57
Topic sentences: as headings, 245; as signposts, 46; revising, 55–56
Topical headings, 222–24
Topics for periodical articles, 302–3; 317–20
Traditional style for letters, 193
Transmittal memos: discussion, 115–16; example of, 117
Typeface, 83–84
Typing, 78

Unintended offenses. *See* Offensive language
Unparallel sentence construction, 338
Unsolicited manuscripts, 294
Update memos: discussion of, 116, 119; example of, 120–21
Upward communication, 16
Usage, problems in, 334–36

Verbatim transcript in minutes, 271, 273
Verbs: inconsistent verb tense, 60–61; passive voice, 59; revising vague or passive verbs, 58–60

When to write: guidelines, 10–11; institutional practice, 11; memos, 95–96
White space: as element of design, 85; as technique for making memos easy to read, 101; in office documents, 87
Word choice: exercise in, 67; revising, 61–67
Word processing: discussion, 78–79; ease of revision, 75; provision of for all who write, 75–76
Wordy constructions: discussion of, 64–65; exercise, 67
Writing checklists. *See* Professional writing process
Writing, effective. *See* Effective writing
Writing equipment, 75, 76
Writing support: models for writing support, 76; types of writing support, 75

Jana Bradley was most recently director of libraries at DePauw University and is now a doctoral candidate in library and information science at the University of Illinois. She also has worked as an editor for both trade and professional magazines, and has taught university courses and workshops on writing articles for publication, effective communication for managers, and problems in professional writing. Larry Bradley is an associate professor of English at Butler University, where he teaches courses in composition and English literature.